Research on e-Learning and ICT in Education

Athanassios Jimoyiannis
Editor

Research on e-Learning and ICT in Education

Springer

Editor
Athanassios Jimoyiannis
Department of Social and Educational Policy
University of Peloponnese
Korinthos, Greece
ajimoyia@uop.gr

ISBN 978-1-4614-1082-9 e-ISBN 978-1-4614-1083-6
DOI 10.1007/978-1-4614-1083-6
Springer New York Dordrecht Heidelberg London

Library of Congress Control Number: 2011935523

Printed on acid-free paper

Springer is part of Springer Science+Business Media (www.springer.com)

Editing of this book would not had been
possible without the support from
Natassa, Marianthi and Valentini,
who recognized that the time devoted
and missing from them was worthwhile.
This dedication belongs to them rightfully.

Editorial

During the last decades, Education and *Information and Communications Technologies (ICT)* have developed a growing symbiotic relationship. In a variety of educational contexts, educators, learners and researchers are turning to ICT-based practices to design learning materials, to structure new educational methods, to enhance learning experiences and develop novel approaches in supporting learning and instruction. Nowadays, ICT have been widely perceived and commonly used as the lever that would leads to significant educational and pedagogical outcomes and support students' development of the knowledge and skills needed to succeed in the twenty-first century society.

The increasing growth in the use of learning environments in which education is delivered and supported through ICT has brought new challenges. Academics, researchers, educators and policy makers have advocated that the emerged applications of ICT and the Web have the potential to offer enhanced learning opportunities for both students and teachers and support lifelong competence development. They transform the learning context by providing multiple opportunities for shared content and resources, self-directed learning, collaborative learning, ubiquitous and lifelong learning, among others.

In this sense, ICT applications and e-learning environments are becoming common elements of contemporary educational institutions, allowing both teachers and students to build strong learning communities around a common subject or field of interest. ICT and the new generation of Web technologies (blogs, wikis, social media etc.) offer enhanced learning resources and virtual learning spaces that are expected to exert a significant impact on education, since they change the boundaries between school and home; formal, non-formal and informal learning; teachers and learners; education and entertainment. In addition, the emergent Web 2.0 applications promote a new relationship between learners and teachers (but also learners), since the first are becoming potential authors of a new type of content.

Consequently, the debate about e-learning involves students, teachers, pedagogies, technologies and the related content. Undoubtedly, ICT have a number of affordances that change the key aspects of the *nature of knowledge* and the way people access it. But what knowledge do we need in the twenty-first century? It is already apparent that the way we construct knowledge is still embedded in past perceptions of knowledge, schooling and learning. It is worth considering how *educational thinking* moves within a broader agenda, which is fundamentally affected by technology and the changes it induces in society. This justifies why there is a real need to rethink the whole framework of instruction and learning though the lens of ICT; the elements above as the constitutional components of any educational process cannot be independently managed.

Reflecting the current trends, this book comprises a set of high-quality scientific papers, sourced from a wide international community, that present theoretical perspectives, pedagogical innovations, original empirical investigations, case studies and practical applications regarding e-learning and ICT in education. Bringing together contributions from different educational systems and cultures around the world (from the UK, Canada, Spain, Italy, Bulgaria, Cyprus and Greece), this book serves as a multidisciplinary forum and gives an explicit view of the current international trends regarding the research and the application of ICT in educational practice.

The papers included were originally presented at the Seventh Pan-Hellenic Conference with International Participation *Information and Communication Technologies in Education (HCICTE 2010)*, organized by the Department of Social and Educational Policy, University of Peloponnese, Greece and the Hellenic Association of ICT in Education (HAICTE), September 23–26, 2010, Korinthos, Greece, http://korinthos.uop.gr/~hcicte10. The original papers received positive criticism and suggestion from, at least, two independent reviewers, experts in the various fields, after a blind review process.

The result is a book that does not focus on a specific issue. Reflecting a variety of thematic areas across e-learning, the 22 chapters included fall into four main categories as follows:

Part I: Twenty-first century education and e-learning
Part II: E-Learning and teachers' professional development
Part III: ICT-enhanced learning
Part IV: Learning environments and technologies

Our ultimate ambition is that this book will have a positive impact and will be a valuable contribution, internationally, to the fields of e-learning and ICT in Education.

Part I Twenty-First Century Education and E-Learning

The first part of the book and under the name of *Twenty-First Century Education and E-Learning*, presents five papers that address the current trends and perspectives regarding ICT and e-learning in twenty-first century educational settings, in various educational contexts ranging from primary education to university level.

In the first chapter, Neil Selwyn debates the future of formal schools and schooling in an increasingly digital age. He argues that, despite the ambitious promises and discussions on the impact of ICT in transforming educational settings, the organizations and institutions that relate to education have displayed less obvious evidence of change over the last few decades. This chapter outlines and critiques the radical forms of digital "re-schooling" and "de-schooling" that are often argued for within current academic debates over educational technology community. In conclusion, the chapter suggests a more modest approach that seeks to use digital technologies to work with schools as they currently are, rather than against them.

Chapter 2 by Christina Preston and John Cuthell presents the MirandaMod model of "unconference", an informal partly facilitated participant-driven meeting focused on a theme or a purpose. This model reflects the complex, social, intellectual and practical process of teachers' professional learning and facilitates this under three headings: the opportunities for teachers to record changes in their beliefs and understandings in relation to changing practice and developing skills; the variety of locations and modes that reflect different cultural contexts for learning; and the potential for professionals to re-evaluate their identity in relationship to their role and their pedagogical observations.

Our collection proceeds with a third chapter oriented toward the difficulties people from communities with distinct religious or cultural identities have to engage with or be welcomed into citizenship in European democracies. In this chapter, Stewart Martin presents a project in secondary schools in the northeast of England, UK, using a virtual environment to understand how such technology can explore and develop young people's conceptualization of a citizenship in harmony with cultural and religious convictions in contemporary British society. The chapter also presents initial findings from an investigation suggesting that a revealing alternative approach is afforded through the use of immersive virtual worlds by applying experiential learning and ethnographic simulation.

The fourth chapter, by Antonio Cartelli, reports on the Italian experience and the InnovaScuola project for the introduction of digital technologies in Italian schools. His analysis focuses on the difficulties that students meet while approaching discipline topics and on the importance of digital literacy in helping students to overcome their problems. As a result a framework for digital competence assessment is reported, and the data obtained from a competition made at different school levels are shown. The results suggest and highlight the importance of problem-solving strategies for the improvement of everyday teachers' work.

Chapter 5, by Eleni Sianou-Kyrgiou and Iakovos Tsiplakides discuss the digital divide issue and the different sociological perspectives through which it is examined and interpreted. The authors present the findings of an empirical research, conducted with first year university students, showing that the digital divide is a divide in use rather than in access; new social inequalities emerge and are reproducing in different ways than in the past. They concluded that any attempts to examine social inequalities in higher education need to focus on the issue of the digital divide, as it constitutes a critical parameter which determines academic knowledge, students' performance and their transition to the labour market as well.

Part II E-Learning and Teachers' Professional Development

Part II presents an additional five papers, under the title *e-learning and teachers' professional development*, that deal with the issue of teacher's preparation and professional development programs aimed at the integration of ICT in school practice and supporting students learning and development.

In chapter six, Yannis Dimitriadis analyzes the multiple problems teachers face at when orchestrating technology-enhanced classrooms, and especially when dealing with complex pedagogies such as collaborative learning. His approach focuses on the extensive knowledge, both in pedagogy and technology, teachers need to design and put in practice computer-supported collaborative learning lesson plans. The chapter reports on the Spanish experience and deals with enhanced and shared teacher practices, as well as the support that may be provided in order to achieve the goals of effective and sustainable creation and use of CSCL lesson plans or scripts.

In the next chapter, Vassilios Makrakis presents a wiki technology, named WikiQuESD, and its application as a scaffolding hypermedia tool to enhance pre-service teachers' education for sustainable development (ESD) project-based learning. The study presented revealed that the use of WikiQuESD allowed pre-service teachers to design and upload interactive ESD projects online, through discussing and sharing ideas, collecting, assessing and integrating digital material available in the Web. The chapter concludes with the need to revise teacher education curriculum in order to provide authentic learning environments helping student teacher to develop their instructional skills, actively and experientially, within realistic and problem-solving learning scenarios.

Chapter 8, by Thierry Karsenti and Simon Collin, reports on the Canadian experience regarding the potential benefits of ICT for practical teacher training and professional induction. Results are presented from two pilot studies conducted in the province of Quebec during the internship of student teachers and the professional induction of new teachers. They identified the difficulties that interning and new teachers encounter and how ICT can help them overcome these challenges. The analysis of the results suggests that ICT help student teachers cope with pedagogical and other challenges encountered during their internship and the professional induction in various ways, while supporting student teachers to maximize their academic performance and to become more confident.

The next chapter, by Nikleia Eteokleous-Grigoriou, Garifalos Anagnostou and Simeon Tsolakidis, presents a case study in Cyprus regarding pre-service elementary teachers' use of the Online Dictionary of Standard Modern Greek, the Modern Greek Text Corpora and the Corpus of Greek Texts as alternative tools for teaching basic notions of Physical Education. Using the Technology Acceptance Model, the study describes usefulness of the tools, difficulties encountered, teaching philosophies and pedagogical beliefs, and educational use of the tools as the key-parameters determining pre-service teachers' profiles and future technology use.

In the last chapter of this part, Kyriacos Charalambous and Photos Papaioannou present a study exploring self perceived competence and use of ICT, by primary school principals in Cyprus, for personal, teaching and administrative–managerial purposes. Their results revealed that primary school principals, generally, do not feel very competent in using ICT, although the majority of them have received in-service training on ICT. It appears that they use computers for personal purposes, mainly word-processing and information seeking on the Internet, rather than for administrative and for teaching purposes.

Part III ICT-Enhanced Learning

Part III includes seven papers that address trends and perspectives regarding ICT-enhanced and ICT-supported learning. Most of the empirical studies presented use educational software (e.g. concept mapping tools, simulations, programming environments) and Web 2.0 applications to support and enhance students' engagement, inquiry and collaborative learning.

The first chapter under this heading, by Sofia Hadjileontiadou, Georgia Nikolaidou and Leontios Hadjileontiadis, proposes an instructional design within a computer-supported collaborative learning setting to examine if the provision of illusionary adaptive support could be perceived as such and cause intrinsic motivation towards better collaborative performance. Extending previous relative work, the authors applied two conditions of collaborative concept mapping to 11 groups of dyads of undergraduate teacher students, i.e. control and experimental. The groups during the experimental condition, unlike the control one, received an illusionary type of support. According to the experimental results, they produced better collaborative performance, on the basis of relevant indicators, as compared to their performance during the control condition.

The effective integration of wikis in undergraduate education is considered in the investigation by Ilias Karasavvidis and Sevasti Theodosiou. This chapter presents data from a longitudinal research project which aims at the progressive refinement of a wiki task using a design experiment method. The effect of a third version of a wiki task on student participation, online collaboration and interaction was examined in an undergraduate course with 56 participants. The results indicated that, while student participation rates and online interactions were substantially improved, compared to an earlier version of the task, student on-line collaboration remained minimal.

Sophia Angelaina and Athanassios Jimoyiannis report on the investigation of educational blogging using the Community of Inquiry framework. The study presented in this chapter used a blog as a project-based learning environment to engage secondary education students (15 years aged), coming from two separate K-9 classes. The results shed light on the multiple ways of students' engagement and presence into the blog learning space, namely their social and cognitive presence, that support the development of a community of inquiry though which students achieved higher cognitive levels and enhanced their communication and collaboration skills.

The next chapter, by Maria Latsi and Chronis Kynigos, is oriented toward how mathematical meaning-making can be integrated with spatial navigation and orientation in 3D digital media. They report on the findings of a classroom research investigating 12 year-old pupils' construction processes as they worked with a 3D Logo/Turtle Geometry environment. The results show that the simulated 3D space was experienced by the pupils through two distinct perspectives on the way the available viewing angle manipulation tools were used: (a) an intrinsic perspective, according to which the simulated space was viewed from inside, through the turtle's viewpoint, and (b) an extrinsic, from the view point of an external observer who looked at the figural results of turtle's movement.

Anthi Karatrantou and Chris Panagiotakopoulos report on the value of educational robotics, considering that computer programming is a difficult cognitive task for most students. In this chapter, they present three case studies where Lego Mindstorms educational kits are used by small groups of junior high school students, students in vocational secondary education and prospective primary teachers. The findings of the case studies are briefly described and seem very promising with regard to the use of educational robotics to promote understanding of the basic programming principles.

The last chapter, by Athanasios Taramopoulos, Dimitris Psillos and Evripides Hatzikraniotis, presents a study comparing the learning outcomes of 15–16 year-old students of the Greek junior high school in the field of simple electric circuits, when they are subjected to a teaching-by-inquiry intervention in a real and in a virtual laboratory environment. A pre–post comparison study design was used with two groups, who used the same inquiry-based curriculum materials with different in nature equipment (real vs. virtual environment). The findings indicate a similar conceptual improvement for both groups after the intervention.

Part IV Learning Environments and Technologies

The fourth part of the book deals with new technological environments and their applications in practice; namely virtual reality and virtual spaces, technological issues and standards development, as well.

The first chapter under this heading, by Mark Stansfield, Thomas Connolly, Thomas Hainey and Gavin Baxter, explores the contribution that computer games and Web 2.0 technologies can provide to enhance learner motivation and engagement. The chapter highlights the main advantages and problems associated with computer games in education. In addition, a recent project is presented, the Web 2.0 European Resource Centre which is aimed at enabling the mass of educators who find ICT confusing and frightening to have a simple and secure environment to use Web 2.0 technologies within their class.

This part proceeds with another chapter, by Ioannis Vrellis, Nikiforos M. Papachristos, Antonis Natsis and Tassos A. Mikropoulos, presenting an exploratory study regarding the educational affordances of virtual environments and the related students' learning experiences. The empirical data gathered, using the Temple

Presence Inventory questionnaire, in order to investigate the sense of presence (spatial and social) that emerges while students collaborate in a problem-based physics learning activity through Second Lifes. The results indicate higher scores of social presence than of spatial presence. Correlations were found between dimensions of presence, subjective computer expertise and tendency to become involved in activities.

Konstantina Chatzara, Charalampos Karagiannidis and Demosthenes Stamatis present an empirical study regarding a pedagogical agent that imitates human behaviour for enhancing e-learning applications through emotional intelligence. The results of the study reveal that agents can improve the quality of education. In particular, the agent can successfully diagnose the emotional state of the students and help them to complete their learning tasks. On the other hand, students enjoyed using the agent, they exhibited a sense of communicating with the agent, and they had positive emotions through this communication.

In chapter 20, Pavel Boytchev reports on digital visualization and presents several software applications designed and implemented by the author as an attempt to represent the mathematical concept of conic sections. The applications utilize virtual reality to represent the basic properties of conic sections in a way easily to understand by a non-mathematician. The applications cover several different perspectives that correspond to a multidisciplinary approach. The paper describes how conic sections can be generated by using objects from everyday life and how to design virtual mechanical devices that draw conic sections.

The potential value of sharing and reusing digital resources among educational communities is deeply studied in the next chapter by Demetrios Sampson, Pãnagiotis Zervas and George Chloros. Within this framework, a popular way for describing digital educational resources is the IEEE Learning Objects Metadata (LOM) Standard. The authors present an extended overview of existing tools for developing and managing IEEE LOM Application Profiles, and a comparison grid to identify their strengths and weaknesses.

The learning environments and technologies theme concludes with a paper, by Ioannis Kazanidis and Maya Satratzemi, on personalized instruction and the difficulties to develop reused content by conventional systems and platforms. The adoption of SCORM technological standard results in some restrictions to system design and the provided adaptivity. The chapter focuses on the restrictions, which are related to the production of educational content, and investigates ways for developing dynamic and adaptive educational material that conforms to SCORM's specifications. Finally, an adaptive learning management system, named ProPer, is presented which supports further course adaptation.

I want to thank the authors for submitting their contributions to this book; especially because they reworked their manuscripts to the final form presented here. I am most grateful to the reviewers for their comprehensive review. Their constructive comments and suggestions contributed to the improvement of the quality of the chapters in this book.

Korinthos, Greece Athanassios Jimoyiannis

Contents

Contributors

Garifalos Anagnostou Department of Primary Education, Frederick University, Limassol, Cyprus
pre.ag@frederick.ac.cy

Sophia Angelaina Department of Social and Educational Policy, University of Peloponnese, Korinthos, Greece
sangelaina@gmail.com

Gavin Baxter School of Computing, University of the West of Scotland, Paisley, UK
gavin.baxter@uws.ac.uk

Pavel Boytchev Sofia University, Sofia, Bulgaria
boytchev@fmi.uni-sofia.bg

Antonio Cartelli University of Cassino, Cassino, Italy
cartan@unicas.it

Kyriacos Charalambous School of Education, Frederick University, Nicosia, Cyprus
pre.ck@frederick.ac.cy

Konstantina Chatzara Department of Special Education, University of Thessaly, Volos, Greece
chatzara@sed.uth.gr

George Chloros Department of Digital Systems, University of Piraeus, Piraeus, Greece
gchloros@tellas.gr

Simon Collin University of Quebec in Montreal, Montreal, QC, Canada
collin.simon@uqam.ca

Thomas Connolly School of Computing, University of the West of Scotland, Paisley, UK
thomas.connolly@uws.ac.uk

John Cuthell MirandaNet Fellowship International, London, UK
john.cuthell@mirandanet.ac.uk

Yannis A. Dimitriadis Department of Signal Theory, Communications and Telematics Engineering, School of Telecommunications Engineering, University of Valladolid, Valladolid, Spain
yannis@tel.uva.es

Nikleia Eteokleous-Grigoriou Department of Primary Education, Frederick University, Limassol, Cyprus
pre.en@frederick.ac.cy

Leontios Hadjileontiadis Department of Electrical & Computer Engineering, Aristotle University of Thessaloniki, Thessaloniki, Greece
leontios@auth.gr

Sofia Hadjileontiadou School of Humanities, Hellenic Open University, Patra, Greece
shadji@ee.duth.gr

Thomas Hainey School of Computing, University of the West of Scotland, Paisley, UK
thomas.hainey@uws.ac.uk

Evripides Hatzikraniotis Department of Physics, Aristotle University of Thessaloniki, Thessaloniki, Greece
evris@physics.auth.gr

Athanassios Jimoyiannis Department of Social and Educational Policy, University of Peloponnese, Korinthos, Greece
ajimoyia@uop.gr

Charalampos Karagiannidis Department of Special Education, University of Thessaly, Volos, Greece
karagiannidis@sed.uth.gr

Ilias Karasavvidis Department of Preschool Education, University of Thessaly, Volos, Greece
ikaras@uth.gr

Anthi Karatrantou Department of Primary Education, University of Patras, Patras, Greece
a.karatrantou@eap.gr

Thierry Karsenti University of Montreal, Montreal, QC, Canada
thierry.karsenti@umontreal.ca

Ioannis Kazanidis Department of Accountancy, Kavala Institute of Technology, Kavala, Greece
kazanidis@teikav.edu.gr

Chronis Kynigos School of Philosophy, National and Kapodistrian University of Athens, Athens, Greece
kynigos@ppp.uoa.gr

Maria Latsi School of Philosophy, National and Kapodistrian University of Athens, Athens, Greece
mlatsi@ppp.uoa.gr

Vassilios Makrakis Department of Primary Education, University of Crete, Crete, Greece
makrakis@edc.uoc.gr

Stewart Martin School of Social Sciences and Law, Teesside University, Middlesbrough, UK
s.m.martin@tees.ac.uk

Tassos A. Mikropoulos Department of Primary School Education, University of Ioannina, Ioannina, Greece
amikrop@uoi.gr

Antonis Natsis Department of Primary School Education, University of Ioannina, Ioannina, Greece
anatsis@cc.uoi.gr

Georgia Nikolaidou Direction of Primary Education of Eastern Thessaloniki, Thessaloniki, Greece
msa0848@uom.gr

Chris Panagiotakopoulos Department of Primary Education, University of Patras, Patras, Greece
cpanag@upatras.gr

Nikiforos M. Papachristos Department of Primary School Education, University of Ioannina, Ioannina, Greece
npapachr@grads.uoi.gr

Photos Papaioannou Ministry of Education and Culture of Cyprus, Nicosia, Cyprus
fotospap@hotmail.com

Christina Preston MirandaNet Fellowship International, London, UK
christina@mirandanet.ac.uk

Dimitris Psillos Department of Elementary Education, Aristotle University of Thessaloniki, Thessaloniki, Greece
psillos@eled.auth.gr

Demetrios G. Sampson Department of Digital Systems,
University of Piraeus, Piraeus, Greece

Informatics and Telematics Institute, Centre for Research
and Technology Hellas, Athens, Greece
sampson@unipi.gr

Maya Satratzemi Department of Applied Informatics,
University of Macedonia, Thessaloniki, Greece
maya@uom.gr

Neil Selwyn London Knowledge Lab, Institute of Education,
University of London, London, UK
n.selwyn@ioe.ac.uk

Eleni Sianou-Kyrgiou Department of Philosophy, Education and Psychology,
University of Ioannina, Ioannina, Greece
esianou@uoi.gr

Demosthenes Stamatis Department of Informatics,
Alexander TEI of Thessaloniki, Thessaloniki, Greece
demos@it.teithe.gr

Mark Stansfield School of Computing,
University of the West of Scotland, Paisley, UK
mark.stansfield@uws.ac.uk

Athanasios Taramopoulos Department of Elementary Education,
Aristotle University of Thessaloniki, Thessaloniki, Greece
ttar@sch.gr

Sevasti Theodosiou Department of Preschool Education,
University of Thessaly, Volos, Greece
theodosiou@uth.gr

Iakovos Tsiplakides Department of Philosophy, Education and Psychology,
University of Ioannina, Ioannina, Greece
tsiplakides@hotmail.com

Simeon Tsolakidis Department of Primary Education,
Frederick University, Limassol, Cyprus
pre.st@frederick.ac.cy

Ioannis Vrellis Department of Primary School Education,
University of Ioannina, Ioannina, Greece
ivrellis@uoi.gr

Panagiotis Zervas Department of Digital Systems,
University of Piraeus, Piraeus, Greece

Informatics and Telematics Institute, Centre for Research
and Technology Hellas, Athens, Greece
pzervas@iti.gr

Part I
Twenty-First Century Education and e-Learning

School 2.0: Rethinking the Future of Schools in the Digital Age

Neil Selwyn

Introduction

Despite all of the talk of technology transforming organizations and institutions, it could be argued that the organizations and institutions that relate to education have displayed less obvious evidence of change over the last few decades than those in other areas of society. In particular, many people would argue that a slow pace of change is especially evident with the "traditional" institutions of education – not least the school. In this chapter, we shall consider the significance of educational institutions in contemporary education. How can educational institutions such as the school be said to be coping with the demands of digital technology? Is there a continued need for formal institutions in education? Does digital technology in fact render the educational institution obsolete?

In addressing these questions, we need to consider all of the formal and informal elements of "the school" – in other words, we need to approach schools and digital technology both in terms of structure and in terms of process. For example, with regard to defining the "structure" of schools, most people would think of the material aspects of schools as places – i.e., their buildings, corridors, and classrooms. Yet schools are based around a range of social and cultural structures – including the hierarchical roles that people assume within the school organization, the hierarchies of knowledge that constitutes the school curriculum, and the organization of time that constitutes the school time table. All of these structures – although often out-of-sight and rarely talked about – are integral elements of the organization of schools and schooling. Similarly, with regard to the "processes" of schooling most people would immediately think of explicit processes such as teaching, learning, communication, and decision-making. However, schooling should also be seen as involving

N. Selwyn (✉)
London Knowledge Lab, Institute of Education, University of London, London, UK
e-mail: n.selwyn@ioe.ac.uk

A. Jimoyiannis (ed.), *Research on e-Learning and ICT in Education*,
DOI 10.1007/978-1-4614-1083-6_1, © Springer Science+Business Media, LLC 2012

more implicit processes of socialization, regulation, and control. All of these processes and structures highlight the fact that schools should certainly not be seen simply as neutral contexts within which digital technologies are implemented and then used. Instead, we need to consider how digital technologies "fit" with these structures and processes. How do digital technologies complement or challenge the established processes and structures of school organization? In what ways do digital technologies appear to support the "reconstitution" of schools and schooling?

Technology and the Reconstitution of Schools and Schooling

In exploring the relationship between technology and the structures and processes of schools and schooling, we should first consider the ways in which digital technology is being used around the world to reconfigure the nature and form of educational institutions. These efforts tend to take three main forms. The first one is the use of digital technology to represent the structures and processes of school – what is often referred to as "virtual schooling." The second one is the use of digital technology to reconstitute the structures and processes of school – what can be referred to as a digitally driven "reschooling." The last one is the use of digital technology to replace the structures and processes of school altogether – what can be termed a digitally driven "deschooling."

Technology and Virtual Schooling

There is a relatively long history of using technology to set the provision of schooling free from the physical and spatial confines of school buildings, while retaining the major structures and processes of schooling such as curriculum, assessment, and certification. Throughout the 1990s and 2000s, a large number of internet-based virtual schools were established to provide online "out-of-school" schooling. Perhaps the most widespread use of the internet to provide institutional support and provision of teaching and learning has occurred in the United States. One of the first major instances of this was the now defunct "Virtual High School" program. This program was sponsored by $7.4 million of federal funding and, at its peak, boasted students from ten countries. From these beginnings a large majority of US states now operate online learning programs for children and young people involved in compulsory schooling. Many states support individual "cyber schools" as well as having district level online programs where between 20 and 80% of a student's academic instruction can be delivered via the internet (Watson et al. 2008; Ellis 2008). In this way, it is estimated that over one million US school students will take online courses alongside their classroom lessons each year (Means et al. 2009).

These forms of virtual schooling are often justified as introducing the benefits of market efficiency and competition into compulsory school systems. As the brief examples provided above suggest, virtual schools tend to be run by a variety of providers – from school districts and universities, to private companies and corporate commercial entities. Growing numbers of commercial companies also act as vendors for the delivery of courses and the licensed use of course materials. This "learning marketplace" is bolstered by the wealth of content developed by educators and schools themselves. All told, virtual schooling is seen to make school systems more diverse and more competitive. Besides these system-wide improvements, proponents of virtual schooling also celebrate the benefits of choice and flexibility for the individual learner. For example, virtual schools are seen to provide individual instruction that better meets the specific needs and learning styles of students. Virtual schooling is seen to allow flexibility in terms of scheduling and place, as well as expanding educational access to individuals and groups who would otherwise be unable to engage in high quality learning. While some students (or their parents) will actively choose virtual schooling, these methods are also seen to play a compensatory role for students who are physically unable to attend "bricks-and-mortar" schools. As such virtual schooling is justified as a ready alternative for students who have long-term illness, have been excluded from school or where schools are considered as unsuitable for them to attend.

Technology and Re-Schooling

Whereas virtual schooling takes place outside of the conventional school, another approach has been the use of technology as an impetus to "remix" the major structures and process of schooling *within* the physical and spatial confines of the school. This technology-driven reconstitution of the school can be referred to as a digitally driven "reschooling." In other words, although the school may look the same from the outside, what goes on within it may be substantially different from before. Of course, efforts have long been made at the margins of educational systems to reconstitute and reconstruct the school. Throughout the twentieth century a number of high-profile "experimental" and "free" schools such as Summerhill, Fernwood, and the Vancouver New Schools all attempted to reinvent the structures and processes of schooling. Now digital technologies are seen to allow for the wide scale reconstitution of educational institutions across entire school systems – albeit in less radical and overtly political ways.

Many of these proposals for "digital reschooling" involve the reconfiguration of curriculum and assessment. For example, efforts have been made in many countries to design new forms of digitally driven assessment to support learners – especially in terms of assessing areas of learning such as decision-making, adaptability, and cooperation. Attempts have been made to develop technology-based forms of "peer assessment," as well as collaboratively produced work. Steps are being taken in countries such as Denmark and Norway to allow pupils full access to the internet during school examinations. Similarly, in terms of reconstituting the school curriculum, many educationalists are striving to find ways of foregrounding technology-based practices of collaboration, publication, and inquiry within the classroom. Current discussions in the academic educational technology literature will often conclude with proposals and manifestos for the redefinition of curriculum and pedagogy – sometimes through radical models of "mash-up pedagogy" and a "remix of learning" (e.g., Fisher and Baird 2009; Mahiri 2011).

Besides issues of curriculum and assessment, attempts are also being made by some academics to recast education institutions as sites of technological exploration. An obvious area for change here has been the remodeling of the physical boundaries of schools to fit with the needs and demands of modern technology. From William Mitchell's (1995) suggestions for a "recombinant architecture" in schools, to proposals for the re-design of the school environment into "collaboration-friendly" and "really cool spaces" (e.g., Dittoe 2006) the idea of redesigning and rebuilding the physical environment of schools to better accommodate digital technology use continues to gain popularity and support. For example, it has been suggested that the planning and design of new schools is less rigidly "zoned," with schools becoming "learning spaces" that are "blended" in with other spaces and sites within the community (Harrison 2009). All told, the reconstitution of the physical work environment of the school to accommodate the demands of digital technology use is seen to be long overdue.

Technology and De-Schooling

While these ideas of reschooling and virtual schooling have obvious merit, other academics, educationalists, and technologists have chosen to pursue an even more radical agenda of change – what can be termed the digitally driven "deschooling" of society. From this perspective, digital technology is seen to offer a means of escaping the physical and spatial confines of the school, as well as providing an alternative to the major structures and processes of schooling such as curriculum, assessment, and qualifications. These forms of technology-based deschooling take a variety of guises. For example, a growing number of online institutions now exist that are based on an ethos of using digital technologies to bypass traditional education institutions. This approach is evident in online services such as the *School of Everything*. This is a prominent online space in the UK designed to put people in the community who wish to "teach" with people who wish to "learn." This form of teaching and learning exchange has therefore been described as "an *eBay* for stuff that does not get taught in school" (Leadbeater 2008a, p. 26).

Digital technology has also been used to further support and extend the "home schooling," "unschooling", and "self-directed learning" movements where children and young people are educated by family and community members. For example, the "Free World U" has been developed as an online alternative learning community for home-schooled young children – offering online "accelerated learning" resources to be shared between communities of parents and learners. The development of online alternative schooling is an increasingly significant part of the efforts of neo-conservative and fundamentalist religious groups in the US to support alternative forms of home-schooling outside of state control of the curriculum (Peters and McDonough 2008). As Michael Apple observed at the beginning of the 2000s, "there are scores of websites available that give advice, that provide technical and emotional support, that tell the stories of successful home schoolers, and that are more than willing to sell material at a profit" (Apple 2000, p. 71).

Reasons for the Technology-Driven Reconstitution of Schools and Schooling

Although all of these examples challenge the traditional concept of "the school," in a practical sense they remain on the periphery of contemporary educational provision. For the time being, at least, the main significance of such efforts is symbolic rather than substantial. As such it is worth considering the implications of the ideas and arguments that underpin these examples in further detail. All of the examples covered in this chapter certainly reflect a strongly held belief among some academics and educational technologists that profound and significant changes to the organization and arrangements of schools and schooling are imminent. Arguments along these lines are made regularly and forcefully in educational technology discussions and debate – especially by academic commentators. In fact it could be argued that much of the current discussion and debate about education and technology is tinged with an underlying "down with school" sentiment. We therefore need to ask why this is, and whether such reactions are justified?

Looking back over the recent academic literature on education and technology (or to be more accurate, the English language academic literature), it would seem that people's enthusiasms for different forms of schooling are usually driven by two interrelated beliefs. The first one is the widely held assumption among some academics and technologists that digital technology offers a better way of "doing education" – what could be referred to as a technological "pull" factor. The second one is a general dissatisfaction with current types of schools and schooling – what could be described as an institutional "push" factor. Together, these beliefs can be seen as underpinning most people's desire for the technology-driven redefinition of schools. In the spirit of all our other discussion up until now, it therefore makes sense to give further consideration to the ideas, beliefs, values, and agenda that inform these arguments. Is the school as it currently stands really a dysfunctional institution? Do digital technologies really offer a better way of organizing and providing educational opportunities?

Technology as a Better Means of "Doing" Education

One recurring theme throughout the educational literature is the assumption that digital technologies offer as a ready means of supporting better forms of teaching and learning than can usually be found in formal educational settings. Technology-based education is seen to provide a more conducive way than "traditional" schooling to facilitate the informal, collective, and communal forms of learning that many educationalists believe to be important. Some people therefore reckon digital technology to be capable of superseding the educational opportunities that can be provided by schools and other formal institutions. This is not to say that technology-driven provision will necessarily replace formal education institutions. Nevertheless, digital technology is certainly seen as able to fulfill many of the same functions and roles. As Allan Collins and Richard Halverson reason:

> We see the question of where education is headed in terms of the separation of schooling and learning. We are not predicting the collapse of your local elementary school. Young people will not be forced to retreat behind computer screens to become educated. Rather, we see the seeds of a new education system forming in the rapid growth of new learning alternatives, such as home schooling, learning centers, workplace learning, and distance education. These new alternatives will make us rethink the dominant role of public schools in education as children and adults spend more time learning in new venues (Collins and Halverson 2009, pp. 3–4).

This enthusiasm for digital technology supporting a set of "new alternatives" to the school reflects a number of beliefs and values about what education should be. Firstly, many people's interest in the technology-based reconfiguration of schooling reflects a belief in increased individual freedom. As can be seen throughout the educational technology literature, many people are convinced of the capacity of digital technologies to make education more flexible, fluid, and ultimately more empowering for the individual learner. For many commentators it therefore no longer makes sense to retain "pre-digital" models of organizing learning through institutions that are focused on the rigidly hierarchic mass delivery of static content. Instead, people are now beginning to question how best to develop forms of learning that can be negotiated rather than prescribed and discovered rather than delivered. More often than not, digital technology is seen to provide a powerful means of supporting education that is driven by individual learner's needs and based on learners taking control of managing and accessing knowledge for themselves (Facer and Green 2007).

In this sense, growing numbers of authors are now discussing the value of what Jonathan Edson (2007) terms "user-driven education" – i.e., allowing learners to take an active role in what they learn as well as how and when they learn it. Of course, this "pick and mix approach" to curricular content and form presents a challenge to the professional roles, identities, and cultures of teachers and other educators. It also presents a fundamental challenge to the concept of the formal educational establishment as a whole. As McLoughlin and Lee (2008, p. 647) conclude, all of these ideas and arguments imagine a radically different education system – one where "learners are active participants or co-producers of knowledge rather than passive consumers of content and learning is seen as a participatory, social process supporting personal life goals and needs."

These enthusiasms are often coupled with enthusiasm for the power of "informal" learning – i.e., learning that takes place outside of the control of the formal education system. Digital technologies such as the internet and mobile telephony are seen as especially conducive to informal learning through their ability to support enhanced connections between people, places, products, and services. Above all, technology-supported informal learning is seen to be more empowering in comparison to formal schooling, with young people able to learn in spite (rather than because) of their schools (Ito et al. 2009). As Nicole Johnson concluded from a study of Australian teenage "expert" technology users, with informal learning …

> … the [students] were able to choose what they learned and when they learned. They viewed the medium in which they did it as a form of leisure. They were also able to choose who and

> what they learned from – not just what has been set up as exclusive and privileged. They were able to both learn and receive pleasure from their engagement and not have to be concerned about the hierarchization and failure in relation to how traditional schooling determines competence (Johnson 2009, p. 70).

The School as a "Dysfunctional" Technology

As this last quotation implies, much of the enthusiasm for the power of technology-based informal and collective learning is often accompanied by a complementary set of concerns over the failings of "traditional schooling" and formal school systems. Of course, "school-bashing" occurs throughout all aspects of educational debate and is by no means a recent phenomenon. The rise of mass education throughout the twentieth century was accompanied by trenchant critiques of "the school nightmare" and accusations of schools causing intellectual "death at an early age" (see Gross and Gross 1969). Many of these critiques centered on fundamental issues of knowledge, relationships, diversity, community engagement, and social justice (e.g., Postman 1996). More recently, these long-standing discontentments about schools appear to have been amplified and accelerated by the rise of digital technology. In many ways, digital technology now provides a high-profile filter for many long-standing criticisms of formal educational institutions. The support for technology-related changes to education is therefore driven more by the "push" factor of the supposed inadequacies of the formal educational institution rather than the "pull" factor of technology's promise.

Criticism of the failings of contemporary forms of schools and schooling is varied. In a technological sense, it is argued that schools as they currently stand do not offer an adequate context for "doing technology" properly. The conclusion reached by many commentators is that schools, at best, assimilate and incorporate digital technology into their existing practices and processes. As Wilhelm (2004, p. 3) puts it, schools' technology adoption can be seen as being "largely hewn to established practice." Many people therefore see schools as unable or even unwilling to respond to the more radical demands of digital technology use outlined earlier. Schools are seen to be stuck in a position of lacking what it takes "to go with the technological flow" (Dale et al. 2004).

As far as many commentators are concerned, the extent of the technological intransigence of schools is considerable. For instance, many school buildings have been criticized as being architecturally unsuitable for widespread networked and/or wireless technology use. School leaders and administrators have been accused of lacking the required "vision" to make the most of the educational potential of digital technology. School curricula have been observed widely as being too rigid and entrenched in "pre-information age" ways of thinking. School assessment procedures are seen to be overly concerned with the development and assessment of scholastic aptitude rather than "softer" or creative skills.

These criticisms often focus on what is seen as the rigid organizational arrangements and social relations within schools. A perennial concern among many academics, technologists, and policymakers relates to the apparent incompatibility between digital technology and what has been variously termed the "industrial-era school"

(Toffler 1970) or the "Henry Ford model of education" (Whitney et al. 2007) – i.e., a school system that is based around the needs of mass production and centralized factory-like workplaces. Many educational technologists therefore continue to denounce the industrial-era school as a profoundly unsuitable setting for the more advanced forms of learning demanded digital technology and the "knowledge society" (e.g., Miller 2006; Warner 2006). In particular, schools' continued reliance on "broadcast" pedagogies of various kinds, their structured hierarchical relationships, and formal systems of regulation are all seen to render them incapable of responding adequately to the challenges posed by digital technology. All told, many people simply do not consider schools to be the best places for technology-based learning to take place.

Digital Technology and the Growing Rejection of the School

So far this chapter has outlined a range of arguments, ideas and proposals relating to school change and digital technology. To date, much of the established academic thinking has focused on the "reschooling" view of adjusting and reconfiguring the main structures and processes of schooling along more "technology-friendly" lines. For example, there is broad agreement within the academic literature, that the educational potential of digital technology is more likely to be realized through a redefinition of the processes and practices of contemporary schooling. Indeed, the need to develop "school 2.0" is an increasingly common topic of educational technology debate, with digital technology positioned as offering "a simple, clean approach" to redesigning schools (Apple 2008, p. 4). It is now becoming a fairly orthodox position within educational technology debates to argue that the processes and structures of schools are in need of being updated and rethought in light of digital technology use. However, some of the arguments covered in the last section of this chapter hinted at a creeping frustration among some educational technologists with the general concept of the school altogether. Indeed, some commentators are now openly hinting that they consider schools to be beyond salvation. Why then is there a growing rejection of school-based learning within some sections of the educational technology community?

As we saw earlier on in this chapter, powerful arguments are being advanced that children and young people may well be better off learning among themselves through the support of digital technologies. In particular, internet technologies have been promoted as providing a ready basis for young people's circumvention of the traditional structures of their schools and generally "finding something online that schools are not providing them" as Henry Jenkins (2004, n.p.) has put it. Digital technologies are seen to be able to move schooling away from being "a special activity that takes place in special places at special times, in which children are instructed in subjects for reasons they little understand" (Leadbeater 2008b, p. 149). In this respect, a great deal of faith continues to be vested in digital technologies as a catalyst for the total discontinuation of twentieth century forms of schools and schooling.

Indeed, a subtle rejectionist line of thinking can be found in quite a few accounts of educational technology and schools. This can be seen if we think back to the writing of the technologist Seymour Papert – one of the guiding lights of educational technology thinking over the past 40 years. It could be argued that Papert has promoted an often overt anti-school agenda throughout all these works. Take, for instance, his contention that schools and schooling are "are relics from an earlier period of knowledge technology" (Papert 1998, n.p.) or that new technology will "overthrow the accepted structure of school, the idea of curriculum, the segregation of children by age and pretty well everything that the education establishment will defend to the bitter end" (Papert 1998, n.p.). Perhaps Papert's most memorable proclamation in this respect was ...

> the computer will blow up the school. That is, the school defined as something where there are classes, teachers running exams, people structured in groups by age, and following a curriculum – all of that. The whole system is based on a set of structural concepts that are incompatible with the presence of the computer (Papert 1984, p. 38).

Such sentiments have implicitly informed the work of many other educational technologists over the past 30 years. More often than not, the rejection of school-based education is presented in a celebratory way that moves education nearer to harnessing the informal learning potential of digital technology. Yet on occasion some educational technologists cannot resist the urge to express their essentially negative view of the school. This sense of terminal incompatibility between technology and school was perhaps best encapsulated in Lewis Perelman's (1992) observation that any attempt to integrate computing into schools "makes about as much sense as integrating the internal combustion engine into the horse." Over 20 years later, polemic of this sort continues to be an accepted part of mainstream thinking about education and technology, with many commentators willing to denounce schools as "anachronistic" relics of the industrial age that are now rendered obsolete by contemporary digital technology. As Juha Suoranta concludes:

> in their current forms it might be that schools no longer belong to the order of things in the late modern era, and are about to vanish from the map of human affairs (Suoranta and Vadén 2010, p. 16).

In the minds of some commentators, then, the seriousness of the "school problem" has now passed a point of no return and leaves little choice but to argue for the dissolution of the school as it currently exists. Indeed, there would seem to be an implicit willingness within certain elements of the educational technology community to "give up" on the notion of the industrial-era school. The idea that technology-based learning could replace the idea of school altogether is becoming an increasingly serious proposition. Yet as with all debates about the "future" of education, it is important that we take time to properly consider and challenge these proposals and assumptions. Suggesting that the concept of formal schooling is abandoned altogether is a substantial proposal, and not to be taken lightly. It is worthwhile to therefore consider the roots of these contemporary arguments for the digital "deschooling" of society – not least their ideological origins.

In particular, parallels should be drawn between current calls for a digitally driven dismantling of the school and the earlier deschooling arguments of writers such as Paul Goodman (1962), Jonathan Kozel (1968), John Holt (1969), Everett Reimer (1971), Ian Lister (1974) and, most prominently, Ivan Illich (1971). In particular, Ivan Illich was at the forefront of debates toward the end of the 1960s as educationalists began to consider the emergence of what was being described as "post-industrial" society. In his 1971 book on *Deschooling Society* Illich challenged the structures, myths, and rituals that underpin all of contemporary capitalist society, not least educational institutions such as schools, colleges, and universities. Above all, much of the deschooling literature of the 1960s and 1970s resonates with – and often informs – present debates over digital technology and education. This is especially the case in the interest shown by writers such as Illich in re-appropriating technologies (from networks of tape recorders and computers to "mechanized donkey" vehicles) for providing learning opportunities along "convivial" rather than "manipulative" lines – thus reflecting a faith in the notion of placing new technology at the heart of communities as a ready way to give people the opportunity to access a range of educational objects, skill exchanges, peer-matching, and "educators-at-large" (see Illich 1971).

Reconsidering the Ideology of Digital Deschooling

It is evident that many of the twenty-first century arguments outlined earlier in this chapter for the discontinuation of schooling in favor of technological means (un) consciously update the arguments of Ivan Illich. At the first glance, Illich's thinking fits well with many of the issues raised throughout current debates over technology and schools. Take, for example, his condemnation of institutionalized learning as inhibiting individual growth due to its emphasis on "progress" through mass production and consumption. This reading of school and schooling fits well with contemporary discussion of digital technologies and education. As Charles Leadbeater (2008b, p. 44) reasoned, "in 1971 [deschooling] must have sounded mad. In the era of *eBay* and *MySpace* it sounds like self-evident wisdom." As Leadbeater then goes on to admit, "the self-help" philosophy of his own thinking on social media and education "is an attempt to realize some of Illich's ideals" (Leadbeater 2008b, p. 45). Similarly, as Juan Suoranta concludes:

> Illich's utopia is turning out to be more of a topical scenario for our so-called information age than anyone imagined. Illich's learning web metaphor is in itself interesting. It represents the current trend nicely that it is as if all the best minds in education are found in the virtual world of the worldwide web (Suoranta and Vadén 2010, p. 19).

The linkages between current educational technology thinking and the arguments advanced by writers such as Illich 40 years earlier reflect the highly ideological nature of debate over the schools and digital technology. Illich himself was a politically fluid but essentially anarchistic thinker who in later years argued against the entire notion of "education" altogether. Indeed, he reasoned that as people have historically always known many things without enforced and compulsory forms of education then current generations therefore would do better to learn outside the aegis of the state altogether. Of course, the intentions of many commentators on education and technology may well be rooted in similar counter-cultural sensibilities – especially among more idealistic elements of the computer programming community. Yet one of the key differences between the original deschooling debates of the 1970s and those in the 2010s is the diversity of often conflicting ideological standpoints of those interests that are currently arguing for such change. As such, the people arguing for the digitally driven deschooling of 2010s' society are doing so for a variety of reasons and rationales, not all counter-cultural or anarchic in intention.

Many of these ideological agendas relate back to wider efforts to re-configure the provision of education along market-driven, neo-liberal lines. Indeed, the prospect of the digital replacement of the school is being increasingly used to support neo-liberal arguments for the "end of school" and the realization of the "dream of education without the state" (Tooley 2006). Here digital technology is valorized in decidedly different terms than with Illich – i.e., as an ideal vehicle for the establishment of "a genuine market in education, where there was no state intervention of any kind, in funding, provision or regulation" (Tooley 2006, p. 26). From this perspective, digital technology is celebrated as a means to re-position education around the power of radical individualism, market forces, and the rational pursuit of self-interest.

So while the general premise of technology being used to replace the school may be seductive, it should be remembered such arguments are also used to support a number of more "laissez-faire" arguments for the dismantling of the state and public sector. Of course, we are not suggesting that these neo-liberal arguments should be rejected out of hand any more than Illich's arguments should be agreed with. It may well be that the convenience of digital technology allows the "privilege and convenience" of education to be provided through the power of the market and "without the unsightly mess" of state provision (Dean 2002). Yet, if these terms are accepted as the basis for the (re)organization of contemporary education, then it could be argued that a number of important principles of mass schooling in society are weakened – in particular, the principles of collective responsibility and empowerment. Indeed, the counter-argument could be made that there are a number of very good reasons to argue for the continuation – rather than dismantling – of the school in the twenty-first century.

Above all, it could be said that digital technologies should not be allowed to overshadow the basic social importance of formal schooling. From a social justice perspective alone, the argument could be advanced that educational technologists (however well-intentioned) have no right to legitimize calls for the alteration or dismantling of the publically provided "industrial-era" school. It could be argued that, for all their faults, current forms of mass schooling play a significant role in the improvement of life chances for all children and young people. As Michael Young has argued, academic commentators should remain mindful that schools fulfill a societal purpose as a valuable source of "powerful knowledge" and social mobility for all children and young people – not just the technologically privileged few (Young and Muller 2009). It could be argued that there are key differences between gaining knowledge and gaining experience, and that for many children and young people the most powerful forms of specialist knowledge cannot be acquired easily at home or in the community. In the case of these forms of powerful knowledge, it could be argued that the school plays a crucial enabling and supporting role.

Conclusions

All of these discussions and arguments highlight the complex nature of debates over the continuation of schools and schooling in the digital age. As this chapter has illustrated, these debates are often ideological in nature and are driven by wider arguments over what education is for and how society should be arranged. As Levinson and Sadovnik (2002, p. 2) observe, "schools are a Pandora's box for visualizing a number of conundrums currently facing liberal democratic societies." In particular, while the idea of a digitally driven displacement of schools may be justified on technical grounds of increasing the efficiency, economy, and even conviviality of education, there are a number of other socially focused arguments for not radically altering schools and schooling. Although it is easy to denounce many technological frustrations of the "industrial-era" school, we should be wary of setting a precedent where the interests of technology outweigh all other social, cultural, and political concerns. It could be argued that there are actually few compelling reasons to assume that formal schooling is set to lose significance and status in contemporary society. In fact, the continued persistence of a top–down, hierarchal configuration of formal schooling could be seen as testament to what Steven Kerr identified as the "historical flexibility of schools as organizations, and of the strong social pressures that militate for preservation of the existing institutional structure" (Kerr 1996, p. 7). Whether we like it or not, there is little historical reason to anticipate the imminent institutional decline of the "industrial-era" school in the near future.

That said, many of the issues raised in this chapter would seem to point toward the need for *some* degree of change in order for educational institutions to make the most of digital technology and, indeed, to get the most from digital technology-using learners. It could well be that these changes can be achieved through relatively modest "readjustments" to technological practices that do not disrupt existing institutional structures and boundaries. We should be wary of giving up on the entire notion of the industrial-era school or university as it currently exists. Instead, it may be more productive – and certainly more practical – to set about addressing the "problem" of formal education and technology in subtler and less disruptive ways than radically altering educational institutions or even disposing of them altogether. In this sense, we need to think carefully about the future shape and forms of technology-based education in more modest and far less radical terms than are presently being argued for.

In this sense, educational technologists may be best advised to explore ways of "loosening up" in-school technology use and introducing a degree of informality to current digital practices *without* undermining the overall institutionalized social order of the school. While many education technologists may well consider this to be a disappointingly compromised agenda for change, this may be a more realistic and achievable approach than the radical discourses of technological reschooling and retooling currently being proposed by others in the field. As such, careful thought now needs to be given as to exactly how the relationships between formality and informality within schools may be adjusted and altered in ways that can shift the frames of in-school technology use without undermining basic institutional structures and interests.

References

Apple Corporation (2008). *Apple classrooms of tomorrow – today*. Cupertino CA: Apple Corporation.

Apple, M. (2000). Away with all teachers. *International Studies in Sociology of Education*, 10, 61–80.

Collins, A., & Halverson, R. (2009). *Rethinking education in the age of technology*. New York: Teachers College Press.

Dale, R., Robertson, S., & Shortis, T. (2004). You can't not go with the technological flow, can you?. *Journal of Computer Assisted Learning*, 20, 456–470.

Dean, J. (2002). *Publicity's secret*. Ithaca NY: Cornell University Press.

Dittoe, W. (2006). Seriously cool places. In D. Oblinger (ed.), *Learning Spaces* (n.p.). Washington DC: Educause. Retrieved 9 March 2011 from http://www.educause.edu/learningspacesch3.

Edson, J. (2007). Curriculum 2.0: user-driven education. *The Huffington Post*. Retrieved 9 March 2011 from www.huffingtonpost.com/jonathan-edson/curriculum-20-userdri_b_53690.html.

Ellis, K. (2008). Cyber charter schools. *Educational Horizons*, 86, 3, 142–152.

Facer, K., & Green, H. (2007). Curriculum 2.0: educating the digital generation. *Demos Collection*, 24, 47–58.

Fisher, M., & Baird, D. (2009). Pedagogical mashup: Gen Y, social media, and digital learning styles. In L. Hin & R. Subramaniam (eds.), *Handbook of research on new media literacy at the K-12 level* (pp.48–71). Hershey PA: IGI Global.

Goodman, P. (1962). *Compulsory mis-education*. New York: Vintage.

Gross, R., & Gross, B. (1969). *Radical school reform*. London: Penguin.

Harrison, A. (2009). *Changing spaces, changing places*. Paper for the Beyond Current Horizons Project. London: Department for Children, Schools and Families.

Holt, J. (1969). *How children fail*. Harmonsworth: Penguin.

Illich, I. (1971). *Deschooling society*. London: Marion Boyars.

Ito, M., Baumer, S., Bittanti, M., & Boyd, D. (2009). *Hanging out, messing around, geeking out*. Cambridge MA: MIT Press.

Jenkins, H. (2004). Why Heather can write. *Technology Review* [BizTech], 6th February. Retrieved 9 March 2011 from http://www.technologyreview.com/business/13473.

Johnson, N. (2009). Teenage technological experts' views of schooling. *Australian Educational Researcher*, 36(1), 59–72.

Kerr, S. (1996). Toward a sociology of educational technology. In D. Jonassen (ed.), *Handbook of Research on Educational Communications and Technology* (pp. 143–169). New York: Macmillan.

Kozel, J. (1968). *Death at an early age*. Harmonsworth: Penguin.

Leadbeater, C. (2008a). People power transforms the web in next online revolution. *The Observer*, 9th March (p.26).

Leadbeater, C. (2008b). *We-think*. London: Profile.

Levinson, D., & Sadovnik, A. (2002). Education and society: an introduction. In D. Levinson, P. Cookson & A. Sadovnik (eds.), *Education and Sociology* (pp.1–16).London: Taylor and Francis.

Lister, I. (1974). *Deschooling.* Harmonsworth: Penguin.
Mahiri, J. (2011). *Digital tools in urban schools.* Ann Arbor MI: University of Michigan Press.
McLoughlin, C., & Lee, M. (2008). Mapping the digital terrain. *Proceedings Ascilite 2008.* Retrieved 9 March 2011 from http://www.ascilite.org.au/conferences/melbourne08/procs/mcloughlin.pdf.
Means, B., Toyama, Y., Murphy, R., Bakia, M., & Jones, K. (2009). *Evaluation of Evidence-based Practice in online Learning.* Washington DC: U.S. Department of Education.
Miller, R. (2006). Equity in a twenty-first century learning intensive society. *Foresight,* 8(4), 13–22.
Mitchell, W. (1995). *City of bits.* Cambridge MA: MIT Press.
Papert, S. (1984). Trying to predict the future. *Popular Computing*, 3(13), 30–44.
Papert, S. (1998). Does easy do it? Children, games, and learning. *Game Developer,* Jun./Sept., 88–92, Retrieved 9 March 2011 from www.papert.org/articles/Doeseasydoit.html.
Perelman, L. (1992). *School's out.* New York: Avon.
Peters, M., & McDonough, T. (2008). Editorial. *Critical Studies in Education*, 49(1), 127–142.
Postman, N. (1996). *The end of education.* New York: Vintage.
Reimer, E. (1971). *School is dead.* Harmonsworth: Penguin.
Suoranta, J., & Vadén, T. (2010). *Wikiworld.* London: Pluto Press.
Toffler, A. (1970). *Future Shock.* London: Bodley Head.
Tooley, J. (2006). Education reclaimed. In P. Booth (ed.), *Towards a Liberal Utopia?* (pp.22–30). London: Continuum.
Warner, D. (2006). *Schooling in the Knowledge Era.* Victoria: Australian Council for Education Research.
Watson, J., Gemin, B., & Ryan, J. (2008). *Keeping Pace with K–12 Online Learning 2008.* Philadelphia PA: Evergreen Consulting Associates.
Whitney, P., Grimes, J., & Kumar, V. (2007). *Schools in the digital age.* Chicago: MacArthur Foundation.
Wilhelm, A. (2004). *Digital Nation.* Cambridge MA: MIT Press.
Young, M., & Muller, J. (2009). *Three Scenarios for the Future.* Paper for 'Beyond Current Horizons' programme London: Department for Children, Schools and Families.

MirandaMods: From Practice to Praxis in Informal Professional Learning Contexts

Christina Preston and John Cuthell

Introduction

Marshall McLuhan, one of the first prophets of the electronic age, made some striking pronouncements in the 1960s. Two of the best known, "the medium is the message" and "the world is a global village" focused on the potential effects of new communication technologies as they related to popular culture, and how this in turn would affect human behaviour and relationships within and across established communities (http://www.marshallmcluhan.com). Fifty years later, one observation about human behaviour is that despite the pervasive power of digital technologies in society today there are still socio-cultural barriers and training issues that prevent many educators in all phases of education from using these technologies with the facility shown by their pupils (Facer et al. 2003; Downes 2004; Somekh 2004; Preston and Cuthell 2007; Pachler et al. 2011). This chapter illustrates how the paucity of well-designed Continuing Professional Development (CPD) programmes in digital technologies is being remedied. Educators themselves are taking charge of an emerging mode of professional online communication that engages educators in knowledge creation. This mode of communication is a modification of the "unconference". The "unconference" is a democratic knowledge exchange where all professional participants are considered to have expertise, rather than invited speakers. The derivative designed by educators, called a MirandaMod, is a themed debate where issues of practice and theory are raised on equal terms. These terms are explained more fully in the next section.

C. Preston (✉) • J. Cuthell
MirandaNet Fellowship International, London, UK
e-mail: christina@mirandanet.ac.uk

A. Jimoyiannis (ed.), *Research on e-Learning and ICT in Education*,
DOI 10.1007/978-1-4614-1083-6_2, © Springer Science+Business Media, LLC 2012

Key Terms

This section defines several terms as they are used in this chapter: educator; digital technologies; the unconference and its derivative, the MirandaMod.

The term "educator" has been chosen as a collective noun for the subjects of this developmental project in order to embrace the roles of all teachers who also teach other teachers about digital technologies, formally or informally: senior managers, teacher educators, staff trainers, network managers, regional advisers and teaching assistants.

The global term "digital technologies" is used to encompass all the technologies that teachers might use for teaching and learning within their classrooms. This term also refers to technologies that are used for teaching and learning remotely, such as Virtual Learning environments. The term "Information and Communications Technology" (ICT) is used both in the UK and in South Africa for the subject as it is both taught in the classroom and deployed as part of pedagogy. However, in other countries, this curriculum subject is often called Information Technology or Informatics. Internationally, these terms imply a concentration on the computer science aspects of computer application: the implication in the UK is that ICT refers to the ways of using computers for information retrieval, communications and pedagogy, rather than how computers are controlled through programming and how hardware operates. Across the world, however, computer science is still taught in schools where learning to programme a computer as well as learning to use the packages in detail are key elements in computer lessons although computers are not deployed elsewhere in the curriculum.

The term "MirandaMod" is used for a virtual debate between professionals who are seen as equals. These innovative opportunities for exchange meet the demands of emerging cultures of professional learning in this digital age. While learning remotely and informally is largely what has been understood about mobile learning, the concept can now be extended to include the informal spaces in which learning takes place – the liminal spaces that those who push the boundaries of digital possibilities now inhabit intellectually (Preston et al. 2009). The term "liminal space (Cuthell et al. 2011)" is a term drawn from anthropology that describes a rite of passage, in which a person moves from one state to another. The anthropological view sees the liminal state as involving a period of time in which an individual may oscillate between old and new states, involve a range of emotions including anticipation, difficulty and anxiety, and at times require the mimicry of the new state until it becomes "natural". ICT users are transformed in the liminal space by acquiring new knowledge, a new status and a new identity in the community. This is of critical importance if ICT CPD is to be successful.

The mode of learning that takes place in this liminal space has recently been modified by professional educators in two versions. The TeachMeet[1] participants are called in random order to offer a 2- or 5-min focus on the teachers' knowledge and craft, rather than on theory and abstraction. Each teacher speaks about their

[1] http://wiki.scotedublogs.org.uk.

achievements in the classroom from their own perspective. There is no theme established. In a MirandaMods,[2] however, the Fellows chose a theme beforehand. Some lead participants set the tone in a 5-min talk, usually without presentation software, and further contributions are selected by the chairperson of the debate to achieve a balance in participation between teachers, researchers and teacher educators. This chapter explores the emergence of the MirandaMod in more detail, but first the relevant literature on professional learning will be covered – largely from the British point of view.

Literature Review

Three literature strands are relevant to the development of the MirandaMod: social and cultural contexts that look at the impact of digital technologies in informal learning; professional learning issues; and, the basic pedagogic principles that underpin CPD programmes and their relationship to the principles of an unconference.

Social and Cultural Contexts

The new demands of digital technologies are challenging traditional, social and cultural practices as well the agency of teachers and learners (Pachler et al. 2010). Kress and Pachler (2007) warn, however, that associated social, political and economic changes, linked with globalisation, are taking place with a speed that militates against careful reflection within the education profession. These authors balance the attractions of such benefits as democratisation of education through greater access against the transfer of power in the digital realm from state to market. They point to large-scale social consequences where digital technologies and their affordances have already become a prosthesis for some users and are generally influencing our notions of self and society. They ask some "troubling" questions about the gains and losses that are occurring because of the prevalence of technologies in education. "Mobile learning", "e-learning", "online learning", "virtual learning", "anywhere anytime learning" are typical of phrases that are linked to hardware and software rather than a process change. In contrast, they prefer not to refer to the technology that is being used, but to distinctly new conditions and environments created by technology that are impacting on the experience of learning. The engagement of activist professionals in the policy and practice agenda is essential if the concerns of Kress and Pachler (2007) are to be heeded.

Kress and Pachler (2007) outline learning processes that shift from the notion that learning is about acquiring information to the idea that the learner shapes their own knowledge from their own sense of the world – and that this new knowledge

[2] http://www.mirandanet.ac.uk/mirandamods.

created by the learner is valuable. Central are their reflections on the issues of meta-collaboration – the circumstances that allow people to communicate remotely across boundaries of status, nationhood and culture that have not been so readily available in the past. However, Kress and Pachler (2007) point out that this widespread opportunity for communication for all does not presuppose that the agents have a critical understanding of the potential partners in knowledge creation and how their abilities and status might relate. I make a similar point in comparing the differences between social networking in the general sense and deliberate knowledge creation in a Community of Practice (CoP), where there is trust between members with similar approaches to learning and mutual aims to support each other. However, strategies for leveraging this community trust still have to be mutually developed and understood (Preston 2007).

Professional Learning

"Professional learning" is the outcome of the transformational change described by Friere (1968) in his definition of "praxis", the evidence that the professional as the agent has forged together theory and practice (Infed 2011). Praxis, is a high-level mode of professional operation where the practitioner does not only possess skills but a deep knowledge and understanding of the theories that underpin practice. This can lead to a profound change in the professional's sense of identity that is the aim of the best professional development.

As a term, "professional learning" is widely used to cover the activities in CPD programme designs that put educators who are motivated by the prospect of professional change in control of their learning agenda (Pickering et al. 2009; Johns-Shepherd and Gowing 2007). The term emphasises teachers learning actively rather than being passive recipients of an expert teaching agenda. In the ICT CPD Landscape: Literature Review (Daly et al. 2009) the phrase, "professional learning", is used frequently in the context of change. The researchers explain the challenges for the designers of CPD programmes for professionals who aim to promote change:

> ICT CPD, therefore, needs to be recognised as a complex, social, intellectual and practical activity which brings about change in teachers' beliefs and understandings in relation to changing practice and developing skills. It takes place within a range of locations and modes which provide cultural contexts in which to learn. It involves re-evaluating learner–teacher roles and overall classroom pedagogies. It brings changes in aspects of professional identity. For these reasons, simplistic models of ICT CPD are not helpful – it is highly situated and success is subject to many inter-related human and social factors which vary across locations, strategies and relationships (Daly et al. 2009, pp. 69–70).

In 2010, a further government survey of the UK ICT CPD Landscape indicates that there is an even greater diversity of ICT CPD programmes mostly running at a skills level rather than addressing the need for transformative change (Pachler et al. 2011). In this chapter, the MirandaMod is investigated as a means of providing widely available and cost effective CPD for those leaders who are willing to learn informally from each other.

Pedagogical Models Underpinning CPD

The underlying pedagogical mode of the traditional conference is "information transmission". This popular phrase is used to denote the communication of expert knowledge that is one way only. Chandler (1994) complains that the information transmission model assumes communicators are isolated individuals. No allowance is made for differing purposes, differing interpretations, unequal power relations and situational contexts. The traditional role of expert educators around the world is to pass on their expertise to students who learn this information and reproduce it for examinations and tests without necessarily processing it to change their practice.

The "unconference" model eschews this approach to learning in favour of demanding that all the participants are actively engaged in generating knowledge and knowledge exchange. In this innovative mode of professional learning, the traditional power relationships between the expert and the learner are unbalanced. The underlying pedagogical approaches "social interaction" promoted by Lave and Wenger in the development of the "community of practice (CoP)" concept over nearly two decades (Lave and Wenger 1991, 1999; Wenger 1998, 2004; Wenger et al. 2002). These are groups of professionals who chose to learn together informally. Thus two related theories expand Wenger's vision about CoP practices: Communal Constructivism and Braided Learning. Communal Constructivism emphasises teachers' knowledge building role as they work together often across national boundaries (Holmes et al. 2001; Leask and Younie 2001, 2002).

This "social interaction" approach to learning relates to Freire's notion of the wider value of collaborative learning in social and cultural contexts for professionals who want to take charge of their own agenda (Friere 1968). As CoPs mature, the MirandaNet observation has been that an interesting form of social learning emerges underpinned by the use of technologies (Cuthell 2005). Salmon (2002) has analysed the five steps of learning that take place when a course is run online: access and motivation; online socialisation; information exchange; knowledge construction; and development. Salmon comments that knowledge construction tends to happen when students are writing their essays in isolation. It would be fruitful in the development stage, the fifth step, if they came back to the classroom and shared collaboratively what has been learnt in their individual studies in order to gain new insights into learning together. This rarely happens because students begin new modules at this stage in new groupings.

Braided Learning theory (Haythornthwaite et al. 2007; Cuthell and Preston 2007; Preston 2008) picks up on the individual learning in Salmon's step four and then considers how the development step, five, might be an activity like an unconference that is collaborative, community-focused and voluntary. This contrasts with the activity of a group of individual learners moving towards accreditation on a formal course. Braided Learning is an emergent theory that is tracing how this kind of informal dynamic knowledge creation works in a collaborative online context. Braided Learning refers to a meaning-making process that is emerging from the observation of online communication. Cuthell (2005) has traced the development of students' collaborative knowledge sharing in a MirandaNet online course on e-facilitation in a virtual learning environment in detail. The second Braided Learning studies looked at the productive use of email texts and e-facilitation processes (Preston 2007, 2009; Cuthell and Preston 2008; Cuthell 2008, 2009). In this third study, undertaken as communities of professionals mature in digital competence, the MirandaMod has become a crucible where social learning can find expression using virtual meeting software transcripts, i-chat, remote multi-authored digital concept mapping, microblogging and video streaming.

The MirandaMod development is one answer to the approach to ICT CPD recommended by the Landscape Review: a greater concentration on the role of groups of professionals who meet informally to exchange the theories and practices (Daly et al. 2009). In MirandaNet research the investigators are members researching members and themselves. This ethnographical method was developed by Adler and Adler (1987): the Complete Member Researcher. Originally international MirandaNet researchers were engaged in simply observing the email discussions taking place in professional CoPs, ITTE (http://www.itte.org.uk) and Naace (http://www.naace.org.uk) are two influential UK professional organisations relating to digital technologies in education. Their members' use of email indicate how online professional learning is orchestrated by the members of the CoP in accordance with their own agenda (Preston 2007; Preston and Cuthell 2009; Preston et al. 2009). In this chapter, the newest iteration of informal learning, the MirandaMod, is the focus of investigation. The MirandaMod extends the opportunities for collaborative learning practised in a "community of practice".

MirandaMod Format

In brief, a themed MirandaMod is an occasion when like-minded educators aim to explore an emerging professional issue and collaboratively create new knowledge. This knowledge is then disseminated through the website to inspire new grassroots practice.

MirandaNet members define the MirandaMod on their website as an informal, loosely structured unconference of like-minded educators sharing ideas about the use of technology to inspire others. The term "Mod" that was offered by a Scottish member historically comes from the Gaelic word for a gathering, assembly or parliament. MirandaMod is usually (but not always) a fringe event following or attached to a formal MirandaNet seminar/workshop or meeting. The format includes a wiki, streamed webcasts, chat facilities, online collaborative concept maps and linked Twitter streams, means that there is an international dimension to these events. Like wikis, blogs, chat and email, this online multimodal communication is unlike previous modes of knowledge construction because remote participation reduces time and cost commitments. In these unstructured activities software such as Flash Meeting, linked to microblogging and instant communication streams, empower digital visitors to engage remotely with those at the terrestrial meetings, even to the point of placing a convivial pint of beer next to their terminal. The virtual world, Second Life, is also being considered as a welcoming MirandaMod location.

These creators of the MirandaMod programme, as well as the participants, value the mix of perspectives at the meetings. Some of them are also members of Naace, or ITTE, or TeachMeet, or all three; users of Twitter. They have engaged in a variety of experiments with "unconference" models in relationship to the topic, the location and the technology available. The MirandaMod format is constantly being adjusted according to the topic.

Typically, a conventional seminar might take place from 1400 to 1700 at the "home" of MirandaNet, the WLE Centre at the Institute of Education, University of London. Some well-known experts are given 30 minutes to talk about their subject at length, followed by time for questions. For example, the MirandaMod on educational games covered different perspectives on games in education by researchers, teachers, teacher educators and games developers.

In a MirandaNet seminar the room is organised without a speakers' platform. Speakers and participants sit round a table, so that the barriers between speakers and their listeners are broken down and the participants can look at one another in the eye and see reactions. All participants are also invited to introduce themselves, whereas speakers in conferences often do not ask their audience who they are: sometimes because the audience is too big, sometimes because the speakers are keener to talk than to learn. Each MirandaNet seminar will be filmed and hosted on the MirandaNet website, assuming that funds are available. In this way international and national members who could not be in London have asynchronous access to the meeting and can learn from the topics.

In planning the programme, complex decisions by the team have to be made that take account of what is topical, who is available to lead the sessions and what technology is appropriate. "Low cost and no frills" is the norm; speakers are asked to give their time free. So this early seminar and the MirandaMod are free to anyone who has an interest. Supper follows; it is sponsored by companies and by government agency supporters and the WLE Centre where the London MirandaMods are held and continues from 1700 to 1830. During the supper some of the audience leave and others stay; some go shopping for books and return. More participants appear for the MirandaMod who could not attend the afternoon session; these are members of MirandaNet as well as staff and students at the host university, members of ITTE, Naace and attendees at TeachMeet. Where possible MirandaMods are held during school holidays or on a Friday evening, so practising teachers have a chance of attending. Obtaining support cover for teachers in classrooms is increasingly difficult. The "expert" seminar speakers are expected to stay on as well to contribute to the more relaxed MirandaMod. Speakers are invited to see this as an opportunity to learn from the participants as well as contribute.

MirandaMods, lasting from about 1830 to 2100, are open to all students and teachers from the Institute of Education, University of London, MirandaNet and other appropriate professional groups. The full programme for the academic year 2009/2010 can be found in Appendix one, where the range of formats and approaches can be seen even over one season. The full resources can be accessed on http://www.mirandanet.ac.uk/mirandamods. Speakers and participants are asked to make their materials freely available and the collaborative maps prove to be a good place for useful but less obvious resources to be posted.

All the iChat text, video stream and Twitter feeds are then posted in the MirandaNet web space so that those who could not participate have a record of proceedings and asynchronous access. Currently, this material is also being used for research, in order to develop the Braided Learning framework more comprehensively.

In specific terms, participants elect to present for 2 or 7 min on the theme of the session. The use of standard presentation software (like PowerPoint) is discouraged in order to minimise the possibility of didactic presentations, and to empower engagement with colleagues. On the evening, the order of speakers is random. Time factors may prevent some from speaking depending on the incidental discussions that evolve about the presentations. The international dimension is made possible by the use of wikis, FlashMeeting, real time video streams, iChat and a Twitter stream (Preston and Cuthell 2010) – all of which can be embedded in a Second Life seminar space. The last half hour of the MirandaMod and time afterwards will be taken up by the collaborative creation of an online multi-authored concept map that will outline the group judgements that have been made on the topic under debate. These maps form the basis of the professional distribution of knowledge and the reports.

The Findings: Achieving Praxis

The evidence for changes in praxis was divided under the key characteristics of an effective ICT CPD programme design described in the Landscape review (Daly et al. 2009) that reflects the complex, social, intellectual and practical process of professional learning. The conclusions have been grouped under three headings:

Under the first heading, "the opportunities for teachers to record changes in their beliefs and understandings in relation to changing practice and developing skills", there are several observations:

- The MirandaMod is proving valuable in the creation of professional knowledge as opposed to socialising online. This instant communication between work-based experts is a valuable mode for professional learning, where all the participants define the agenda before and during the event.
- In particular, a MirandaMod programme addresses some of the issues raised in the Becta reports on the UK ICT landscape (2010). First, the emphasis on intellectual debate about digital technologies emphasises a deep understanding and application of skills to developing learning and teaching rather than just a discussion of skills. Additionally, teachers' knowledge and craft are recognised, rather than relying on a crude estimate of their skills.
- Teachers at any level are sharing in a MirandaMod the development of an appropriate "vision" focused on pedagogy. Even if their own focus is skills, other participants can open minds to other perspectives. The teacher development aspect is given in the information experience that they have.

Under the second heading "a variety of locations and modes that reflect different cultural contexts for learning" are these observations:

- Because presentation software is discouraged each participant has to think hard about less linear ways in presenting information and deploy greater use of multimodal forms of presentation. Persuasion simply through eye contact with the audience is also seen to be powerful in terms of performance.
- The way in which a MirandaMod can be set up means that the costs and time required for conventional CPD do not apply. The teachers are, in effect, teaching themselves. They do not need to meet face-to-face in order to keep up their knowledge. The MirandaMod can help to dissipate the "policy tensions" that prevent coherent and consistent development of pedagogy using technologies, and that create conflicts over how time and resources are used to embed technologies within schools.
- This knowledge creation activity is important because the technology is sufficiently transparent to empower all members to set the agenda at the grassroots. This mirrors young peoples' mobile learning activity outside school in easy to use virtual environments, such as ThinkQuest, Bebo and Facebook, that allow them to follow their interests and to develop and extend their existing talents.
- Teachers can utilise the attendant resources in any way or time they wish. They can use these resources for self study or to share with peers and pupils. They can also author resources for others which change their perception of their role.

Under the third heading "potential for professionals to re-evaluate their identity in relationship to their role and their pedagogical observations" MirandaMods can:

- Encourage democratic debate rather than just promote socialisation.
- Challenge the usual model of conferences for teachers where there is limited interaction, if any, between "experts" on stage and the experts in the audience. This mix helps teachers to see themselves in the wider professional context and, perhaps, open up interests that they were not aware that they had.
- Challenge the usual model of conferences for teachers where there is limited interaction, if any, between "experts" on stage and the experts in the audience. In the MirandaMod, professionals have equal input regardless of their differing status in the world of education, which challenges their understanding of their identity.

In questions about revaluating their identity the practitioner participants particularly valued the research input which is not normally available to teachers in classrooms. They also found contact with researchers and the chance to question them particularly revealing and mind changing.

Conclusions

The MirandaMod is a new mode of professional learning that employs digital technologies in innovative ways to enrich collaborative knowledge creation processes. The main message is that it is the knowledge gathering agenda that should take precedence over the demands of digital technologies.

Five ways have been identified overall that show how MirandaMods have the potential to promote changes in professional praxis through:

- Reflection
- Collaboration
- Access to collaborative resources
- Publishing new professional knowledge based on collaboration
- Changing existing frames of thought and patterns of behaviour

What is probably most important for the future is the extra dimension MirandaMods add to learning through social interaction, especially when the opportunities for professionals to engage in face-to-face meetings are reduced because of economic constraints. Costs are not high: investment in this form of ICT CPD may be the only way that many educators have access to professional learning in the years to come.

References

Adler, P. A. & Adler P. (1987). *Membership roles in field research.* Newbury Park C.A.: Sage.

Chandler, D. (1994). *The transmission model of communication.* Retrieved 19 March 2011 from http://www.aber.ac.uk/media/Documents/short/trans.html.

Cuthell, J. (2005). Beyond collaborative learning: Communal construction of knowledge in an online environment Paper presented at the Web Information Systems and Technologies International Conference (WEBIST), Miami, Retrieved 19 March 2011 from http://www.virtuallearning.org.uk/?page_id=414.

Cuthell, J. (2008). The Role of a Web-based community in teacher professional development. *International Journal of Web Based Communities*, 2(8), 115–139.

Cuthell, J. (2009). Thinking and changing practice: Collaborative online professional development. In: R. Carlsen, K. McFerrin, R. Weber & D. A. Willis (eds.), *Proceedings of SITE 2009* (pp. 2264–2269). Norfolk, VA: AACE.

Cuthell, J., & Preston, C. (2007). Braided learning: Developments in an online community of practice. In: Kinshuk, D. G. Sampson, M. J. Spector & P. Isaias (eds.), *Proceedings of the IADIS International Conference on Cognition and Exploratory Learning in Digital Age, CELDA 2007* (pp.79–84). Algarve: IADIS Press.

Cuthell, J., & Preston, C. (2008). Expert ICT advisers considering their own ICT CPD experiences. In R. Carlsen, K. McFerrin, R. Weber & D. A. Willis (eds.), *Proceedings of SITE 2008* (pp. 3247–3250). Norfolk, VA: AACE.

Cuthell, J. P., Cych, L., & Preston, C. (2011). Learning in Liminal Spaces. Paper presented at "Mobile learning: Crossing boundaries in convergent environments" Conference, 21–22 March 2011, Bremen, Germany. Retrieved 15 May 2011 from http://www.virtuallearning.org.uk/?p=555.

Daly, C., Pachler, N., &. Pelletier, C. (2009). *Continuing professional development in ICT for teachers: A literature review. Becta,* London: WLE Centre. Retrieved 19 March 2011 from http://www.wlecentre.ac.uk/cms/files/becta/becta-ict-cpd-literaturereview.pdf.

Downes, T. (2004). *Playing and learning with digital technologies - at home and at schoo*l. In N. Davis & A. Brown (eds.), *Digital Technologies, Communities and Education* (pp. 115–131). London. New York. Routledge Falmer.

Facer, K., Sutherland, R., Furlong, J., & Furlong, R. (2003). *Screenplay: Children's Computing in the Home.* London: Routledge Falmer.

Friere, P. (1968, reprinted 1970) *Pedagogy of the Oppressed.* London: Continuum International Publishing Group.

Haythornthwaite C., Andrews R., Kazmer M. M., Bruce B. C., Montague R.-A., & Preston C. (2007). *New International Theories and Models of and for Online Learning.* First Monday, 12(8), 6 August 2007, Retrieved 22 March 2010 from http://firstmonday.org/article/view/1976/1851.

Holmes, B., Tangney, B. et al. (2001). Communal constructivism: students constructing learning for as well as with others. *Proceedings of the 12th International Conference of the Society for Information Technology & Teacher Education, SITE 2001* (pp. 3114–3119). Charlottesville, VA, USA, Association for the Advancement of Computing in Education.

Infed (2011). Retrieved 15 December 2010 from http://www.infed.org/biblio/b-praxis.htm.

Johns-Shepherd, L., & Gowing, E. (2007). Beyond the classroom door, beyond the school gates: the imperative for school-to-school networks for professional learning. In J. Pickering, C. Daly & N. Pachler (eds.), *New Designs for Teachers' Professional Learning* (pp. 116–133). London: Bedford Way papers.

Kress, G., & Pachler, N. (2007). Thinking about the 'm' in learning. *Mobile Learning: towards a research agenda.* N. Pachler. London, WLE centre. Retrieved 16 March 2011 from http://www.wlecentre.ac.uk/cms/files/.../mobilelearning_pachler2007.pdf.

Lave, J., & Wenger, E. (1991) *Situated Learning: Legitimate Peripheral Participation.* Cambridge University Press.

Lave, J., & Wenger, E. (1999). Learning and pedagogy in communities of practice. In J. Leach & B. Moon (eds.), *Learners and Pedagogy* (pp. 21–33). Open University: SAGE Publications Inc.

Leask, M., & Younie, S. (2001). Building on-line communities for teachers: ideas emerging from research. In M. Leask (ed.), *Issues in Teaching Using ICT* (pp. 223–232). London: Routledge.

Leask, M., & Younie S. (2002). Communal constructivist theory: ICT pedagogy and internationalisation of the curriculum. *Journal of Information Technology for Teacher Education*, 10(1/2), 117–134.

Pachler N., Bachmair, B., & Cook, J. (2010). *Mobile Learning: Structures, Agency, Practices.* New York: Springer.

Pachler, N., Preston, C., Cuthell, J., Allen, A., & Pinheiro Torres, C. (2011). *The ICT CPD Landscape: Final Report.* Becta, Retrieved 15 March 2011 from http://www.wlecentre.ac.uk/cms/files/becta/becta-ict-cpd-landscapereport.pdf.

Pickering, J., Daly, C., & Pachler N. (2009). *New Designs for Teachers Professional Learning.* London: Bedford Way Papers.

Preston, C. (2007). Social networking between professionals: what is the point?. In J. Beishuizen, R. Carneiro & K. Steffens (eds.), *Proceedings of the KALEIDOSCOPE-TACONET Conference "Self-regulated Learning in Technology Enhanced Learning Environments: Individual Learning and Communities of Learners"* (pp. 71–75). Aken: Shaker Verlag.

Preston, C. (2008). Braided learning: an emerging practice observed in e-communities of practice'. Special Issue: Online Learning Communities in Context. *International Journal of Web Based Communities,* 4(2), 220–243.

Preston, C. (2009). Exploring semiotic approaches to analysing multidimensional concept maps using methods that value collaboration. In P. Torres and R. Marriott (eds.), *Handbook of Research on Collaborative Learning Using Concept Mapping* (pp. 256–283). Hershey, PA: IGI Global.

Preston, C., & Cuthell, J. (2007). *The Perspectives of Professional Educators' on ICT CPD: Past, Present, Future.* N. Pachler (ed.). London: WLE, Institute of Education, University of London. Retrieved 19 March 2011 from http://www.wlecentre.ac.uk/cms/files/cpreston_report.pdf.

Preston, C., & Cuthell J. (2009). *Towards collaboration: knowledge creation in Web 2.0 environments.* An unpublished report for Becta, Coventry.

Preston, C., & Cuthell J. (2010). *Towards collaboration: knowledge creation in Web 2.0 environments.* An unpublished report for Becta, Coventry.

Preston, C., Cuthell, J., Keuchel T., Cych L., Thomas D., Buddie D., & Allen A. (2009). New professional cultures: Braided gatherings in the third space. In N. Pachler & J. Seipold (ed.), *Proceedings of 3rd WLE Mobile Learning Symposium* (pp.135–137). Institute of Education,

University of London, Retrieved 19 May 2011 from http://www.londonmobilelearning.net/symposium/downloads/3rd_wle_mlearning_symposium_-_book_of_abstracts_single_page_display.pdf.

Salmon, G. (2002). *E-tivities: the key to active online learning.* London: Kogan Page.

Somekh, B. (2004). Taking the Sociological Imagination to School: an analysis of the (lack of) impact of information and communications technologies on education systems. *Technology, Pedagogy and Education* 13(2), 163–179.

Wenger, E. (1998). *Communities of Practice: learning, meaning and identity.* Cambridge University Press.

Wenger, E. (2004). *Learning for a small planet: a research agenda.* Retrieved 29 July 2010 from http://www.ewenger.com/research/LSPfoundingdoc.doc.

Wenger, E., McDermott, R., & Snyder, W. (2002). *Cultivating communities of practice: a guide to managing knowledge.* Boston: Harvard Business School Press.

Synthetic Worlds and Virtual Citizens: Experimental Ethnographic Simulation, Virtual Autotopography and Emerging Citizenship Identity in Young People

Stewart Martin

Introduction

Concerns have risen sharply in recent years about the level of public disengagement with political and civic life in the UK, as evidenced by falling turnout at national and local elections, rising cynicism and lack of trust in politicians and a perceived increase in the alienation and marginalisation of some groups. Particular anxiety has been expressed, both by governments and in the media, about the radicalisation of some young people and the association of this with the growth of cultural and religious fundamentalism (Home Office 2001a, b, 2004, 2006; Bradford Metropolitan District Council 2001). Such concerns have been fuelled and given greater credence by international events, especially when perceived to be associated with political instabilities and terrorism and by rising levels of threat to individual nation states from military developments worldwide.

Such anxieties are not unique to any one country and many governments have responded to concerns about the perceived fragmentation of and threat to political and national identity (Deakin et al. 2005). Some governments have reacted by increasing the attention given to producing citizens with appropriate senses of self, community and citizenship often through changes to their educational systems, via "citizenship education" under various guises (Martin and Feng 2006; Goldsmith 2008).

In the case of England the intellectual, legislative and political legacy of British colonialism, the subsequent growth of the UK as a multicultural democracy and the development of trans-national political structures have over time increased concerns about entitlement to and the nature of British citizenship. This contentious area has promoted considerable debate about what should constitute the appropriate responses through educational policies and outcomes.

S. Martin (✉)
School of Social Sciences and Law, Teesside University, Middlesbrough, UK
e-mail: s.m.martin@tees.ac.uk

A. Jimoyiannis (ed.), *Research on e-Learning and ICT in Education*,
DOI 10.1007/978-1-4614-1083-6_3,

The UK has one of the lowest voter turnouts of any western democracy and there is rising anxiety about the lack of political engagement with the state; "Concern about youth alienation from democratic processes has led, at least in part, to the introduction of citizenship education in schools. This has stemmed, in part, from angst about the low levels of voter participation by young citizens in the 18-24 age bracket, in particular" (MacFarlane 2005: 298). This matters because one of the outcomes of increased international interconnectedness is that global tensions are being reflected on the streets of local communities. Particular anxieties exist about the disengagement and marginalisation of groups such as Muslims (Osler and Starkey 2003; Gallup 2009), heightened by the growth of economic globalisation, international terrorism and high-profile extremist events. Media reporting of such factors can compound the resulting anxieties and confusion:

> 'Of Muslims in the 16-24 age group, our poll found 37 per cent wanted Islamic sharia law in the UK, 31 per cent wanted heretics put to death and 74 per cent wanted Muslim women to wear the full-face niqab veil or the hijab headscarf'. Sharia law 'specifies stoning, amputations and executions as routine punishments. Religious police bring suspects before special courts' (Daily Mail 2007).

Young people from communities with distinct religious or cultural identities have traditionally found it difficult to engage with or be welcomed into an inclusive sense of national citizenship, as considered by McGhee (2005). In the UK in particular, there is no strong sense of inclusive national identity or of a sense of citizenship which embraces Europe comfortably, and the need for the development of a contemporary and more inclusive conception of citizenship and a wider participatory democracy has been noted both in government policy and more widely (McGhee 2005; MORI 2007).

However, the desire to develop a stronger, more cohesive sense of British citizenship by implementing Citizenship Education in schools has met with limited success. The intentions for citizenship education remain contested and misunderstood, its delivery often makes little reference to significant local and national issues and how politicians, the media and the wider society deals with these and in many schools the general provision for citizenship education is inadequate. Teachers find the topic problematic to teach, often due to poor knowledge, training and resources, overall attainment in citizenship education is poor when compared with other subjects, and the National Curriculum for citizenship education is also ambiguous, lacks coherence and is unmanageable (Ofsted 2006). There has been sustained criticism that "citizenship education is the worst taught subject in secondary schools" (Independent 2006) and, despite improvements made since its introduction, the Chief Inspector of Schools' most recent Annual Report concedes that it "remains fragile" in many schools (Chief Inspector's Annual Report 2008).

There a growing recognition that citizenship education in the UK needs to be more about empowerment and "performativity" (Braidotti 1994; Commission on Integration and Cohesion 2007), about the society we want to see (The Equalities Review 2007) and less about the study of academic content, citizenship duties, the institutions of government, "the rule of law" (Ofsted 2006) or citizenship as an act of social compliance and contribution, as is sometimes found when countries take a more overtly political approach to promoting social integration (Martin and Feng

2006; Goldsmith 2008). But engaging young people in civic and political life via an active citizenship is not of only advantage for them but:

> Being taught to respect the law without learning how bad laws can be changed and better ones promoted tends to create apathetic subjects rather than active citizens. At the worst, disengagement can lead to acts of delinquent rebellion against a social order that young people feel powerless to influence. Sir Bernard Crick (Quoted in Ofsted 2006: 5).

A series of large-scale studies with secondary school age young people by the International Association for the Evaluation of Educational Achievement (IEA) into citizenship and civic education across Europe (e.g. the International Civic and Citizenship Education Study, ICCS, and the Civic Education Study, CIVED, see http://www.iea.nl) found that students in most EU countries have an understanding of basic democratic values and institutions although females are more supportive than males of the political rights of women and immigrants. While young people are sceptical about traditional forms of political engagement (except voting) these studies found that they are open to other types of civic involvement such as collecting money for good causes or joining non-violent protest marches. Many students, especially as they get older, seem to trust news media more than government-related institutions and have less positive feelings about their countries. These studies also found that the home environment had a substantial impact on civic knowledge but that schools that used democratic practices were more successful in promoting civic knowledge and engagement (Torney-Purta et al. 2001; Amadeo et al. 2002).

These studies used metrics from questionnaire scores that asked about particular pre-identified areas of knowledge and understanding (Schultz et al. 2008) but did not collect significant amounts of qualitative data or engage young people in exploring the degree to which their individual citizenship identity emerged over time during adolescence. They found that young peoples' concepts of democracy and of what makes a good citizen consistently identified the most important features to be obeying the law, voting and following political issues, although this was established from the predetermined topics explored and questions answered (Amadeo et al. 2002). The views of younger and older secondary age students did not differ markedly, suggesting that by age 14 the views of young people have already been influenced by their cultural, historical and educational context. However, over a 10-year period, citizenship skills and knowledge appeared to have declined significantly in the age group studied (Amadeo et al. 2002).

As with other large-scale studies, the ICCS study of 24 EU countries (Kerr et al. 2010) and the IEA study of 38 countries (Schultz et al. 2010a, b) were based on the premise that citizenship education involves helping young people develop relevant knowledge and understanding and positive attitudes towards being a citizen and towards participating in activities related to civics and citizenship. The results showed considerable variation in civic knowledge among and within European countries for facts about the EU, knowledge of EU laws and policies and knowledge about the euro currency. This study sought to identify the degree to which participants engaged with and were interested in: European citizenship and identity; Intercultural relations in Europe; Free movement of citizens in Europe; European policies, institutions and participation and European language learning.

Many students participating in these studies had a strong sense of European identity, although in some countries this was weaker in those with immigrant backgrounds. Those with positive attitudes towards their country tended also to have a stronger sense of European identity. Most held positive attitudes towards equal rights for other European citizens living in their country as well as for racial/ethnic minorities. Most also supported citizen's rights to free movement to live, work and travel anywhere in Europe, although a minority in some countries were in favour of restrictions on this.

Most teachers thought knowledge and skills were the most important aim of citizenship education, including knowledge of social, political and civic institutions; skills and competencies in conflict resolution; knowledge of citizens' rights and responsibilities; and critical and independent thinking. Only a few thought that "preparing students for future political participation" and "supporting the development of effective strategies for the fight against racism and xenophobia" were important aims of citizenship education. These studies, as a group, concluded that learning about the EU therefore needed more emphasis within citizenship education and that knowledge and skills should be emphasised above the importance of participation. Emphasis was placed heavily on "knowing facts" and reasoning about them.

Teachers in many countries appear to have tended to emphasise a didactic approach to citizenship education with an associated emphasis on content over process and on a transmissive pedagogy over one more strongly founded on collaborative learning, constructionism and student empowerment. The degree to which curricula are prescribed within government policy varies from country to country and is likely to be a contributing factor to this, producing a variety of approaches between and within countries and their individual educational institutions. However, the reports discussed above emphasise that, in general, active participation was not something that most teachers promoted and although they were usually receptive to open student discussion in classrooms, they provided only limited choice of citizenship topics and activities. Most students said they participated in class or school elections and about two fifth said they participated in debates, decision-making and student assemblies. Active citizenship community involvement by schools focused on sports events and cultural activities. Few teachers reported student involvement in human rights projects or activities to help the underprivileged. These factors suggest the presence of a relatively modest degree of participatory democracy within educational institutions, despite arguments that this is an essential pre-requisite for effective citizenship education (Kohlberg 1985; Torney-Purta et al. 2001; Amadeo et al. 2002) and also further highlights for many professional educators the unresolved and uncomfortable tension in their practice between professional autonomy, research-led pedagogy and their increasing accountability to external audit systems (Martin 2010).

The IEA study of 38 EU countries (Schultz et al. 2010a) noted that the wide variation it found in student citizenship knowledge was most strongly associated with parental occupational status, although the degree of variation among groups with both similar and different parental occupations was wide in some countries but narrow in others. A significant unexplained decline in students' knowledge was found in 7 of the 15 countries that this study shared with an earlier study 10 years earlier

(Torney-Purta et al. 1999), which measured students' citizenship perceptions across four domains: value beliefs, attitudes, behavioural intentions and behaviours.

These studies indicate that despite some limited success, citizenship education is increasingly characterised by declining achievement over time across the range of (desired) measured skills and knowledge. This parallels the British experience and difficulties in raising achievement in citizenship education, or of sustaining levels of performance and outcomes comparable with other subjects. In many countries in Europe achievement in citizenship education shares a tendency to be associated with prescribed curricula promoting predetermined elements of knowledge, skill and understanding relatively uninformed or guided by the contemporary concerns, problems and identified concerns and needs of students. The lack of, or declining, success of present approaches suggests the need for an alternative which, given the relative lack of unanimity about citizenship identity and the emergence of increasingly pluralistic democracies, would seem to be most likely to succeed if based upon a more qualitative, exploratory methodology. Such an approach could more effectively explore how citizenship and civic education might be configured to promote a vision for citizenship based upon a consultative participatory model designed to reveal how far citizenship identities may be evolving over time in line with the growth of globalisation and the complexities and changes in demographics, migration and political consensus.

During adolescence, young people are heavily engaged in the exploration of identity (Erikson 1950), but schools are not generally able to afford students access to a rich resource of material and conceptual tools to support the development of workable prototypes and roles. The research reported here is developing an artefact and methodology for use in educational settings to help young people in their exploration and development of cultural and citizenship identity for an inclusive society. It makes imaginative use of technologies known to be attractive to young people, many of whom routinely use similar digital environments such as online social networking to develop and maintain relationships, communicate with others and (re)present themselves. The present research allows young people to practice citizenship in a safe environment that, while virtual, represents real-world contexts dealing with issues of relevance to them, their lives and their development en route to full citizenship.

Experimental Environment

The software used in the present study is a purpose built technology developed from the commercial version of Second Life (OpenSim) but represents a significant development of both. Additional functionality facilitates the creation of communal values, personal diaries, legacy recording and the expression of emotion. It also facilitates communal discussion of citizenship issues and the recording and storage of the collective values and associated definitions that emerge. The environment includes many of the useful and attractive features of Second Life but at the same time addresses and overcomes the perceived barriers to its use by educational institutions inherent in the public access version's lack of user activity monitoring, weak data protection, minimal privacy controls, exposure to "griefing" (cyber-bullying) and prevalence of mature content. These factors make the commercial platform attractive to the wider public but create severe obstacles for educational use. The approach used in this project ensures that at its conclusion the research is able to access a route to adoption by providing educational and other institutions with a technology that draws upon those features known to be engaging and motivating in Second Life but that overcomes the commercial version's inherent limitations, addresses anxieties expressed about its use by young people and provides secure and safe configurations for institutions to implement on their own servers.

Despite the introduction of citizenship into the school curriculum in several countries including England, there has been little debate about what content, tools, pedagogy, or assessment methods are most appropriate. The present research uses an interventionist environment to study how citizenship education can adopt new approaches to explore such relevant issues. Prior work has shown how immersive virtual environments can facilitate the study of cultural and personal values (Csikszentmihalyi and Rochberg-Halton 1981; Bisaillon 1989; Bers and Urrea 2000) while others have focussed on the value of multi-user environments and collaborative virtual spaces (e.g. Bruckman 1998) to show that constructionist approaches maximise the learning, content production and creative expression of individuals in learning communities (Martin and Vallance 2008). However, the present research also uses a relatively small, virtual community to avoid the problems that tend to appear in large platforms (Kollock and Smith 1996).

This project's innovative use of an immersive virtual environment to study citizenship draws on the work of Turkle and Erikson on identity formation and the tensions between the individual's need for social integration into family, culture and society (identification) and the search for boundaries between the self and others (differentiation) (Erikson 1950, 1968; Turkle 1995). The research also makes use of "virtual autotopography" (Gonzalez 1995; Bers 2001) to represent identity through participants' selection of symbolically significant objects. Participants' virtual dwellings are used to study individual re-presentations of self (differentiation). Their involvement with the built environment (e.g. virtual civic spaces, artefacts or "temples" representing religious traditions or cultural/group interests) is used to map their integration into the virtual society and culture (identification). The attachment of values and stories to these artefacts and reflections upon them by participants and on their experiences and on introduced scenarios provides data for studying the tensions between differentiation and identification and emerging perspectives on citizenship.

The imperative given to each participant is to develop a harmonious environment within which each individual feels welcome and empowered. This draws on the idea that individual moral development is critically shaped by participation in democratic social institutions designed to encourage self-government and group decision-making (Kohlberg 1985). In the present research, participants test moral and personal values through conversations and actions in everyday behaviour.

This empirical research focuses on a significant research, policy and practice gap in this area (Deakin et al. 2004) and on how immersive virtual technologies can facilitate and support reflection and discussion about citizenship choices and related ethical issues. The project has high potential for impact on citizenship education, education for multicultural understanding, the understanding of personal identity in relation to that of others and for how these can be used to promote a fairer and more tolerant society which has a more coherent and inclusive sense of what it is to be British.

Methodology

Small-scale trials followed pre-pilot testing with several religious/cultural groupings to validate scenario effectiveness, environmental instrumentation and resource suitability. The trials used pre/post-16 young people and their teachers, drawn from regional schools and colleges and explored the concept of "citizen" and its expression in national identity ("being British").

The research employs experimental ethnographic simulation through immersion of participant teaching groups in a virtual world environment for approximately 2 h/week for 6 weeks. Participants create an avatar to represent how they see themselves; through this they participate as "citizens" in the environment, helping to form an ordered, harmonious community to represent the kind of Britain they would like to see established. Each avatar is provided with a habitat and access to artefacts (e.g. furniture, household objects, clothing) and actions (e.g. "tell a story", "make an argument") from a communal database. Using these, each participant is required to furnish a provided "dwelling" (an installation) to represent what matters to them, and what they value in their life as a citizen.

Avatars use the affordances of the object-oriented environment to move around (walk, fly, run, etc.) and interact with it (by selecting, creating and using objects, artefacts and structures such as community centres, temples or personal homes) and with other avatars (e.g. synchronously via real-time graphical chat, or asynchronously via postings on a communal discussion forum). Participants upload images of their own and incorporate these into the environment as objects added to the common database. Avatars are provided with a range of "emoticons" to signal emotion when responding to others or to scenarios.

Each artefact or image that is used, selected or created (including the avatar) requires the assignment of attributes from three different categories: presentation attributes (graphical appearance; dynamic capabilities); ownership attribute (to control who can copy, modify and own the object) and narrative attributes that provide its description, associated story/biography and an explanation of the personal and/or moral values and purpose that the individual ascribes to it – in the case of a created avatar each owner is required to categorise it as a hero or villain and to provide its biography. Copied objects retain inherited attached values but new owners must attach their own definitions so that objects increasingly are "collective repositories of meaning" (Bers 2001: 383).

Participants will develop both abstract and universal expressions of their values separate from those they attach to any particular experience or instance by recording them and their explanations and definitions of them in the communal values dictionary, which is empty at the start of the experiment but progressively includes all the values and any multiple definitions of those developed by the community. Participants are encouraged to comment on any perceived conflict between the definitions provided; to explore values and behaviours in concrete ways grounded in experiences and through more abstract means and to explore the dictionary and develop conversations with the rest of the community about differing definitions of values, or to enter new values and definitions.

Participants are asked to interact through their avatar with other inhabitants using synchronous and asynchronous "chat" and text in response to a series of experimenter-introduced situations and scenarios. These present contentious "citizenship-related" issues and events, representative of those in the media, and participants respond to these and in so doing help develop social rules and contribute to a participatory community environment. Participants are asked to comment on scenarios with a view to reaching a communal agreement about them and their social implications. Participants can suggest additional scenarios. This approach is designed to minimise the possibility of assumptions being inferred by participants from the nature and design of the experimental environment about whether moral development proceeds universally from concrete to abstract thinking (Kohlberg 1976), or may be differentiated by gender (Gilligan 1982) or is conditional upon particular different ways of individual thinking (Papert 1987; Turkle and Papert 1992).

Participants keep a semi-structured private online reflective diary that encourages them to note ideas, thoughts and observations using guide headings. At the end of the experiment, participants complete a "legacy document" for subsequent visitors, which asks them to summarise what they have learned about citizenship and themselves through using this technology and invites comment about comparisons with their more usual experiences of citizenship education. At this time, they also become "virtual tourists" in the "homes" (or of the installations) created by others and produce a written response to each of them. Participants complete an exit interview (structured questionnaire, given verbally, with some pre-coded answers) to gather opinions and user experiences of the project and reflections on the comments of others about their created home. This method of data collection is effective with young people who may need prompting and encouragement to articulate abstract ideas and insights into how they see their own identity, and needs experienced research staff to facilitate this. Analysis of this data will inform the project's future work, aid understanding of how individuals construct citizenship identity and how personal, religious and cultural values inform this. Implications for citizenship and citizenship education will be explored. Ready for later reconstruction and evaluation, the environment logs all user activity, "chat" and action, with dates and times to enable classification and ordering of activity and events. Participant activity is monitored (tracking the frequency of use of "negative" emotional icons) to ensure that participants do not experience distress. Exit interviews are used to identify and offer appropriate support to those who report negative effects from participating.

Discussion and Conclusions

Key project partners include schools and colleges in the northeast of England, whose teachers and students are collaborating with the research team to explore, develop and articulate new ways for learning about adolescents' emerging adult identities and for developing more effective pedagogies and technologies for teaching citizenship in the twenty-first century. These kinds of collaborative engagements are essential if researchers are to bridge the traditional gulf between their work and educational policy and practice. This gulf is well documented within the UK where in education we seek to overcome the historically strong influence of a utilitarian approach to educational pedagogy (Alexander 2008), but the deep disconnect between research, policy and classroom practice also appears to be an international phenomenon of some concern (Hattie 2009). The current project aims to bridge this gulf and demonstrate to teachers and policy makers the advantages of evidence led practice that is informed by research rather than by inherited views of "what works" or political dogma.

The project expects to produce impact not only within the formal educational curriculum but also more widely within local and faith communities and at the policy level within national government. For projects such as the one reported here, the engagement of an appropriate audience to ensure full dissemination, local and national influence, the clear identification of immediate and potential future benefit and a sympathetic reception with the national political discourse is of great importance. The project is producing greater understanding of how individuals construct their internal sense of identity in the context of wider social structures and cultural influences, and how novel uses of emerging technologies can be applied to the experimental study of these areas. The technical innovations embedded in the design of the virtual environment and the project's use of mixed-methodology will be relevant to researchers working in fields exploring the individual–social interface and to researchers in other disciplines such as computing, sociology and psychology who will gain more understanding of how experimental designs can be realised to explore individual and collective values and behaviours, and model these in simulated real-world contexts, using immersive virtual worlds.

Preliminary findings from the current project are drawn from 705 students aged between 12 and 19 (male=24%, female=76%; white=60%, Pakistani=18%, other Asian or African=22%) in over 40 "virtual" focus groups in schools and colleges in the northeast of England. Most said their ethnic origin had little impact on their everyday life (54%), 34% said it had an impact "sometimes" and 11% said it had a lot of impact. Students in the sample gave their religion as: none (38%); Christian (26%); Muslim (24%); Sikh (6%); Jewish (1%); other (4%). Most said their religious orientation had no influence on their daily life (56%), while 29% said it had some impact, and 15% said it often or always had an impact on this (all figures rounded).

Young people did not find it easy to find consensus on criteria for national identity ("being British") and became conscious that for most suggested criteria there were many circumstances under which each could not apply. Criteria that initially seemed useful became less reliable when participants realised that classmates who they thought of as sharing their own national identity were excluded when sorted by criteria such as "place of birth" – i.e. classmates born outside the UK because their parents had been on holiday or working abroad, or because parents had been in the armed forces or diplomatic service. Despite these exceptions, most young people characterised being British as largely defined by residence or birthplace (24%). However, some felt that national identity required a preference for a certain diet (14%) or particular shared beliefs or allegiances such as support for law enforcement agencies or the military (13%). Many young people associated national identity with patriotism, support for the principles of free speech and equality and an acceptance of other cultures. Significant minorities also prioritised the possession of a relatively neutral accent and high verbal fluency in the dominant national language (11%) or possession of legal documentation such as a UK national passport (9%). These five criteria covered 71% of the responses. Much less emphasis was given to criteria based on appearance (white or non-white), lifestyle, religion, wealth or education.

Criteria for "a good citizen" attracted much greater consensus across fewer domains. Over 83% of young people in the virtual focus groups concluded that a good citizen was defined mostly by personal behaviour and character, key elements of which (in order of priority) included being helpful, friendly, kind, polite, caring, honest, respectful, law abiding and trustworthy. The emphasis throughout was that a good citizen was essentially someone who was morally good, fair and compassionate and was tolerant and unprejudiced in their approach to others. Next in importance were closely related behaviours and actions (11%) such as involvement in voluntary activity that helped the community or individual groups such as the elderly, caring for the environment (not "green" but averse to graffiti, litter, etc.) and generally not indulging in anti-social behaviour (i.e. being non-confrontational; not behaving badly, not taking drugs or committing crime). Deemed of much less importance to being a good citizen were an individual's job, appearance, education, religious beliefs or abilities and skills and this group of factors accounted for less than 6% of responses.

These focus groups also discussed the Life in the UK examination that all aspirant citizens and permanent residents are required to pass (Stationery Office 2011a), and the preparation booklet for it published by the government (Stationery Office 2011b). These tests include questions on a range of topics from knowledge of civic institutions and responsibilities to questions about historical issues or statistical information about contemporary society. These questions and the criteria they supported were in many cases rejected by young people, who saw many of them as unworkable or ridiculous, irrelevant, elitist and likely to be failed by a majority of existing UK citizens; examples particularly criticised included questions requiring knowledge of why the Huguenots left France for Britain in the sixteenth and eighteenth centuries and whether more boys than girls smoke in the UK.

Because of its exploration of whether the developed technology and its design has potential to promote empathy with others and better management of intolerance, community and Faith groups (local and national) also anticipate that they will benefit from greater awareness of how faith and cultural heritage support civil society and of how individuals see themselves and the impact of culture and belief on their self-identity.

A greater understanding of how cultural values and heritage contribute to group and individual identity may help illuminate the impact of these factors on an individual's construction of national identity and by more clearly articulating the dynamics within this help to map the possibilities for an inclusive sense of "Britishness". For politicians, community and faith representatives and educationalists alike, these issues are of more than passing interest in a modern post-industrial pluralist democracy where there is uncertainty as to how individuals understand and relate to community, politics and values and how these influence identity and citizenship.

The policy makers and charities who form the community of direct interest for the research project and who are involved in its development through representation on its steering group also have a direct interest in seeing how this research may improve understanding of how social policy is articulated in civil society, how it shapes citizenship and how perceptions of individual rights and responsibilities are active in framing citizenship identity. The relationship between personal responsibility and engagement with political issues in a participatory democracy is a source of continuing tension and intervention not just within the UK but more widely where countries have at times adopted highly directive approaches to citizenship education (Martin and Feng 2006).

By the completion of this 18-month project, the technology will be refined to the point where its software and associated resources can be used in educational institutions, by faith groups and registered charities and be exploited commercially. By the end of this phase of the project a model of citizenship identity formation will be developed that aids our understanding of the complex processes at work within young people from a variety of backgrounds as they reflect upon their entry into the adult world and especially as they approach or undertake their first experience of democratic participation through voting. This model will map the key contribution to citizenship identity that is made by cultural, religious and other values and will contribute to the development of an understanding of how these articulate within the family, the local community and civil society more generally. This model and its associated instrumentation will provide the foundation for wider studies to follow and will aid the construction of a unidimensional Citizenship Assessment Scale to be used in that phase, which by the use of methodologies such as item response theory will generate a data set that will inform an understanding of national identity in young people and illuminate more clearly our understanding of national identity and its implications for a pluralistic capitalist democracy.

References

Alexander, R. (2008). Pedagogy, curriculum and culture. In K. Hall, P. Murphy & J. Soler (eds.), *Pedagogy and Practice* (pp. 3–27). London: Sage.

Amadeo, J., Torney-Purta, J., Lehmann, R., Husfeldt, V., & Nikolova, R. (2002). *Civic knowledge and engagement: An IEA study of upper secondary students in sixteen countries.* Amsterdam: International Association for the Evaluation of Educational Achievement.

Bers, M.U. (2001). Identity construction environments: developing personal and moral values through the design of a virtual city. *Journal of the Learning Sciences*, 10(9), 4, 365–415.

Bers, U. & Urrea, C. (2000). Technological prayers: Parents and children working with robotics and values. In A. Druin & J. Hendler (eds.), *Robots for kids: Exploring new technologies for learning experiences* (pp. 194–217). San Francisco: Morgan Kaufmann.

Bisaillon, D. (1989). *Logo computer culture and children's development: The influence of socio-moral atmosphere.* Unpublished doctoral dissertation. Harvard University, Cambridge, MA.

Bradford Metropolitan District Council (2001). *Community Pride not prejudice*. Bradford: Bradford Council.

Braidotti, R. (1994). Embodiment, Sexual Difference, and the Nomadic Subject. *Hypatia*, 8(1), 1–13.

Bruckman, A. (1998). Community support for constructionist learning. *Computer Supported Cooperative Work*, 7(1–2), 47–86.

Chief Inspector of Schools (2008). *Annual Report*, 2008, 29. London: Ofsted.

Commission on integration and cohesion (2007). *Our shared future*. London: The Stationery Office.

Csikszentmihalyi, M. & Rochberg-Halton, E. (1981). *The meaning of things*. Cambridge: University Press.

Daily Mail (2007). January 29th.

Deakin C.R., Coates, M., Taylor, M. & Ritchie, S. (2004). A systematic review of the impact of citizenship education on the provision of schooling. *Research Evidence in Education Library.* London: EPPI-Centre, Social Science Research Unit, Institute of Education. Retrieved 1 March 2011 from http://eppi.ioe.ac.uk/cms/Default.aspx?tabid=127&language=en-US.

Deakin C.R., Taylor, M., Tew, M., Samuel, E., Durant, K., & Ritchie, S. (2005). A systematic review of the impact of citizenship education on student learning and achievement. *Research Evidence in Education Library.* London: EPPI-Centre, Social Science Research Unit, Institute of Education. Retrieved 01 March 2011 from http://eppi.ioe.ac.uk/cms/Default.aspx?tabid=129.

Erikson, E.H. (1950). *Childhood and Society*. New York: Norton.

Erikson, E.H. (1968). *Identity: Youth and crisis.* New York: Norton.

Gallup (2009). *The Gallup Coexist Index 2009: A Global Study of Interfaith Relations*. London: Gallup.

Gilligan (1982). *In a different voice: Psychological theory and women's development.* Cambridge, MA: Harvard University Press.

Goldsmith, L. (2008). *Citizenship: Our Common Bond*. London: The Stationery Office.

Gonzalez, J. (1995). Autotopographies. In J. Brahm & M. Driscoll (eds.), *Prosthetic territories: Politics and Hypertechnologies* (pp. 133–150). San Francisco: Westview Press Inc.

Hattie, J.A.C. (2009). *Visible Learning*. London: Routledge.

Home Office (2001a). *Building cohesive communities: a report of the Ministerial Group on Public Order and Community Cohesion*. London: The Stationery Office.

Home Office (2001b). *Community Cohesion: A Report of the Independent Review Team*. London: The Stationery Office.

Home Office (2004). *Strength in diversity*. London: The Stationery Office.

Home Office (2006). *Strong and prosperous communities (white paper).* London: The Stationery Office.

Independent (2006). *Citizenship: Is this the worst taught subject?*. Retrieved 1 March 2011 from http://www.independent.co.uk/news/education/education-news/citizenship-is-this-the-worst-taught-subject-406760.html.

Kerr. D., Sturman, L., Schultz, W., & Burge, B. (2010). ICCS 2009 *European Report: Civic Knowledge, attitudes, and engagement among lower-secondary school students in 24 European countries*. Amsterdam: International Association for the Evaluation of Educational Achievement. Retrieved 1 March 2011 from http://www.iea.nl/iea_publications.html.

Kohlberg, L. (1976). Moral stages and moralization: The cognitive-developmental approach. In T. Lickona (ed.), *Moral development and behavior* (pp. 31–53). New York: Holt, Reinhart & Winston.

Kohlberg, L. (1985). The just community approach to moral education in theory and practice. In M. Berkowitz & F. Oser (eds.), *Moral education: Theory and application* (pp.27–87). Hillsdale, NJ: Lawrence Erlbaum Associates, Inc.

Kollock, P. & Smith, M. (1996). Managing the virtual commons: Cooperation and conflict in computer communities. In S. Herring (ed.), *Computer-mediated communication* (pp. 109–128). Amsterdam: Benjamins.

MacFarlane, B. (2005). The Disengaged Academic: the Retreat from Citizenship, *Higher Education Quarterly*, 59(4), 296–312.

Martin, S. (2010). Teachers using learning styles: caught between research and accountability? *Teaching and Teacher Education*, 26(8) 1583–1591.

Martin, S. & Feng, A. (2006). The construction of citizenship and nation building: the Singapore Case, *Education for Intercultural Citizenship: Concepts and Comparisons* (pp. 47–66). Multilingual Matters.

Martin, S., & Vallance, M. (2008). The impact of synchronous inter-networked teacher training in information and communication technology integration. *Computers & Education*, 51(1), 34–53.

McGhee, D. (2005). Patriots of the future? A critical examination of community cohesion strategies in contemporary Britain. *Sociological Research Online*, 10(3).

MORI (2007). *What works in community cohesion.* London: The Stationery Office.

Ofsted (2006). Towards consensus? Citizenship in secondary school. The Stationery Office.

Osler, A., & Starkey, H. (2003). Learning for Cosmopolitan Citizenship: Theoretical debates and young people's experiences, *Educational Review*, 55(4), 243–254.

Papert, S. (1987). The value of logic and the logic of values. In B. Inhelder, D. de Caprona & A. Cornu-Wells (eds.), *Piaget today* (pp. 101–110). Mahwah, NJ: Lawrence Erlbaum Associates, Inc.

Schultz, W., Fraillon, J., Ainley, J., Losito, B. & Kerr, D. (2008). *International Civic and Citizenship Education Study: Assessment Framework. Amsterdam*: International Association for the Evaluation of Educational Achievement. Retrieved 1 March 2011 from http://www.iea.nl.

Schultz, W., Ainley, J., Fraillon, J., Kerr, D. & Losito, B. (2010a). *Initial Findings from the IEA International Civic and Citizenship Education Study.* Amsterdam: International Association for the Evaluation of Educational Achievement.

Schultz. W., Ainley, J., Fraillon, J., Kerr, D. & Losito, B. (2010b). *ICCS 2009 International Report: Civic Knowledge, attitudes, and engagement among lower-secondary school students in 38 countries.* Amsterdam: International Association for the Evaluation of Educational Achievement. Retrieved 1 March 2011 from http://www.iea.nl/iea_publications.html.

Stationery Office (2011a). Retrieved 1 March 2011 from http://www.lifeintheuktest.gov.uk/htmlsite/index.html.

Stationery Office (2011b). Retrieved 1 March 2011 from http://www.tsoshop.co.uk/bookstore.asp?FO=1240167&trackid=002353.

The Equalities Review (2007). *Fairness and Freedom: The Final Report of the Equalities Review.* London: The Stationery Office.

Torney-Purta, J., Lehmann, R., Oswald, H., & Schultz, W. (2001). *Citizenship and Education in Twenty-eight Countries: Civic Knowledge and Engagement at Age Fourteen.* Amsterdam: International Association for the Evaluation of Educational Achievement.

Torney-Purta, J., Schwille, J., & Amadeo, J.A. (eds.) (1999). *Civic Education Across Countries: Twenty-Four National Case Studies for the IEA Civic Education Project.* Delft: IEA.

Turkle, S. (1995). *Life on the screen: Identity in the age of the internet.* New York: Simon & Schuster.

Turkle, S., & Papert, S. (1992). Epistemological Pluralism and the Revaluation of the Concrete. *Journal of Mathematical Behavior*, 11(1), 3–33.

Teaching in the Knowledge Society: Between Technology and Competences

Antonio Cartelli

Introduction

The Internet and all services on it have changed and are continuously changing mankind and human society, due to the effects they have on information management and communication; otherwise stated, they are influencing individuals' learning, knowledge development and, more generally, interpersonal and intra-personal relationships. The phenomenon has been widely analyzed since its origins, and many studies have confirmed that the IT/ICT provided deep changes on learning environments, either formal, non-formal or informal (Conner 1995, 2004); it is useful to recall here, that the influence of the above environments on the different stages of human development is changed too, together with the effects of digital technologies on intentional and unexpected learning.

Furthermore, the Internet has been considered responsible for the differences affecting people in their access to information and its management. More specifically, the words "digital divide", once identifying the lack of communication equipment in underdeveloped countries, are today used to describe a growing problem in the developed countries (Bindé et al. 2005; Guidolin 2005); they describe at least:

(a) The gap in the pre-existing personal differences, between people who can use technologies (i.e. those who are able in the use of IT/ICT), and those who cannot
(b) The gap in the content management between people who master it (i.e. they can use the IT/ICT to manage information, knowledge, know how etc.), and those who do not

In this context, the analysis of Bauman (2006) regarding today's society has a special relevance, together with his definition of "liquid modernity"; following Bauman's idea,

A. Cartelli (✉)
University of Cassino, Cassino, Italy
e-mail: cartan@unicas.it

A. Jimoyiannis (ed.), *Research on e-Learning and ICT in Education*,
DOI 10.1007/978-1-4614-1083-6_4,

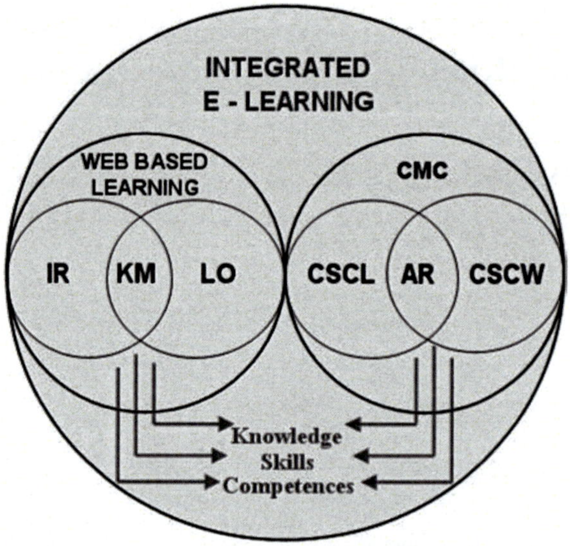

Fig. 1 Model for integrated e-learning strategies (by L. Galliani)

the destruction of the certainties in the liquid life forces the subjects to adapt to group behaviour, to avoid exclusion. It well explains the explosion of the phenomenon of social networks and the reinforcement of the definition of "digital natives" (Prensky 2001), for the young generations, against the definition of "digital immigrants", used for elder people or at least for those who were not born in the digital era.

As a result of the above issues the following questions arise:

- How many theories and models coming from educational research are used by public institutions and governments to produce real innovation or, at least, better results in everyday teaching?
- What role the school has in today's society in helping students to develop self-learning skills, meta-cognitive abilities and lifelong learning strategies?
- What role do digital technologies have in everyday teaching-learning processes for the improvement of the quality of teaching and to help students overcome their problems and difficulties?

A first answer to the above questions has been given by Galliani (2004), who proposed an integrated model for the e-learning instruments and methods to be used at school. In his model two main elements determine the development of students' knowledge, skills and competences: web-based learning (WBL) and computer-mediated communication (CMC).

Both of them have a complex structure and are based on other elements. For the features of the web, the most relevant elements to be used for students' learning are in the following: information retrieval (IR), knowledge management (KM) and the use of learning objects (LOs). The CMC, on the other hand, induces and improves social actions, like computer supported collaborative learning (CSCL), computer supported collaborative work (CSCW) and action research (AR). Figure 1 synthesizes the structure of that model, which is used here as framework for the analysis of the experience the author had with the schools taking part in an Italian project for teaching innovation (i.e. the *Innovascuola* project).

The most relevant aspects to focus on in that experience have been:

(a) The involvement of the author in the schools' projects, that is: the analysis of teachers' backgrounds, the planning of training activities, the proposal of the instruments and strategies to be adopted and the support to the creation of learning units for students
(b) The results from an investigation on digital competence assessment, which has been used to obtain suggestions and ideas on new teaching units of learning in everyday school work

Each of them will be better analyzed in the following sections.

The *InnovaScuola* Project and the Teachers Working on It

The work the author made with the teachers engaged in the *Innovascuola* project has been the result of the agreement between the Laboratory for Teaching and Learning Technologies, in the University of Cassino, and the funded schools.

The laboratory, managed by the author, had to support the schools in the choice of the instruments to be used for teaching, helped them in planning the strategies to be adopted in everyday school work and supported them in the production of learning units.

The constraints for the decisions to be adopted by the teachers were as follows:

- The introduction of new instruments and processes in the schools had to respect the commitment of the projects, which were approved by the Public Agency charged of their evaluation
- Teachers' training had to be based on the knowledge and skills that the same teachers involved in the project already had

The InnovaScuola *Project*

Since 2006, the Italian Ministry of Education has proposed the introduction of Interactive Whiteboards (IWBs) in the schools, to produce direct and effective changes in teaching-learning processes. This choice came after may be 20 years of projects for the introduction of computer science, and more generally multimedia, IT/ICT and new technologies in education (Cartelli 2002). The main differences with past experiences were as follows: (a) no computing topics (i.e. computer structure and functions, algorithm development, computer programming etc.) were now introduced in study curricula, (b) teachers were directly involved in the digital revolution, which had the students at its core attention, because they had to actively and collaboratively involve students in the construction of their knowledge and skills, and had to use the strategies of web 2.0 for hitting this target (DIT 2010).

Table 1 Basic computing knowledge and skills held by teachers

Topics and skills needed	% of positive answers
1. Basic structure and operation of a computing system (creating folders, copying files, saving information etc.)	100
2. Advanced operation on a computing system (back-up and restore of data, clearing and defragmenting the system, connecting and managing devices etc.)	9
3. Using a word processor (at home and at school)	100
4. Using a spreadsheet (at home and at school)	31
5. Using a presentation manager (at home and at school)	56
6. Browsing the web frequently	75
7. Communicating by e-mail periodically (at least once or twice a week)	53
8. Editing of images	12
9. Web editing	3

The project started in 2008, when the Ministry of Education provided the equipment and the funds to the schools winners of the national competition for the best teaching projects. Main obligations for the competitor schools were:

- To propose and carry out a biennial educational project, centred on the use of learning objects (LOs)
- To make up at least 20 LOs/year (by each school) and upload them on a national virtual space (i.e. on a platform for LOs distribution)
- To make LOs Scorm 1.2 compliant and based on Open Source software

The schools could subscribe agreements with firms, corporate, associations and universities to carry out their projects; the agreements had to guarantee the support for the choice of the equipment and the training of the teachers. At last, it has to be noted that teachers could be rewarded for the extra work they made to create LOs.

The Schools and the Teachers Involved in the Project

As soon as the competition ended, four school networks (i.e. groups of schools made of at least one public institution), three in Southern Latium and one in Molise (Central Italy regions), could start their projects in cooperation with the laboratory managed by the author.

In the first joint meeting with all stakeholders a survey was made to investigate teachers' features and basic skills, and the following data were collected:

- Thirty-six teachers (may be 10% of the whole set of teachers in the schools), were working on the school projects; they were from Primary Schools and Junior High Schools
- The answers to the questionnaire showed that almost all the teachers had the basic computing skills and knowledge, but only a little minority among them had the pre-requisites for their immediate involvement into the projects. The data from the questionnaire are synthesized in Table 1, where the percentage of positive answers to the various questions is reported

The interviews the author had with the teachers, after they answered the questionnaire, produced the following supplement of information:

- Only three teachers (9%), knew of the existence of Open Source software (e.g. the suite of office automation Open Office), and only one teacher really used it
- Those who responded positively to question eight had in mind MS Paint (included in the MS Windows operating system), which is not a proper image editor
- No teacher had former experiences with e-learning platforms
- Almost all teachers had preconceptions on the use of IWBs (Interactive White Boards); they thought they could use IWBs only to show multimedia materials to the class

As a result, teachers had to be trained on the use of most common digital instruments and on their introduction in teaching processes. On the side of the instruments the following Open Source tools complying to the requests of the project were adopted: Open Office, as the tool for office automation; Gimp and/or Paint.net, for image editing; Exe-learning, for learning objects management (it can create LOs SCORM 1.2 compliant), Moodle has been the e-learning platform suggested to teachers for online activities.

To let teachers experience the features of the e-learning platform they were allowed access to a Moodle platform, and all the materials used both in the kick-off meeting and during the different lectures have been put online and made available in that environment.

A few meetings on the description of the features of the software followed, and two lectures with the main aim of soliciting the teachers' interest on the following topics were made. First, the dependence of the creation of learning objects from the different involvement of the various actors (i.e. students and teachers) was showed; otherwise stated, different psycho-pedagogical paradigm which could inspire the use of LOs were reported, depending on the students and teachers involvement in teaching-learning work. Second, suitable topics to focus on for the planning and the development of suitable disciple and cross-discipline units of learning in the classes had to be found (all based on the creation of LOs and the use of IWBs).

The approach described above led teachers to be persuaded that:

- The equipments and the LOs could be used in different ways in the classes
- The choice of a given psycho-pedagogical approach in teaching–learning activity does not exclude other approaches (i.e. other psycho-pedagogical paradigms), also in the same activity

Before passing to the planning and creation of LOs by the teachers, the following topics were proposed for discussion:

- The results from the OECD-PISA surveys, which showed the low level of the scores obtained by Italian students to verbal-linguistic and logical-mathematical questions
- The data coming from an international competition called "Beaver", used for the assessment of students' digital competences. This last issue was the natural consequence of the discussions on the features of the net generation and the differences between digital natives and digital immigrants (Prensky 2001; Mantovani and Ferri 2008)

The last two arguments are widely analyzed in the next section and the guidelines for the development of learning objects to be created collaboratively in the classes are proposed soon after.

Students' Learning and Digital Competence Assessment

The discussions on the low level of the Italian students' performance in the OECD-PISA surveys have been very useful to introduce the more general question of students' learning difficulties.

Knowledge Construction, Meaningful Learning and Students' Problems

When looking at knowledge construction, two main positions must be considered. On one hand, individuals' learning is compared with the structure of scientific disciplines and evaluation/assessment strategies are used to express the compliance of the subject's personal knowledge with the scientific knowledge. On the other, when knowledge development is mainly analyzed from social constructivist and cultural viewpoint, the comparison with scientific knowledge is on the background, and self-consistency, activity, support and scaffolding elements are paramount. Otherwise stated, in the first case the teachers/scholars attention is centred on discipline knowledge, in the last case individual knowledge phenomena are the main object of analysis.

The above approaches have their counterpart in the definitions used to describe the problems that students meet in explaining natural phenomena, especially when there is a comparison with the right scientific explanations.

By adopting the first viewpoint, Driver and Erickson (1983) defined nomothetic – the studies which evaluate the correctness of people's ideas with respect to the scientifically accepted paradigms; on the other hand, they called ideographic – the studies on the ideas that people show when they explain phenomena with no dependence from scientific paradigms (i.e. only the internal coherence of the people's concepts and ideas is evaluated).

Together with the work of Driver and Erickson, many investigations and researches have been made all over the world in the 1970s and in the 1980s, to find instruments and strategies helping people overcome the difficulties they meet in the study of scientific disciplines and in learning new topics (i.e. recent investigations have shown that misconceptions and mental schemes do not affect only natural sciences and/or technical knowledge like IT and ICT, they are also present in history, literature and other cross-disciplinary fields).

Despite the lack of a unique approach to the solution of the students' learning problems, many situated analyses and *ad hoc* instruments and strategies (Jonassen 1994) have been proposed during last decades (i.e. those experiences were mostly based on interactive and social constructivist approaches, often based on the use of special equipments, and produced very good effects on the classes involved in the experiments). Traces of the fragmentation of the interventions can be found in the educational chapters and special interest groups of the different scientific associations (like those of mathematicians, physicians, biologists, computer scientists etc.). The most successful experience in the creation of a cross discipline, which studied people's learning, has been made by the Meaningful Learning Research Group (MLRG, http://www.mlrg.org); within it, four international conferences were organized, many hundreds of papers on the above topics were published, and Novak ideas on knowledge maps were developed and proposed to teachers (Novak and Gowin 1984).

At last, it must be noted that no final answer has been given to students' learning problems. An explanation for the above statement can be found in the result from the studies the author lead in computer science with high school students (Cartelli 2003): when preconceptions and misconceptions appear defeated, also by the use of technology and the application of constructivist strategies, they can reappear in special cases.

Digital Literacy, Digital Competence and Beaver Competition

On the basis of the issues reported above, the different meanings of digital divide proposed in the introduction assume now the features of special learning difficulties that people may have. With respect to other knowledge fields, different proposals of literacy have been recently developed, with the help of computer science and information technology, under the hypothesis that they could prevent people's difficulties.

Computing literacy, information literacy, IT/ICT literacy and media literacy are the most famous ones, and they have also been compared by Tornero (2004), who proposed the definition of digital literacy as the literacy for the knowledge society.

The most recent and comprehensive definition for this literacy is as follows: "Digital Literacy is the awareness, attitude and ability of individuals to appropriately use digital tools and facilities to identify, access, manage, integrate, evaluate, analyze and synthesize digital resources, construct new knowledge, create media expressions, and communicate with others, in the context of specific life situations, in order to enable constructive social action; and to reflect upon this process" (Martin 2005).

Very recently the attention of researchers and institutions has focussed on how people use digital resources and processes, more than on the things they must know and be able to do with technologies. This new approach to the analysis of the impact of new technologies on mankind led to the concept of competence, and on the active involvement of subjects in the interaction with digital equipments, without forgetting the representations of reality, the knowledge and the skills that people manifested (Le Boterf 1990).

On this side, the European Commission issued in 2005 the "Recommendation on key competences for lifelong learning" and stated the features of the digital competence, the fourth among them (Commission of the European Parliament 2005).

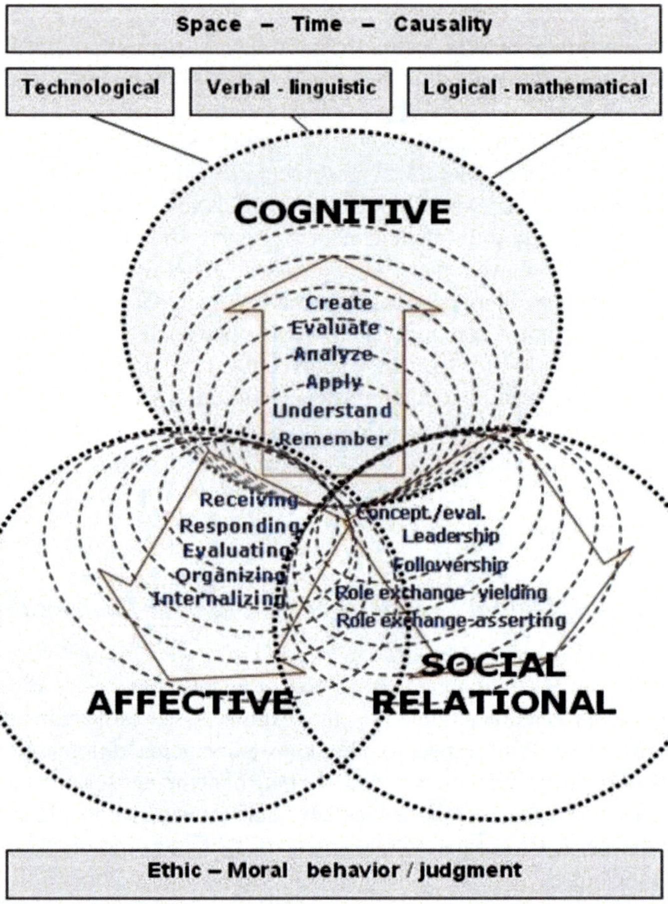

Fig. 2 The digital competence assessment framework

For the European Commission, the development of digital competence is based on the confident and critical use of Information Society Technology (IST) for work, leisure and communication and is underpinned by basic skills in ICT: that is the use of computers to retrieve, assess, store, produce, present and exchange information, and to communicate and participate in collaborative networks via the Internet.

The above issues have led to the definition of work plans for the creation of suitable frameworks for digital competence assessment and the development of strategies helping students build sound digital competence. Among the most recent proposals there is one that is reported in Fig. 2 (Cartelli 2010). It is based on three dimensions (strictly related to well-known taxonomies): cognitive, affective and socio-relational. The cognitive dimension is the better analyzed and is made of three main sections: technological, verbal-linguistic and logical-mathematical (the last two mostly due to Gardner (1993)), all under the umbrella of the categories of space, time and causality (Piaget 1970).

It is behind the aims of this chapter the detailed discussion of all the features of the framework, but it has to be remarked here that cognitive dimension is very important in the analysis of people's ways of thinking and knowing. It can suggest hypotheses for the mistakes and the errors that people make in interpreting natural and scientific phenomena.

The Beaver competition, the international contest for the assessment of computing, logic and mathematical skills in the students of the 15 countries today involved in the same competition, has been used in 2009 by the author to verify the structure of the model, and especially the correctness of the structure of the cognitive dimension.

In the Italian experience of the Beaver competition, which has been held the first time in 2009, two different categories of students have been investigated: Benjamins (10–12 years old) and Juniors (13–15 years old). From the solutions the students gave to the different problems emerged very similar behaviours; in both cases, in fact, there was a relevant number of positive answers to single questions, but only 3–5% of the students gave the right answers to all the questions. More specifically, it could be shown that in both categories of students, less than 50% of them succeeded in managing the same information through different languages (i.e. the verbal and iconic languages), and may be 50% among them did not use space, time and causality categories of the cognitive dimension in the right way.

The above data led to the following conclusions:

- The structure of the cognitive dimension looked good enough to show that the students are differently skilled in each section
- The less developed sections and categories in the cognitive dimension are the possible reason for students' problems in knowledge development and in the acquisition of meaningful knowledge
- Sound teaching–learning activities can be planned and carried out to help students recover the gap in the underdeveloped dimensions and build the digital competences needed in the knowledge society

The main consequence of the above issues for the *InnovaScuola* project has influenced teachers' work by leading to the collaborative creation of at least two learning objects:

- The first one centred on binary logic and its use in the research and affordability of information
- The second one focussed on the representation of reality (i.e. texts with different subjects and actions) by means of different languages (especially verbal and iconic) and on the use of instruments and strategies for the hitting of this target

Both of them have been developed by teachers in the second part of the project and the corresponding LOs have been made publicly available on the Internet (http://elf.let.unicas.it).

Conclusion and Future Work

The above issues led to the following remarks, especially centred on to the instruments proposed for the *InnovaScuola* project and the definition of strategies and processes for teaching innovation. On the side of the instruments proposed for teachers' training the following elements were judged by teachers very positively:

- The framework centred on the integrated e-learning environment (i.e. the model based on WBL and CMC), which has proven very successful for the proposal of materials and the development of the activities in the project
- The Open Source instruments were considered very useful and would have been adopted for everyday work by the teachers
- The framework for digital competence assessment, and especially its cognitive dimension, which has been considered very useful to discover undeveloped or less developed languages and skills in the students

As regards the processes experimented in the teachers' training activity the following issues emerged:

- The use of the integrated e-learning environment was considered useful for the introduction of deeper innovation in the class work, but adequate help was needed from teachers for the management of the e-learning platforms and for the use of social networking instruments
- The lack of instruments involving students and families in the continuous monitoring of school processes and in the updating of students learning and educational data, was considered negatively affecting the evolution of teaching-learning activities
- The planning of teaching activities based on problem finding, problem searching and problem building, has been considered essential for students' successful learning (i.e. for their direct connection to the development of problem solving features); the hypothesis underlying this issue is that contextual and situated learning can be reconciled with scientific/discipline learning and, what is more, students can be helped in the overcoming of the problems they usually show when approaching scientific knowledge

What has been reported in the above issues has also been considered a very good basis for future development. It is especially true for the possible influence of problem solving based teaching on the development of students' autonomous strategies and ways of learning.

The main topics considered here are Personal Knowledge Management (PKM) and Personal Strategic Thinking (PST), both strongly based on digital technologies and skills. As showed by the scholars who introduced the first definition at UCLA and Millikan University (Sorrentino 2008), the instruments and the information skills that people need for retrieving, storing, analyzing and more generally managing information, can help them in improving individual's performances and intra-personal/inter-personal relations. Furthermore, it has to be noted that

Table 2 Basic features of personal strategic thinking (PST)

Elements to be considered for corporate strategic thinking	PST
Competencies and skills	Competences, know how
Products and offerings	Subject's specialization and capabilities
Environment and industry	Communities/society the subject belongs to, behavioural/ personal features, knowledge/communication features
Markets and customers	Knowledge sources/clients
Competitors and substitutes	Internal and external sources and conflicting needs must be compared
Suppliers and buyers	Subjects' specialization within the community and ability in supporting other people in the community

the instruments and the tools that people use for PKM, rarely motivate the actions that people undertake, not necessarily imply the thinking about the processes people are involved in and, what is more, do not help the creation of knowledge management strategies. For those reasons, the application to subjects of the ideas developed for corporate and firms on strategic thinking have been hypothesized (Cartelli 2008).

Table 2 reports on the right column the translation and application to subjects of the well-known features of corporate strategic thinking. Furthermore, the features of the processes that corporate must carry out can be applied to subjects; that is, they must be *aligned, goal-oriented, fact-based, lying on broad thinking, focused etc.*

The questions to be answered in further studies become:

- How much digital competences are useful for the development of PKM?
- How much digital competences can influence the development of PST?

Otherwise stated, if it is true that further studies are needed to better analyze the features of the framework for digital competence assessment and the relevance of the impact of LOs introduction on students learning, they have also to analyze the influence they can have on the development of PKM and PST.

References

Bauman, Z. (2006). *Vita liquida*. Rome-Bari: Laterza.

Bindé, J. Cotbett, J., & Verity, B. (2005). *21st-century talks: Towards knowledge society*. New York: UNESCO.

Conner, M. L. (2004). *Learn More Now: 10 Simple Steps to Learning Better, Smarter, and Faster*. New York (NJ): John Wiley & Sons.

Conner, M. L. (1995). *How Adults Learn*. Ageless Learner, 1997–2007. Retrieved 15 June 2010 from http://agelesslearner.com/intros/adultlearning.html.

Cartelli, A. (2002). Computer science education in Italy: A survey. *InRoads SIGCSE Bullettin*, 34(4), 36–39.

Cartelli, A. (2003). Misinforming, misunderstanding, misconceptions: What informing science can do. In E. Cohen & E. Boyd (eds.), *Proceedings of IS+IT Education 2003 Conference* (pp. 1259–1273). Pori, Finland. Retrieved 6 April 2010 from http://proceedings.informingscience.org/IS2003Proceedings/docs/156Carte.pdf.

Cartelli, A. (2008). E-learning and E-citizenship: Between PKM and PST. In D. Remenyi (ed.), *Proceedings of the 7th European Conference on e-Learning, ECEL2008* (vol. 1, pp. 168–177). Agia Napa, Cyprus. Reading: Academic Publishing Limited.

Cartelli, A. (2010). Theory and practice in digital competence assessment. *International Journal of Digital Literacy and Digital Competence*, 1(3), 1–17.

DIT, 2010. Dipartimento Innovazione e Tecnologia. Iniziativa InnovaScuola. Retrieved 6 April 2010 from http://www.innovascuola.gov.it.

Driver, R., & Erickson, G. (1983). Theories in action: some theoretical and empirical issues in the study of students' conceptual frameworks in science. *Studies in Scientific Education*, 10, 37–60.

European Parliament and Council (2005). *Recommendation on key competences for lifelong learning*. Retrieved 15 June 2010 from http://ec.europa.eu/education/policies/2010/doc/keyrec_en.pdf.

Galliani, L. (2004). *La scuola in rete*. Bari (Italy): Laterza.

Gardner, H. (1993). *Multiple Intelligences: The Theory in Practice*. New York (NJ): Basic Books.

Guidolin, U. (2005). *Pensare digitale. Teoria e tecniche dei nuovi media*. Milan, Italy: Mc Graw-Hill.

Jonassen, D. H. (1994). Thinking technology. Towards a constructivist design model. *Educational Technology*, 34(4), 34–37.

Le Boterf, G. (1990). De la compétence: Essai sur un attracteur étrange. Paris: Les Ed. de l'Organisation.

Mantovani, S., & Ferri, P. (2008). *Digital kids. Come i bambini usano il computer e come potrebbero usarlo genitori e insegnanti*. Milan, Italy: Etas.

Martin, A. (2005). DigEuLit: A European Framework for Digital Literacy. A Progress Report. *Journal of eLiteracy*, 2(2). Retrieved 4 December 2009 from http://www.jelit.org/65/01/JeLit_Paper_31.pdf.

Novak, J. D., & Gowin, D. B. (1984). *Learning how to Learn*. New York (NJ): Cambridge University Press.

Piaget, J. (1970). *Lo sviluppo mentale del bambino*. Turin, Italy: Einaudi.

Prensky, M. (2001). Digital natives, digital immigrants. *On the Horizon,* 9(5), Retrieved 15 June 2010 from http://www.twitchspeed.com/site/Prensky%20-%20Digital%20Natives,%20Digital%20Immigrants%20-%20Part1.htm.

Sorrentino, F. (2008). From knowledge to personal knowledge management. In A. Cartelli & M. Palma (eds.), *Encyclopaedia of Information Communication Technology* (pp. 510–517). Hershey (PA): IGI Global.

Tornero, J. M. P. (2004). *Promoting Digital Literacy: Final report (EAC/76/03).* Barcelona: UAB. Retrieved 15 June 2010 from http://ec.europa.eu/education/archive/elearning/doc/studies/dig_lit_en.pdf.

Digital Divide: Students' Use of the Internet and Emerging Forms of Social Inequalities

Eleni Sianou-Kyrgiou and Iakovos Tsiplakides

Introduction

The emergence of the Information and Communication Technologies (ICT), their dramatic diffusion, and the growth of the Internet as an information conduit were accompanied by a general enthusiasm concerning their exploitation in education. According to the official rhetoric, in the modern knowledge and information societies, ICT constitute an extremely useful tool in education, which can improve students' academic performance and help young people in the transition to the labor market (Eamon 2004). It has been suggested that the exploitation of the Internet and interactive multimedia, in particular, can improve teaching, increase the sources of knowledge and promote students' engagement and motivation to learn (Pascarella and Terenzini 1998; Bransford et al. 1999; Chen 2008). They provide all students, regardless of socioeconomic background, with the opportunity to access a vast bulk of information, which can help them improve their academic achievement and can therefore contribute to the reduction of social inequalities in education (Heemskerk et al. 2005).

Such views are based on ideas concerning the future of industrial societies elaborated since the 1970s and the transition from the industrial to the knowledge and information society. In this society, the social and economic relationships are not organized on the basis of material goods but on the basis of the exploitation of knowledge and information. At the "heart of information society (as mediated by the Internet) is a radical decentring of communication," and in the information economy "we work primarily with our minds rather than with our hands" (May 2002, p. 10, 14). According to Van Dijk (2005, p. 133), the notion of the information society is "a *substantial* characterization of societies in which information increasingly is the primary means and product of all processes" (emphasis in the original).

E. Sianou-Kyrgiou (✉) • I. Tsiplakides
Department of Philosophy, Education and Psychology, University of Ioannina, Ioannina, Greece
e-mail: esianou@uoi.gr

A. Jimoyiannis (ed.), *Research on e-Learning and ICT in Education*,
DOI 10.1007/978-1-4614-1083-6_5,

The concept of knowledge society was introduced by Drucker who argued that in modern societies the basic financial resources are not the capital, nor the natural resources, nor work, but knowledge. Developments after World War II and especially the emergence of new technologies have led to "the emergence of knowledge as the new capital and as the central resource of an economy" (Drucker 1992, p. xiii). Daniel Bell uses the term post-industrial society to refer to a new form of society, the post-industrial society, in which the basis is not "raw muscle power, or energy, but information" (Bell 1976, p. 127). The new society is now defined "by its novel methods of acquiring, processing and distributing information" (Kumar 1998, p. 97). As a result, young people should "be able to access, understand, and use the computer and Internet in order to develop the skills necessary to succeed individually and to contribute to future growth and prosperity of the information society" (Cleary et al. 2006, p. 354).

In this framework, Castells (1996) has proposed that ICT create a new kind of social structure, the network society. His core argument is that we are undergoing a shift from the industrial mode of development, in which the main source of productivity is the introduction of new sources of energy, to the informational mode of development in which "the source of productivity lies in the technology of knowledge generation, information processing, and symbol communication" (Castells 1996, p. 17). The network society consists of "networks of production, power and experience, which construct a culture of virtuality in the global flows that transcend time and space" (Castells 2000, p. 381). This is likely to accentuate social inequalities, since the networks have the ability to transcend place and time compared to other ways of organization, while not all workers are connected to networks or have positions with few connections (Castells 2000; Van Dijk 2005).

The information society idea has been severely debated. Frank Webster, for instance, reviews varying definitions of the concept of information society and concludes that "whether it is a technological, economic, occupational, spatial or cultural conception, we are left with highly problematical notions of what constitutes, and how to distinguish, an information society" (Webster 2006, p. 21). Similarly, it has been argued that there is not enough evidence to support the argument that we are moving towards a knowledge society (Sianou-Kyrgiou 2006).

The Digital Divide

The "optimist rhetoric" concerning technology-enhanced learning, which argues that ICT has the capacity to increase pupil achievement underpins the policies adopted by governments in many countries, their commitment to promoting ICT and the vast amounts of money allocated for the incorporation of new technologies in all stages of education (Reynolds et al. 2003). In Britain, for example, the government is equipping schools with multimedia blackboards (Hall and Higgins 2005), and is investing £45 billion in the "Building Schools for the Future" program (Facer and Sandford 2010, p. 74), with the hope of improving students' academic performance. In Greece, the effective pedagogical exploitation of ICT in education is considered a basic priority of the "New School" announced recently by the Ministry of Education, Lifelong Learning and Religious Affairs. Substantial investments target at equipping all schools with interactive whiteboards and broadband Internet access.

From the end of the 1990s, however, a critical issue of the rise of ICT appeared on the scene and became the focal point of the public, political, and scholarly debate, the issue of the so-called digital divide (Van Dijk 2005). The term was originally used in the mid-1990s to refer to "the divide between those with access to the Internet and those without" (Witte and Mannon 2010, p. 4) in relation to age, race, gender, and socioeconomic background (Mason and Hacker 2003; Van Dijk 2006). The concept of the digital divide comprises three distinct aspects: (a) the global divide, (b) the social divide, and (c) the democratic divide, which refers to "the differences between those who do, and do not, use the panoply of digital resources to engage, mobilize, and participate in public life" (Norris 2001, p. 4). According to OECD, the "digital divide among households appears to depend primarily on two variables, income and education. Other variables, such as household size and type, age, gender, racial and linguistic backgrounds and location also play an important role" (OECD 2001, p. 5).

In recent years, with the rapid spread of Internet technology and the fact that it constitutes an important part of the daily lives of many people, the interest has shifted towards the difference in use among individuals from different socioeconomic backgrounds (Bonfadelli 2002; Warschauer 2004; Van Dijk 2005; Peter and Valkenburg 2006; Livingstone and Helsper 2007; Hargittai 2008). It has been argued that beyond differences in access to ICT, differential uses are also likely to contribute to social inequality, since the effective exploitation of the Internet is related to a person's socioeconomic status (Hargittai 2007; Hargittai and Walejko 2008, p. 240). ICT may exacerbate existing social inequalities, since computer and Internet skills are essential in education and the labor market (Attewell and Battle 1999; Rideout 2000; DiMaggio et al. 2001), in "the service and trade sectors and most jobs in the finance, technology, and manufacturing sectors" (Cleary et al. 2006, p. 355). A society characterized by differentiated skills in the use of ICT, and especially the Internet, may lead to different and unequal positions within it (Van Dijk 2005). It is now widely recognized that "the digital divide must be understood as incorporating a broad range of variables," such as "language and literacy ability, computer skills, suitability of online content, and availability of instruction or social support that enable or constrain meaningful ICT use" (Warschauer 2010, p. 1552).

Inequalities of ICT Access and Use in Higher Education

The study of digital inequalities in education has expanded to include higher education (HE). It is widely recognized that digital technology has affected HE, and that within it there has been more technological change compared to other sectors of education (Selwyn 2010). HE institutions are now investing substantial resources to provide students with Internet-based information and to equip classrooms and libraries with high-spec Internet connectivity (Selwyn 2008). Indeed, it has been suggested that "Information and communication technologies have become nearly as integral to teaching and learning as books. Rare is the course that does not utilize some form of IT, from using electronic resources in the library to conducting Internet research to delivering grades and other content through a course management system" (Smith and Caruso 2010, pp. 73–74). It is often thought that ICT can support learning in HE more effectively than traditional recourse-based learning methods (Breen et al. 2001). In addition, since "the worldwide web is now established as a key setting where students access and interact with information" it could be argued that ICT use is increasingly linked to their academic performance, their employment, and their social, political, cultural and political involvement in modern society and HE (Selwyn 2010, p. 35).

Research has also dealt with inequalities in ICT access and use within HE. In Smith and Caruso's recent survey of college and university freshmen at over 100 institutions, it was found that "respondent ownership of computers has remained steady at around 98% for the last four years" (Smith and Caruso 2010, p. 9). They also found that students report spending 21.2 h/week on the Internet for school, work or recreation, while they report persistent gender differences in the use of certain technologies. Using data gathered by a web-based survey conducted on 232 college freshmen in the United States which was designed to determine whether a digital divide in Internet usage exists among college students, Cotten and Jelenewicz report differences in terms of race, and conclude that "Internet experience and gender affect particular types of Internet usage, suggesting that the digital divide is multilayered" (Cotten and Jelenewicz 2006, p. 497). Nevertheless, although "digital technologies are felt to support forms of university teaching and learning that are more efficient, engaging and equitable," the notion of the digital divide in HE "is now notable only by its absence in contemporary education debate" (Selwyn 2010, p. 34).

Conceptual Frameworks

The above concerns lie at the heart of the scholarly debate about the digital divide and the interplay between Internet access and use and social inequalities. The issue is usually examined on the basis of the classic sociological perspectives, such as the functionalist, the conflict, and Bourdieu's cultural perspective.

According to the functionalist perspective the digital divide can decrease when the disparities in Internet access decrease. When access differences become minimal, all people regardless of socioeconomic background will have equal opportunities to use the Internet as a source of information, learning, and communication (Compaine 2001). This is already happening to young people who have familiarized themselves with the Web (Negroponte 1995). Explanations which draw from the conflict perspective point to the relationship between the digital divide and social inequalities and support the view that new forms of digital inequalities emerge. If the inequalities in Internet access decrease, then new divides will be created, so that people from the most privileged social classes will be at an advantage. As a result, the reduction of Internet inequalities is important, since Internet inequalities deprive a great number of people of access to knowledge, information and lead to social exclusion (Van Dijk and Hacker 2003; Peter and Valkenburg 2006).

Some researchers who examine the digital divide in education draw on Bourdieu's theory of the different forms of economic, social, and cultural capital (Bourdieu 1998; Bourdieu and Passeron 1977). Cultural capital exists mainly in the form of academic qualifications, while social capital refers to "the actual or potential resources which are linked to possession of a durable network of more or less institutionalized relationships of mutual acquaintance and recognition" (Bourdieu 1998, p. 51). Economic capital, that is, money wealth can be "'cashed' in any part of society" (Grenfell and James 1998, p. 20). There is a relationship between the students' academic performance and the economic, cultural, and social capital of their family. These forms of capital are interconnected and can convert "from one type to another" (Bourdieu 1998, p. 54). For example, the economic capital can be used to buy computer and Internet access, educational goods and services so that it becomes cultural capital (Grenfell and James 1998).

The above conceptual approaches provide useful contributions to the understanding of the relationship between the Internet and inequality and also highlight the importance of examining ICT access and use from a sociological perspective. However, a constructive scholarly debate has not flourished in Greece. Most research studies focus on statistical analyses concerning Internet access, or the effective exploitation of ICT in the classroom. While useful, this body of literature concentrates on technical issues, and is usually technocratic and simplified (Gouga and Kamarianos 2007). It also focuses on primary or secondary school students, and fails to take into account the digital divisions in HE. There is, therefore, a gap of solid empirical data that could examine, for example, what HE students actually do when they are connected to the Internet and the relationship between Internet use and socioeconomic background. We also aim to contribute to the international debate by providing useful insights into the interplay between HE students' use of the Internet and their socioeconomic background. The research study we present here is distinctive in that it can provide policy makers with a useful tool in their effort to reduce disparities in Internet access and use among HE students. In addition, collecting both quantitative and qualitative data enables us to uncover the students' attitudes toward modern technology, at a time when household Internet access and especially broadband connection has increased significantly in recent years (Greek Information Society Observatory 2008, 2010). For example, broadband connections marked a considerable increase going from 56% in 2007 to 67% in 2008 and, by now, they constitute "the more popular connection type," although well below the EU27 average (Greek Information Society Observatory 2008, p. 6).

The Research Study

Research Questions

The theoretical considerations outlined above and the lack of empirical studies about the digital divide in HE from a sociological perspective in Greece, led us to pose the following research questions:

(a) Is there a relationship between socioeconomic background and access to a computer and the Internet?
(b) Is there a relationship between socioeconomic background and Internet use?

We hypothesize that students differ in terms of Internet access and use, and that socioeconomic background explains the greater part of this difference.

Data and Methodology

The sample included 100 first year students, 50 from the Medical School of the University of Ioannina and 50 from the Department of Early Childhood Care and Education from the Technological Educational Institute of Epirus. The sample included equal numbers of male and female participants. We decided to focus on these two departments for the following reasons. First, because according to official data they have different social class composition of students. More specifically, the Medical School is dominated by upper middle-class students, while the majority of students in the Department of Early Childhood Care and Education come from lower middle-class or working-class backgrounds. Second, these two departments admit students with different performance in the national university entrance examinations. In the academic year 2009–2010, the medical school in the University of Ioannina admitted students who achieved a general access mark of 19,105 points and above, out of a maximum possible number of 20,000 points. Students who were admitted in the Department of Early Childhood Care and Education achieved a general access mark of 13,847 points and above, a difference of 5,258 points.

Both qualitative and quantitative methods of data collection were employed, since "they involve differing strengths and weaknesses" and "constitute alternative, but not mutually exclusive, strategies for research" (Patton 2002, p. 14). A self-completed questionnaire was administered to first-year students in the spring semester of the academic year 2009–2010. It consisted of a number of predetermined response categories with close and open questions with the aim of investigating students' experiences and attitudes towards the Internet and the impact of their socioeconomic background. We also conducted ten semi-structured interviews. Semi-structured interviews were utilized because they "result in a true and accurate picture of the respondents' selves and lives" (Fontana and Frey 2005, pp. 698–699) and provide in-depth, detailed data collection, and allow researchers "to enter into the other person's perspective" (Patton 2002, p. 341).

In our study we used the OPCS (1991) scale to assign socioeconomic status based "on occupation in the Standard Occupational classification system developed by the Office of Population Censuses and Surveys" (Power et al. 2003, p. 161). We employed this scale because it is widely employed in many empirical studies. We also accept that for people under the age of 25 their position is defined in relation to their parents' occupation. To assign social class we used parental socioeconomic status. We have employed a pattern of six social and occupational categories that involves the hierarchical classification of occupations on the basis of education and professions (Crompton 1998).

As far as the social composition of the students in the sample is concerned, the Department of Early Childhood Care is dominated by lower middle-class or working-class students, while the majority of the students in the Medical School come from upper middle-class or middle-class backgrounds. More specifically, 4% of the students from the Department of Early Childhood Care come from the upper middle-classes, 26% are middle-class students, while 70% are working-class students. By contrast, 10% of the students from the Medical School come from the upper middle-classes, 54% are middle-class students, while 36% are working-class students.

Findings

Computer and Internet Access

All but 2% of the sample reported having access to a personal computer at home. This is not surprising, given the fact that in recent years prices have fallen, so that even students from poorer families can afford a personal computer. However, different findings emerge if we examine the relationship between Internet access at home and students' socioeconomic background. Research data show that all upper middle-class students have Internet access. By contrast, 70% of middle-class students have Internet access at home, while for working-class students the percentage is only 53%. According to official data for 2010, 46.4% of Greek households have an Internet access at home, while 53.4% of households have a computer, of any type, at home (Hellenic Statistical Authority 2010). As far as the diffusion of new technologies is concerned, in the last 5 years Internet access at home increased by 100%, computer access has increased by approximately 45%, and broadband connections have increased by approximately 435% (Hellenic Statistical Authority 2010).

When asked whether their parents are familiar with Internet use, 71.5% of upper middle-class respondents reported that their parents can use the Internet, while the percentages for middle-class students and working-class students are 55% and 21%, respectively.

Internet Use

Research findings provide evidence of a relationship between the students' socioeconomic background and Internet use. Upper middle-class students reported a wider range of Internet uses compared to students from the lower middle-class and working-class students. More specifically, the former reported the following Internet uses: downloading software, online submission of forms, communication via e-mail, Internet telephony, voice calls, video calls via the Internet, reading online newspapers, reading online books, blogs, discussion forums, accessing websites which will help them for their university assignments, seeking information about goods or services, using RSS service, buying goods from online stores, creation of a personal website, listening to Internet radio stations, etc. By contrast, lower middle-class and working-class students have a more restricted Internet use. They use it primarily for communication through e-mail, discussion forums, playing online video games, downloading music, and blogs. They also use it to read the news and to find information, but they do it far less frequently. Few students reported that they use it for online buys or in order to find information relevant to their studies.

Apart from the variety of Internet uses, interesting findings emerged in relation to the use of the Internet for educational purposes. All but one upper middle-class students reported using the Internet frequently in order to find information from scientific journals, scientific articles and for buying books from online stores. They also reported that they use it to find information about their studies and university assignments, and that they visit the official website of their university department or the website of the university library almost every day. The percentage is 47.5% for middle-class students and 40% for lower middle-class and working-class students. A significant finding was that working-class students often respond that they do not distinguish between reliable and not reliable websites in relation to information finding, while very few mentioned the reliability of the Internet-based sources they use. As a working-class student from the Department of Early Childhood Care and Education said: "I use search engines to find information for my assignments ... I simply type the word I am looking for." By contrast, students from more privileged social classes often report that they look for information: "from international medical websites ... information from Medical Schools abroad" (female Medical School student with a mother with postgraduate studies). These students seem to be more able to distinguish between reliable and not reliable websites. It is also interesting to note that, at least as far as educational uses of the Internet are concerned, students from higher socioeconomic backgrounds seem to have more Internet literacy skills, being "computer virtuosi," while students with families with a lower educational background are simply "ordinary computer users" (Attewell 2001, p. 257).

This differentiation is significant, as an important aspect of the digital divide concerns the differentiation of Internet users in relation to the ability to assess and evaluate the reliability of the information contained in it (DiMaggio et al. 2001). Such disparities in Internet skills are important because they have consequences for the academic performance of students. Given the fact that Internet skills are indispensable for university assignments, searching for bibliography, students who are not able to have access to reliable sources of information will be at a disadvantage compared to students who have access to reliable information sources.

Research data also revealed that use of the Internet as an information medium is patterned according to students' socioeconomic background. For example, most upper middle-class students reported that they use the Internet frequently to read the news from online newspapers/magazines. As a Medical School upper middle-class female student said: "I rarely watch the news on TV, I trust the Internet most." The percentage was 35% for middle-class students and 21% for working-class students. Similar results have been found in other studies. Peter and Valkenburg (2006, p. 300) examined Dutch adolescents' Internet use and found that "adolescents' use of the Internet as an information medium was influenced by their socioeconomic and cognitive resources."

As far as using the Internet as a means of communication is concerned, differences were also found. While most students in the sample use the Internet for communication, regardless of socioeconomic background, the majority of working-class students prefer more "traditional" uses, such as the e-mail, while students from the upper social classes more often use more sophisticated ways of communication through the Internet, such as video conferencing.

Finally, as regards the use of the Internet as a source of entertainment, little differences were found among students from different socioeconomic backgrounds. More specifically, about 85% of the students in the sample reported that they often use the Internet for entertainment purposes, regardless of socioeconomic background. The following response of a working-class student is a recurring pattern of attitudes toward the Internet "You can have a good time, listen to music, play games, it's just so good."

Discussion and Conclusion

The first research question we posed concerned HE students' socioeconomic background and access to a computer and the Internet from home. The research findings suggest that disparities in access to computer technology are almost nonexistent and that the penetration rate of computer technology is very high. The narrowing of the divide in access to a computer can be attributed to the fact that prices have fallen significantly in recent years. Another factor is that most families buy computers for their children because computers are considered as a means that will increase their children's academic performance and provide them with more educational opportunities and useful, lifelong skills. Research data also show that there is still a divide in relation to Internet access at home among students from socioeconomic background, especially for working-class students.

An important finding was that HE students from more privileged socioeconomic backgrounds make more frequent use of the Internet for educational and academic purposes. It could be argued that they are more likely to gain more educational benefits from it, for the following reasons. First, effective use of the Internet as a medium for accessing information is indispensable for successfully completing university assignments. Second, divisions in Internet use for accessing information are important for the students' transition to the labor market, since "employers increase the emphasis they place on the ability to acquire, manipulate and apply information, and reduce the emphasis on memorizing facts" (Breen et al. 2001, p. 96).

Findings also provide preliminary evidence that students from families with higher socioeconomic background are more critical users of the Internet and have more skills than their counterparts from families from lower socioeconomic background, or with no history of participation in HE. Similar results were found in other studies which document "the appearance of a usage divide between parts of the population systematically using and benefiting from advanced digital technology and the more difficult applications and services, and other parts only using basic digital technologies for simple applications with a relatively large part of entertainment" (Van Dijk and Hacker 2000).

Even if the small sample means that care should be taken in generalizing the research findings, the empirical data presented provide evidence that universal access to computers and the Internet does not necessarily lead to a reduction in the digital divide. We argue that the digital divide widens, despite the fact that the problem of physical access to a computer no longer exists. The digital divide is now a divide in use rather than access (Bucy 2000; Warschauer 2003; Peter and Valkenburg 2006). Our research findings are in line with other studies which conclude that "Internet access alone obviously does not automatically guarantee an informed and knowledgeable public" (Bonfadelli 2002, p. 81) and that "obtaining a PC does not confer, at a stroke, the skills and experience enjoyed by those who have a longer standing acquaintance with such technology" (Hull 2003, p. 132). The increasing diffusion of the Internet among the population means that in the examination of inequalities in relation to the Internet it becomes less useful to simply focus on binary classifications of who is online, but rather we need to start examining differences in how those who have access make use of the medium, that is, differences in people's online skills (Hargittai 2002).

In relation to the opposing arguments about the "social consequences of Internet use," we found initial support for the view that socioeconomic background remains a key parameter of differential Internet use, since research findings do not seem to support the argument that widened access to the Internet is "enabling and egalitarian, promoting social inclusion" (Willis and Tranter 2006, p. 43). We therefore propose a new interpretation of the concept of digital divide in contemporary HE. We need to take into account the emerging digital inequality which refers not only to differences in access, or binary distinctions between "information-rich and the information-poor" (Angus et al. 2004, p. 3), but also to "the purposes for which the technology is employed" (DiMaggio and Hargittai 2001, p. 1). In other words, the divide acquires qualitative characteristics and is related to social class (Iske et al. 2005). We argue that any attempts to examine social inequalities in HE need to examine the issue of the digital divide in relation to Internet use, as it constitutes a critical parameter which has an effect on academic knowledge, students' academic performance, and their transition to the labor market.

Implications for further research are clear. Since our study provided evidence that inequalities in modern technology use in HE are not diminishing, there is a clear need for the debate to address the issue of digital divide within HE in more sophisticated terms. Researchers should focus on the digital divide in relation to such factors as household residence, and examine who uses the Internet, for which purpose and in what ways, as well as the ways through which social inequalities are exacerbated (Chen and Wellman 2005). The investigation of the characteristics of digital divisions which manifest themselves among HE students, such as inequalities stemming from effective use of ICT to access information, gender, race, and/or technological experience, also merit a sustained program of future research (Selwyn 2008, 2010). In addition, this study has not examined all four dimensions which make up digital inequality: access, digital literacy, intensity of use, and purpose of use (Castaño-Muñoz 2010, p. 45); nor has it dealt with parameters such as "age, gender, race, ethnicity" which are "relevant to one's ICT experiences" (Hargittai 2008, p. 939). Future research should thus focus on these parameters.

Finally, in relation to policy implications, we believe that disparities in Internet use among HE students merit policy attention. Second, public policy needs to target both Internet access and use, since factors such as educational background, income, occupation, age, gender, and race impact strongly on the instrumental uses of the Internet. There is an urgent need for policy efforts to focus on helping students from disadvantaged socioeconomic backgrounds to acquire not only physical access to the Internet, but also information-age skills necessary for its effective exploitation. Of course, as it is widely accepted, no intervention will be effective unless measures are introduced which aim at reducing existing social inequalities.

References

Angus, L., Snyder, I., & Sutherland-Smith, W. (2004). ICT and educational (dis)advantage: families, computers and contemporary social and educational inequalities. *British Journal of Sociology of Education*, 25(1), 3–18.

Attewell, P. (2001). The first and second digital divides. *Sociology of Education*. 74(3), 252–259.

Attewell, P., & Battle, J. (1999). Home Computers and School Performance. *The Information Society*, 15(1), 1–10.

Bell, D. (1976). *The Coming of Post-Industrial Society: A Venture in Social Forecasting*. New York: Basic Books.

Bonfadelli, H. (2002). The Internet and knowledge divides. A theoretical and empirical investigation. *European Journal of Communication*, 17(1), 65–84.

Bourdieu, P. (1998). The forms of capital. In A. H. Halsy, H. Lauder, P. Brown, & A. S. Wells (eds.), *Education. Culture, Economy, Society* (pp. 47–56). Oxford and New York. Oxford University Press.

Bourdieu, P., & Passeron, J.C. (1977). *Reproduction in Education, Society and Culture*. Beverly Hills, CA: Sage.

Bransford, J., Brown, A., & Cocking, R. (1999). *How People Learn. Brain, Mind, Experience, and School*. Washington: National Academy Press.

Breen, R., Lindsay, R., Jenkins, A., & Smith, P. (2001). The role of Information and Communication Technologies in a university learning environment. *Studies in Higher Education*, 26(1), 95–114.

Bucy, E. P. (2000). Social access to the Internet. *The Harvard International Journal of Press/ Politics*, 5(1), 50–61.

Castells, M. (1996). *The Information Age: Economy, Society and Culture. Volume I, The Rise of the Network Society*. Oxford, UK, and Cambridge, Massachusetts: Blackwell Publishing.

Castells, M. (2000). *The Information Age: Economy, Society and Culture. Volume III, End of Millennium*. Oxford, UK, and Cambridge, Massachusetts: Blackwell Publishing (2nd edition).

Castaño-Muñoz, J. (2010). Digital Inequality among university students in developed countries and its relation to academic performance. *Revista de Universidad y Sociedad del Conocimiento (RUSC)*. 7(1), 43–52. Retrieved 2 April 2011 from http://rusc.uoc.edu/ojs/index.php/rusc/article/view/v7n1_castano/v7n1_castano.

Chen, Y. L. (2008). Modeling the determinants of Internet use. *Computers & Education*, 51(2), 545–558.

Chen, W., & Wellman, B. (2005). Minding the cyber-divide: The Internet and social inequality. In M. Romero & E. Margolis (eds.), *The Blackwell Companion to social inequalities* (pp. 523–545). Oxford: Blackwell Publishing.

Cleary, P. F., Pierce, G., & Trauth, E. M. (2006). Closing the digital divide: understanding racial, ethnic, social class, gender and geographic disparities in Internet use among school age children in the United States. *Universal Access in the Information Society*, 4(4), 354–373.

Compaine, B. M. (2001). Declare the war won. In B. M. Compaine (ed.), *The digital divide. Facing a crisis or creating a myth?* (pp. 315–335). Cambridge, MA: MIT Press.

Cotten, S. R., & Jelenewicz, S. M. (2006). A disappearing digital divide among college students? Peeling away the layers of the digital divide. *Social Science Computer Review*, 24(4), 497–506.

Crompton, R. (1998). *Class and stratification. An introduction to current debates*. Cambridge: Polity Press.

DiMaggio, P., Hargittai, E., Russell Numan, W., & Robinson, J. P. (2001). Social implications of the Internet. *Annual Review of Sociology*, 27, 307–336.

DiMaggio, P., & Hargittai, E. (2001). *From the 'digital divide' to 'digital inequality': Studying internet use as penetration increases*. Working Paper 15. Princeton University, Center for Arts and Cultural Policy Studies.

Drucker, P. F. (1992). *The Age of Discontinuity: Guidelines to our Changing Society*. USA: Harper & Row.

Eamon, M. K. (2004). Digital divide in computer access and use between poor and non-poor youth. *Journal of Sociology and Social Welfare*, 31(2), 91–112.

Facer, K., & Sandford, R. (2010). The next 25 years?: future scenarios and future directions for education and technology. *Journal of Computer Assisted Learning*, 26(1),74–93.

Fontana, A., & Frey, J. H. (2005). The Interview. In N. K. Denzin & Y.S. Lincoln (eds.), *Handbook of Qualitative Research* (pp. 695–728). Thousand Oaks, CA: Sage.

Gouga, G., & Kamarianos, I. (2007). Exploring the digital gap: technology, culture and society. *The International Journal of Technology, Knowledge and Society*, 3(4), 75–80.

Greek Information Society Observatory (2008). *Project: Study for measuring the indicators of the i2010 initiatives for the year 2008. Research findings among private individuals-households*. Athens. Retrieved 5 April 2011from http://www.observatory.gr/files/meletes/i2010_Report_Households_2008_EN.pdf.

Greek Information Society Observatory (2010). *11th report on broadband connections*. Athens. Retrieved 5 April 2011 from http://www.observatory.gr/files/meletes/11_Broadband_report_a10.pdf.

Grenfell, M., & James, D. (1998). Theory, practice and pedagogic research. In M. Grenfell & D. James (eds.), *Bourdieu and education: Acts of practical theory* (pp. 6–26). London: Falmer Press.

Hall, I., & Higgins, S. (2005). Primary school students' perception of interactive whiteboards. *Journal of Computer Assisted Learning*, 21(2), 102–117.

Hargittai, E. (2002). Second-level digital divide: differences in people's online skills. *First Monday*, 7(4).

Hargittai, E. (2007). Whose space? Differences among users and non-users of social network sites. *Journal of Computer-Mediated Communication*, 13(1), 276–297.

Hargittai, E. (2008). The digital reproduction of inequality. In D. Grusky (ed.), *Social Stratification* (pp. 936–944). Boulder, CO : Westview Press.

Hargittai, E., & Walejko, G. (2008). The participation divide: Content creation and sharing in the digital age. *Information, Communication & Society*, 11(2), 239–256.

Heemskerk, I., Brink, A., Volman, M., & Ten Dam, G. (2005). Inclusiveness and ICT in education: a focus on gender, ethnicity and social class. *Journal of Computer Assisted Learning*, 21(1), 1–16.

Hellenic Statistical Authority (2010). *Survey on the use of information and communication technologies by households: 2010*. Retrieved 20 December 2010 from http://www.statistics.gr/portal/page/portal/ESYE/BUCKET/A1901/ PressReleases/A1901_SFA20_DT_AN_00_2010_01_F_EN.pdf.

Hull, B. (2003). ICT and social exclusion: the role of libraries. *Telematics and Informatics*, 20(2), 131–142.

Iske, S., Klein, A., & Kutscher, N. (2005). Differences in internet usage: social inequality and informal education. *Social Work & Society*, 3(2), 215–223.

Kumar, K. (1998). The post-modern condition. In A. H. Halsy, H. Lauder, P. Brown & A. S. Wells (eds.), *Education. Culture, Economy, Society* (pp. 96–112). Oxford and New York. Oxford University Press.

Livingstone, S., & Helsper, E. (2007). Gradations in digital inclusion: Children, young people, and the digital divide. *New Media and Society*, 9(4), 671–696.

Mason, S. M., & Hacker, K. L. (2003). Applying communication theory to digital divide research. *IT and Society*, 1(5), 40–55.

May, C. (2002). *The Information Society. A Skeptical View*. Cambridge: Polity Press.

Negroponte, N. (1995). *Being Digital*. London: Hodder & Stoughton.

Norris, P. (2001). *Digital divide: Civic engagement, information poverty, and the Internet worldwide*. Cambridge: Cambridge University Press.

OECD (2001). *Understanding the digital divide*. Paris: OECD.

OPCS (1991). *Standard Occupational Classification, Volume 3*. London: HMSO.

Pascarella, E., & Terenzini, P. (1998). Studying college students in the 21st century: Meeting new challenges. *Review of Higher Education*, 21(2), 151–165.

Patton, M.Q. (2002). *Qualitative research & evaluation methods*. Thousand Oaks, CA: Sage Publications (3 rd edition).

Peter, J., & Valkenburg, P. M. (2006). Adolescents' internet use: Testing the "disappearing digital divide" versus the "emerging digital differentiation" approach. *Poetics*, 34(4–5), 293–305.

Power, S., Edwards, T., Whitty, G., & Wigfall, S. (2003). *Education and the middle class*. Buckingham, UK: Open University Press.

Reynolds, D., Treharne, D., & Tripp, H. (2003). ICT-the hopes and the reality. *British Journal of Educational Technology*, 34(2), 151–167.

Rideout, V. (2000). Public access to the Internet and the Canadian digital divide. *Canadian Journal of Information and Library Science*, 25(2–3), 1–21.

Selwyn, N. (2008). An investigation of differences in undergraduates' academic use of the internet. *Active Learning in Higher Education*, 9(1), 11–22.

Selwyn, N. (2010). Degrees of digital division: reconsidering digital inequalities and contemporary higher education. *Revista de Universidad y Sociedad del Conocimiento*, 7(1), 33–42. Retrieved 2 April 2011 from http://rusc.uoc.edu/ojs/index.php/rusc/article/view/v7n1_selwyn/v7n1_selwyn.

Smith, S. D., & Caruso, J. B. (2010). *The ECAR study of undergraduate students and Information Technology, 2010*. Educause Center for Applied research.

Sianou-Kyrgiou, E. (2006). Knowledge society and widening of participation in higher education. Upgrading of skills or degrading of degrees?. *Proceedings of the Scientific Conference "Knowledge Society. Ideology and Reality"* (pp. 35–49). Ioannina: University of Ioannina (in Greek).

Van Dijk, J. (2005). *The Deepening Divide: Inequality in the Information Society*. Thousand Oaks CA, London, New Delhi: Sage Publications.

Van Dijk, J. (2006). Digital divide research, achievements and shortcomings. *Poetics,* 34(4–5), 221–235.

Van Dijk, J., & Hacker, K. (2000). *The digital divide as a complex and dynamic phenomenon.* Paper presented at the 50th Annual Conference of the International Communication Association, Acapulco, 1–5 June 2000.

Van Dijk, J., & Hacker, K. (2003). The digital divide as a complex and dynamic phenomenon. *The Information Society*, 19(4), 315–326.

Warschauer, M. (2003). Social capital and access. *Universal Access in the Information Society*, 2(4), 315–330.

Warschauer, M. (2004). *Technology and Social Inclusion: Rethinking the Digital Divide.* Cambridge, MA: MIT Press.

Warschauer, M. (2010). Digital Divide. *Encyclopedia of Library and Information Sciences. Third Edition*, 1(1), 1551–1556.

Webster, F. (2006) *Theories of the Information society*. New York: Routledge (3 rd edition).

Willis, S., & Tranter, B. (2006). Beyond the 'digital divide': Internet diffusion and inequality in Australia. *Journal of Sociology*, 42(1), 43–59.

Witte, J. C., & Mannon, S. E. (2010). *The Internet and Social Inequalities*. New York: Routledge.

Part II
e-Learning and Teachers' Professional Development

Supporting Teachers in Orchestrating CSCL Classrooms

Yannis A. Dimitriadis

Introduction

A pedagogically effective and sustainable use of Information and Communications Technologies (ICT) in education is far from being a reality, in spite of the huge advances in ICT, the investments and political plans, and especially all promising research results in the field (Cuban 2001). One of the reasons for such a delay can be found in the lack of understanding on how teachers orchestrate their classrooms, taking into account the technology-enhanced classroom complex ecosystem (Dillenbourg et al. 2009). Teachers have to deal with context factors, such as time pressure and insufficient infrastructure or deficiencies in knowledge about technology affordances and in skills for ICT management. The introduction of ICT in classrooms, with face-to-face, blended, or remote interactions, has added several degrees of complexity, since the new technology affordances allow for new teaching/learning opportunities. These problems are getting even worse when innovative pedagogies are sought, such as those of collaborative, inquiry, or project-based learning. *Knowledge, Goals, and Beliefs* (KGB) of the teachers have to match the new technological affordances (Chen et al. 2009), together with an efficient classroom management at several social levels in order to increase the chances of pedagogical effectiveness. Thus, teachers need to accomplish a very difficult task, i.e., to orchestrate their technology-enhanced classrooms dealing with ICT and non-ICT artifacts and tools, as well as social interactions at various levels (Dillenbourg et al. 2009).

The case of computer-supported collaborative learning (CSCL) has attracted a lot of attention in the last two decades with promising results at a research level (Stahl et al. 2006; Dillenbourg et al. 2009). However, the production of effective learning interactions is not guaranteed in a "free" and unconstrained environment.

Y.A. Dimitriadis (✉)
Department of Signal Theory, Communications and Telematics Engineering,
School of Telecommunications Engineering, University of Valladolid,
Valladolid, Spain
e-mail: yannis@tel.uva.es

A. Jimoyiannis (ed.), *Research on e-Learning and ICT in Education*,
DOI 10.1007/978-1-4614-1083-6_6, © Springer Science+Business Media, LLC 2012

Scaffolding of learners in such an environment, either by the teachers themselves and/or the technological system has been found to be especially helpful, while *scripting* has been used as an alternative term to express structuring of groups, timing, tasks, or resources (Fischer et al. 2007).

Independently of the term employed, scripting, or scaffolding, there is a wide consensus that there is a need for additional planning for CSCL based on good practices and existing knowledge in order to increase the chances of effective teaching/learning processes. However, there is a need to solve several important tensions (Tatar 2007) and achieve in practice a balance between a flexible and creative constructivist class and one guided by effective knowledge stemming from instructional design-oriented practices (Dillenbourg 2002).

Orchestration of CSCL classrooms requires a careful production of lesson plans, scripts, or scaffolds that need to be enacted and managed in concrete context conditions. However, as mentioned above, there exist several challenges for an effective and sustainable support of the complete lifecycle of such an orchestration. There is a need to understand better existing practices probably through ethnographical studies, analyze the alternative mediating artifacts that may support a more effective and efficient lifecycle, and eventually construct and evaluate the most appropriate mediating artifacts.

This paper, as a support and evolution of the associated keynote talk at the HCICTE 2010 conference (HCICTE 2010), addresses some of the aforementioned challenges related to the effective and sustainable support of orchestration in CSCL classrooms. It aims to provide a better understanding of such a problem, in both theoretical and practical terms, together with some proposals that have been analyzed during the last decade in the frame of the GSIC/EMIC group (GSIC/EMIC 2011) and the broader research and practice CSCL and TEL communities.

The following section deals with the concepts of orchestration, learning design, and the lifecycle of CSCL scripts so that we can get a better understanding of the most appropriate mediating artifacts for the support of CSCL scripting. Later, some specific proposals are studied in light of experiences and cases studies. Special focus is put on the use of learning and assessment patterns in higher education at the University of Valladolid, Spain, as well as design and enactment routines in a primary school at Cigales, Spain. A broader literature review and similar research efforts are presented and discussed in the next section. The lifecycle of CSCL scripts in blended environments is discussed with a special focus on the sustainability issues, which may be dealt through the Glue! Architecture proposed by the GSIC-EMIC group.

Mediating Artifacts in CSCL Scripting

A *CSCL classroom*, in its broad sense employed in this paper, may involve various elements that have to be taken into account in its management. These elements of CSCL classrooms include: ICT-based (e.g., a generic concept map tool, an interactive digital blackboard or a learning management system) or non-ICT-based (e.g., post-its or traditional blackboards) tools; face-to-face, distance or blended interactions at home, classes or museums through different media; and work in small groups, at a whole-class classroom and community level, or individually.

Orchestration of all these elements has been acknowledged as one of the major research challenges in the technology-enhanced learning (TEL) field by the *Stellar* network of excellence (Stellar 2010). The effective "coordination of supportive interventions across multiple learning activities occurring at multiple social levels" (Dillenbourg et al. 2009) by teachers is especially complex, given the great number of elements to be controlled and the associated trade-offs. The term of "orchestration" has attracted a lot of attention recently in the TEL community, although there are several interpretations assigned to it (Prieto 2010; Prieto et al. 2011b), either at the musical metaphor, or at the instructional design and computer science levels. The metaphor of musical orchestration may be attractive given the role of the teacher as "director" of the classroom, or of the students as self-orchestrators of their own activities. However, the metaphoric use of the term in TEL may be inspiring but at the same time it can be misleading and confusing, as the ones of theater plays or choreographies. Some more useful interpretations of the term may be related to the real-time monitoring and adaptation of teacher interventions in a computer-integrated classroom (Dillenbourg and Jermann 2010) or a more general view that includes modeling, planning, enacting, adapting, and evaluating lesson plans. In any case, it is expected that the TEL and CSCL communities may reach a consensus in the short term, based on peer-reviewed publications (Dillenbourg et al. 2009) or face-to-face interactions in conferences (Dillenbourg 2009; Nussbaum et al. 2011).

Scaffolding of learners may be based on micro- or macro-scripts that regulate the processes, through the sequencing and distribution of roles and activities (Weinberger et al. 2009). However, such regulation should be sufficiently flexible and adaptable, fading in time as learners internalize the external *scripts*. Additionally, such guidance should not be excessively prescriptive and reflect existing research knowledge that could be understood by the educational practitioners. From a technical point of view, these scripts might be partially or completely formalized using an appropriate educational modeling language (EML), such as IMS-LD (IMS 2003), so that they can be interpreted by computational systems. In this case, teachers should be able to find the balance between socially and technologically mediated coordination, so that emergent situations could be adequately handled.

In any case, independently of the use of terms and metaphors, such as scaffolds, scripts, or orchestration, expert instructional designers or educational practitioners need to produce *learning designs* or lesson plans for their CSCL classes. At the same time, they have to choose adequate tools, think of the specific conditions of their classes, and instantiate their designs while being able to reuse their generic designs. Finally, practitioners have to enact their instantiated designs, being able to monitor and regulate the evolution of the interactions. There is no consensus in the literature on the model and stakeholders of the lifecycle of orchestration or scripting, but it is generally accepted that it is complex, nonlinear, and iterative (Gómez-Sánchez et al. 2009; Jullien et al. 2009).

Although there are several educational, technological, and research trends, one framework for the analysis of the aforementioned issues is the Cultural Historical Activity Theory (CHAT). The associated concept of "mediating artefacts," i.e., instruments, signs, language, and machines has been analyzed especially in the task of learning design (Conole 2008). Thus, our research objective is to understand the processes and the mediating artifacts that are currently employed, using ethnographical methods, formalize them, and eventually construct *mediating tools* that might better support the lifecycle of orchestrating CSCL classes. Conole (2008) identifies several mediating artifacts that correspond to models, vocabularies, patterns, iconic representations, or case studies. Such artifacts support the decisions made by the practitioners, either isolated or aggregated to other artifacts, thus forming meta-mediating artifacts. Examples of meta-mediating artifacts include repositories of patterns, toolkits, pedagogical planners, or scaffolds in the form of hints, advisors, etc. Isolated or aggregated artifacts are typically implemented in software tools that are especially adequate for a technology-enhanced class.

In the following section, we focus on one type of artifacts, i.e., pedagogical patterns (Goodyear 2005) as a means to support the design and enactment phases of the lifecycle.

A Pattern Oriented Approach to CSCL Scripting

Pedagogical patterns form a special category of design patterns, and as such they capture and communicate good practices in learning and teaching processes (Dimitriadis et al. 2009a). Design patterns have been used broadly in several fields, starting with the pioneer work of Alexander in architecture and going through Human Computer Interaction to the Gamma design patterns in software engineering. They capture reusable knowledge about a contextualized problem and its associated, broadly accepted, solution. Although patterns may be used individually, typically they are grouped in networks of interconnected patterns, thus forming pattern languages that provide solutions to broader problems.

Pedagogical patterns are especially relevant to our research objective, since the ultimate actors in CSCL classroom orchestration are educational practitioners, who might be more familiar with the practice-oriented knowledge represented in pedagogical patterns. According to Retalis et al. (2006), pedagogical design patterns could be elicited in a lifecycle that merges bottom–up and top–down approaches. On the one hand, case studies in authentic contexts or other more controlled experiences capture practices, while literature and theory-driven work looks for evidence and wider support of these patterns and the associated pattern languages.

In our case, a CSCL scripting pattern language was proposed in (Hernández-Leo et al. 2010a) that focuses on *Collaborative Learning Flow Patterns* (CLFP), i.e., flows of activities, such as jigsaw, pyramid, or think-pair-share. This type of patterns, whose visual representation is shown in Fig. 1, has been shown to be effective in

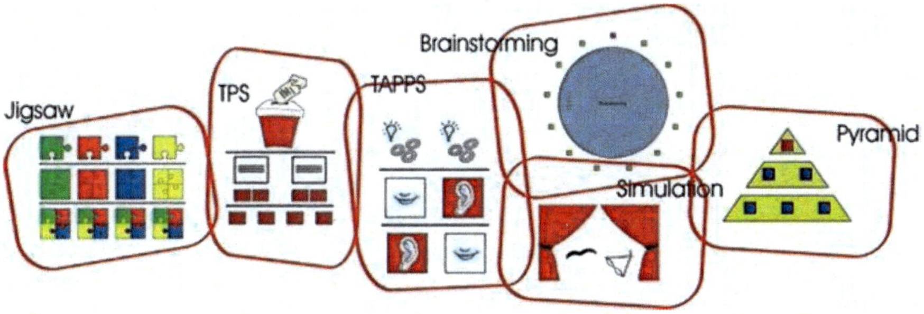

Fig. 1 Visual representations of collaborative learning flow patterns (CLFP)

several contexts, as e.g., in repurposing existing Open Educational Resources for collaborative learning (Dimitriadis et al. 2009b). Later, such a pattern language evolved in an assessment-aware scripting language that includes *assessment patterns* (Villasclaras-Fernández 2010). The following subsection discusses the use of the learning and assessment pedagogical patterns and the associated software tools in the context of higher education. On the other hand, similar research has been conducted in a primary school environment with respect to design and enactment patterns. A brief report of the associated research is presented in the second subsection.

Learning and Assessment Patterns in Higher Education

Use of ICT in higher education is typically associated with blended (or distance) learning settings in which courses are delivered using *Learning Management Systems* (LMS). While collaborative activities are especially appropriate for problem- or project-based learning, university professors are reluctant and several times unaware of collaborative techniques, such as the ones described in CLFP.

On the other hand, technology mediated coordination in CSCL scripting could be especially appropriate for the production and delivery of such courses. However, existing EML, and especially IMS-LD, are rather far away from a practitioner's mindset, and therefore they should be "hidden" to final users. Thus, it seems reasonable to think of employing CLFP and other elements of the CSCL scripting language as mediating artifacts for design and enactment of collaborative learning activities in higher education.

The first generation of tools created in the context of the GSIC/EMIC group included *Collage* (Hernández-Leo et al. 2006) for the support of the authoring phase and *InstanceCollage* (Villasclaras-Fernández et al. 2009) for the instantiation phase, while scripts could be deployed either in an LMS with an IMS-LD player or in a service-oriented environment, such as *Gridcole* (Bote-Lorenzo et al. 2008). Thus, the complete lifecycle of CSCL scripting and orchestration can be supported by this

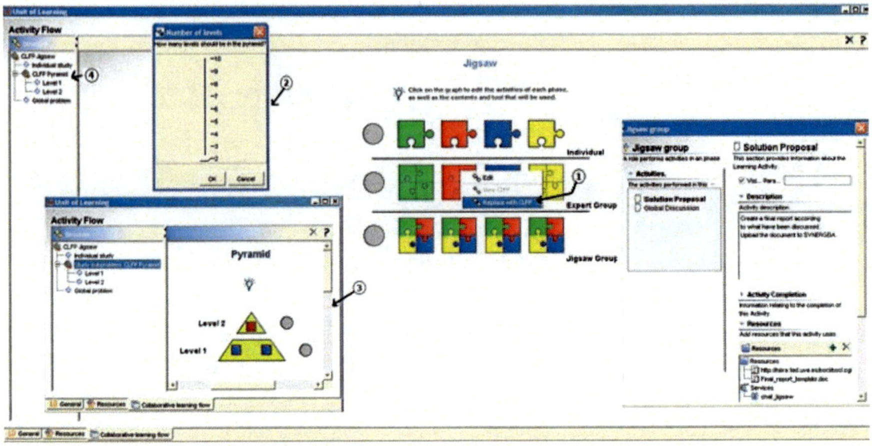

Fig. 2 Authoring a computer-supported collaborative learning (CSCL) script based on the Jigsaw and Pyramid CLFP in Collage

set of tools, or meta-mediating artifacts. Figure 2 illustrates part of the pattern-based design process supported by *Collage* for a CSCL script used in the context of a real course in University of Valladolid (Hernández-Leo et al. 2010b).

In this case, the teacher is using the jigsaw CLFP so that students may work on different parts of a complex technical document. Such pattern is adequate since the aforementioned document is divisible and the teacher wants to promote positive interdependence together with individual accountability. Thus, students need to work individually and then join the expert groups for each part of the document, while in the last phase super groups are formed in order to deal with the complete document. However, the teacher does not want to have expert groups with many students that are not typically effective in tasks of joint production. Thus, she selects the pyramid CLFP in order to implement the expert phase of the jigsaw CLFP, hoping that it will promote the quest for consensus among students.

The *Collage* tool supports this process of selecting patterns, combining and configuring them, assigning adequate services (tools) for the activities, and finally producing a reusable IMS-LD compliant file. Such support is implemented through advices and empty building blocks, with a strong emphasis in visual representations. Finally, the *InstanceCollage* tool is employed in order to instantiate this script for a specific context, taking into account all intrinsic features of the patterns, while *Gridcole* or an LMS such as *.LRN* and the associated IMS-LD player are employed for the enactment of the CSCL script.

From the above short presentation of the illustrating example, it can be seen that this set of ICT-based tools may be effective and efficient as mediating artifacts for orchestration of CSCL classes. Indeed, the process has been evaluated through a multi-case study that covers seven experiences that took place in the period 2005–2007

(Hernández-Leo et al. 2010b). The first set of workshops with professors at several Spanish universities showed that practitioners were able to create CSCL scripts for their own context. On the other hand, a workshop held in an international conference allowed us to show that the tools were able to implement a scenario proposed by a third-party, while several case studies in courses showed that the whole process could be carried out in real settings.

However, several elements were missing from the above process and the associated toolset, and especially in relation to adaptation (Karakostas and Demetriadis 2009) and flexibility (Dillenbourg and Tchounikine 2007), or the effective use of monitoring and regulation (Soller et al. 2005). The second generation of tools focused on the inclusion of assessment plans in the scripts. It is widely accepted that assessment is an integral part of any teaching/learning process and there is a significant body of knowledge related to production and use of assessment (Chan and Van Aalst 2004). We were especially interested in understanding and supporting the alignment between learning and assessment flows in scripts. In collaborative learning settings it is expected that formative assessment may be used employing assessment evidence produced in various activities. The use of appropriate assessment techniques could provide input for the adoption of further actions in other learning and support activities.

As mentioned above, the pattern-based approach was used again in order to formulate a set of assessment patterns and produce an expanded assessment-aware CSCL scripting language. On the other hand, a new information model has been proposed together with a design process that aligns learning and assessment patterns. This proposal has been implemented in the new *WebCollage* tool and has been evaluated through four workshops with university professors, two complete case studies in real settings, as well as a controlled evaluation experience with practitioners and experts in the period 2007–2010 (Villasclaras-Fernández 2010).

Figure 3 illustrates the interweaved learning and assessment flows for a concrete script implemented through *WebCollage*. The results (reports) of the first phase of the jigsaw CLFP are used as a source for the assessment pattern REPORT REVIEW (top-right icon) while the expert phase is employed as a source for the pattern OBSERVATIONS OF COLLABORATIVE WORK (bottom-right icon). *WebCollage* supports visualization of the complete set of patterns and the associated documentation, configuration of the templates for each pattern, and especially provides advices on the set of actions for an effective use of the patterns, the information model and the design process (see e.g., the advice provided through an exclamation mark for a missing element in the first phase of jigsaw).

The evaluation process confirmed that the process is especially complex, when learning and assessment are considered together in collaborative settings. Practitioners and experts acknowledged the usefulness and effectiveness of the support provided by WebCollage, although several actions were recommended with respect to user interface or even the process itself.

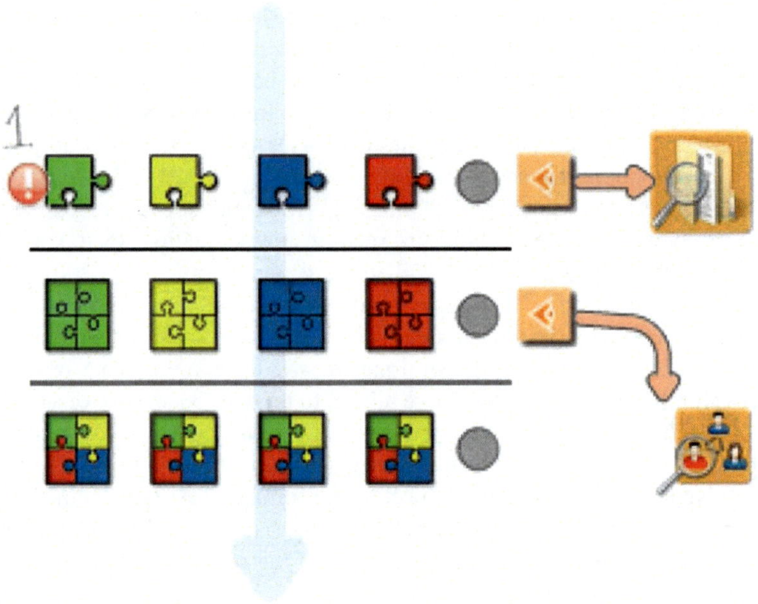

Fig. 3 Defining learning and assessment flows in WebCollage

Design and Enactment Patterns in a Primary Education School

Another parallel thread of our research in CSCL classroom orchestration refers to primary education classrooms that are significantly different from those described in the previous subsection. We have been conducting since 2008 a long case study in the "Ana de Austria" rural school at Cigales, Spain. In this case, we have focused on the problems of orchestrating face-to-face interactions in K6–8 classes, using typical non-ICT tools and communication media, together with wireless tablet PCs connected in a local network and interactive digital boards. We were especially interested in understanding improvisation and social coordination mechanisms, through the introduction of the *GroupScribbles* collaborative learning software tool (SRI 2006). Additionally, the qualitative case study that took place aimed at detecting routines (or patterns) that are recurrently used during the design and enactment of collaborative activities. Finally, we have been looking for an effective use of these patterns by teachers in new activities.

A significant result of this study shows that several patterns have been detected in both design and enactment phases (Prieto et al. 2010) in line with independent research results published by SRI research staff (DeBarger et al. 2010). A joint analysis of the GSIC/EMIC and SRI projects (Prieto et al. 2011a) has shown that such good practices may enable effective teaching strategies or moves in a contingent pedagogy context. Also, results from a recent workshop with teachers have

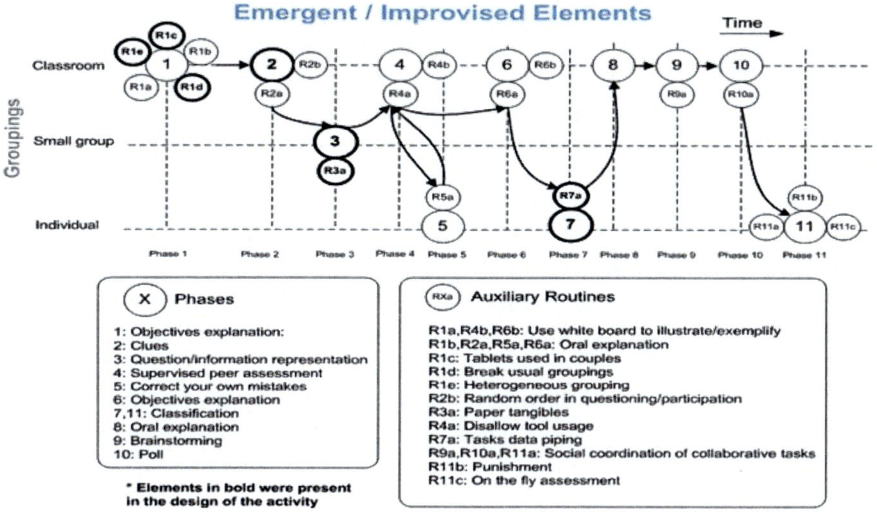

Fig. 4 Visual representation of orchestration in a face-to-face CSCL activity, together with the design, enactment, and improvisation routines

shown a clearly positive perception of the usefulness of these patterns as means to enrich new collaborative learning activities (Prieto et al. 2011c).

As an illustration of the orchestration held in classroom and the associated routines, Fig. 4 presents a visualization of an activity carried out in the "Ana de Austria" primary school during the 2008–2009 academic year. We may observe the different social levels of interaction (individual, small group and whole classroom), as they are unfolded in time. On the other hand, we may notice the phases in which the activity (script) was based, as well as the enactment routines that were associated to each phase. In bold, we can also detect some elements that were not designed by the teacher and therefore they emerged during enactment. Such emergent/improvisation actions could be better understood within the "disciplined improvisation" framework (Sawyer 2004). Overall, it can be seen that orchestration in CSCL classrooms is complex enough, although there are recurrent routines/patterns that enable a compact description of the activities. Recent evidence shows that these patterns were adequate mediating artifacts that enabled better orchestration by the teachers (Prieto et al. 2011c).

Conclusions

This paper based on the associated keynote talk (HCICTE 2010) deals with some issues related to orchestration of CSCL classes, and especially in supporting educational practitioners through appropriate mediating artifacts. Orchestration of technology-enhanced classes is relevant in the case of collaborative learning activities, due to the complexity of this pedagogical approach and the excessive number of aspects and trade-offs that have to be controlled by the teachers.

Patterns have been analyzed as a particularly promising set of mediating artifacts, for the support of the design, instantiation, and enactment phases of the orchestration lifecycle. In spite of the positive results of the evaluation studies, many issues are still open. Flexibility, adaptation, and improvisation need to accompany adequately these structuring, scaffolding, or scripting approaches. On the other hand, other mediating artifacts, such as visual representation or social software may be analyzed and integrated (see the *CompendiumLD* and *Cloudworks* tools developed in the Open University). Also, a seamless integration of scripts, LMS, and external tools has to be accomplished in order to provide a sustainable use of these solutions (see the *Glue!* Architecture proposed by the GSIC/EMIC research group, or similar initiatives at the IMS Global Consortium). Finally, the complexity of the orchestration process has to be handled adequately in the framework of pragmatic theoretical approaches.

Acknowledgments The author would like to acknowledge the contributions of the GSIC/EMIC group at the University of Valladolid, Spain and especially E. Villasclaras, J.I. Asensio, D. Hernández, L.P. Prieto, S. Villagrá, and I.M. Jorrín. Special thanks to the teachers and students of the "Ana de Austria" primary school at Cigales, Spain, as well as all other participants in the workshops and courses at University of Valladolid, Spain and other universities around Spain. The work presented in this paper has been partially funded by the Spanish Ministry of Science and Innovation (TIN2008-03023/TSI) and the regional Government of Castilla and León (VA106A08 and VA107A08).

References

Bote-Lorenzo, M., Gómez-Sánchez, E., Vega-Gorgojo, G., Dimitriadis, Y., Asensio-Pérez, J., & Jorrín-Abellán, I. (2008). Gridcole: a tailorable grid service based system that supports scripted collaborative learning. *Computers & Education*, 51(1), 155–172.

Chan, C. K. K., & Van Aalst, J. (2004). Learning, assessment and collaboration in computer-supported environments. In J. W. Strijbos, P. A. Kirschner, & R. L. Martens (eds.), *Computer-supported collaborative learning: What we know about CSCL and implementing it in higher education, Volume 3* (pp. 87–112). Boston, MA: Kluwer Academic Publishers.

Chen, F.-H., Looi, C.-K., & Chen, W. (2009). Integrating technology in the classroom: a visual conceptualization of teachers' knowledge, goals and beliefs. *Journal of Computer Assisted Learning*, 25(5), 470–488.

Conole, G. (2008). Capturing practice, the role of mediating artefacts in learning design. In L. Lockyer, S. Bennett, S. Agostinhi and B. Harper (eds.), *Handbook of learning designs and learning objects* (pp. 187–207). Hershey, PA: IGI Global.

Cuban, L. (2001). *Oversold and underused: Computers in the classroom*. Cambridge, MA: Harvard University Press.

DeBarger, H., Penuel, W., Harris, C. J., & Schank, P. (2010). Teaching routines to enhance collaboration using classroom network technology. In F. Pozzi & D. Persico (eds.), *Techniques for fostering collaboration in online learning communities: theoretical and practical perspectives* (pp. 224–244). Hershey, PA: IGI Global Publishing.

Dillenbourg P., & Jermann, P. (2010). Technology for classroom orchestration. In M. S. Khine and Saleh I. M. (eds.), *New Science of Learning: Cognition, Computers and Collaboration in Education* (pp. 525–552). New York: Springer.

Dimitriadis, Y., Goodyear, P., & Retalis, S. (2009a). Using e-learning design patterns to augment learners' experiences. Guest editors' introduction to "Design patterns for augmenting e-learning experiences". *Computers in Human Behavior*, 25(5), 997–1188.

Dimitriadis, Y., McAndrew, P., Conole, G., & Makriyannis, E. (2009b) New design approaches to repurposing Open Educational Resources for collaborative learning using mediating artefacts. In R. J. Atkinson & C. McBeath (eds.), *Proceedings of the Australasian Society for Computers in Learning in Tertiary Education* (pp. 200–207). Auckland: The University of Auckland, Auckland University of Technology, and Australasian Society for Computers in Learning in Tertiary Education (ASCILITE).

Dillenbourg, P. (2002). Over-scripting CSCL: The risks of blending collaborative learning with instructional design. In P. A. Kirschner (ed.), *Three worlds of CSCL: Can we support CSCL?* (pp. 61–91). Heerlen: Open Universiteit Nederland.

Dillenbourg, P. (2009). Exploring neglected planes: Social signs and class orchestration. *Proceedings of the International Conference of Computer-Supported Collaborative Learning (CSCL2009)* (pp. 6–7). Rhodes, Greece: International Society of the Learning Sciences.

Dillenbourg, P., Järvelä, S., & Fischer, F. (2009). The evolution of research in computer-supported collaborative learning: From design to orchestration. In N. Balacheff, S. Ludvigsen, T. de Jong, A. Lazonder & S. Barnes (eds.), *Technology-Enhanced Learning: Principles and products* (pp. 3–19). Amsterdam, the Netherlands: Springer.

Dillenbourg, P., & Tchounikine, P. (2007). Flexibility in macro CSCL scripts. *Journal of Computer-Assisted Learning*, 23(1), 1–13.

Goodyear, P. (2005). Educational design and networked learning: Patterns, pattern languages and design practice. *Australasian Journal of Educational Technology*, 21(1), 82–101.

Fischer, F., Kollar, I., Mandl, H., & Haake, J.M. (2007). *Scripting Computer-Supported Collaborative Learning: Cognitive, Computational and Educational Perspectives*. Berlin: Springer.

Gómez-Sánchez, E., Bote-Lorenzo, M. L., Jorrín-Abellán, I. M., Vega-Gorgojo, G., Asensio-Pérez, J. I., & Dimitriadis, Y. (2009). Conceptual framework for design, technological support and evaluation of collaborative learning. *International Journal of Engineering Education*, 25(3), 557–568.

GSIC/EMIC (2011). *Interdisciplinary Research Group on Intelligent and Cooperative Systems / Education, Media, Informatics and Culture*. Retrieved 15 February 2011 from http://www.gsic.uva.es.

HCICTE (2010). *7th Pan-Hellenic Conference with International Participation "ICT in Education"*. Invited speakers, Retrieved 15 February 2011 from http://korinthos.uop.gr/~hcicte10/speakers.html.

Hernández-Leo, D, Villasclaras-Fernández, E. D., Asensio-Pérez, J. I, Dimitriadis, Y., Jorrín-Abellán, I. M., Ruiz-Requies, I., & Rubia-Avi, B. (2006). Collage: A collaborative learning design editor based on patterns. *Educational Technology & Society*, 9(1), 58–71.

Hernández-Leo, D., Asensio-Pérez, J. I., Dimitriadis, Y., & Villasclaras, E. D. (2010a). Pattern languages for generating CSCL scripts: from a conceptual model to the design of a real situation. In P. Goodyear and S. Retalis (eds.), *E-learning, design patterns and pattern languages* (pp. 49–64). Rotterdam, the Netherlands: Sense Publishers.

Hernández-Leo, D., Jorrín-Abellán, I. M. Villasclaras, E. D., Asensio-Pérez, J. I., & Dimitriadis, Y. (2010b). A multicase study for the evaluation of a collaborative learning pattern-based visual design approach. *Journal of Visual Languages and Computing*, 21(6), 313–331.

IMS Global Learning Consortium. *IMS learning design v1.0 (2003) - Final specification*. Retrieved 31 August 2010 from http://www.imsglobal.org/learningdesign.

Jullien, J., Martel, C., Vignollet, L., & Wentland, M. (2009). OpenScenario: A flexible integrated environment to develop educational activities based on pedagogical scenarios. In I. Aedo (ed.), *Proceedings of the ninth IEEE International Conference on Advanced Learning Technologies, ICALT 2009* (pp. 509–513). Riga: IEEE Computer Society Press.

Karakostas, A., & Demetriadis, S. (2009). Adaptation patterns in systems for scripted collaboration. *Proceedings of the 8th International Conference on Computer Supported Collaborative Learning* (pp. 477–481). Rhodes: International Society of Learning Sciences.

Nussbaum, M., Dillenbourg, P., Fischer, F., Looi, C.K., & Roschelle, J. (2011). Workshop on "How to integrate CSCL in classroom life: Orchestration". *Pre-conference event at the 9th International Conference on Computer-Supported Collaborative Learning (CSCL 2011)*. Hong-Kong, China, July 2011.

Prieto, L. P. (2010). *The many faces of orchestration: Towards a (more) operative definition.* Unpublished manuscript, University of Valladolid, Spain.

Prieto, L. P., Villagrá-Sobrino, S., Dimitriadis, Y., Jorrín-Abellán, I. M., Martínez-Monés, A., & Anguita-Martínez, R. (2010). Recurrent routines in the classroom madness: pushing patterns past the design phase. In L. Dirckinck-Holmfeld, V. Hodgson, C. Jones, M. de Laat, D. McConnell & T. Ryberg (eds.), *Proceedings of the 7th International Conference on Networked Learning* (pp. 499–507). Aalborg: Aalborg University.

Prieto, L. P., Villagrá-Sobrino, S., Dimitriadis, Y., Schank, P., Penuel, W., & DeBarger A.H. (2011a). *Mind the gaps: Using patterns to change everyday classroom practice towards contingent CSCL teaching*. Paper accepted at the 9th International Conference of Computer-Supported Collaborative Learning (CSCL2011). Honk Kong.

Prieto, L. P., Villagrá-Sobrino, S., Jorrín-Abellán, I. M., Martínez-Monés, A., & Dimitriadis, Y. (2011b). Recurrent routines: Analyzing and supporting orchestration in technology-enhanced primary classrooms. *Computers & Education*, 57(1), 1214–1227.

Retalis, S., Georgiakakis, P., & Dimitriadis, Y. (2006). Eliciting design patterns for e-learning systems. *Computer Science Education*, 16(2), 105–118.

Sawyer, R. K. (2004). Creative teaching: Collaborative discourse as disciplined improvisation. *Educational Researcher*, 33(2), 12–20.

Soller, A., Martínez, A., Jermann, P., & Muehlenbrock M. (2005). From mirroring to guiding: A review of the state of the art in interaction analysis. *International Journal on Artificial Intelligence in Education*, 15, 261–290.

SRI (2006). Group Scribbles official website. Retrieved 31 August 2010 from http://groupscribbles.sri.com.

Stahl, G., Koschmann, T., & Suthers, D. (2006). Computer-supported collaborative learning: An historical perspective. In R. K. Sawyer (Ed.), Cambridge handbook of the learning sciences (pp. 409–426). Oxford, UK: Cambridge University Press.

Stellar Network of Excellence in TEL (2010). *WP1: The grand research challenge for TEL.* Retrieved 31 August 2010 from http://www.stellarnet.eu/programme/wp1.

Tatar, D. (2007). The design tensions framework. *Human Computer Interaction*, 22(4), 413–451.

Villasclaras-Fernández, E. D., Hernández-Gonzalo, J. A., Hernández-Leo, D., Asensio-Pérez, J. I., Dimitriadis, Y. & Martínez-Monés, A. (2009). InstanceCollage: A tool for the particularization of collaborative IMS-LD scripts. *Educational Technology & Society*, 12(4), 56–70.

Villasclaras-Fernández E. D. (2010). *A design process supported by software authoring tools for the integration of assessment within CSCL scripts.* Doctoral dissertation. University of Valladolid, Spain.

Weinberger, A., Collar, I., Dimitriadis, Y., Mäkitalo-Siegl, K., & Fischer, F. (2009). Computer-supported collaboration scripts: Perspectives from educational psychology and computer science. In N. Balacheff, S. Ludvigsen, T. de Jong, A. Lazonder & S. Barnes (eds.), *Technology-Enhanced Learning: Principles and products* (pp. 155–174). Amsterdam, the Netherlands: Springer.

Reorienting Teacher Education to Address Sustainable Development Through WikiQuESD

Vassilios Makrakis

Introduction

UNESCO (2006) indicated that Faculties of Education and teacher training institutions, in particular, need to reorient their study programs to address the quest for Sustainable Development. The latter is an evolving and dynamic concept in terms of its conceptual definition. According to the World Commission on Environment and Development (1987, p. 43) "Sustainable development is development that meets the needs of the present without compromising the ability of future generations to meet their own needs." In a recent panel review of 37 experts (Makrakis 2011, p. 411) sustainable development was consensually defined as "to making informed, contextual and conscious decisions driven by the principles of solidarity, justice, accountability, equity and transparency for the good of present and future generations, locally and globally and to act upon those decisions for advancing social, economic and environmental wellbeing." The link between Information and Communication Technologies (ICTs) and sustainable development is being addressed by extensive debates and research which recognize the challenge new technologies bring to the reorientation of education towards learning to live sustainably (Makrakis 2006, 2008, 2011; Paas 2008). Sustainable development is generally perceived as an overlapping of four pillars, dimensions or components, namely environment, society, culture, and economy. According to UNESCO (2005), environmental dimension encompasses key areas such as natural resources, climate change, rural transformation, sustainable urbanization, and disaster prevention and mitigation, while societal dimension embraces human rights, peace and human security, gender equality, indigenous knowledge, cultural diversity and intercultural understanding, health, HIV/AIDS, and governance. Economic dimension, by contrast, includes poverty reduction, corporate

V. Makrakis (✉)
Department of Primary Education, University of Crete, Crete, Greece
e-mail: makrakis@edc.uoc.gr

A. Jimoyiannis (ed.), *Research on e-Learning and ICT in Education*,
DOI 10.1007/978-1-4614-1083-6_7, © Springer Science+Business Media, LLC 2012

responsibility and accountability, fair trade, and market economy. Finally, cultural dimension is referred to as both "an underlying dimension of and 'inter-linkages' or 'inter-connections' between the other three pillars of sustainable development" (UNESCO 2008). In fact, cultural elements are indeed present in each of the environmental, economic, and social pillars of sustainable development.

The United Nations passed a resolution in December 2002 to adopt the Decade of Education for Sustainable Development (DESD) as endorsed by the Johannesburg World Summit on Sustainable Development (WSSD). The DESD (2005–2014) was adopted as a Resolution 57/254 at the UN General Assembly 57th Session in 2002. According to the Resolution, education is considered as a primary capacity to transform their visions for society into reality. It has been also stated that education not only provides scientific and technical skills, it also provides the motivation, justification, and social support for pursuing and applying education for sustainability (UNESCO 2005, 2006; Lawale and Bory-Adams 2010). Education for sustainability has been defined "as the learning needed to maintain and improve our quality of life and the quality of life of generations to come. It is about equipping individuals, communities, groups, businesses and government to live and act sustainably, as well as giving them an understanding of the environmental, social and economic issues involved" (Makrakis 2011, p. 411). This vision of education emphasizes a holistic, interdisciplinary, and cross-disciplinary approach to developing the knowledge and skills needed for a sustainable future as well as changes in values, behavior, and lifestyles.

Hence, in order to achieve sustainability through education, we need teachers who are well-prepared and committed to the principles of sustainability (UNESCO 2006; Makrakis 2010b). In this context, the use of ICTs, can offer exciting new possibilities to promote the changes in teaching methodologies called for education for sustainable development (ESD) (Makrakis 2008; Paas 2008). However, when looking specifically for research on the use of ICTs in ESD, including educational policies, pedagogical approaches and classroom uses of ICTs for ESD, there is not much available to date (Tella and Adu 2009). Integration of ESD in higher education, especially as it concerns pedagogical practice, has been slow (Everett 2008; Rode and Michelsen 2008); except initiatives for campus greening and research where there is more progress (Sterling and Scott 2008; Wals 2009).

In recent years, the concept of WikiQuESD has been developed by the author to combine a Wiki platform and its technologies, the idea of WebQuest (Dodge 1998) and an ESD approach. The template developed is divided into three parts (Fig. 1). The left hand side displays five main nodes: (1) activation, (2) learning tasks, (3) learning processes, (4) reflective feedback/assessment, and (5) extensions, each of which can be used for planning and constructing WikiQuESD lesson interventions. There are also secondary nodes, which provide information about the sources (learning objects) used and creators. The main right pane is the screen that holds the HTML content associated with each node. In the upper bar space, the creators place the title of the instructional project and in the right part, the UNESCO Chair's logo as well as additional nodes related to online tools that can be used such as Cmap; Blog etc. These mindtools repurpose ICTs to engage learners in critical and reflective thinking (Jonassen 1996; Jonassen and Reeves 1996) and ESD (Vanhear and Pace 2008). WikiQuESD is envisioned to contribute into bridging this gap.

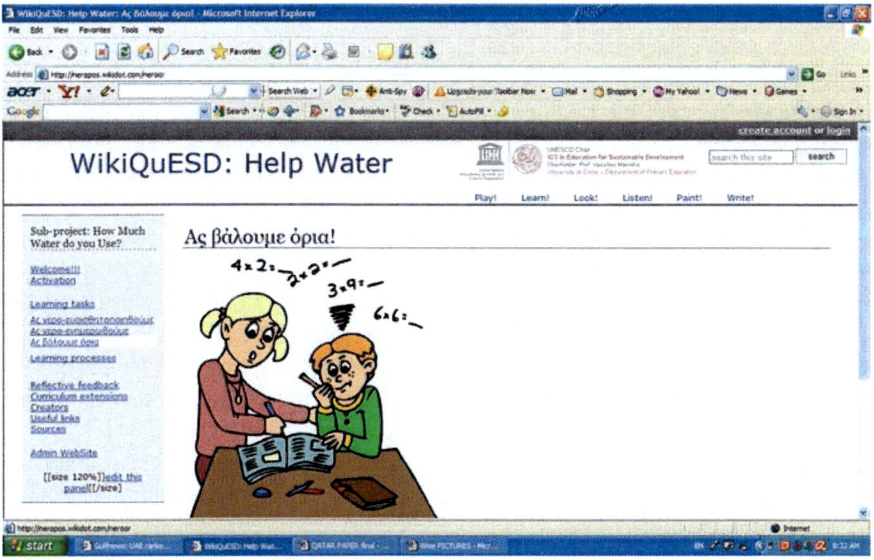

Fig. 1 WikiQuESD template

WikiQuESD is based on theoretical insights from critical or emancipatory constructivist research and transformative/reflective learning with particular reference to education for sustainability (Sterling 2001; Wals and Blaze Corcoran 2006; Huckle 2010). Emancipatory constructivism implies that meaning is shaped and knowledge is constructed through discussion with peers and teachers, and through reflection that leads to learning-based change (Kostoulas-Makrakis and Makrakis 2008).

The principal idea behind WikiQuESD is that teaching and learning should focus on the study of real-life problems and the learning process should be learner-centered. To support these features, WikiQuESD includes strategies such as: activation though various means such as conceptual mapping, Webloging, brainstorming etc. It continues through problem identification, identification of learning needs and tasks, processing and refinement of needs and tasks, construction and reconstruction of new knowledge, and continuous reflective feedback. These descriptors clearly call for pedagogical processes that are participatory, reflective, and emancipatory. It also assumes that an attempt to reorienting teacher education to address sustainability needs to be based on three interrelated pedagogical concepts: (1) contextual learning, (2) authentic learning, and (3) transformative learning (Makrakis 2006). All of these are critical to transforming unsustainable values and actions into sustainable ones. The main technological and pedagogical characteristics built into WikiQuESD can be summarized as follows (Makrakis 2010a):

- *Multiple types and levels of scaffolding*: Support comes from online instructional material (http://www.wikitipsgr.wikidot.com) that is monitored by a mentor or facilitator to assist our preservice teachers' engagement in producing WikiQuESD learning activities. Some of the examples include templates, descriptive assessment rubrics, and guidelines that help them develop and design their WikiQuESD instructional projects.

- *Authentic content, curriculum, and learning tasks*: To ensure that content is authentic and learning is meaningful, preservice teachers are encouraged to select and/or negotiate an ESD local/global topic and engage in learning tasks which are real-world and situated within realistic contexts. Content is thus learner-generated, interdisciplinary, and hypermedia-based largely built through multimodal open education resources available in the Web.
- *Multimodal texts and literacies*: Using the affordances available in the source social software of the WikiQuESD learning and authoring environment, preservice and in-service teachers are guided to develop web-based instructional interventions merging various modes of representation such as spoken and written language, still or moving images, sounds, designs, animation, and videos.
- *Reflective feedback/assessment*: Through a set of guiding questions, pre/in-service teachers are empowered to monitor and take ownership of their learning guided by prompt questions.
- *Active constructive and meaning making reflective process*: Pre/in-service teachers are guided to actively engage in knowledge and meaning construction through reflection.
- *Meaningful cooperation, collaboration, and communication*: This process engages pre/in-service teachers to learn to negotiate, compromise, compare, share, revise, and scaffold each others' learning.
- *Transferability and replicability*: Pre/in-service teachers working within the WikiQuESD learning and authoring environment produce multimodal content that can be up-scaled, adopted and adapted to various settings and to suit social, cultural and language learner's needs and making learning more customized.

Learning and behavioral change are essential for achieving sustainable thinking and living (learning to live sustainably), which is inextricably connected to transformative perceptions of learning (Aubusson et al. 2007; Goodfellow and Sumsion 2000; Pilling-Cormick 1997). Transformative learning, in that sense, focuses on learning-based change that involves "learning to be," "learning to live together," "learning to know" and "learning to do" (Delors 1996). It is a shift of consciousness that alters: our way of being in the world (learning to be), our way for discovering others by discovering ourselves (learning to live together), our way of learning how to learn as well as acquiring, constructing, disseminating and managing knowledge (learning to know), and our way of putting knowledge into action (learning to do). It is above all learning that "transforms problematic frames of references – sets of fixed assumptions and expectations – to make them more inclusive, discriminating, open reflective and emotionally able to change" (Mezirow 2003, pp. 57–58). To put all these together, all these educational goals or pillars for the twenty-first century need to be integrated with another pillar that is "learning to transform oneself and society."

Context of the Study and Method

This study examined preservice teachers' use of WikiQuESD Web 2.0 environment in an undergraduate education course entitled "Design and Develop Web-based Instructional Material" at the Department of Primary Education, University of Crete during the fall of 2009 semester. The course took place over a 13-week period and consisted of a weekly 3-h lecture supplemented by five 2-h tutorials. The teaching process was supported through online instructional material (http://www.wikitipsgr.wikidot.com) that was monitored by a mentor or facilitator. Participants in the course were 30 preservice teachers: 90% were females and 100% had access to Internet either at the University and/or at home and all of them had previous experience using ICTs. Only, a 4% had previous experience with Wikis. The course activities were designed to promote ESD across the primary school curriculum through the support of ICTs integrated into the WikiQuESD authoring environment. It was also designed to promote critical reflection and collaborative learning through the affordances (e.g., weblogs, Cmap, Hotpotatoes) integrated into the WikiQuESD platform (Makrakis 2010a).

A naturalistic inquiry was used to guide the research process for this study. This approach implied that meaning was socially constructed by individuals through interaction with the setting environment and their personal beliefs, theories, practices, and perceptions (Creswell 2003). The research methods used were: participant observation, focus group discussions, reflective journals prepared by course participants, and project-based assignments (Ellis and Weekes 2008; Everett 2008; Clarke 2004). Priest and Sturgess (2005, p. 2) claim that reflection in a group setting provides a richer experience by enabling "the individual to subject their personal beliefs to critical analysis in a safe environment." Sockman and Sharma (2008) show that through peer feedback and reflective journal writing, teachers could uncover the obstacles and discover how their personal learning theories and teaching beliefs need to change in order to implement transformative teaching strategies. Brandt (2008) also indicates that when feedback and reflection are integrated in the form of reflective conversations between teachers and students, both teachers and students could benefit from the reflective practice. Therefore, reflective practice not only makes change possible, but also provides necessary information to develop guidelines for setting new needs, goals, and plans (Liou 2001; Yang 2009). Content analysis was used to analyze the presence, meanings and relationships of key words, and concepts related to constructs or categories and then make inferences about the messages (Krippendorff 2004). A category was defined as a group of words with similar meaning or connotations, which must be mutually exclusive and exhaustive. Three types of texts were used: (1) texts derived from the participants' answers to a set of open-ended questions elicited through focus group discussion and reflective journals, (2) the instructor's notes taken through participant observation, and (3) the texts of the 16 submitted WikiQuESD projects. Some of the questions asked during the focus group discussions were: What did you expect from the course? What has changed in terms of pedagogy and personal theory after finishing the course?

If something changed, why did it not happen before? The content was examined using two methods: conceptual analysis and relational analysis (Carley 1993). The former was used to look into the existence of concepts associated with critical constructivism in the texts. The latter was used to examine whether the instructional strategies and the activities adopted, especially in the WikiQuESD projects were related to critical constructivist principles.

To make valid inferences from the content of the projects examined, double checking has been carried out and no ambiguity of word meanings and category definitions had been revealed. To cross-validate the findings, two techniques were employed: first, the results were communicated to a sample of respondents to get a sense of the extent to which they are truly reflected in the project works and second, the project works and the open-ended questions upon which analysis was made were cross-referenced (Miles and Huberman 1994). Both revealed a high consistency with the constructs developed and the interpretations and inferences made.

Results of the Study

The themes or main categories that emerged from the analysis could be assigned to the following concepts: motivation, multimodality, authenticity, interdisciplinarity, use of distributed resources, transferability, empowerment, and meaningfulness. Motivation was enabled through using stories, videos, pictures, or cartoons. It was assumed that such anchors could stimulate the learners' curiosity about the topic, challenge their perceptions, and motivate them to explore further the sustainability issue. In some cases, the use of video-clips was used together with the use of blogs or forums. Previous research shows that the use of such networking media contributes positively to empowerment and learning (Williams 2004). These results can be substantiated by previous research which shows that it can be difficult to motivate learners when it comes to reading texts (Dewitt 1996; Davis 1997) and that Internet access and use could motivate students (Stiler and Philleo 2003; Liaw et al. 2007).

To ensure that content is authentic and learning is meaningful, preservice teachers participated in the study were encouraged to select and/or negotiate an ESD local/global topic and engage in learning tasks which were real-world and situated within realistic contexts. Themes developed in the project works dealt with types of energy, desertification, renewal resources, overconsumption, bioclimatic schools, and climate change. The content of the WikiQuESD projects submitted was interdisciplinary and largely built on multimodal open education resources available in the Web. A sample of representative projects developed can be accessed from the following URL addresses:

http://aioliki-energeia.wikidot.com
http://desertification-energy.wikidot.com
http://overconsumption.wikidot.com
http://bioclimatic-schools.wikidot.com
http://renresources.wikidot.com/start
http://energy-ngos.wikidot.com

http://recycle-saveenergy.wikidot.com
http://energy-green-health.wikidot.com
http://bioclimatic-houses.wikidot.com
http://energy-globalwarming.wikidot.com
http://energy-airpollution.wikidot.com
http://saveenergy-recycling.wikidot.com
http://climatechange1.wikidot.com

The WikiQuESD projects submitted show that the learning activities integrated into projects were associated with an extensive use of ICT affordances and extensive use of Web-based open education resources. The amount of open education resources integrated into the WikiQuESD projects ranged about 40–50% of the total content. All of the participants used both home and university campus networked facilities, mostly for asynchronous collaborative learning, although synchronous collaborative networking facilities were available through the WikiQuESD platform. This is largely due to the fact that most participants were not accustomed to this type of communication; added to that such activity was not demanded by the course.

Based on the analysis of focus group discussions, course participants' instructional design models elicited at the beginning, in the middle, and at the end of the course changed significantly. When participants were asked to indicate their instructional design model at the start of the course, the most common instructional design models exhibited were largely divided into four stages: stating goals and objectives, turning objectives into learning tasks, use of ready-made content, and learning assessment at the end to be delivered mostly through structured tests. This reflects a traditional objectivist instructional design model that has the following characteristics: the process is sequential and linear, predefined learning objectives guide lesson planning and development, didactic material is prescribed, and implementation is largely teacher-centered and summative learning assessment is dominant. The shift to an alternative instructional design model was evidenced in the middle of the course when participants were asked to present the progression of their projects tasks. By the end, almost all WikiQuESD projects developed can be characterized by the following design characteristics: recursive and nonlinear, learning objectives are negotiated (emerge through activation and learning processes), didactic material is constructed and reconstructed based on OERs, and instruction focuses on contextual and meaningful learning.

This shift in instructional design paradigm also reflects a "change agency" principle that can be interpreted in a threefold way. First, all the participants in this study expressed a positive image about themselves and confidence in their engagement with WikiQuESD technologies. Indicative expressions supporting this assumption elicited through focus group discussions and the personal reflective journals are the following: "Feel more confident," "can do things without support," "I will use wiki in class" etc. Second, it was also revealed that merging ICT-based reflective pedagogies, such as webloging was perceived as a tool that can empower them to change their personal theories and practices.

The following replies elicited through focus group discussions and reflective journals seem to be indicative in supporting this assumption: "using themes that reflect real-life problems, teachers take investigative roles that help them discover and construct new understandings and knowledge," "real-life problems made me think over of my personal beliefs and actions." It is also worth pointing out that almost all participants indicated that through this course they learned how to construct knowledge rather than acquiring knowledge. It was also revealed by more than half of them that the knowledge and skills acquired through the WikiQuESD projects could be transferred to other situations. The core assumption of constructivism is that learners actively create their own knowledge, vs. acquiring it, and that this active engagement is thought to promote a deeper understanding that may be transferred to new and different situations (Tobias 2010; Evans 2006). Looking into the WikiQuESD projects, it is also evidenced that participants used a mixture of assessment tools such as concept mapping, weblogs, and interactive exercises. Previous research shows that concept mapping has been used extensively in teaching and learning (Raymond 1997; Novak 1990; Novak and Cañas 2008) as well as a tool to monitor and promote meaningful learning, thinking, and acting in courses related to sustainable development for teacher education (Åhlberg 2004).

Evidence through focus group discussions shows that the paradigm shifts have been empowered by discussions on the three dominant paradigms of learning (transmissive, transactual and transformative) in the context of three corresponding models of curriculum: (1) product, (2) process, and (3) praxis (Grundy 2003). However, the reflective journals submitted by participants varied: a few revealed deep and critical reflection but most focused on describing events, with relatively narrow analysis. However, almost all the participants stated that they plan to integrate WikiQuESD in their future work. In terms of problems encountered, the great majority of participants indicated that the most demanding in working with WikiQuESD is the learning of codes. This may be explained by the fact that most of the participants had little previous experience with wiki environments.

Conclusion

Three of the major forces shaping and driving the twenty-first century education are (Makrakis 2008): (1) the development and diffusion of ICTs, (2) the increasing demand for new educational approaches and pedagogies that foster transformative and lifelong learning, and (3) the reorientation of educational curricula to address sustainable development (SD). Education systems, at all levels, and especially Higher Education and Teacher Education bear their own responsibility for building a more sustainable future. If higher education fails to educate students for sustainability, future teachers and leaders cannot be qualified agents for sustainable development. In the field of education, ICTs are increasingly deployed as tools to extend the learner's capacity to learn and teacher's capacity to deliver quality teaching and develop professional skills. One emerging area concerns merging ICTs with the United Nations (UN) call for the DESD to create a more sustainable development future. While increasing the quality of education through ESD, the use of ICTs pose many challenges for innovative and creative ways in reorienting teacher education to address sustainability. From this study, although limited to a case study, it is quite clear that building constructivist learning environments enabled by ICTs had an important influence on the preservice teachers' learning both in terms of what and how to teach. Analyzing the content of the WikiQuESD projects submitted at the end of the course, it is evident that ICTs when merged with sound pedagogical principles may contribute to educational innovative and education for sustainability. Besides the learning outcomes gained by preservice teachers while developing these projects, they can also be seen as good examples of curriculum innovation and evidence of the changing their instructional design roles. These projects can also provide a useful teaching resource for other preservice and in-service teachers to be used for modeling similar developments. Rethinking and revising education to address the knowledge, skills, perspectives, and values related to sustainability is of paramount importance to current and future societies. This implies a review of existing curricula in terms of their objectives and content with the aim to develop interdisciplinary and cross-disciplinary understanding and knowledge of social, cultural, economic, and environmental sustainability. These include skills for problem-based learning (PBL), creative, reflective and critical thinking, using appropriate ICTs, and reforming teacher training practices so that transformative lifelong learning is fostered. PBL is preferred as the methodology because of its compatibility with ESD and the strengths and advantages it offers for supporting teachers' professional development and learning. First, PBL builds on the use of learners' reflective practice in teaching and learning based on real-life and authentic problems and issues (Stewart et al. 2007; Neo and Neo 2001). Through this, teachers are encouraged to take more ownership of their professional development in a highly creative and stimulating way supported by hypermedia-based cognitive tools (Jonassen et al. 2003; Brush and Saye 2002).

Through a PBL process, teachers have an opportunity to develop skills in problem definition and problem solving, to reflect on their own learning, knowledge and practices, and develop a deep understanding of the content domain learning. In a PBL approach, the problem is often stated in the form of key questions, such as the following:

- How can I use computerized graphic organizers to teach vocabulary relevant to environmental sustainability issues?
- How can I use datahandling tools (e.g., Excel) to construct knowledge and promote learning-based action on ESD local/global issues?
- How can I use ICT to develop my ecological footprint towards sustainable water use?

In light of these questions, there is need to merge new technology with new pedagogy that addresses sustainability. Teaching local/global sustainable issues also requires teachers to be creative, critical, resourceful, and informed on these issues. The interactive nature of hypermedia technology provides unique capabilities for the implementation of problem-based environments. This suggests a high degree of learner control. Hypermedia tools, such as video-based scenarios, ecological footprints, visual graphic organizers, electronic notebooks, and communication tools help learners explore and address problems in a real-life situation as well as being used as critical reflective scaffolds on the problem-solving process. Media, interaction tasks, navigation etc. should follow sound interface design principles.

Our experiences in carrying out teaching interventions dealing with ESD themes and PBL methods supported by ICTs indicate that such an interface should take into consideration: (1) using PBL scenarios linked to local sustainability issues in audio-visual/hypermedia format, (2) employing critical thinking scaffold as knowledge elicitation systems that could also assist teachers as action researchers, (3) exploring the advantage of technology to provide opportunity for support and reflection on both the content learned and the learning process, and (4) connecting ICTs with learning techniques that foster higher-order thinking skills, support decision making and involve participatory learning. Our teaching and research experiences through this study imply that there is need for teacher education curriculum revision which will aim at:

- Empowering future teachers to develop their instructional skills actively and experientially, in a variety of learning environments, both individually and collaboratively.
- Providing an authentic learning environment so that future teachers engage in concrete tasks within realistic and problem-solving learning scenarios.
- Emphasizing ways that technology can facilitate and enhance future teachers' professional roles.

References

Åhlberg, M. (2004). Concept mapping for sustainable development. In A. J. Cañas, J. D. Novak &. M. González (eds.), *Concept Maps: Theory, Methodology, Technology. Proceedings of the First International Conference on Concept Mapping,* Vol. 1 (pp. 34-44). Pamplona, Spain.

Aubusson, P., Steele, F., Dinham, S., Brady, C. (2007). Action learning in teacher learning community formation: Informative or transformative? *Teacher Development,* 11(2), 133–148.

Brandt, C. (2008). Integrating feedback and reflection in teacher preparation. *ELT Journal,* 62(1), 37–46.

Brush, T. A., & Saye, J. W. (2002). A summary of research exploring hard and soft scaffolding for teachers and students using a multimedia supported learning environment. *Journal of Interactive Online Learning,* 1(2), 1–12.

Carley, K. (1993). Coding choices for textual analysis: A comparison of content analysis and map analysis. *Sociological Methodology*, 23, 75–126.

Clarke, M. (2004). Reflection: journals and reflective questions: a strategy for professional learning. *Australian Journal of Teacher Education*, 29(2), 11–23.

Creswell, J.W. (2003). *Research design. Qualitative, quantitative and mixed methods approaches.* London: Sage Publications.

Davis, J.N. (1997). Computer and L2 reading: Student performance, student attitudes. *Foreign Language Annals,* 30(1), 58–72.

Delors, J. (1996). *Learning – The treasure within.* Report to UNESCO of the International Commission on Education for the twenty-first century. Paris: UNESCO Publ.

Dewitt, S. L. (1996). The current nature of hypertext research in computers and composition studies. *Computers and Composition,* 13(1), 69–84.

Dodge, B. (1998). *WebQuests:* A strategy for scaffolding higher level learning. *Paper presented at the National Educational Computing Conference*, San Diego, June 22-24, Retrieved 22 January 2011 from http://webquest.sdsu.edu/necc98.htm.

Ellis, G., & Weekes, T. (2008). Making sustainability 'real': Using group-enquiry to promote education for sustainable development. *Environmental Education Research,* 14(4), 482–500.

Evans, J. (2006). Building bridges: Reflections on the problem of transfer of learning in mathematics. *Educational Studies in Mathematics*, 39(1–3), 23–44.

Everett, J. (2008). Sustainability in higher education: Implications for disciplines. *Theory and Research in Education,* 6(2), 237–251.

Goodfellow, J., & Sumsion, J. (2000). Transformative pathways: Field-based teacher educators' perceptions. *Journal of Education for Teaching: International Research and Pedagogy,* 26(3), 245–257.

Grundy, S. (2003). *Curriculum: product or praxis?*. Athens: Savvalas (in Greek).

Huckle, J. (2010). ESD and the current crisis of capitalism. *Journal of Education for Sustainable Development,* 4(1), 135–142.

Jonassen, D. H. (1996). *Computers in the classroom: Mindtools for critical thinking*. Columbus, OH: Merrill/Prentice-Hall.

Jonassen, D. H., & Reeves, T. C. (1996). Learning with technology: Using computers as cognitive tools. In D.H. Jonassen (ed.), *Handbook of research for educational communications and technology* (pp. 693–719). New York: Macmillan.

Jonassen, D., Howland, J., Moore, J., & Marra, R. (2003). *Learning to solve problems with technology: A constructivist perspective*. Upper Saddle River, NJ: Merril Prentice Hall (2nd ed.).

Kostoulas-Makrakis, N., & Makrakis, V. (2008). *Interculturality and education for a sustainable future*. Heraklion: E-media University of Crete (in Greek).

Krippendorff, K. (2004). *Content analysis: An introduction to its methodology*. London: Sage Publications.

Lawale, S., & Bory-Adams, A. (2010). The decade of education for sustainable development: Towards four pillars of learning. *Development*, 53(4), 547–550.

Liaw, S. S., Huang, H. M., & Chen, G. D. (2007). Surveying instructor and learner attitudes towards e-learning. *Computers and Education*, 49(4), 1066–1080.

Liou, H. C. (2001). Reflective practice in a pre-service teacher education program for high school English teachers in Taiwan, ROC. *System, 29*, 197–208.

Makrakis, V. (2006). *Preparing United Arab Emirates teachers for building a sustainable society*. University of Crete: E-Media publications.

Makrakis, V. (2008). An instructional design module of ICT that empowers teachers to integrate education for sustainable development across the curriculum. In C. Angeli & N. Valanides (eds.), *Proceedings of the 6th Panhellenic Conference with International Participation on Information and Communication Technologies in Education* (v.1, pp. 391–398). University of Cyprus.

Makrakis, V. (2010a). The challenge of WikiQuESD as an environment for constructing knowledge in teaching and learning for sustainable development. *Discourse and Communication for Sustainable Education,* 1(1), 50–57.

Makrakis, V. (2010b). Strategies to reinforce the role of ICT in teaching and learning for sustainability. In M. Witthaus, K. Candless & R. Lambert (eds.), *Tomorrow Today* (pp. 169–171). Leicester: Tudor Rose.

Makrakis, V. (2011). ICT-enabled education for sustainable development: Merging theory with praxis. In M. Youssef & S.A. Anwar (eds.), *Proceedings of the 4th Conference on e-Learning Excellence in the Middle East* (pp. 410–419). Hamdan Bin Mohammed e-University, Dubai, UAE.

Mezirow, J. (2003). *Transformative learning*. Athens: Metaixmio (in Greek).

Miles, M. B., & Huberman, A. (1994). *Qualitative data analysis: An expanded sourcebook.* Thousand Oaks, CA: Sage.

Neo, M., & Neo, K. (2001). Innovative teaching: using multimedia in a problem-based learning environment. *Educational Technology & Society*, 4(4), 19–31.

Novak, J. D., & Cañas, D. A. (2008). *The theory underlying concept maps and how to construct and use them*. Technical Report IHMC CmapTools 2006-01, Rev 01-2008, Florida. Institute for Human and Machine. Retrieved 12 March 2011 from http://cmap.ihmc.us/Publications/ResearchPapers/TheoryUnderlyingConceptMaps.pdf.

Novak, J. D. (1990). Concept mapping: A useful tool for science education. *Journal of Research in Science Teaching,* 27(10), 937–949.

Paas, L. (2008). *How ICTs can support education for sustainable development: Current uses and trends.* Retrieved 12 March 2011 from http://www.iisd.org/pdf/2008/ict_education_sd_trends.pdf.

Pilling-Cormick, J. (1997). Transformative and self-directed learning in practice. *New Directions for Adult and Continuing Education*, 74, 69–77.

Priest, A.M., & Sturgess, P. (2005). But is it scholarship? Group reflection as a scholarly activity. *Studies in Learning, Evaluation, Innovation and Development*, 2(1), 1-9. Retrieved 12 March 2011 from http://www.sleid.cqu.edu.au/viewissue.php?id=6.

Raymond, A. (1997). The use of concept mapping in qualitative research: A multiple case study in mathematics education. *Focus on Learning Problems in Mathematics*, 19(3), 1–28.

Rode, H., & Michelsen, G. (2008). Levels of indicator development for education for sustainable development. *Environmental Education Research,* 14(1), 19–33.

Sockman, B., & Sharma, P. (2008). Struggling toward a transformative model of instruction: It's not so easy!. *Teaching and Teacher Education,* 24(4), 1070–1082.

Sterling, S., & Scott, W. (2008). Higher education and ESD in England: A critical commentary on recent initiatives. *Environmental Education Research,* 14(4), 386–398.

Sterling, S. (2001). *Sustainable Education: Revisioning, Learning and Change.* Totnes: Green Books.

Stiler, G. M., & Philleo, T. (2003). Blogging and blogspots: An alternative format for encouraging reflective practice among preservice teachers. *Academic Research Library,* 123(4), 789–798.

Stewart, T., Maclntyre, W., Galea, V., & Steel, C. (2007). Enhancing problem-based learning designs with a single e-learning scaffolding tool: Two case studies using challenge FRAP. *Interactive Learning Environments*, 15(1), 77–91.

Tella, A., & Adu, E. (2009). Information Communication Technology (ICT) and curriculum development: the challenges for education for sustainable development. *Indian Journal of Science and Technology*, 2(3), 55–59.

Tobias, S. (2010). Generative learning theory, paradigm shifts, and constructivism in educational psychology: A tribute to Merl Wittrock. *Educational Psychologist*, 45(1), 51–54.

Vanhear, J., & Pace, P. J. (2008). Integrating knowledge, feelings and action: Using vee heuristics and concept mapping in education for sustainable development. *Journal of Teacher Education for Sustainability,* 10, 42–55.

UNESCO Netherlands National Commission (2008). *Culture and sustainable development: Executive summary.* Netherlands National Commission for UNESCO.

UNESCO (2005). *Guidelines and Recommendations for Reorienting Teacher Education to Address Sustainability, UNESCO Education for Sustainable Development in Action.* Technical Paper No 4, Retrieved 12 March 2011 from http://unesdoc.unesco.org/images/0014/001433/143370e.pdf.

UNESCO (2006). *Higher Education for Sustainable Development Education.* UN Decade, 2005-2014-Section for Education for Sustainable Development (ED/PEQ/ESD). Paris: UNESCO Publ.

Wals, A.E.J. (2009). A mid-DESD review: Key findings and ways forward. *Journal of Education for Sustainable Development,* 3(2), 195–204.

Wals, A., & Blaze Corcoran, P. (2006). Sustainability as an outcome of transformative learning. In J. Holmberg & B. E. Samuelsson (eds.), *Drivers and Barriers for Implementing Sustainable Development in Higher Education* (pp. 103-110). UNESCO Education for Sustainable Development in Action Technical Paper N°3.

Williams, G. (2004). Evaluating participatory development: tyranny, power and (re)politicization. *Third World Quarterly*, 25(3), 557–579.

World Commission on Environment and Development (1987). *Our common future*. Oxford: Oxford University Press.

Yang, S.-H. (2009). Using blogs to enhance critical reflection and community of practice. *Educational Technology & Society*, 12(2), 11–21.

Can ICT Reduce Drop-Out Rates Among New Teachers? A Qualitative Study in Canadian Student Teachers

Thierry Karsenti and Simon Collin

Introduction

A paradox has arisen in the literature on information and communication technologies (ICT) appropriation by teachers during their internship and professional induction. On the one hand, some studies show that, at the completion of their basic training, new teachers have a good grounding in technology skills (Clausen 2007; Karsenti et al. 2007), feel fairly confident about using ICT (Moore and Chae 2007; Slaouti and Barton 2007; Russell et al. 2003), and use ICT regularly in their personal life and professional practice, albeit mainly for lesson planning (Clausen 2007; Karsenti et al. 2007; Slaouti and Barton 2007). On the other hand, studies show that new teachers hold more negative beliefs about how ICT impact students than more experienced teachers do (Russell et al. 2003). They also show little ability to integrate ICT pedagogically and a low tendency to introduce them into the classroom (Karsenti et al. 2007). Here again, there is a significant difference from experienced teachers (Russell et al. 2003).

This finding is all the more surprising in light of the fact that new teachers have been trained according to a socioconstructivist vision of learning, as defined by the ministry of education in Quebec, Canada (Ministère de l'Éducation du Québec (MEQ) 2001a, b). According to some authors, teachers who adhere to this approach should be in favor of the pedagogical integration of ICT (Becker 2001; Ravitz et al. 2000). They would also be expected to turn to their peers to help them learn how to do this. However, this is apparently not happening.

In fact, the recent research has shown that, in addition to being somewhat reluctant to integrate ICT pedagogically, new teachers are also slow to use ICT for their professional development and to seek support when they need it (Moore and Chae 2007;

T. Karsenti (✉)
University of Montreal, Montreal, QC, Canada
e-mail: thierry.karsenti@umontreal.ca

S. Collin
University of Quebec in Montreal, Montreal, QC, Canada

A. Jimoyiannis (ed.), *Research on e-Learning and ICT in Education*,
DOI 10.1007/978-1-4614-1083-6_8, © Springer Science+Business Media, LLC 2012

Schuck 2003). On this subject, Schuck (2003) confirms that new teachers use the Internet in the same way they used it during their basic training, that is, mainly to look for information and resources, and considerably less to keep in touch with their peers through online communities.

This underuse of ICT to obtain support is particularly troubling during the professional induction phase, referred to by some as the "survival" period, when inexperienced teachers are especially in need of backing and encouragement. The problem can be seen in the excessively high numbers of teachers who quit the profession in the first 5 years, not only in Quebec [between 15 (MELS 2006, cited in Martineau et al. 2008) and 25% (Tardif 2001)], but also in North America [46% in the U.S. (Ingersoll 2002)], and around the world [40% in the first 3 years in the U.K. (Stoel and Thant 2002)]. Moreover, teaching has one of the highest drop-out rates of all professions (Ingersoll 2002).

For all these reasons, the Conseil supérieur de l'éducation (Quebec's superior council of education) (CSE 1997), the MEQ (1992), and the Ontario College of Teachers (2003) have addressed the issue of professional induction and recognized the urgent need for action. In the wake of their pronouncements, the Comité d'orientation de la formation du personnel enseignant (Quebec's advisory committee on teacher training) (COFPE 2002) drew up a set of recommendations for the professional induction of teachers and submitted them in a brief to the MEQ. The brief included a specific recommendation for "a process for induction into the teaching profession" (Recommendation 9). On this point, Chen (2008) affirms that it is important for researchers to help teachers "to cope with the difficulties and the complexities of classroom life" (p. 74). In this empirical study, we take a look at how ICT can support teachers in the professional induction phase.

Objective

We wanted to deepen our understanding of the potential benefits of ICT for practical teacher training and professional induction. More specifically, we aimed (1) to identify the difficulties that interning and new teachers encounter; and (2) to better understand how ICT can help them overcome these challenges. Results are presented from two pilot studies conducted in Canada during the internship of student teachers and the professional induction of new teachers.

Context

To set the context for our study, we begin by underscoring the important role of the internship in initial teacher training programs in Quebec and some of the inherent problems. We then discuss the issue of teacher drop-out during the professional induction. Finally, we discuss the potential of ICT to support student teachers and new teachers.

The Teaching Internship in Quebec: A Challenging Context

Practical training is an important aspect of university teacher training programs in Quebec, Canada. Student teachers spend 120 days of their 4-year university program interning in secondary schools to develop their professional skills. According to Nault and Nault (2001), internships give teachers-to-be an opportunity to test themselves in real schools. In Canada, teacher training programs focus on the development of professional skills that are grounded in professional practice. School internships are opportunities to apply professional competencies to real situations and assess performance. Therefore, it became essential that "the university community must have more opportunities to experience real-life teaching firsthand" (MEQ 2001, p. 27). This gives student teachers a chance to show that they possess the skills to become effective professionals.

During the internship, student teachers are supervised by two educators: (1) the university supervisor, who makes regular visits to observe student teachers in practice; and (2) the cooperating teacher, usually a classroom teacher, who temporarily mentors the student teacher. The university supervisor is therefore key to helping future teachers transfer their academic knowledge into practice. At the other end, the cooperating teacher plays a front-line role, coaching future teachers day-to-day and integrating them into the classroom and the teaching team. These two educators collaborate to assess the student teacher. The assessment is based on a set of 12 professional teaching competencies, each made up of various components (MEQ 2001). The eighth competency is "To integrate ICT in the preparation and delivery of teaching/learning activities and for instructional management and professional development purposes" (MEQ 2001). Thus stated, ICT skills are transferable skills that can be applied to several teaching areas.

Nault and Nault (2001) point out that university supervisors are often required to leave the university in order to observe interning students in the classroom, even when the schools are located far away. In Quebec, aside from the traveling that generates considerable time loss, supervisors have increasing numbers of interns and are required to visit each one more often. When students intern in areas so remote that a visit can take all day, assuming that the weather allows a same-day return, supervision can be a daunting task. In these circumstances, it is also difficult for university supervisors to maintain continuous collaboration with the cooperating teachers and their students between visits.

This situation is not only highly inconvenient for university supervisors, it is also frustrating for the students and cooperating teachers, who have complained about the decreased availability of professors and other university staff (Bourbeau 1997). Furthermore, many studies, e.g., by Barker (1986), Zeichner (1992), O'Neill (1996), and Venn, Moore and Gunter (2001), have shown that interns often feel isolated during their internship, when they have few, if any opportunities to share their experiences with their peers. Nault and Nault (2001) suggest that one way for students to escape this isolation would be to share their daily classroom experiences with others in the same situation.

Professional Induction of Teachers in Quebec and the Problem of Teacher Drop-Out

Drawing from Macdonald (1999), we define teacher drop-out as premature departure from the teaching profession, whether voluntary or not. In fact, the studies we consulted (see Karsenti et al. 2008) clearly show that teacher attrition (referred to as drop-out in the present study), far from being confined to retiring veterans, is connected to the issue of induction into the teaching profession. In this perspective, novice teachers (those having less than 7 years of experience), not experienced veterans, are the ones who are quitting most frequently. Teacher drop-out is not without consequences in terms of both education costs (Alliance for Excellent Education 2004; OECD 2005) and education quality (OECD 2005; Stoel and Thant 2002). This is particularly due to the need to hire more teachers, who are themselves in the process of building their skills, such that they have not yet developed optimal teaching practices. Moreover, teacher drop-out is also an international problem (see, e.g., Borman and Dowling 2008; Dolton and Van der Klaauw 1995; Ingersoll 2002; Stoel and Thant 2002), albeit to a varying degree. The question therefore arises as to why new teachers drop out, which leads in turn to the question of drop-out factors. The literature on teacher drop-out reveals a number of factors, as follows:

(a) Task-related factors: a demanding and time-consuming job, management of difficult classrooms, unsatisfactory work conditions, inappropriate teaching subjects, restrictive administrative policies, and unappealing tasks.
(b) Individual factors: emotional and psychological characteristics those are incompatible with the teaching profession, and sociodemographic and professional factors.
(c) Social environment factors: difficult relations with education and social actors and difficult students and workplace conditions.
(d) Socioeconomic conditions.

We also decided to add a fourth, more general category called *socioeconomic conditions*. Macdonald (1999) notes that socioeconomic conditions can be more or less conducive to attrition in young teachers. In other words, tough economic times might compel some young teachers to remain in the profession, despite any difficulties encountered. Alternatively, very positive economic conditions, in which other jobs are easy to find, might encourage teachers to quit.

Integrating ICT: How Do They Support Interning and New Teachers?

With the increasing disparity between technology's relatively modest presence in the classroom and its ever increasing popularity in society at large, it has become imperative for universities, and especially education faculties and departments, to bridge this technological gap. In the wake of the reform of teacher training programs in 2001 (MEQ 2001), and considering the importance placed on integrating ICT into these programs, the need to promote the potential benefits of ICT and their use by future teachers is self-evident. They should not be introduced as an appendage to academic training, but rather as an integral component of a global, cross-curricular approach throughout the entire teacher training process. In this perspective, the pedagogical integration of ICT into teacher training programs is promising for two reasons: (1) it gives future teachers a chance to develop their skills in integrating ICT into their teaching practice in real classroom situations; and (2) it could help them overcome some of the problems identified in this study. For example, online interactive environments would enable future teachers to escape the isolation of their internship, in addition to making it easier for university professors to monitor their progress (Karsenti et al. 2002). The potential of ICT support would apply equally to new teachers in the professional induction phase. Studies have shown that two of the most important factors in adequate mentoring are access to computer equipment and human support at all times. Almås and Krumsvik (2007) reported that the most effective way to foster skill development in teachers was to provide them with a laptop computer. Schuck (2003) even recommended giving a laptop computer with Internet access to all new teachers for the duration of the professional induction year, to provide them with continuous access at any time and in any place. Many studies have confirmed that continuous access to pedagogical and technical support is a crucial facilitating factor in overcoming obstacles (Allaire 2006), for both ICT integration (Granger et al. 2002) and professional induction (Nault 2005). In addition, some support mechanisms, including mentoring (Vallerand and Martineau 2006), online practice communities (Nault 2005), and a virtual teachers group (Shoffner 2009) appear to facilitate professional induction. Thus, as the entry into teaching is often marked by professional isolation, ICT can be used as networking tools to help new teachers buy into a collective vision of peer-supported professional development (Lieberman 2000).

Method

The aim of this study was (1) to identify the difficulties that interning and new teachers encounter; and (2) to better understand how ICT can help them overcome these challenges. This section presents the methodology used in two exploratory empirical studies: one addressing teacher internship and the other, the problem of new teacher drop-out.

Subjects and Data Collection

Study on teacher internship: A total of 800 preservice teachers (682 women, 118 men) enrolled in a 4-year teacher training program were selected to participate in the study. Subjects had a mean age of 22 years. They were enrolled in the second, third, and fourth year of a 4-year secondary school teacher-training program.

First-year students were not included in the study because they have little internship experience at that stage. A questionnaire was administered to all teacher interns in the second, third, and fourth years of a secondary school teacher training program, for a total of 1,140 potential participants. We received 800 completed questionnaires, which is 70% response rate. The questionnaire comprised two main sections: one addressing problems that teacher interns encountered in their internship, and the other addressing the role and importance of ICT in overcoming these problems. Most of the questions were open-ended (aside from those designed to gather socio-demographic information) so as not to direct the respondents' answers. This was consistent with our exploratory approach. We then performed a content analysis of the responses, as described below.

Study on new teacher drop-out: To better understand the factors at play in the problem of new teacher drop-out, we used an online questionnaire, which has the advantage of being administered via the Internet, thereby, transcending limitations of time and space. The questionnaire is based primarily on our literature review, from which we retained the most frequently cited drop-out factors. It was tested on 26 teachers and 11 school staff (school principals and pedagogical counselors), whose comments helped us improve the questions. Several themes were addressed, such as reasons for quitting, conditions for preventing drop-out, human support available to drop-out teachers experiencing problems, teaching as a career choice, professional aspirations to become a teacher, and the degree of satisfaction of drop-out teachers prior to leaving the profession. The questionnaire contained both open-ended and closed questions. We mobilized all the members of the Canadian Association of Immersion Teachers so that the questionnaire would be widely distributed. To complete the distribution procedure, we published ads in five newspapers in two languages (French and English) in the cities of Halifax, Toronto, Calgary, Vancouver, and Montreal. In this way we were able to reach participants across the country for a Canada-wide survey. The questionnaire was posted online for 3 weeks, and 34 drop-out teachers responded.

Data Analysis

Study on teacher internship: Data were analyzed using a grounded theory approach, more precisely, an ethnographic content analysis (Altheide and Johnson 1994). This type of content analysis includes many of the traditional content analysis procedures (e.g., Huberman and Miles 1994) in addition to a group feedback analysis and constant comparison methods, as used in grounded theory studies (Tesch 1990). Under this general qualitative analysis framework, the collected data were coded in order to generate concepts. "Coding represents the operations by which data are broken down, conceptualized, and put back together in new ways. It is the central process by which theories are built from data" (Strauss and Corbin 1990, p. 57). We performed the data coding in three phases: induction (reading all the data to allow concepts or codes to emerge), deduction (coding all data and labeling each segment), and verification (verifying all coded data). We used an initial analytical induction (e.g., Strauss and Corbin 1990) to derive categories of meaning from the data, called coding concepts. We then reiteratively verified the coding to further define and refine the concepts. In the end, nine concepts emerged to represent the problems that teacher interns encountered in their internship (see section "Results" below), as well and the potential for ICT to overcome these problems.

Study on new teacher drop-out: The data obtained from the questionnaires comprise both Likert scores and open-ended responses. Accordingly, the analysis of results is mixed. The quantitative analysis includes descriptive and inferential statistics, developed using SPSS 13. This enabled us to draw a sociodemographic portrait of the participants and uncovered some interesting facts concerning teacher drop-out. The initial results were further investigated by a qualitative analysis using QDAMiner. It consisted of a content analysis (see Huberman and Miles 1994; L'Écuyer 1990) with semi-open coding, initially constructed from the various factors influencing drop-out (see the section "Professional Induction of Teachers in Quebec and the Problem of Teacher Drop-Out"), as follows: task-related factors, individual factors, and social environment factors. The qualitative analysis aimed to highlight the relationships between the different moderators of drop-out identified in the quantitative analysis.

Results

In this section, we first present a summary of the challenges that teacher interns and new teacher drop-outs encountered during the internship or profession induction, as reported in the questionnaires. We then outline how ICT could help them overcome these challenges.

Main Challenges Encountered by Teacher Interns and New Teacher Drop-Outs

As shown in Table 1, the main obstacle that teacher interns faced in their internship was overall classroom management. Thus, almost 37% of respondents reported classroom management as a major difficulty. Assuming authority, being assertive, enforcing rules, and dealing with difficult students are some examples of classroom management challenges. Almost 25% of respondents mentioned planning and evaluation. The quality and quantity of material resources were also problematic. More than 10% of respondents stressed that teaching materials were often outdated, inaccessible, or imposed by the cooperating teacher. The school where the internship took place, including the school's pedagogical organization (e.g., number of students per class), and student or community characteristics (multi-ethnic clientele, at-risk students, underprivileged environment) posed further challenges. About 14% of the respondents mentioned at least one of these characteristics as a problem. It is noteworthy that a significant number of respondents (3%) reported that the greatest

Table 1 Main problems encountered by student teachers during the internship ($n=800$)

Problem	Percentage
Classroom management	36.4
General teaching abilities (planning, evaluation)	24.9
Guidance provided by and teaching philosophy of cooperating teacher or university supervisor	13.7
Teaching circumstances (e.g., number of students per class, social and cultural context, multi-level classrooms, parents, types of students, teaching subjects)	13.5
Teaching resources	11.1
Personal characteristics (e.g., self-confidence, anxiety, openness)	8.8
Internship organization (e.g., placement, distance, evaluation, length)	6.1
Integration into the workplace (e.g., communication with other teachers in the school)	3.4
Language (e.g., code mastery, communication)	2.6

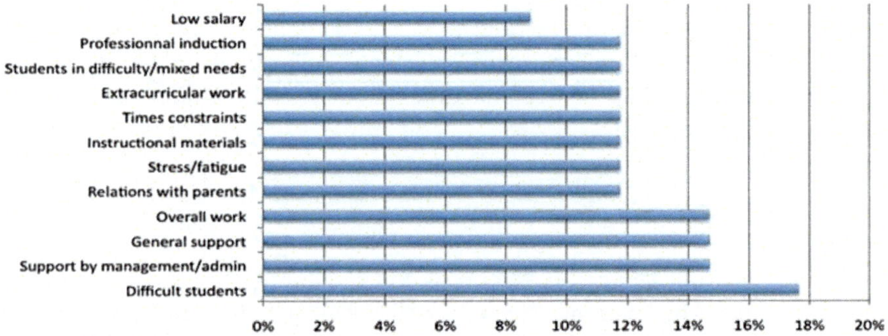

Fig. 1 Main reasons for leaving the profession according to the drop-out teachers ($n=34$)

challenge was their insufficient mastery of the teaching language, oral or written, in order to carry out their teaching activities.

Another problem stemmed from the internship experience itself. 13% of respondents mentioned that the cooperating teacher (and less often, the university supervisor) posed an obstacle by providing insufficient guidance in terms of feedback, support, availability, or interest; by granting the student teacher insufficient leeway; by presenting a counter-model, with a negative, bitter, or inappropriate attitude toward the students; or by creating conflicts between the cooperating teacher and the student teacher. Other aspects related to the internship arrangements created problems for approximately 7% of respondents, particularly the distance between their home and the school, as well as certain internship requirements (e.g., writing a report, attending seminars). Finally, more than 10% of respondents mentioned personal problems, such as lack of self-confidence, stress caused by the internship arrangements, or financial difficulties and the challenge of reconciling internship requirements with paid employment. Note that other problem categories were cited, but by fewer respondents, for instance, the challenge of fitting in with the school staff.

It is noteworthy that the difficulties encountered by new teacher drop-outs (see Fig. 1) are similar to those encountered by teacher interns, as we explore next.

Table 2 How information and communication technologies (ICT) helped teaching, as reported by student teachers ($n = 800$)

How ICT helped teaching	Percentage
Helped them create a variety of learning activities	60.0
Increased access to a variety of teaching resources	29.0
Helped them present new concepts, theories, ideas, etc.	22.0
Helped motivate learners	21.0
Helped them communicate with education and school stakeholders	15.0

Thus, the first set of drop-out factors includes difficult students, relationships with parents, and students in difficulty or with mixed needs, all of which are closely connected to the problems of classroom management and the teaching circumstances mentioned by teacher interns (see Table 1). All these factors are related to the social environment factors presented in the section "Professional Induction of Teachers in Quebec and the Problem of Teacher Drop-Out." The second set of drop-out factors concerns the overall lack of support, and more particularly support by the school administration, which may be related to the problems with the mentoring teacher or the university supervisor and integration into the workplace encountered by teacher interns (see Table 1). These factors are again related to the social environment factors. A third set of drop-out factors concerns problems related to professional induction, such as the workload and the lack of time that stresses new teachers, especially as they are in the process of building their professional skills. These factors may also be related to the inadequate teaching skills that hinder teacher interns (see Table 1). This set of factors relates to the task-related factors mentioned in the section "Professional Induction of Teachers in Quebec and the Problem of Teacher Drop-Out." Still other factors identified by new teachers, such as stress, fatigue, and the lack of instructional materials, are also factors that affect teacher interns (see Teaching resources and Personal characteristics, Table 1).

In view of the similarity observed between the problems encountered by teacher interns during the internship and the drop-out factors for new teachers, we may posit that the challenges of the internship remain much the same during professional induction.

How ICT Helped Teaching

As shown in Table 2, ICT appear to have helped student teachers cope with many of the teaching tasks and challenges encountered during the internship. The greatest advantage of using ICT appears to be the variety of activities that teachers can do in the classroom, as reported by 60% of all respondents. ICT appear to help them diversify both their teaching strategies and their students' tasks.

As reported by 29% of respondents, ICT helped them to be more professional and gave them increased access to a wide variety of up-to-date resources, so they could improve their teaching and learning activities. More than 20% of the respondents emphasized that ICT helped them present new concepts, theories, and ideas. Many noted that ICT helped them motivate their students, a considerable challenge, especially in secondary school. Moreover, 21% reported that their students were interested in ICT, and that ICT made learning more relevant and fun. Some respondents (15%) also reported that ICT were very useful ways to increase their communication with the various actors involved in their internship (e.g., cooperating teacher, university supervisor, colleagues, other teachers, parents). They appreciated having ICT to communicate, as it allowed them to share ideas, talk over problems, and get past difficult moments, which, according to most, were easier to deal with when they knew that others were facing them as well. Finally, it is noteworthy that less than 4% of respondents reported that ICT were useless in helping them overcome the teaching challenges they encountered in their internship. Our findings on the number and content of interactions reveal that student teachers tend to participate actively in online interactions, wherever they are located. The frequently mentioned collaboration and sharing of experiences promote solidarity and mutual assistance. Teacher interns develop bonds within a dynamic learning community, providing them with the encouragement and confidence to develop their professional skills.

Discussion and Conclusion

Based on the literature, our findings on the problems of teacher interns are similar to those for teachers in the transition to professional practice, and are particularly relevant to the issue of teacher drop-out. Classroom management heads the list of problems reported by our surveyed teacher interns. This result is consistent with the literature on new teachers, for whom classroom management is the greatest concern (Evertson and Weinstein 2006; Kagan 1992; Veenman 1984). Other general teaching abilities, such as planning and evaluation, are also considerable problems for teacher interns. This is understandable, given that they are in the process of building their professional skills at this point. The lack of guidance and the teaching philosophies of cooperating teachers and university supervisors constitute the third most often reported problem by our teacher interns. The literature review by Hobson et al. (2009) on mentoring beginning teachers concurs with this finding. These authors noted that successful mentoring depends on a number of conditions in the environment, and that these conditions vary considerably across educators. They identified three potential limitations of mentoring: lack of support by the educator; inversely, lack of autonomy granted to the teacher intern in developing professional skills; and an exaggerated focus on technical aspects of teaching, to the detriment of more fundamental pedagogical issues.

In our case, some of the results, such as lack of feedback, support, availability, or interest and insufficient leeway granted to the teacher intern, appear to fall under the first limitation identified by Hobson et al. (2009) (lack of support). On the other hand, we obtained some more extreme results that were not covered in the literature review by Hobson et al. (2009). For instance, one educator was characterized as a counter model: someone who is negative, bitter, or who displays an inappropriate attitude toward the students or who creates conflicts between cooperating teachers and student teachers. The challenge of teaching circumstances, which we identified as the fourth problem that teacher interns encountered, appears to echo several motives cited in the literature on teacher drop-out, for example, difficult relationships with parents (Certo and Fox 2002; Gonzales 1995; Macdonald 1999; OECD 2005) or with students (Chaplain 2008; Gonzales et al. 2008; Kirsch 2006; Ingersoll 2001; Macdonald 1999; OECD 2005). From the similarities between the problems encountered by teacher interns and new teachers, we may cautiously argue that the problems that future teachers face in their internships remain much the same as they enter professional practice. In this view, the teaching internship would be an integral part of the transition to professional practice, i.e., professional induction.

Concerning the potential of ICT to overcome problems encountered by teacher interns, it is noteworthy that the second potential benefit of ICT (increased access to a variety of teaching resources) appears to respond directly to the fourth most often mentioned problem by teacher interns (teaching resources), and to the seventh drop-out factor mentioned by new teacher drop-outs (instructional materials). ICT as a source of motivation for learning constitutes our fourth potential benefit. This finding is well supported by the literature on ICT in education (see the literature review by Balanskat et al. 2006). The same holds true for the last potential benefit of ICT (helped them communicate with education and school stakeholders), which is also frequently cited in the literature (Karsenti 2005; Lameul 2008), and which appears particularly relevant for rural schools (Fry and Bryant 2007).

An analysis of the data gathered so far suggests that ICT help student teachers cope with pedagogical and other challenges encountered during their internship and the professional induction in various ways. ICT allow student teachers to take advantage of a vast network in order to maximize their academic performance and to become more confident and comfortable in the sometimes difficult situations that can occur in schools. This also holds true for new teachers during professional induction. Although ICT may be challenging for internship supervisors, these challenges should be met head-on through innovative pedagogical practices and further research.

References

Allaire, S. (2006). *Les affordances socionumériques d'un environnement d'apprentissage hybride en soutien à des stagiaires en enseignement secondaire. De l'analyse réflexive à la coélaboration de connaissances.* Doctoral dissertation, Québec: Université Laval. Retrieved 15 April 2011 from http://www.theses.ulaval.ca/2006/23829/23829.pdf.

Alliance for excellent education. (2004). *Tapping the potential: Retaining and developing high-quality new teachers.* Retrieved 15 April 2011 from http://www.all4ed.org/publication_material/reports/tapping_potential.

Almås, A. G., & Krumsvik, R. (2007). Digitally literate teachers in leading edge schools in Norway. *Journal of In-Service Education, 33*(4), 479–497.

Altheide, D. L., & Johnson, J. M. (1994). Criteria for assessing interpretive validity in qualitative research. In N. K. Denzin & Y. S. Lincoln (eds.), *Handbook of Qualitative Research* (pp. 485–499). London: Sage.

Balanskat, A., Blamire, R., & Kefala, S. (2006). *The ICT impact report. A review of studies of ICT impact on schools in Europe*. Brussels: European Schoolnet.

Barker, B. (1986). *Efforts to improve the preparation of teachers for rural schools*. Paper presented at the Annual Conference of the Southwest Educational Research Association. ERIC (ED265993).

Becker, H.J. (2001). *How are teachers using computers in instruction?* Paper presented at the 2001 Meetings of the American Educational Research Association. Retrieved 15 April 2011 from http://www.msu.edu/course/cep/807/zOld807.1998Gentry/snapshot.afs/*cep240studyrefs/beckeraera2001howtchrsusing.pdf.

Borman, G. D., & Dowling, N. M. (2008). Teacher attrition and retention: A meta-analytic and narrative review of the research. *Review of Educational Research, 78*(3), 367–409.

Bourbeau, L. (1997). *La formation pratique à l'enseignement: l'organisation des stages en milieu scolaire: rapport d'enquête*. Québec: Fédération des enseignantes et enseignants de commissions scolaires.

Certo, J. L., & Fox, J. (2002). Retaining quality teachers. *High School Journal,* 86(1), 57–75.

Chaplain, R. P. (2008). Stress and psychological distress among trainee secondary teachers in England. *Educational Psychology,* 28(2), 195–209.

Chen, C.-H. (2008). Why do teachers not practice what they believe regarding technology integration? *The Journal of Educational Research*, 102(1), 65–75.

Clausen, J.M. (2007). Beginning teachers' technology use: first-year teacher development and the institutional context's affect on new teachers' instructional technology use with students. *Journal of Research on Technology in Education,* 39(3), 245–261.

Comité d'orientation de la formation du personnel enseignant (COFPE) (2002). *Offrir la profession en héritage. Avis du COFPE sur l'insertion professionnelle.* Québec: Gouvernement du Québec.

Conseil Supérieur de l'Éducation (1997). *L'insertion sociale et professionnelle, une responsabilité à partager. Rapport annuel 1996–1997 sur l'état et les besoins de l'éducation.* Sainte-Foy: Gouvernement du Québec.

Dolton, P., & Van der Klaauw, W. (1995). Leaving teaching in the UK: A duration analysis. *Economic Journal,* 105, 431–444.

Evertson, C. M., & Weinstein, C. S. (2006). Classroom management as a field of inquiry. In C. M. Evertson & C. S. Weinstein (eds.), *Handbook of classroom management: Research, practice, and contemporary issues* (pp. 3–16). Mahwah, NJ: Lawrence Erlbaum Associates.

Fry, S., & Bryant, C. (2007). Using distance technology to sustain teacher education for student teachers in isolated areas: The technology supported induction network. *Journal of Computing in Teacher Education,* 23(2), 63–69.

Gonzales, P. (1995). *Factors that influence teacher attrition.* Alexandria, VA: National Association of State Directors of Special Education. Retrieved 15 April 2011 from ERIC database (ED389127).

Gonzales, L., Brown, M. S., & Slate, J. R. (2008). Teachers who left the teaching profession: A qualitative understanding. *The Qualitative Report,* 13(1), 1–11.

Granger, C. A., Morbey, M. L., Lotherington, H., Owston, R. D., & Wideman, H. H. (2002). Factors contributing to teachers' successful implementation of IT. *Journal of Computer Assisted Learning,* 18(4), 480–488.

Hobson, A., Ashby, P., Malderez, A., & Tomlinson, P. (2009). Mentoring beginning teachers: What we know and what we don't. *Teaching and Teacher Education,* 25(1), 207–216.

Huberman, A. M., & Miles, M. (1994). Data management and analysis methods. In N. K. Denzin & Y. S. Lincoln (eds.), *Handbook of Qualitative Research* (pp. 428–444). London, England: Sage.

Ingersoll, R. (2001). Teacher turnover and teacher shortages: An organizational analysis. *American Educational Research Journal,* 38(3), 499–534.

Ingersoll, R. M. (2002). The teacher shortage: A case of wrong diagnosis and wrong prescription. *NASSP Bulletin,* 86, 16–30.

Kagan, D. M. (1992). Professional growth among preservice and beginning teachers. *Review of Educational Research,* 62(2), 129–169.

Karsenti, T. (2005). Développer le professionnalisme collectif des futurs enseignants par les TIC : bilan de deux expériences réalisées au Québec. *Recherche et Formation,* 45, 73–90.

Karsenti, T., Raby, C., Villeneuve, S., & Gauthier, C. (2007). *La formation des maîtres et la manifestation de la compétence professionnelle à intégrer les technologies de l'information et des communications (TIC) aux fins de préparation et de pilotage d'activités d'enseignement-apprentissage, de gestion de l'enseignement et de développement professionnel.* Rapport détaillé de recherche. Centre de recherche interuniversitaire sur la formation et la profession enseignante, Montreal: CRIFPE.

Karsenti, T., Collin, S., Villeneuve, S., Dumouchel, G., & Roy, N. (2008). *Pourquoi les nouveaux enseignants d'immersion ou de français langue seconde quittent-ils la profession? Résultats d'une enquête pancanadienne.* Ottawa: Association canadienne des professeurs d'immersion.

Karsenti, T., Lepage, M., & Gervais, C. (2002). Accompagnement des stagiaires à l'ère des TIC: forum électronique ou groupe de discussion? *Formation et profession,* 8(2), 7–12.

Kirsch, R. (2006). *L'abandon volontaire de la carrière chez des enseignants débutants du primaire et du secondaire au Québec.* Unpublished master's thesis, Université de Montréal, Montreal.

L'Écuyer, R. (1990). *Méthodologie de l'analyse développementale du contenu. Méthode GPS et concept de soi.* Québec: Presses de l'Université du Québec.

Lameul, G. (2008). Les effets de l'usage des technologies d'information et de communication en formation d'enseignants, sur la construction des postures professionnelles. *Savoirs,* 17, 73–94.

Lieberman, A. (2000). Networks as learning communities: Shaping the future of teacher development. *Journal of Teacher Education,* 51(3), 221–227.

Macdonald, D. (1999). Teacher attrition: A review of literature. *Teaching & Teacher Education,* 15(8), 835–848.

Martineau, S., Gervais, C., Portelance, L., & Mukamurera, J. (2008). L'insertion professionnelle des enseignants : une problématique complexe qui requiert un regard multiple. In L. Portelance, J. Mukamurera, S. Martineau et C. Gervais (eds.), *L'insertion dans le milieu scolaire. Une phase cruciale du développement professionnel de l'enseignant* (pp. 1–8). Québec: Les Presses de l'Université Laval.

Ministère de l'Éducation du Québec (1992). *Réforme du mode d'insertion professionnelle des nouveaux enseignants et des nouvelles enseignantes.* Québec: Gouvernement du Québec.

Ministère de l'Éducation du Québec (2001a). *Programme de formation de l'école québécoise. Version approuvée. Éducation préscolaire. Enseignement primaire.* Québec: Gouvernement du Québec.

Ministère de l'Éducation du Québec (2001b). *Teacher training: Orientations, Professional Competencies – New Directions for Success.* Québec: Gouvernement du Québec.

Moore, J. A., & Chae, B. (2007). Beginning teachers' use of online resources and communities. *Technology, Pedagogy and Education,* 16(2), 215–224.

Nault, G. (2005). *Étude du fonctionnement et du potentiel d'une communauté de pratique en ligne pour le développement professionnel d'enseignantes novices.* Unpublished doctoral thesis. Université du Québec à Montréal, Montreal.

Nault, T., & Nault, G. (2001). Quand les stages attrapent les TIC. In T. Karsenti & F. Larose (Eds.), *Les TIC... au cœur des pédagogies universitaires* (pp. 145–164). Québec: Presses de l'Université du Québec.

O'Neill, A. (1996). Increasing reflective instructional decision-making by clinically supervising teachers using telecommunications. In D. Ingham (ed.), *Proceedings of the annual National Educational Computing Conference* (pp. 299–302). Eugene, OR: International Society for Technology in Education. Retrieved 15 April 2011 from ERIC database. (ED398893).

OECD (2005). *Teachers matter: Attracting, developing and retaining effective.* Paris, France: OECD Publications.

Ontario College of Teachers (2003). *New teacher induction: growing into the profession.* Retrieved 15 April 2011 from http://www.oct.ca/publications/pdf/induction_white_paper_e.pdf.

Ravitz, J.L., Becker, H.J., & Wong, Y.T. (2000). *Constructivist-compatible beliefs and practices among U.S. teachers* (Report # 4). Teaching, Learning, and Computing: 1998 National Survey.

Russell, M., Bebell, D., O'Dwyer, L., & O'Connor, K. (2003). Examining teacher technology use implications for preservice and inservice teacher preparation. *Journal of Teacher Education*, 54(4), 297–310.

Schuck, S. (2003). Getting help from the outside: Developing a support network for beginning teachers. *Journal of Educational Enquiry,* 4(1), 49–67.

Shoffner, M. (2009). Creating a community of support for beginning English teachers. In C. D. Maddux (ed.), *Research Highlights in Teacher Education and Technology 2009* (pp. 311–318). Chesapeake, VA: SITE.

Slaouti, D., & Barton, A. (2007). Opportunities for practice and development: newly qualified teachers and the use of information and communications technologies in teaching foreign languages in English secondary school contexts. *Journal of In-service Education,* 33(4), 405–424.

Stoel, C. F., & Thant, T. S. (2002). *Teachers' professional lives – A view from nine industrialized countries.* Washington, DC: Milken Family Foundation.

Strauss, A., & Corbin, J. (1990). *Basics of qualitative research: Grounded theory procedures and techniques.* Newbury Park, CA: Sage.

Tardif, M. (2001). Quelques indicateurs de l'attrition des nouveaux enseignants de la formation professionnelle au Québec. In A. Beauchesne, S. Martineau et M. Tardif (eds.), *La recherche en éducation et le développement de la pratique professionnelle en enseignement* (pp. 131–141). Sherbrooke: Éditions du CRP.

Tesch, R. (1990). *Qualitative Research.* New York, NY: The Falmer Press.

Vallerand, A-C., & Martineau, S. (2006). *Plaidoyer pour le mentorat comme aide à l'insertion professionnelle des nouveaux enseignants.* Retrieved 15 April 2011 from Carrefour National de l'Insertion Professionnelle en Enseignement's website http://www.insertion.qc.ca/cnipe_2/spip.php?article89.

Veenman, S. (1984). Perceived problems of beginning teachers. *Review of Educational Research,* 54(1), 51–67.

Venn, M. L., Moore, R. L., & Gunter, P. L. (2001). Using audio/video conferencing to observe field-based practices of rural teachers. *Rural Educator,* 22(2), 24–27.

Zeichner, K. (1992). Rethinking the practicum in the professional development school partnership. *Journal of Teacher Education*, 43(4), 296–307.

Examining the Use of Text Corpora and Online Dictionaries as Learning Tools: Pre-Service Teachers' Perspectives

Nikleia Eteokleous-Grigoriou, Garifalos Anagnostou, and Simeon Tsolakidis

Introduction and Theoretical Background

Factors That Influence Technology Integration in Education: Teachers' Role

A result of the invasion of Information and Communications Technology (ICT) in society is that the education agendas of world organizations and curricula of a lot of countries include the embedding of new technologies in schools. More than a few studies (Earle 2002; Eteokleous 2008; Angeli and Valanides 2005) evaluated ICT integration in different educational settings, suggesting that elementary teachers use technology rather extensively for personal and classroom preparation purposes and less frequently for teaching and learning purposes. Additionally, when they do use them in their classroom practices, it tends to be in a rather sporadic fashion, more as "extras" or fancy chalkboards than as true learning tools. Few teachers were found to use computers as learning tools in any sort of constructivist or progressive way. The above happens due to a number of factors such as: lack of equipment, support and help from the officials, inadequate training, teachers' pedagogical beliefs, knowledge, skills, and attitudes toward technology integration within classroom practices (Carvin 1999; Earle 2002; Eteokleous 2008). In addition, researchers (Ertmer 2005; Carvin 1999) argue that teachers' instructional styles, pedagogical beliefs, and teaching philosophies influence the way technology (patterns of technology) is integrated and the degree of technology integration success within classroom practices. A well-known differentiation related to the above is: teacher-centered and traditional-pedagogical beliefs, and learner/student-centered and constructivist-oriented belief (Schuh 2004). Thus, teachers whose philosophies favor constructivist-oriented beliefs and student-centered approaches

N. Eteokleous-Grigoriou (✉) • G. Anagnostou • S. Tsolakidis
Department of Primary Education, Frederick University, Limassol, Cyprus
e-mail: pre.en@frederick.ac.cy

A. Jimoyiannis (ed.), *Research on e-Learning and ICT in Education*,
DOI 10.1007/978-1-4614-1083-6_9, © Springer Science+Business Media, LLC 2012

are more likely to integrate technology in their classrooms in a substantial and intellectually fruitful way (Ertmer 2005; Eteokleous 2008). Finally, it is suggested that successful technology integration into classrooms requires the continuous and adequate professional development and training of teachers (Carvin 1999). More important than simply learning how to use technology is the training in technology curriculum-integration. Consequently, teachers who had received both kinds of training are likely to feel more prepared and comfortable to integrate technology in their classroom practices (Carvin 1999; Earle 2002). Given the above, in-service teacher training and pre-service teacher training are equally important. This study, therefore, qualitatively examined pre-service teachers' experiences, while using three online language tools within an interdisciplinary environment.

Technological Acceptance

Teachers' contribution is very important for the implementation and success of any innovation, thus the investigation of their perceptions and attitudes toward technology integration is extremely valuable (Mitra 1998; Rozell and Gardner 2000). A similarly important element in the literature related to technology and education is the acceptance and actual use of technology by school teachers. Another group of studies examined factors that affect teachers' attitudes toward computers (e.g., Seyal et al. 2002) and teachers' actual use of computers (e.g., Mitra 1998; Rozell and Gardner 2000). Studies examined the influence of numerous variables on computer use such as age, prior computer training, computer literacy (e.g., Seyal et al. 2002), gender (e.g., Whitley 1997), computer experience (e.g., Rozell and Gardner 2000), and openness to experience. Equally important is the investigation of future teachers' perceptions and attitudes toward technology integration. Several studies (Ma et al. 2005; Hu et al. 2003) consider in their findings and adopt the Technological Acceptance Model (TAM; Davis 1989), suggesting that teachers' perception in regards to the usefulness of new technologies is direclty related to the intention of use and indirectly with the ease of use. This model has been widely used to investigate various ICT integration approaches (computer, internet, or any educational software), as well as various factors that might influence users' perceptions regarding the ease of use and usefulness (see Fig. 1).

Technology and Literacy Education

An accumulating body of research has produced useful conclusions concerning the use of computers in various aspects of literacy education (Coiro et al. 2008; Koutsogiannis 2001, 2002). Furthermore, a number of studies highlight the connection between the broad diffusion of ICT and the notion of literacy (Cope and Kalantzis 2009; Lemke 1998). It is usually pointed out that because of the great changes in the

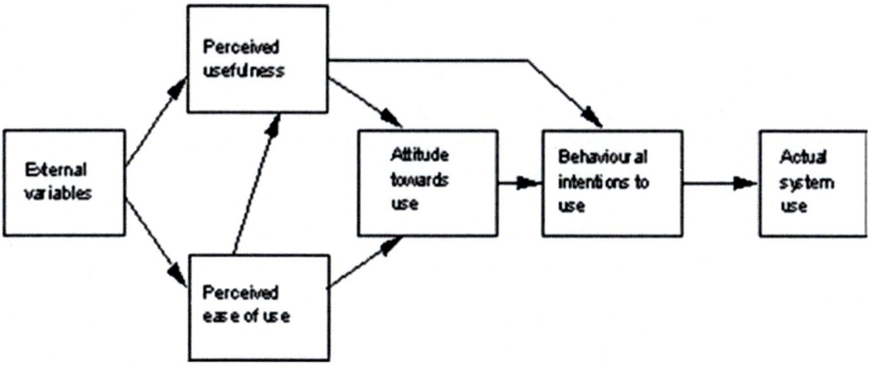

Fig. 1 The Technology Acceptance Model (TAM)

social and technological characteristics of communication, there is a need to extend the range of literacy pedagogy so that it does not unduly privilege alphabetical representations but bring into the teaching practice representations typical of the new, digital media. In a context like this, the familiarization with the use of tools like the online dictionaries (OD) and text corpora (TC), as well as the critical technological currency should become basic elements of a modern curriculum (Koutsogiannis 2007). According to Kazazis and Koutsogiannis (2002), the ultimate goal of the development of the Online Dictionary of Standard Modern Greek (2002) and the Modern Greek Text Corpora (2002) by the Centre for the Greek Language was not merely to serve current school practice but to help change it in accordance to modern trends in literacy education, or, in other words, to transform a closed teacher-centered approach into an open student-centered work environment conduced to the encouragement of discovery learning and the creation of a new generation of students, with skills such as analytical-critical thinking and combinatory-synthetic reasoning.

Concerning concrete pedagogical applications of TC, there is an accumulating body of research (Giagkou 2009; Tan 2002). According to Conrand (1999) at least until the 1980s publications addressed to teachers were focusing almost entirely on concordancing and lexical or lexico-grammatical studies and they were not introducing teachers to more comprehensive types of corpus-based studies. This changed in 1990s, where text corpora could be used in studying multiple characteristics (frequency, semantic category, grammatical structure, placement within the clause, the specific item used, and variation across registers) of English linking adverbials i.e., connecting expressions such as *therefore* and *in other words*. Applications like this made some researchers to speak about "corpus revolution" (Rundell and Stock 1992) or "pedagogical revolution" leading to a shift from the teacher seen as consumer to the teacher as participant in the corpus revolution: TC help teacher not only in deciding what he should teach but also to become a better coordinator or facilitator of the learning process and to stop pretending to be a source of absolute and limitless knowledge or an authority which should be unquestionably trusted (Gavioli and Aston 2001). In Greece or Cyprus this "revolution" is indisputably connected to the development of three major electronic corpora: the *Hellenic National Corpus* (http://hnc.ilsp.gr/) by the Institute of Language and Speech Processing, the *MGTC* by the Centre for the Greek Language, and the *Corpus of Greek Texts* (CGT; http://sek.edu.gr) by the University of Athens and the University of Cyprus (Giagkou 2009). The pedagogical applications of these TC are related mainly with vocabulary teaching (Goutsos 2003; Goutsos and Koutsoulelou-Michou 2009), syntax, and morphology (Giagkou 2009) or, generally, every level of linguistic analysis (Chalisiani 2010).

Technology and Physical Education

In what concerns Physical Education (PE), recent studies: (1) have argued that, because its form includes instructional teaching, demonstration and movement activities' implementation, it seems to constitute a unique field where technology can be used as an instructive tool for teaching cognitive issues and motor skills both in relation to physical activity and sports, and (2) have shown that PE could benefit from the integration of ICT into the educational process, since New Technologies can be a useful tool, affecting and enhancing both the way of teaching and the learning result (Apostolakis et al. 2006; Antoniou et al. 2009).

Main Aim

The study aims to explore and evaluate the educational use of the text corpora and online dictionaries within the educational practice by pre-service teachers. Specifically, the research objectives of the study are the following: (1) to investigate and explain pre-service teachers' experiences, attitudes, and perceptions in relation to the use of the above mentioned electronic language resources for preparation, teaching, and learning purposes; (2) to examine the exploitation of these electronic language resources within the lessons of Literacy and Physical Education, employing an interdisciplinary approach; and (3) to identity the factors that influence teachers integrating technology in the educational practice.

Methodology

A case study design was applied, aiming to collect qualitative data through semi-structured interviews (Kvale 1996; Creswell 2003) as the primary source of data in order to gain thorough understanding of pre-service teachers' experiences. A questionnaire was also used in order to collect basic demographic data (i.e., gender, age, computer use, and ownership). The study focuses on examining and conducting an in-depth analysis of a single process, which, in this case, is the use of the ODSMG, the MGTC, and the CGT as alternative tools for teaching basic notions of PE within a Literacy lesson. The sample of our study was 16 pre-service elementary teachers who were attending the modules of Educational Technology and of Specialization in PE in Frederick University Cyprus during the spring semester of 2010. During the module of Educational Technology, the students developed knowledge and skills related to technology integration within the teaching and learning process. Specifically, they were taught how to use the TC and OD, as well as study and discuss numerous exercises and applications of the TC and OD. During the module of Specialization in PE, the students got acquainted with basic concepts of PE and techniques regarding the teaching of PE in Primary Education. After four to five lectures in every module, a lecture was scheduled, where pre-service teachers (as if they were students in a Literacy lesson) used the TC and OD as learning tools to perform in-classroom activities. Specifically, the pre-service teachers were asked to: (1) search in the OD for entries related to concepts such as "physical activity," "athletics," "health," and "physical fitness"; (2) examine if these entries (or at least certain parts of them) could be used during the teaching or the explaining of the above mentioned concepts. In case that for some concepts there were not proper entries, the students were asked to compose an entry using the material of the Specialization in PE module and the TC, in order to find texts, phrases or sentences where the concept under examination appeared. Pre-service teachers had the chance to practice numerous uses of TC and OD for preparation and teaching purposes (see Figs. 2–4).

The data collection process took place in March 2010. Four semi-structured group interviews were conducted, where all pre-service teachers participated. On average, the duration of each group-interview was 1 h. Open-ended questions were included in the interview protocol in an attempt to provide the opportunity to pre-service teachers to freely express themselves (Kvale 1996). The interviews included questions such as: What are your impressions of the online language tools integration within the teaching and learning process? Did you face any difficulties in learning how to use the tools? Did you face any difficulties while using them as learning tools? Would you use them in developing learning environments enhanced with technology? Why yes? Why not? Would you use them for any other purposes? Follow-up questions occurred naturally to clarify answers and build on the responses. The group interviews were recorded and converted to text. After transcribing the digital audio files, the researchers analyzed pre-service teachers' responses using the method of continuous comparison of data (Maykut and Morehouse 1994). The researchers read and reread the transcriptions of the group interviews, assigning codes and classifying data into categories in order to identify emergent themes. As the analysis progressed, researchers needed to revise the coding system and the categories in order to reflect the emerged themes related to pre-service teachers' experiences. As aforementioned, 16 pre-service teachers participated in the interviews. Ten of them (63%) were girls and the rest six were (37%) boys. All of them were juniors (in their third year of study), and their age

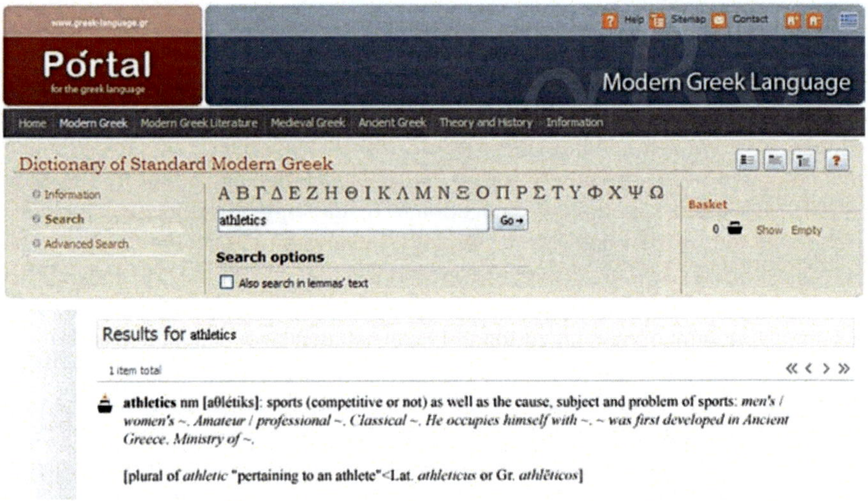

Fig. 2 The lemma "athletics" in ODSMG

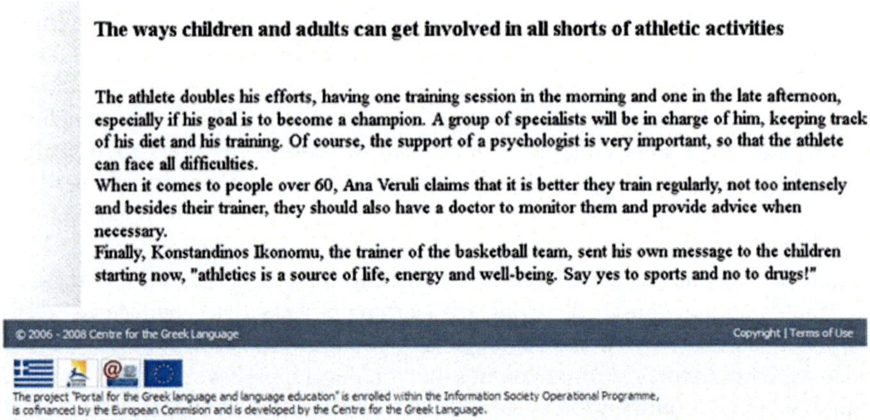

Fig. 3 Data from MGTC concerning "athletics"

ranged from 21 to 25 years old. They were using technology from the age of 15 to 16. All of them owned a personal laptop for the past 3–5 years, using it daily for various purposes. Regarding computer training, they all attended computer lessons at high school and then through the university program of study, they attended the following two courses: Introduction to Information Communication Technology and Educational Technology.

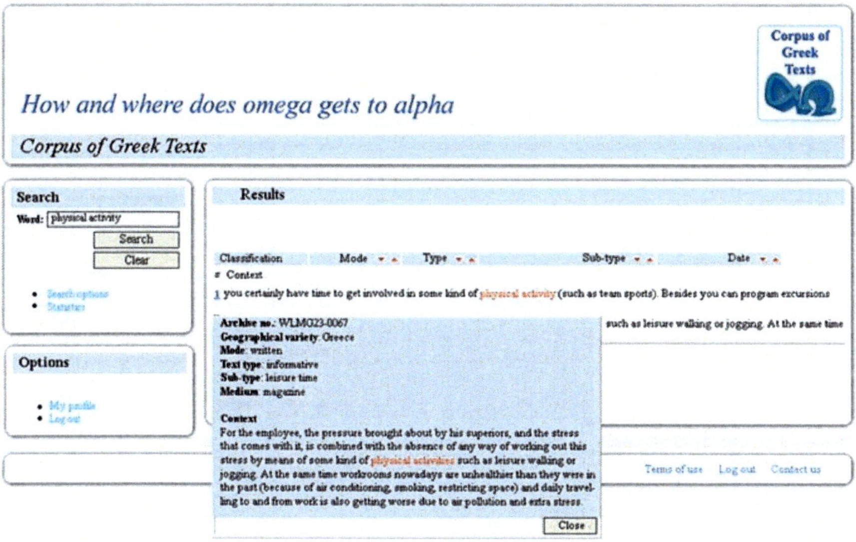

Fig. 4 Data from *Corpus of Greek Texts* (CGT) concerning "physical activity"

Results-Discussion

Pre-Service Teachers' Attitudes Toward Technology Use

Pre-service teachers' responses can be grouped in parameters, where three of them seemed to influence their attitudes toward technology use and consequently their future actual computer use. Those parameters are: (1) pre-service teachers' views about the usefulness of the tools, (2) the difficulties concerning the educational use of the tools, (3) pre-service teachers' teaching philosophies and pedagogical beliefs, and (4) Educational use of the tools. Three of the above parameters are directly related to the TAM model (see Fig. 1). Also, the results of the study revealed two pre-service teachers' profiles. Five of the students participating in our study could be characterized as *technology-supporters* or *techno-positives* and the rest could belong to the category of *social-skeptics* or *techno-skeptics* (see Eteokleous and Pavlou 2010; Raptis and Raptis 2004). The study attempts to relate the aforementioned parameters and pre-service teachers' profiles (see Table 1).

Usefulness of the Tools

Overall, pre-service teachers realize the usefulness and value of both tools; however, several differences revealed between the two groups (see Table 1). Specifically, pre-service teachers, under the social-skeptics group found difficulties in realizing

Table 1 Relating the TAM model with teachers' profiles

Teachers' profiles/parameters *(TAM model)*	Technology-supporters or techno-positives	Social-skeptics or techno-skeptics
Pre-service teachers' views about the usefulness of the tools *(TAM model: Perceived usefulness)*	Realize the usefulness and value of both tools	
	Having less difficulty in realizing TC's usefulness and value within the teaching and learning process	Difficult to realize the added value and possible applications of both tools within the teaching and learning process
	More positive toward the TC as learning tool within the teaching and learning	OD is more user friendly and less time consuming than the TC
The difficulties concerning the educational use of the tools *(TAM model: Perceived ease of use)*	Did not encounter any serious difficulties in learning and using the tools	
	Understood relatively easily the use of OD and TC within the educational practice	
	Minimum trouble in performing the exercises using OD and TC as learning tools	
	Increased time needed in using these tools within the teaching and learning process/time-savers for preparation purposes/"tyranny" of the curriculum	
	Found difficulties in giving examples of using the OD and the TC in other subjects besides Linguistics and Literacy	
	Not easy for them to realize how PE could be related to Linguistics and Literacy	
Pre-service teachers' teaching philosophies and pedagogical beliefs *(Internal Variables – Addition to the TAM model)*	More open-minded	Thinking more traditionally and conservatively
	Focusing more constructivist practices and student-centered approaches	Focused more on traditional pedagogical beliefs and teacher-centered approaches
	Willing to deviate from the traditional way of teaching and the dictates of the curriculum	Preferred to use what they had already learnt – were afraid of not following the "already-known" method of teaching
	Realized the effectiveness of using OD and TC in promoting the involvement of students in learning activities which engage in critical thinking and promote higher order skills	Expressed concerns in integrating the TC and OD as educational tools – did not like to increase students' initiatives, flexibility and freedom and decrease teacher's control
Future use of the tools *(TAM model: Actual technology use)*	More for lesson preparation and less within the teaching and learning process	
	Would use both tools within the educational practice	Supported limited use of the tools and especially the TC within the educational practice
	More positive to use the TC within the teaching and learning process	Would only use the OD during teaching practice

the added value and possible applications of these two tools within the teaching and learning process. In addition, the social-skeptics stated that they would only use the OD during teaching practice, because it was more user-friendly and less time consuming than the TC. One of them mentioned that students using the TC, could not easily distinguish what they are looking for, in contrast to the OD, where they could be helped by the definitions provided in the lemmas. Generally, they argued that it would take the students too long to find and select from the TC, the data that could be relevant, with concepts discussed during the lesson. This point of view resembles traditional pedagogical beliefs and teacher-centered approaches (Schuh 2004). On the contrary, in technology-supporters' point of view, this "waste of time" was an advantage, because they believe that a teacher should give students the chance to search, investigate, select, decide, and choose. Going through the above process, students develop higher-order skills and specifically critical thinking skills (Kazazis and Koutsogiannis 2002).

Generally, their views about the TC as a tool within the teaching and learning practice were more positive, having less difficulty in realizing its usefulness and value. The technology-supporters also emphasized not only on what is taught but also on how it is taught (Gavioli and Aston 2001) focusing more on constructivist practices and student-centered approaches (Schuh 2004).

Difficulties Encountered

Pre-service teachers' responses in both groups were in great alignment regarding this parameter (see Table 1). Overall, they did not encounter any serious difficulties in using the OD and the TC, and they understood relatively easy the application of these tools within the educational practice. Although the vast majority of the pre-service teachers did not know and had never used a TC and many of them had never used an OD of such size and complexity, they easily realized their use and functions, and with not much trouble, they managed to find the answers to the exercises that were given to them during the lesson. Additionally, they reported that both tools would be user-friendly for the students, on the presupposition that they would be acquainted enough with ICT.

As mentioned above, both groups of teachers agreed that the increased time needed in using these tools within the teaching and learning process was another factor to negatively influence their in-classroom integration, however, supporting that these tools would be time-savers for preparation purposes. In addition, time was related to the "tyranny of the National Curriculum," that is, a high volume of educational material to be covered and a demand by education officials that it would be covered on a regularized nationwide basis, something which (in contrast to various government announcements about the need for integration of ICT into the teaching practice) is not aligned with progressive instructional practice and does not really support technology integration (Eteokleous 2008).

Finally, another difficulty revealed was that, although pre-service teachers were familiar with the interdisciplinary approach concept, they found difficulties in giving examples of using the OD and the TC in other subjects besides Linguistics and Literacy or in realizing how PE could be easily related to other subjects. The above could be explained because of pre-service teachers being used to view PE as an exclusively oral process which had nothing to do with the other subjects of an educational system where the emphasis is practically put on the written expression. We could say that the strength of PE's boundary, its classification in relation to the other subjects of Primary Education, leads students to keep a traditional view about "teaching" PE in Primary Education (Bernstein and Solomon 1999).

Pedagogical Beliefs and Teaching Philosophies

Pre-service teachers' pedagogical beliefs, and teaching philosophies were revealed through the data analysis, seemed to be quite different within the two groups of pre-service teachers (see Table 1). More specifically, pre-service teachers' already developed teaching-philosophies, or maybe what we – as teaching staff – had taught them in other modules, as well as the knowledge and the skills they achieved throughout their previous education (using a way of teaching which was similar to the traditional way of teaching in a school), were clearly showed through their approaches toward using the TC and the OD within their future profession as educators (for preparation purposes and as teaching and learning tools). The technology-supporters appeared to be more open-minded, preferring more constructivist practices and student-centered approaches (Schuh 2004), while on the other hand the social-skeptics were thinking more traditionally and conservatively, focusing more on traditional pedagogical beliefs and teacher-centered approaches (Schuh 2004). The social-skeptics preferred to use what they had already learnt and they were afraid of not following the "already-known" method of teaching, and not covering the curriculum. They expressed concerns in integrating the TC and OD as educational tools, since they would be implementing an approach which would increase students' initiatives, flexibility and freedom as well as provide them with the opportunity to search, discuss, choose, and at the same time decrease teacher's control. Consequently, they supported the limited use of the OD and especially TC as learning tools.

On the contrary, the technology-supporters even stated that they were willing to deviate from the traditional way of teaching or from the dictates of the curriculum. This is connected with the fact that they perceived more easily the added value of these tools for the students, since they believed that through the use of this kind of applications students acquire and develop skills and abilities which are important for our era and its challenges. The modern Greek school curricula and the educational legislations always place the development of critical thinking among the priorities of formal education. In practice, however, teaching is based most of the time on the mnemonic abilities of the students. Apparently the technology-supporters emphasized on this matter and realized the effectiveness of using OD and TC in promoting the involvement of students in learning activities which engage in critical thinking (Koutsogiannis 2007).

Use of Technology

In accordance to the existing literature, both pre-service teachers' profiles stated that they would use the tools more for lesson preparation and less during the teaching and learning process (Earle 2002; Eteokleous 2008; Angeli and Valanides 2005). To support the above, they mentioned that through these applications a teacher not only could find a lot of language material which could be easily integrated into the already prepared teaching material, but also he/she could develop new ideas about how to teach, altering at the same time teachers' role to that of a knowledge facilitator (Gavioli and Aston 2001). The views expressed by the pre-service teachers in regards to the use of the technology-based tools are in alignment with the current literature and can be explained based on their pedagogical beliefs and teaching philosophies (Ertmer 2005; Becker and Reil 2000; Carvin 1999) where those that favor constructivist-oriented beliefs and student-centered approaches are more likely to integrate computers in their classrooms in a substantial and intellectually fruitful way (Ertmer 2005; Eteokleous 2008). In addition, the TAM model helps also in explaining and predicting pre-service teachers' use of technology in their practices.

The Suggested Model

Based on the aforementioned results, the study suggests a model (adjusting the TAM model) to be statistically tested (see Fig. 5) in order to measure the factors that influence pre-service teachers to use technology within their educational practice. The study suggests a number of parameters to be added to the original TAM model. Firstly, it recommends the addition of the internal variables such as teachers' pedagogical beliefs and teaching philosophies. Additionally, the model should be examined in relation to the social-cultural environment, the university program of study and the interdisciplinary approach. The above influence the rest of the model parameters (i.e., internal and external variables) and are vital to be included in the analysis in order to reflect society's social-cultural configuration and constant changes. The programs of study at the university should be re-designed in order to educate pre-service teachers on designing modern learning environments enhanced with technology, while employing the interdisciplinary approach. We are in the process of designing the appropriate questionnaire integrating elements from various studies (i.e., Roussos 2003; Pavlou and Vryonides 2009).

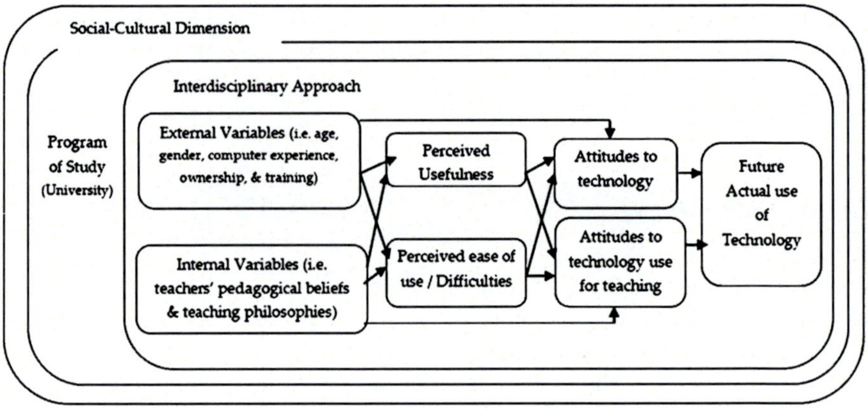

Fig. 5 Factors that influence pre-service teachers' future technology use

Conclusions

On the whole, a positive attitude from future elementary teachers was revealed toward the use of these tools, however, some of them appeared to be somehow hesitant in integrating technology in the teaching and learning process, confirming one more time their preference to using technology as a preparation tool instead as a learning tool. In addition to this, the study's results showed that pre-service teachers' personal teaching philosophies directly influence their beliefs/opinions toward the use, usefulness, and value of the using technology as educational tools. Consequently, it is extremely important for pre-service teachers (future educators) to experience the integration of these internet-based tools, and overall technology, in their teaching practice during their studies at the university. The above would create a strong foundation in developing the appropriate circumstances in integrating technology as a learning tool in their professional teaching career. To achieve the above, pre-service teachers need to further develop their technology literacy level, be trained on how to integrate technology within the curriculum, and realize its value and importance when enclosed in the teaching practice (Carvin 1999; Earle 2002).

Given the above, the study highlights the Schools of Education's decisive role in appropriately preparing pre-service teachers in integrating technology in their teaching practices (Carvin 1999; Earle 2002; Eteokleous and Pavlou 2010). Changes in the philosophy of the School of Education toward technology integration within their programs of study would help to achieve the above. Besides the Introduction to Technology and the Educational Technology courses, the following could also be suggested: offer "Teaching with technology" specialization courses, employ an interdisciplinary approach throughout the School of Education courses concerning technology integration as a learning tool by the lecturers, give the opportunity to the pre-service teachers to experience technology integration in their teaching and learning practice in the elementary schools. It is vital that pre-service teachers make this new learning, communication, work, and collaboration culture their own reality on a personal and professional level prior to transferring it to their students. In this ever-changing, rapid-changing, high-tech, interconnected world we believe that the role of Schools of Education is vital and extremely important to be able to appropriately prepare pre-service teachers to face the challenges of their profession. The pre-service teachers should be provided with these opportunities and experiences since they are one of the most influential factors to technology integration.

Finally, the study not only suggests the need to develop an effective pre-service teachers' training program, but also proposes a model and highlights the need of a quantitative study, where the model will be statistically tested. It constitutes the foundation for further research to be conducted regarding the examination of the factors that influence future technology used by pre-service teachers. Additionally, there is a need to relate the suggested model and the factors that influence teachers to teachers' profiles regarding technology use and consequently reveal elements that might characterize each of the profiles based on the model parameters.

References

Angeli, C., & Valanides, N. (2005). A socio-technical analysis of the factors affecting the integration of ICT in primary and secondary education. In L. T. W. Hin & R. Subramaniam (eds.), *Literacy in technology at the K-12 Level: issues and challenges* (pp. 1590–1610). Heshey, PA: Education Media International.

Antoniou, P., Apostolakis, N., Anastasiaddes, P., & Karipidis, A. (2009). Teaching physical education issues in the compulsory education using digital learning environments. In A. Méndez-Vilas, A. Solano Martin, J. A. Mesa González, J. Mesa González (eds.), *Research, reflections and innovations in integrating ICT in education* (pp. 819–824). Badajoz: FORMATEX.

Apostolakis, N., Antoniou, P., & Karipidis, A. (2006). Evaluation of digital educational material for distance education in basketball. In A. Méndez-Vilas, A. Solano Martin, J. A. Mesa González, J. Mesa González (eds.). *Current Developments in Technology-Assisted Education* (pp. 442–446). Badajoz: FORMATEX.

Becker, H. J., & Reil, M. (2000, April). *The beliefs, Practices, and Computer Use of Teachers Leaders*. Paper Presented at the American Research Association, New Orleans, L.A.

Bernstein, B., & Solomon, J. (1999). Pedagogy, identity and the construction of a theory of symbolic control: Basil Bernstein questioned by Joseph Solomon. *British Journal of Sociology of Education*, 20(2), 265–279.

Carvin, A. (1999). Technology professional development for teachers: Overcoming a pedagogical digital divide. *The Digital Beat,* 16(1). Retrieved 31 January 2011 from http://www.benton.org/DigitalBeat/db093099.html.

Chalisiani, I. (2010). Scenarios for the exploitation of Modern Greek electronic text corpora in L1 teaching. In K. Dinas, A. Chatzipanagiotidi, A. Vakali, T. Kotopoulos & A. Stamou (eds.), *Proceedings of the Panhellenic Conference 'Teaching Greek language'*. Florina: University of Western Macedonia. Retrieved 23 November 2010 from http://linguistics.nured.uowm.gr/Nimfeo2009/praktika/files/down/poster/xalisiani.pdf (in Greek).

Coiro, J., Knobel, M., Lankshear, C., & Leu, D. J. (eds.) (2008). *Handbook of Research on New Literacies*. New York: Lawrence Erlbaum Associates.

Conrand, S. (1999). The importance of corpus-based research for language teaching. *System*, 27(1), 1–18.

Cope, B., & Kalantzis, M. (2009). Multiliteracies: new literacies, new learning. *Pedagogies*, 4, 164–195.

Creswell, J. W (2003). *Research design: qualitative, quantitative and mixed methods approaches*. Thousand Oaks, CA: Sage (2nd edition).

Davis, F. D. (1989). Perceived usefulness, perceived ease of use, and user acceptance of information technology. *MIS Quarterly,* 13(3), 319–339.

Earle, R. S. (2002). The integration of instructional technology: promises and challenges. *Educational Technology*, 42(1), 5–13.

Ertmer, P. A. (2005). Teacher pedagogical beliefs: The final frontier in our quest for technology integration?. *Educational Technology Research and Development,* 53(4), 25–39.

Eteokleous, N. (2008). Evaluating computer technology integration in a centralized educational system. *Computers & Education,* 51(2), 669–686.

Eteokleous, N., & Pavlou, V. (2010). Digital natives and technology literate students: Do teachers follow?. In N. Valanides & C. Angeli-Valanides (eds.), *Proceedings of the Cyprus Association for the Integration of Computer Technology in Education* (pp. 113–124). Nicosia: Culture and Nature Books.

Gavioli, A., & Aston, G. (2001). Enriching reality: language corpora in language pedagogy. *ELT Journal*, 55(3), 238–246.

Giagkou, M. (2009). *Corpora and language education: exploitation potentials in teaching Greek and construction of pedagogical relevant corpora*. PhD thesis, National and Kapodistrian University of Athens, Greece (in Greek).

Goutsos, D. (2003). The use of electronic corpora in the teaching of Modern Greek vocabulary. *Proceedings of the 1st International Conference for Teaching Greek as a Foreign Language* (pp. 259–267). Athens: University of Athens (in Greek).

Goutsos, D., & Koutsoulelou-Michou, S. (2009). The teaching of academic vocabulary in Greek with the use of corpora. *Proceedings of the 3rd International Conference for Teaching Greek as a Foreign Language* (pp. 213–223). Athens: University of Athens (in Greek).

Hu Jen-Hwa, P., Clark,T., & Ma, W. W. (2003). Examining technology acceptance by school teachers: a longitudinal study, *Information & Management,* 41, 227–241.

Kazazis, J., & Koutsogiannis, D. (2002). Tradition and innovation in designing a dictionaries and text corpora electronic environment for literacy education. Offprint from B. Cope & M. Kalantzis (eds.), *Learning for the future. Proceedings of the Learning Conference 2001*. Australia: Common Ground Publishing.

Koutsogiannis, D. (ed.) (2001). *Information–communication technology and literacy: the international experience*. Thessaloniki: Centre for the Greek Language.

Koutsogiannis, D. (2002). Computers and literacy teaching in its cultural context. In B. Cope & M. Kalantzis (eds.), *Learning for the future. Proceedings of the Learning Conference 2001* (pp. 3–19). Australia: Common Ground Publishing.

Koutsogiannis, D. (2007). *Utilization of the electronic dictionaries and text corpora for educational purposes: theoretical framework and teaching applications*. Retrieved 16 November 2010 from http://www.greek-language.gr/greekLang/modern_greek/education/cbt/utilization/theory.html.

Kvale, S. (1996). *Interviews: an introduction to qualitative research interviewing*. Thousand Oaks, CA: Sage.

Lemke, J. L. (1998). Metamedia literacy: transforming meanings and media. In D. Reinking, M. McKenna, L. Laddo & R. Kieffer (eds.), *Handbook of Literacy and Technology* (pp. 269–281). Hillsdale, NJ: Erlbaum.

Ma, W. W., Andersson, R., & Streithw, K. (2005). Examining user acceptance of computer technology: an empirical study of student teachers, *Journal of Computer Assisted Learning,* 21, 387–395.

Maykut, P., & Morehouse, R. (1994). *Beginning Qualitative Research: A Philosophic and Practical Guide*. London, Philadelphia: The Falmer Press.

MGTC (2002). *Modern Greek Text Corpora*. Centre for the Greek Language, Retrieved 20 March 2011 from http://www.greek-language.gr/greekLang/modern_greek/tools/corpora/index.html.

Mitra, A. (1998). Categories of computer use and their relationships with attitudes toward computers. *Journal of Research on Computing in Education, 30*, 281–296.

ODSMG (2002). *Online Dictionary of Standard Modern Greek*. Centre for the Greek Language, Retrieved 20 March 2011 from http://www.greeklanguage.gr/greekLang/modern_greek/education/cbt/utilization/examples.html.

Pavlou, V., & Vryonides, M. (2009). Understanding factors that influence teachers' acceptance of technology and actual computer use for teaching: The case of Greece. *Mediterranean Journal of Educational Studies,* 14(2), 5–25.

Raptis, A., & Raptis, A. (2004). *Teaching and Learning in the Information Era: Educational Activities*. Athens (in Greek).

Roussos, P. (2003). The Project for the Longitudinal Assessment of New Information Technologies in Education: The Case of Greece. In K. Fernstrom (ed.), *Proceedings of 4th International Conference on Information Communication Technologies in Education* (pp. 393–399). Samos, Greece.

Rozell, E. J., & Gardner, W. L. (2000). Cognitive, motivation, and affective processes associated with computer-related performance: a path analysis. *Computers in Human Behavior,* 16, 199–222.

Rundell, M., & Stock, P. (1992). The corpus revolution. *English Today* 30, 9–14; 31, 21–32; 32, 45–51.

Schuh, K. L. (2004). Learner-centered principles in teacher-centered practices?. *Teaching and Teacher Education,* 20(8), 833–846.

Seyal, A. H., Rahman, M. N. A., & Rahim, M. M. (2002). Determinants of academic use of the Internet: a structural equation model. *Behaviour & Information Technology,* 21(1), 71–86.

Tan, M. (ed.) (2002). *Corpus studies in language education*. Bangkok: IELE Press.

Whitley, B. E., Jr. (1997). Gender differences in computer-related attitudes and behavior: A meta-analysis. *Computers in Human Behavior,* 13(1), 1–22.

The Cypriot Public Primary School Principals' Self-Perceived Competence and Use of ICT for Personal, Teaching, and Administrative Purposes

Kyriacos Charalambous and Photos Papaioannou

Introduction

Information and Communication Technologies (ICT) integration in public primary schools is a major priority of the Ministry of Education and Culture (MOEC) of Cyprus. Following the guidelines of the European Union (EU), which promoted the strategic framework "i2010-A European Information Society for growth and employment," many millions of euros have been spent and many more are about to be invested in order to equip schools with the necessary infrastructure, hardware and software; organize in-service training (INSET) for teachers; develop a Learning Management System (LEM) and a School Management System (SMS); create a broad network among schools; and enrich the curriculum with specific goals and activities on ICT (Doratis 2007).

However, results from various studies indicate that ICT integration in primary schools of Cyprus can not be considered as successful yet. A survey from Empirica (2006) revealed that only 7.9% of the primary school teachers use computers in class in more that 50% of their lessons, whereas more than 35% of the primary school teachers use computers in class in less than 10% of their lessons. Moreover, another study that was conducted among primary school teachers in 2004 revealed that 53% of the teachers hold negative attitudes toward computer technology integration in their classroom practices (Eteokleous 2008).

The success or failure of this innovation is very much dependent on the efforts and competence of the school principals. According to Anderson and Dexter (2005) "school's technology efforts are seriously threatened unless key administrators become active technology leaders in a school" (p. 74). Like every innovation, school leaders

K. Charalambous (✉)
School of Education, Frederick University, Nicosia, Cyprus
e-mail: pre.ck@frederick.ac.cy

P. Papaioannou
Ministry of Education and Culture of Cyprus, Nicosia, Cyprus

A. Jimoyiannis (ed.), *Research on e-Learning and ICT in Education*,
DOI 10.1007/978-1-4614-1083-6_10,

are expected to lead the efforts acting as "change agents" (Murphy and Shipman 1999, p. 213) transforming their schools into learning organizations (Reezigt and Creemers 2005) by promoting internal training and an ongoing professional development and by "providing opportunities for meaningful student involvement, developing staff collaboration, securing outside resources to support the school and the forging of links between home and the school" (Reynolds and Teddlie 2000, p. 144).

This study aims to reveal the Cyprus public primary school principals' self-perceived competence and use of ICT for personal, learning, and administrative–managerial purposes and how this competence might influence their workload. In addition, it examines which independent variables (gender; years of service; years of experience as a principal; academic qualifications; access to computer and the Internet at home; INSET on ICT for personal, teaching and learning, and administrative purposes; existence of a computer at the principal's office and the staff room as well as the existence of a computer lab at school; years learning about or working with computers) affect the primary school principals' attitudes toward ICT. The current study is the only one carried out in Cyprus regarding principals' self-perceived ICT competence. Therefore, its results might throw some light to identify whether primary school principals are ready to lead this innovation or whether policy makers should focus their efforts on amplifying principals' capacity to lead effectively ICT integration in schools.

The Educational Context of the Study

The Role of Primary School Principals in the Educational System of Cyprus

The centralized structure of the Cyprus Educational System (CES) deteriorates the role of principals in primary schools. According to official regulations of MOEC about the functioning of public primary schools, the main responsibilities of school principals are to: run their school effectively; promote the implementation of the national curriculum; undertake instructional duties; keep school records, school register, and attendance records; etc. On the other hand, they do not have a say in which school they would like to be appointed. Moreover, they do not have the authority to recruit their teaching personnel and of course, they have no appositeness about the salary of their staff. Additionally, principals – like teachers – are not allowed to stay in a school for more than 6 continuous years. It should also be mentioned that the principals' involvement in curriculum development is very limited (Theofilides et al. 2006). Kithreotis and Pashiardis (2006) concluded that the inflexibility of the centralized educational system of Cyprus is one of the biggest barriers in the efforts of the principals to create effective leadership and to shape a strong positive culture in a school.

The History of ICT Implementation in Primary Schools of Cyprus

MOEC following a centralized approach introduced ICT in primary schools in the early 1990s. Although the innovation was top–down "the strategy for ICT integration involved a combination of centralized initiative and largely decentralized implementation policy" (Karagiorgi and Charalambous 2004, p. 22). According to MOEC, ICT should not be used as a discrete subject but "as a dynamic tool in the teaching and learning process aiming at a more effective implementation of the school curriculum and developing of skills such as problem solving, decision making, communication and information handling" (MOEC 2007, p. 274). Today, almost 20 years after the initial efforts for ICT integration, all classrooms have at least one computer, a scanner, and a printer. It should also be mentioned that INSET programs for using ICT have been developed by the Pedagogical Institute.

Literature Review

The dominance of ICT in schools has inevitably altered the way principals execute their teaching and administrative duties. Using a computer is no longer a benefit for the few gifted ones but a necessity for almost all of those who wish to be effective leaders of their school. Nowadays, the vast majority of principals in developed countries have access to a computer at school. But having access to a computer is not of such importance as using the computer productively for teaching and administrative purposes. Many scholars emphasize that principals must not only use computers extendedly, but additionally they must act as role models (Anderson and Dexter 2005; Gurr 2000) providing to their teachers "visible support and encouragement for the use of the technology" (Murphy and Gunter 1997, p. 138). Stegall (1998) suggested several actions for school leaders who wish to model technology use in their school including: participating in professional training, reading books and journals about computers, going to technology conferences, joining technology organizations, using the Internet, visiting innovative schools, forming a technology committee, finding "experts" to help them, writing a technology plan, etc. BECTA (2003) concludes that school leaders "personally using the technology in their everyday working lives, raise the profile of ICT in their schools" (p. 3).

A main question that emerges is what impact does the use of ICT by the principals have on their work? Does technology really reduce the principals' heavy workload or does it make things worse? Gurr (2000), who interviewed principals from Australia, found that the use of ICT had not necessarily resulted in a decrease in the workload of principals and concluded that "it is not so much that technology has decreased workload, but that technology has facilitated new work, and has improved older work patterns" (p. 16). The above finding is consistent with findings of other researchers who also found out that principals do not necessarily have a decrease in their workload as a result of their use of technology (Bishop 2002) but, on the contrary, the integration of ICT results in an increase of their workload (Schiller 2003). Of course, there are researchers who do not agree with the above findings claiming that technology can reduce the workload of the principal (BECTA 2004; Felton 2006).

The level of ICT use by principals is very much dependent on their self-perceived competence in using ICT. Self-perceived competence in using ICT or computer self-efficacy refers to the belief that individuals hold about their own ability to operate successfully with technology. Bandura (1991) defines self-efficacy as the peoples' "beliefs about their capabilities to exercise control over their own level of functioning and over events that affect their lives" (p. 257). The school leaders' computer self-efficacy is very important for the ICT integration efforts because the stronger the perceived efficacy the higher the goal challenges people set for themselves and the firmer their commitment to them (Bandura 2002).

Increasing their own competence in using ICT is of vital importance for the school leaders who wish to successfully integrate ICT in their school. Actually, principals have a dual role to play concerning the INSET in their school. First, they must ensure that they receive the appropriate training on ICT (BECTA 2007; Dawson and Rakes 2003; Flanagan and Jacobsen 2003) in order to increase their skills and knowledge and effectively inspire and lead the staff in integrating technology across the curriculum (Flanagan and Jacobsen 2003). Dawson and Rakes (2003), through their study on principals' training, came to the conclusion that "the type and amount of technology training principals receive, can make a positive difference in schools" (p. 46) toward ICT integration. Second, principals must promote the professional development of their staff in order to help them integrate ICT successfully in the teaching and learning process (Balanskat et al. 2006; Flanagan and Jacobsen 2003; Mueller et al. 2008).

Research Methodology

The population was comprised of 336 principals who were serving in public primary schools of Cyprus at the school year of 2007–2008. The sample was chosen randomly and was consisted of 250 school principals all over Cyprus. Data were collected through questionnaires, which were mailed to the principals. One hundred and thirty-one questionnaires were received completed (return rate 52.4%).

In order to assess the principals' competence and use of ICT, a special survey instrument was developed. The first part consisted of nine close-ended questions which were relevant to the principals' demographics information (Table 1). The second part contained four questions which investigated the principals' self-perceived competence in using ICT and the frequency of ICT use for personal, teaching, and administrative purposes. Descriptive statistics (means, standard deviations, minimums, maximums, frequencies, percentages) and inferential statistics (t-test, one way ANOVA, and Chi-Square tests) were used to analyze all the variables and assess the principals' self-perceived competence, principals' self-perceived competence in

Table 1 Frequency distribution of principals' and schools' demographics

Variable	*N*(131)	%
Gender		
Males	46	35.1
Females	85	64.9
Years of service		
18–25	19	14.6
26–30	5	3.8
31–35	62	47.7
36+	44	33.8
Highest academic qualification		
Pedagogical Academy	93	71.0
Bachelor	14	10.7
Master's	19	14.5
PhD	5	3.8
Access to a computer at home		
Yes	111	84.7
No	20	15.3
Access to the Internet at home		
Yes	104	79.4
No	27	20.6
In-service training (INSET) for using information and communication technologies (ICT) for personal purposes		
Yes	103	78.6
No	28	21.4
INSET for using ICT in teaching and learning		
Yes	83	63.4
No	48	36.6
INSET for using ICT for administration and management		
Yes	23	17.6
No	108	82.4
Computer experience (years learning about or working with computers)		
1–5	31	27.0
6–10	46	42.7
11–15	19	16.5
16–20	16	13.9
21 and more	1	0.9

undertaking several tasks on computers, principals' frequency of computer use at school and at home, and computer applications that are used for teaching, administrative, and personal purposes by principals. The reliability coefficients were assessed using Cronbach's alpha on the four questions of the second part of the survey instrument. Results indicate that the coefficients were very high for all four questions, i.e., 0.954, 0.912, 0.887, and 0.911 respectively.

Research Findings

Demographics

In Table 1 the demographics of the principals that participated in the research are presented. Of those principals who took part in the quantitative research – 64.9% were females; about eight out of ten of them had access to a computer and the Internet at home; and seven out of ten of them were holders of the Pedagogical Academy diploma only (plus 1 year of completion). Regarding INSET on ICT, the majority of them received training for using ICT for personal purposes (78.6%) and for using ICT in the teaching and learning process (63.4%). On the contrary, a high percentage of them (82.4%) had never attended INSET on ICT for administrative and managerial purposes. Finally, the principals cannot be considered as very computer experienced since only three out of ten of them have been learning or working with computers for more than 10 years. As far as it concerns the schools' background information – 65.6% had a computer in the principal's office; 84.7% had a computer in the staff room; and 60.3% had a computer lab.

Principals' Self-Perceived Competence in Using ICT

The results of the study indicate that, generally, principals did not feel very competent in using ICT. In particular, principals felt fairly competent in using ICT for personal purposes and for lesson planning and preparation (Table 2). This is not surprising since 78.6% have attended INSET on ICT for personal purposes. They felt less competent in performing their administrative duties and this has its explanation since only 17.6% had attended INSET for administrative and managerial purposes. Finally, they perceived to be even less competent in using ICT for teaching purposes, although 63.4% have attended INSET for using ICT in teaching and learning. This can be justified since, on average, principals teach only 11 h a week in classes and usually they teach lessons that are less demanding (Religion, Geography). These lessons have very few software programs available, and it depends mostly on the efforts of each educator to find or prepare the appropriate software. Principals, with their heavy administrative workload and their habitual way of teaching, find it very difficult, time-consuming, and perhaps ineffectual to alter their classroom practice just few years before their retirement.

Table 2 Principals self-perceived competence in using ICT

I feel competent in using ICT for	*N*	Mean	SD
Personal purposes	114	3.26	1.15
Lesson planning and preparation	114	2.98	1.35
Administrative purposes	114	2.77	1.29
Classroom practice	114	2.65	1.24

Scale: 1 = not competent at all; 2 = little competent; 3 = fairly competent; 4 = much competent; 5 = very much competent

Table 3 Principals' self-perceived competence in undertaking several tasks on computers

Tasks	*N*	Mean	SD
Use of basic word processing (Microsoft Word)	114	3.46	1.33
Use a search engine in the Internet	114	3.39	1.40
Write and send an e-mail message	114	2.78	1.54
Create and use a software presentation (PowerPoint)	114	2.67	1.37
Use an educational software	114	2.53	1.28
Use a video projector	114	2.52	1.34
Use a scanner	114	2.50	1.43
Use a digital camera	114	2.25	1.39
Create and use a spreadsheet (Microsoft Excel)	114	2.20	1.20
Create and use a database (Microsoft Access)	114	1.78	1.02

Scale: 1 = not competent at all; 2 = little competent; 3 = fairly competent; 4 = much competent; 5 = very much competent

Table 4 Use of computer at school and at home by principals

Statements	*N*	Mean	SD
I use the computer at school	114	4.03	1.18
I use the computer at home	114	3.95	1.16

Scale: 1 = never used; 2 = few times a year; 3 = few times a month; 4 = few times a week; 5 = everyday

Primary school principals felt more than fairly competent in using word processor and the Internet (Table 3). They also felt competent in writing and sending an e-mail and in creating and using a software presentation (e.g., PowerPoint). Using a digital camera, spreadsheets, and databases are the tasks which principals do not feel competent to deal with. Similar results were found in many researches in other countries (Bishop 2002; Felton 2006; Gurr 2000). The low competence of principals in creating and using spreadsheets and databases is a matter that should make policy makers aware, because these are applications that could facilitate principals' work and decrease their heavy administrative workload.

Principals' Use of ICT at School and at Home

Principals indicated that they use the computer at school and at home few times a week (Table 4). This designates that computer has become part of the principal's life but, still, not a vital one. Researches around the world indicate that the majority of the principals use computers on a daily basis to execute their duties. An explanation of this difference with other countries could be the fact that only 65.6% of the principals had a computer in their office by the time that this survey was carried out. In addition, the absence of administrative software and the lack of training might be another rationale for this result, since principals are still enforced to perform many of their administrative duties in the traditional way. Only those with sufficient knowledge on computers have developed their own programs and use the computers, almost on a daily basis, to fulfill their administrative and managerial duties.

Table 5 Computer applications that are used for teaching, administrative, and personal purposes by principals

	Teaching			Administrative			Personal		
Purpose	*N*	$\overline{X}$	SD	*N*	$\overline{X}$	SD	*N*	$\overline{X}$	SD
Word processing	109	2.75	1.40	108	3.47	1.51	113	3.32	1.40
Internet (use of web search engines, etc.)	108	2.30	1.43	108	2.70	1.58	113	2.82	1.65
Educational software	109	2.02	1.05	107	1.64	0.93	113	1.88	1.00
Video projector	109	2.01	1.07	107	1.67	0.90			
Presentation software (e.g., PowerPoint)	109	1.94	1.01	107	1.80	1.00	113	1.92	1.04
E-mail	108	1.77	1.17	108	2.63	1.52	113	2.73	1.55
Scanner	109	1.70	0.97	108	1.76	1.00	113	1.85	1.05
Digital camera	109	1.66	0.97	107	1.64	1.01	113	1.85	1.15
Spreadsheets (e.g., Microsoft Excel)	108	1.58	0.87	108	1.90	1.09	113	1.85	1.95
Databases (e.g., Microsoft Access)	108	1.35	0.69	108	1.50	0.82	113	1.46	0.78

Scale: 1 = never used; 2 = few times a year; 3 = few times a month; 4 = few times a week; 5 = everyday

Frequency of ICT Use for Teaching, Administrative, and Personal Purposes

Generally, principals appeared to use the computer more frequently for personal purposes, than for administrative purposes and lastly for teaching purposes. Word processor and Internet were the computer programs/applications that were most frequently used by principals for personal, administrative, and teaching purposes (Table 5). On the contrary, scanner, digital camera, spreadsheets, and databases were never used or were used just few times a year for personal, administrative, and teaching purposes. Special reference should be made to the use of spreadsheets and databases for administrative purposes. It is very clear that the principals were not aware of the potentials that these programs can offer concerning the execution of their administrative and managerial duties.

The Impact of the Independent Variables

In this part there will be a brief discussion about the impact of the independent variables (gender, academic qualifications, years of service, years of experience as a principal, access to a computer and the Internet at home, INSET on ICT, access to a computer at the school office, existence of a computer in the staff room, existence of a computer lab at school, and years learning about or working with computers). According to the results, male principals, compared to their female colleagues, were more likely to be more experienced (male: $\overline{X} = 11.22$ years, SD = 5.35; female: $\overline{X} = 8.66$ years, SD = 4.69; ($t(1) = 2.66$, $p < 0.01$)); use computers more frequently at school and at home; have higher self-perceived competence in using ICT (Table 6); and use more

Table 6 Statistically significant differences between self-perceived competence of the principals in using ICT for several purposes and independent variables

	Use a computer for personal purposes			Use a computer for administrative purposes			Use a computer for classroom practice			Use a computer for lesson planning and preparation		
Variables	*N*	$\overline{X}$	SD	*N*	$\overline{X}$	SD	*N*	$\overline{X}$	SD	*N*	$\overline{X}$	SD
Gender												
Male	40	3.73**	1.09	40	3.30**	1.31	40	3.28**	1.13	40	3.43*	1.17
Female	74	3.01	1.10	74	2.49	1.20	74	2.31	1.17	74	2.74	1.39
Years of service												
18–25	19	4.11**	1.10	19	3.79**	1.08	19	3.74**	1.15	19	4.11**	1.05
26–30	5	4.20	0.84	5	3.80	0.45	5	3.40	0.89	5	3.60	1.14
31–35	53	3.08	1.02	53	2.55	1.23	53	2.53	1.07	53	2.75	1.14
36+	36	2.92	1.11	36	2.42	1.25	36	2.14	1.22	36	2.58	1.46
Academic qualifications												
Basic studies	90	3.06	1.10	90	2.51	1.23	90	2.42	1.16	90	2.77	1.29
Postgraduate studies	10	4.04**	1.00	24	3.75**	1.03	24	3.50**	1.18	24	3.79**	1.29
Access to computer at home												
Yes	105	3.37**	1.11	105	2.90**	1.26	105	2.76**	1.22	105	3.13**	1.29
No	9	2.00	0.71	9	1.33	1.33	9	1.33	0.44	9	1.22	0.44
Access to the internet at home												
Yes	99	3.44**	1.07	99	2.95**	1.26	99	2.82**	1.21	99	3.18**	1.28
No	15	2.07	0.88	15	1.60	0.50	15	1.53	0.83	15	1.67	1.05
INSET on using ICT in teaching and learning												
Yes	81	3.47**	1.11	81	2.98**	1.28	81	2.90**	1.19	81	3.22**	1.31
No	33	2.76	1.09	33	2.27	1.21	33	2.03	1.16	33	2.39	1.27

(continued)

Table 6 (continued)

Variables	Use a computer for personal purposes			Use a computer for administrative purposes			Use a computer for classroom practice			Use a computer for lesson planning and preparation		
	N	$\overline{X}$	SD	*N*	$\overline{X}$	SD	*N*	$\overline{X}$	SD	*N*	$\overline{X}$	SD
Existence of a computer in the principal's office												
Yes	83	3.51**	1.08	83	3.04**	1.26	83	2.89**	1.22	83	3.24**	1.28
No	31	2.61	1.09	31	2.06	1.09	31	2.00	1.07	31	2.29	1.30
Years learning about or working with computers												
1–5	27	2.59	1.05	27	2.15	1.20	27	1.93	1.04	27	2.11	1.19
6–10	46	3.22	0.96	46	2.63	1.12	46	2.48	1.03	46	2.96	1.26
11–15	18	3.83	1.15	18	3.67	1.19	18	3.39	1.24	18	3.78	1.22
16–20	17	4.24**	0.75	17	3.65**	1.06	17	3.76**	1.03	17	4.00**	0.79

Scale: 1 = not competent at all; 2 = little competent; 3 = fairly competent; 4 = much competent; 5 = very much competent
*$p<0.01$, **$p<0.001$

Table 7 Frequency of use of several computer resources/applications for teaching, administrative, and personal purposes and independent variables

	Teaching purposes			Administrative purposes			Personal purposes		
Variables	*N*	$\overline{X}$	SD	*N*	$\overline{X}$	SD	*N*	$\overline{X}$	SD
Gender									
Male	39	2.05	0.88**	40	2.49	0.78**	40	2.61	0.90***
Female	70	1.57	0.65	68	1.83	0.76	73	1.95	0.86
Years of service									
18–25	19	2.04	0.86**	19	2.75	0.62***	19	2.98	0.76***
26–30	4	2.60	1.27	4	2.75	0.84	5	2.84	1.00
31–35	51	1.72	0.71	49	1.97	0.81	53	2.06	0.89
36+	34	1.49	0.65	35	1.79	0.73	35	1.86	0.81
Academic qualifications									
Basic studies	86	1.62	0.68**	85	1.89	0.73***	89	1.99	0.84***
Postgraduate studies	23	2.18	0.94	23	2.77	0.80	24	2.92	0.90
Access to computer at home									
Yes	100	1.80	0.78**	99	2.16	0.81***	104	2.27	0.91***
No	9	1.07	0.13	9	1.21	0.20	9	1.20	0.37
Access to the internet at home									
Yes	94	1.82	0.79**	93	2.20	0.81***	99	2.32	0.91***
No	15	1.24	0.35	15	1.33	0.39	14	1.24	0.34
INSET on ICT for teaching and learning purposes									
Yes	79	1.87	0.82**	78	2.19	0.84	81	2.33	0.96**
No	30	1.41	0.50	30	1.78	0.72	32	1.83	0.74
Existence of a computer in the principal's office									
Yes	79	1.82	0.79	78	2.20	0.82**	83	2.31	0.93*
No	30	1.52	0.68	30	1.75	0.74	30	1.85	0.87
Years learning about or working with computers									
1–5	26	1.37	0.56***	26	1.67	0.78***	27	1.64	0.74***
6–10	44	1.67	0.76	43	1.93	0.69	45	2.07	0.82
11–15	17	2.35	0.76	7	2.62	0.70	18	2.85	0.78
16–20	17	2.11	0.69	17	2.69	0.76	17	2.90	0.87

Scale: 1 = never used; 2 = few times a year; 3 = few times a month; 4 = few times a week; 5 = everyday
$^{*}p<0.05$, $^{**}p<0.01$, $^{***}p<0.001$

frequently several ICT resources and applications for teaching, administrative, and personal purposes (Table 7). Principals with fewer years of service were more likely to perceive themselves as more competent (Table 6); use ICT more frequently at school and at home; and use several computer resources and applications for teaching, administrative, and personal purposes more frequently (Table 7).

Principals with postgraduate studies were more likely to be more computer experienced; have higher self-perceived competence in using ICT for personal purposes, administrative purposes, and classroom practice (Table 6); and use the computer and its several resources and applications more frequently (Table 7). Principals with access to a computer and the Internet at home were more likely to have higher computer self-efficacy (Table 6); they use the computer and its resources and applications more frequently (Table 7). Finally, principals who have received INSET on ICT for teaching and learning purposes were more likely to have greater self-perceived competence to undertake several computer tasks for various purposes (personal purposes, administrative purposes, classroom practice, and lesson planning and preparation) (Table 6); use computer more frequently at school; and use several resources and applications of computers more frequently for teaching, administrative, and personal purposes (Table 7).

Principals who have a computer in their school office were more likely to have higher self-perceived competence to undertake several computer tasks (for personal purposes, administrative purposes, classroom practice, and lesson planning and preparation) (Table 6); use the computer more frequently at school and at home; and use several resources and applications more frequently for administrative and personal purposes (Table 7). Principals who have greater computer experience were more likely to have higher self-perceived competence to undertake several computer tasks for personal purposes, administrative purposes, classroom practice, and lesson planning and preparation (Table 6); use the computer more frequently at school and at home; and use several resources and applications more frequently for teaching, administrative, and personal purposes (Table 7).

Discussion and Implications

The findings of this research indicate that, generally, the principals more likely do not feel very competent to use ICT. They appear to feel fairly competent to use ICT for personal and lesson planning and preparation purposes, whereas they appear to feel less competent to use ICT for administrative and teaching and learning purposes. Using a word processor, searching the Internet, and writing and sending e-mails are the computer tasks that they feel more competent to undertake. On the contrary, they seem that they do not feel competent at all in creating and using spreadsheets and databases.

Additionally, the research found that principals use ICT at school and at home few times a week first for personal purposes, then for administrative purposes, and finally for teaching purposes. Based on these findings, it can be inferred that Cyprus primary school principals more likely do not feel competent enough to undertake several tasks on computer and as a result they do not use ICT to the extent that it should be used, especially for administrative purposes. This can be attributed to the low access to a computer at the principal's school office, the insufficient official INSET on ICT for administrative purposes, the absence of any specially designed software programs for administrative purposes, and the resistance to change that some principals show.

Moreover, according to the study, principals use ICT for teaching and learning purposes rarely, although the vast majority of them have attended relevant INSET sessions. Even young principals with postgraduate studies do not use ICT for teaching and learning purposes regularly. The heavy workload, the kind of subjects they teach, the inadequate content of the INSET they received, and the resistance to change are the possible explanations for this reality. Nevertheless, this finding is very worrying, because several researches concluded that modeling computer use and being the instructional leader of the school are two strategies that principals should apply in order to enhance ICT integration in their schools (Anderson and Dexter 2005; Gurr 2000). These two strategies do not seem to be used by the majority of the Cyprus principals. Therefore, the promotion of ICT integration in the teaching and learning process could be achieved only if primary school principals model the routine, intentional, and effective use of technology.

The study indicates that the INSET that is provided to the principals should be enhanced. First of all, special organized sessions about the use of ICT for administrative and managerial purposes should be organized by MOEC. Moreover, it has been found that principals have very low self-perceived competence in creating and using spreadsheets and databases which are programs that could be widely used to fulfill several of their administrative duties. Thus, INSET should focus also on these programs.

A notable finding of the research is that, although INSET for teaching and learning purposes can make the difference, principals, who attended this kind of sessions, to a great extent, indicated that they do not use ICT for teaching and learning purposes in practice. Among other reasons, this could be attributed to the framework of the sessions which were mostly concentrated on providing technical skills to the participants. Thus, INSET sessions should mainly concentrate on practical ways that principals could integrate ICT in their lesson daily and not on the acquisition of more technical skills. Enough money has been spent until now and the desired change through the ICT integration in our schools has not come yet. Maybe, the time has come for investing more in the professional development of the principals in order to strengthen their leadership capability to lead this innovation. After all, "If school principals are to effectively inspire and lead a staff in integrating technology across the curriculum, then professional development opportunities must be available for principals to develop these skills and dispositions" (Flanagan and Jacobsen 2003, p. 140).

References

Anderson, R. E., & Dexter, S. L. (2005). School technology leadership: an empirical investigation of prevalence and effect. *Educational Administration Quarterly*, 41(1), 49–82.

Balanskat, A., Blamire, R., & Kefala, S. (2006). *The ICT impact report: A review of studies of ICT impact on schools in Europe*. Retrieved 5 July 2008 from http://ec.europa.eu/education/pdf/doc254_en.pdf.

Bandura, A. (1991). Social cognitive theory of self-regulation. *Organizational Behavior and Human Decision Processes,* 50(2), 248–287.

Bandura, A. (2002). Growing primacy of human agency in adaptation and change in the electronic era. *European Psychologist,* 7(1), 2–16.

BECTA (2003). *What the research says about strategic leadership and management of ICT in schools*. Retrieved 30 November 2009 from http://partners.becta.org.uk/uploaddir/downloads/page_documents/research/wtrs_stratleaders.pdf.

BECTA (2004). *What research says about ICT and reducing teachers' workload.* Retrieved 30 November 2009 from http://partners.becta.org.uk/uploaddir/downloads/page_documents/research/wtrs_workloads.pdf.

BECTA (2007). *The impact of ICT in schools – A landscape review.* Retrieved 18 December 2009 from http://www.pedagogy.ir/images/pdf/impact_ict_schools.pdf.

Bishop, P. F. (2002). *Information and Communication Technology and school leaders.* Paper presented at the Seventh World Conference on Computers in Education. Copenhagen, Denmark: Australian Computer Society. Retrieved 30 November 2009 from http://crpit.com/confpapers/CRPITV8Bishop.pdf.

Dawson, C., & Rakes, G. C. (2003). The influence of principals' technology training on the integration of technology into schools. *Journal of Research on Technology in Education,* 36(1), 29–49.

Doratis, L. (2007). *ICT projects of the Ministry of Education and Culture of Cyprus.* Retrieved 15 November 2009 from http://www.moec.gov.cy/presentations/ppt/Presentation_for_ICT.ppt.

Empirica (2006). *Benchmarking access and use of ICT in European schools: Final report from head teacher and classroom teacher surveys in 27 European countries.* Retrieved 6 August 2009 from http://ec.europa.eu/information_society/eeurope/i2010/docs/studies/final_report_3.pdf.

Eteokleous, N. (2008). Evaluating computer technology integration in a centralized school system. *Computers & Education,* 51(2), 669–686.

Felton, F. S. (2006). *The use of computers by elementary school principals.* Doctoral dissertation, Virginia Polytechnic Institute and State University, Blacksburg, Virginia. Retrieved 26 July 2008 from http://scholar.lib.vt.edu/theses/available/etd-04242006-144854/unrestricted/FFelton04202006.pdf.

Flanagan, L., & Jacobsen, M. (2003). Technology leadership for the twenty-first century principal. *Journal of Educational Administration,* 41(2), 124–142.

Gurr, D. (2000). *School principals and Information and Communication Technology.* Retrieved 24 November 2009 from http://staff.edfac.unimelb.edu.au/~davidmg/papers/Gurr_Conf_Paper.pdf.

Karagiorgi, Y., & Charalambous, K. (2004). Curricula considerations in ICT integration: Models and practices in Cyprus. *Education and Information Technologies,* 9(1), 21–35.

Kithreotis, A., & Pashiardis, P. (2006). *Exploring leadership role in school effectiveness and the validation of models of principals' effects on students' achievement.* Retrieved 12 May 2008 from http://www.topkinisis.com/conference/CCEAM/wib/index/outline/PDF/KYTHREOTIS%20Andreas.pdf.

Ministry of Education and Culture (2007). *Annual Report-2006.* Nicosia: Ministry of Education and Culture. Retrieved 23 November 2009 from http://www.moec.gov.cy/etisia-ekthesi/pdf/Annual_report_2006_en.pdf.

Mueller, J., Wood, E., Willoughby, T., Ross, C., & Specht, J. (2008). Identifying discriminating variables between teachers who fully integrate computers and teachers with limited integration. *Computers & Education,* 51(4), 1–15.

Murphy, D.T., & Gunter, G.A. (1997). Technology integration: The importance of administrative support. *Educational Media International,* 34(3), 136–139.

Murphy, J., & Shipman, N. (1999). The interstate school-leaders consortium: A standards-based approach to strengthening educational leadership. *Journal of Personnel Evaluation in Education,* 13(3), 205–224.

Reezigt, G., & Creemers B. (2005). A comprehensive framework for effective school improvement. *School Effectiveness and School Improvement,* 16(4), 407–424.

Reynolds, D., & Teddlie, C. (2000). The processes of school effectiveness. In C. Teddlie & D. Reynolds (eds.), *The International Handbook of School Effectiveness Research* (pp.134–159). London: Falmer Press.

Schiller, J. (2003). Working with ICT perceptions of Australian principals. *Journal of Educational Administration,* 41(2), 171–185.

Stegall, P. (1998). *The principal - key to technology implementation.* Paper presented in the 95th Annual Meeting of the National Catholic Education Association, 14–17 April, Los Angeles: CA.

Theofilides, C., Michaelidou, A., Stylianides, M., & Charalambous, K. (2006). *Leadership functions and dysfunctions in Cyprus primary education.* Retrieved 8 May 2009 from http://www.topkinisis.com/conference/CCEAM/wib/index/outline/PDFS/THEOPHILIDES%20Christos.pdf.

Part III
ICT-Enhanced Learning

Instructional Design on Controlling the Quality of Collaboration in a CSCL Setting Through Illusionary Adaptive Support

Sofia Hadjileontiadou, Georgia Nikolaidou, and Leontios Hadjileontiadis

Introduction

According to Reigeluth (1997, p. 44), instruction is "anything that is done to help someone learn", and Instructional Design (ID) aims at offering "guidance for improving the quality of that help". ID refers to the practice of analysis of the learning needs upon which tools and content are systematically built, in order to facilitate learning.

In recent ID, there is a shift from the system-controlled instruction to the learner-controlled one, as learner's control is believed to positively influence learning and motivation (Schnackenberg and Sullivan 2000). In particular, the factor of control refers to the tendency of people to control what happens to them, e.g., of a learner to direct his/her own learning process. Supporting this need for self-determination may refer to helping people to feel that they have choices when they are involved in an educational experience (Reeve et al. 2003). An ID that incorporates such support provides options and gives the learner the ability to control issues such as content, pace of learning, interfaces, and timing; thus, it helps the individual to feel capable of engaging in those activities (Cordova and Lepper 1996; Shroff and Vogel 2009) and be autonomy-oriented to use the provided choices toward his/her self-selected goals (Ryan and Deci 2004). From this perspective, the notion of adaptation can be perceived as one that is focused on the user's control. Furthermore,

S. Hadjileontiadou (✉)
School of Humanities, Hellenic Open University, Patra, Greece
e-mail: shadji@ee.duth.gr

G. Nikolaidou
Direction of Primary Education of Eastern Thessaloniki, Thessaloniki, Greece

L. Hadjileontiadis
Department of Electrical & Computer Engineering, Aristotle University of Thessaloniki, Thessaloniki, Greece

A. Jimoyiannis (ed.), *Research on e-Learning and ICT in Education*,
DOI 10.1007/978-1-4614-1083-6_11,

research has shown that even the mere illusion of control (i.e., illusion of adaptation) can improve learning outcomes; in such a situation, the illusion refers to giving learners a feeling that they control the learning when in fact they do not (Dror 2008). Research in this area that focuses on individual learning (Berger and Schnerring 1982; Vandewaetere 2009; Vandewaetere et al. 2009) reports that the illusion of control (i.e., adaptivity) can be perceived by the learner and trigger better performance, even when the choices provided are irrelevant to learning (Corbalan et al. 2009).

In the present study, the notion of the illusion of control is extended to Computer Supported Collaborative Learning (CSCL) settings, where specific design considerations must be made to produce it. Research in such settings focuses on structuring collaboration, since productive collaboration does not occur when the learners are left to their own devices (Salomon and Globerson 1989). Examples of operationalizing this approach include structuring the problem itself, process scaffolds (i.e., provision of support so as to reduce task management activities in order to allow the learner to focus on tasks related to learning) and scripts (i.e., scenarios that shape the way learners interact with each other), provision of tools, expert help, and adaptive feedback (Stahl 2007; Hadjileontiadou et al. 2010). It is evident that within a CSCL complex social system that incorporates "things", "people", and "outcomes" (Gabriele 2010), ID becomes quite complicated. As far as the designing of the support of the collaboration is concerned, it is easily realized that the "things" (e.g., shared workspaces, timetables, information) are designable subsystems, whereas the "people" are not. However, the illusion of control resides at the "people" subsystem and this makes clear the need to identify the "things" to be designed in order to produce and sustain the illusion.

In this work, the process of making explicit this duality of subsystems is considered under the broad perspective of the Boulding's typology of system complexity (Boulding 1956). This typology was introduced as a "skeleton" of the structure and function of any complex system within a hierarchy of nine level subsystems. Elaboration of the first three levels that comprise the "things" by Checkland (1981) allows for a deeper understanding of their designable character, whereas further elaboration of the typology by Gabriele (1997, 2010) allows for the realization of the structure and function of all the levels, specifically for school and classroom complex systems. The Boulding's typology was extended to the CSCL area by Hadjileontiadou et al. (2010), with the purpose to drive an ID in order to test the impacts of an illusionary adaptive support on the quality of the collaboration (QoC) that was measured on the basis of specific indicators. The results of a pilot study that was conducted to test the efficacy of the proposed approach were promising.

This chapter extends the work of Hadjileontiadou et al. (2010), by verifying its results through a larger-scaled empirical study. Moreover, it presents a more detailed elaboration of the Boulding's typology in the area of the CSCL, aiming at revealing new possibilities of ID in it.

Theoretical Background

The Boulding's Typology

According to the Boulding's typology, the systems of the world are ranked from simple to complex in nine levels as depicted in the top view in Fig. 1 (Boulding 1956): (1) *Frameworks* (systems with static structures), (2) *Clockworks* (simple dynamic systems with predetermined motions), (3) *Thermostats* (cybernetic systems, i.e., self-regulated on the basis of an external prescribed criterion), (4) *Open systems* (systems that are self-maintained on the basis of resources from the environment, e.g., the cell), (5) *Blue-printed growth systems* (systems that contain preprogrammed instructions for development, e.g., the plant), (6) *Internal-image systems* (systems capable of a detailed awareness of the environment through sense organs, e.g., the animal), (7) *Symbol-processing systems* (systems that use language and other symbols, are self-conscious, and can contemplate the past, present, and future, e.g., humans), (8) *Social systems* (comprising actors from level 7 who share a common social order and culture, e.g., social organizations), and (9) *Transcendental systems* (systems where the system goals are met prior to the individual's). Each level in this hierarchy incorporates all below it, as depicted in the front view in Fig. 1 (Boulding 1956).

Elaborations of this typology contributed to the identification of the factors at each level. More specifically (see Fig. 1), levels 1–3 comprise spatial and temporal traits and information respectively (Checkland 1981). Examples of the first two levels in schools are formal goals, participant roles, equipment and rooms for frameworks, calendars, schedules, and routine activities for clockworks (Gabriele 1997).

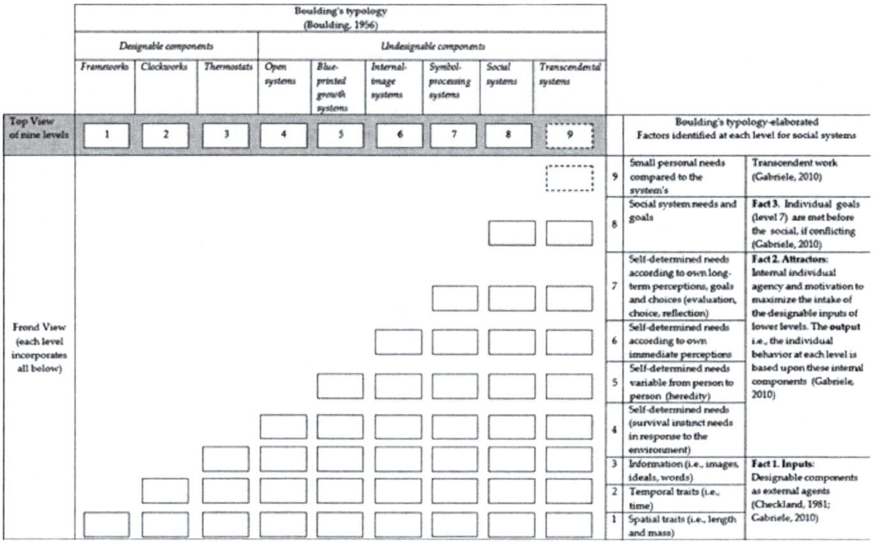

Fig. 1 The Boulding's typology and its elaborations (Checkland 1981; Gabriele 1997, 2010)

Examples of the third, i.e., the level with the thermostat metaphor, are evaluations of the recourses and needs and estimation of the workload in the classroom that leads to self-regulated remedy actions, if needed (Gabriele 1997). Gabrielle discusses the boundaries of this level and proposes to set the function of the thermostat to *off* while planning work, e.g., "when new ideas may come to light while planning a lesson", and set it to *on* during the work process, e.g., "when the classroom interaction takes place" (Gabriele 1997, p. 281). The first three levels comprise the "things" of the system and are either externally (levels 1 and 2) or self-regulated (level 3) to externally prescribed inputs (Checkland 1981). Levels 4–7 comprise the "people", who are self-regulated to internally prescribed criteria (attractors) thus, they are externally undesignable. In level 4, e.g., educational resources, information, and programs should be available to the individual who is acting according to interior criterion (instinct), thus, the input here is described as "intake" (Gabriele 1997). Level 5 realizes the variability of the interior criterion due to the differences of the people (heredity), which is inherited to the response to the stimulus. Furthermore, in level 6, the individual perception intervenes between the stimulus and the response; hence, from this level on, the input/intake is described as "pickup" (Gabriele 1997). The individual "picks up" whatever he/she believes in or understands, otherwise his/her output will be distorted by his/her perception, e.g., instead of learning, memorizing (Gabriele 1997). At level 7 the individual acts consciously to produce the output, not only according to his/her perceptions of the "pickup", but even upon new stimulus he/she can create from the processing of his/her past experiences. The "people" levels are characterized by physical boundaries. Yet, at levels 8 and 9, where the social outcome is expected, only if the individual participation is voluntary and authentic the social intangible system will exist. Moreover, at these levels, individual goals are to be met before the social, otherwise the individual seeks his/her own (Gabriele 2010).

The Boulding's typology (see Fig. 1, facts 1–3) clarifies which levels (subsystems) are predictable and controllable within a system and which are not (fact 1), classifies the relevant types of external (inputs) or internal (attractors) stimuli for their function (fact 2), clarifies that when predictable and designable inputs are designed at levels 1–3, they are expected first to be perceived at level 6 and then reformed to attractors of intrinsic motivation at level 7, toward fulfilling initially individual and then social goals from level 8 and on (fact 3) (Gabriele 2010).

Illusionary Adaptive Support

Within the ID context, the assistance dilemma arises, i.e., when to provide support and when to withhold it, in order to enhance learning (Kapur and Rummel 2009). This dilemma introduces issues concerning the timing, the visibility, and the adaptivity of the support to be provided. Timing may vary in a continuum between the decision of the provision of the support at the beginning of the task and a delayed one. Visibility of the support may be connected to the timing of its provision and have possibly a gradually fading presence. When the timing and visibility are automatically decided by the system that mediates learning, according to the learner's needs, then the support that is provided is of an adaptive character. Moreover, the adaptation issues concerning the assistance dilemma may be extended to issues regarding also the level of the stimuli provision and its type according to the elaborated Boulding's typology. For example, when the effort to support the learner is put at level 7 (i.e., the collaborative performance as outcome), the ID may foresee the design of low-level inputs (i.e., designable "things"), which will be expected to be reformed to internal attractors (i.e., of the collaborating "people") that might maximize the opportunities to produce intrinsic motivation and better learning (i.e., better collaborative performance as "outcome"). Control provided to the learners within a learning setting can serve as an input in the form of support. As Dror (2008, p. 219) states: "the learners' control can take many forms and can be viewed as a continuum. At one extreme, control is totally surrendered to the learners, giving them full freedom to do (or not do) as they please. At the other extreme of the continuum, the learners have no control at all". Yet, if learners are not interested in or do not understand the choices of control provided to them (e.g., level 7 of the Boulding's typology), their involvement in learning may be decreased, which may result in poorer learning outcomes (Paas et al. 2005). Control that is interesting and understood by the learner is therefore suggested as a precursor to both achievement and motivation (Kinzie 1990). Even more, when the offered control is illusionary, choice becomes meaningful if the learner perceives it as such (Corbalan et al. 2009). On the other hand, if choices concerning control are too many, this may cause excessive cognitive load and become detrimental to learning (Dror 2008). Thus, even if the degree of control may be designed as input at the low levels of the elaborated Boulding's typology, be illusionary, it can yet lead to quite effective learning (Dror 2008). In this case, control is perceived by the learners as the adaptivity of the system, which is responding to their choices, whereas the system actually provides only the illusion of control.

The Proposed Instructional Design

The proposed ID elaborates further the Boulding's typology in the area of CSCL as follows (see Fig. 2).

Levels 1 and 2: Stability. At level 1, i.e., the collaborative framework, the individual roles and the group goal are decided. More specifically, collaborative web-based concept mapping, by groups of dyads, is proposed as the CSCL framework. Novak and Gowin (1984, p. 15) defined concept map as a "schematic device for representing a set of concept meanings embedded in a framework of propositions". Each proposition is a statement that contains two or more concepts connected through linking words or phrases to form a meaningful statement. Thus, the role of each collaborator is to contribute to the common-sighted workspace through interactions that can be either submission of entity types, like "concept", "linking phrase", and "connection" or performance of one or more action types, upon each entity type, like "add", "delete", "move", "resize", "modify text", "modify bidirectional" (for the "connection entity type"), and "style". The collaborative character of these interactions is taken into account as a means to estimate the collaborative performance of the peers.

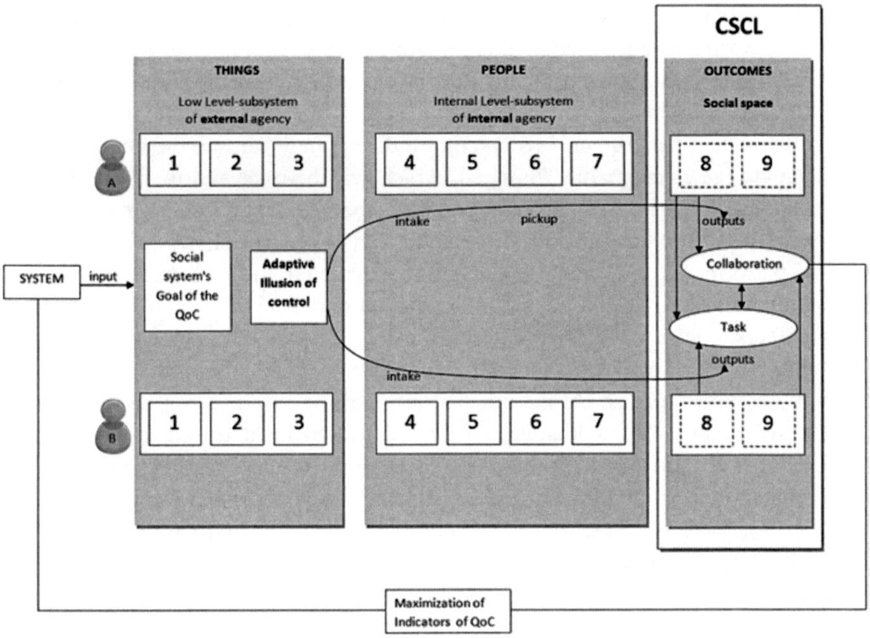

Fig. 2 Depiction of the proposed ID

The goal of the group is to construct collaboratively a concept map upon a theme. At level 2, the timetable of the collaboration is set. Here, the acquaintance period with the CSCL framework and the duration of the main collaboration are decided. In the proposed ID, an intervention by the system is also scheduled at the middle of main collaboration, as it is described in the following level.

Level 3: Adjustability. At this level, the illusion of control is provided in the form of input information. In particular, the collaborators within the web-based concept mapping setting are free to control all the tools that are provided in order to construct the concept map; this control is proposed to be kept as such. An illusionary adaptive support can be decided to increase the perception of control concerning the participation of the collaborators in their evaluation, through appropriate adjustments of their collaborative performance decided by them (thermostat *on*, controlled within the boundaries of the level). In the middle of the predefined duration of the collaboration, the system can reinforce the illusion of control, by an input information in order to sustain it until the end (thermostat *on*, temporarily controlled outside the boundaries of the level).

Levels 4–7: Self-regulation and Variability. At these levels, the illusion of control is expected to be understood and perceived as interesting adaptivity ("intake" at level 4), reformed to attractors of intrinsic motivation ("pick up" at level 6) and processed by each collaborator toward better collaborative performance.

Levels 8–9: Intangibility. At these levels the outcome is produced at the social plain, which in this case of interest is the collaborative performance. Within the proposed setting the quality of the collaborative performance, irrespectively of the content of the concept map, can be promoted through the contribution of the most weighting entity types "concept" and "linking phrase" and the most contributing action types "add" and "modify text". Moreover, a high value of Turn Taking (TT), i.e., the turn of submitting an interaction within the group, can also be indicative of the balance of the interactions between the peers, thus of the commitment to the group work. On the basis of these considerations, simple statistical indicators of the QoC, irrespectively of the content, e.g., the TT value and the total number of the most important entity and action types, weighted according to their contribution to the peers' collaboration, can be calculated. It is evident that from the system perspective, the goal of each group is to maximize the QoC indicators, even when working at level 9.

The hypothesis (H) to be tested through the proposed ID is that the provision of the specific illusionary adaptive support could impact the quality of the collaborative performance, as measured by the QoC indicators. In order to test H, an experimental case was conducted, as it is described in the next subsection.

Experimental Case

The Participants

Two experimental collaborative uses of the IHMC CmapTools version 5.3 (Cañas et al. 2004) (available at http://cmap.ihmc.us) were designed, i.e., the control and the experimental conditions, namely EXP-A and EXP-B, respectively. The participants, who collaborated in 11 groups of dyads (namely G_i, $i=1,2,\ldots,11$) of mixed gender in both experiments, were undergraduate teacher students, aged between 19 and 20 years old. All the students were completely acquainted with the collaborative concept mapping using the IHMC CmapTools about a month before the experiments. A 15 (±1) min duration of the collaborative session was considered adequate enough to keep the procedure intensive, based upon the findings of a previous pilot study (Hadjileontiadou et al. 2010).

The Setting

During the EXP-A, the students collaborated without any perception of being monitored by the system regarding their collaborative activity. The theme of the concept map was left on the choice of the peers and was decided before the beginning of the EXP-A. Two weeks later, the EXP-B was conducted within the same groups and the same content map theme per group, yet they were told that the system continuously monitors their QoC, estimated through their collaborative interactions. This information was illusionary and aimed at causing intrinsic motivation (sense of control) toward better collaboration. The choice of sustaining the same groups and the same concept map theme was decided to make the monitoring of the effect of the illusion

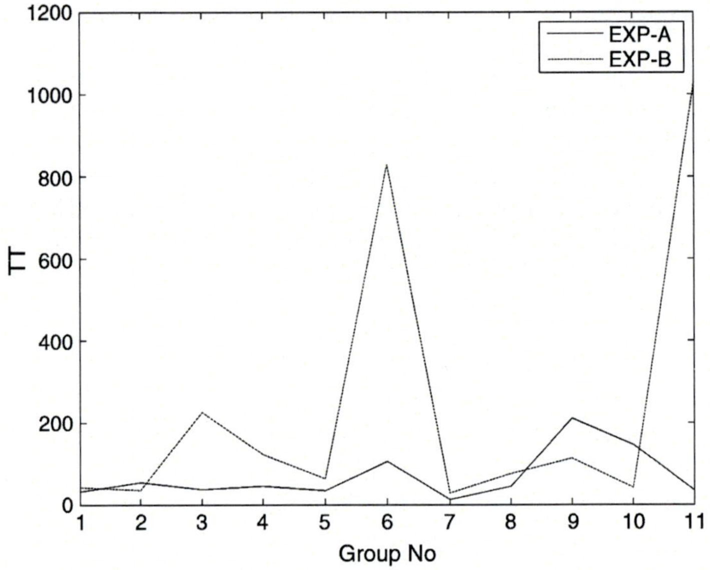

Fig. 3 Total number of Turn Taking (TT) during the experiment duration per group and experiment

of control to the peers independent from the group construction and task content. In order to reinforce the illusion of monitoring the peers' collaborative activity by the system, a text-feedback in a reminder-like form ("Remember! The system keeps records of you collaborative activity") was provided to all groups around the middle of the duration of the collaborative session.

Data Collection and Elaboration

The interactions in both experimental conditions were recorded in IHMC CmapTools and log files were exported in .txt format. For each interaction, the log files included the number, time stamp, user's identity, action type ("add", "delete", "move", "resize", "modify text", "modify bidirectional", and "style"), and entity type ("concept", "linking phrase", and "connection"). The quantitative elaboration of these raw data was followed by a statistical analysis using Matlab R2009b (Mathworks 2009).

Results

In order to accept or reject the H, the values of the indicators of the QoC were calculated as presented in Figs. 3–9. More specifically, Figs. 3 and 4 present the number of TT in both experimental conditions, for the total experiment duration of each group and per minute of the normalized duration (15 (±1) min represent 100%), respectively.

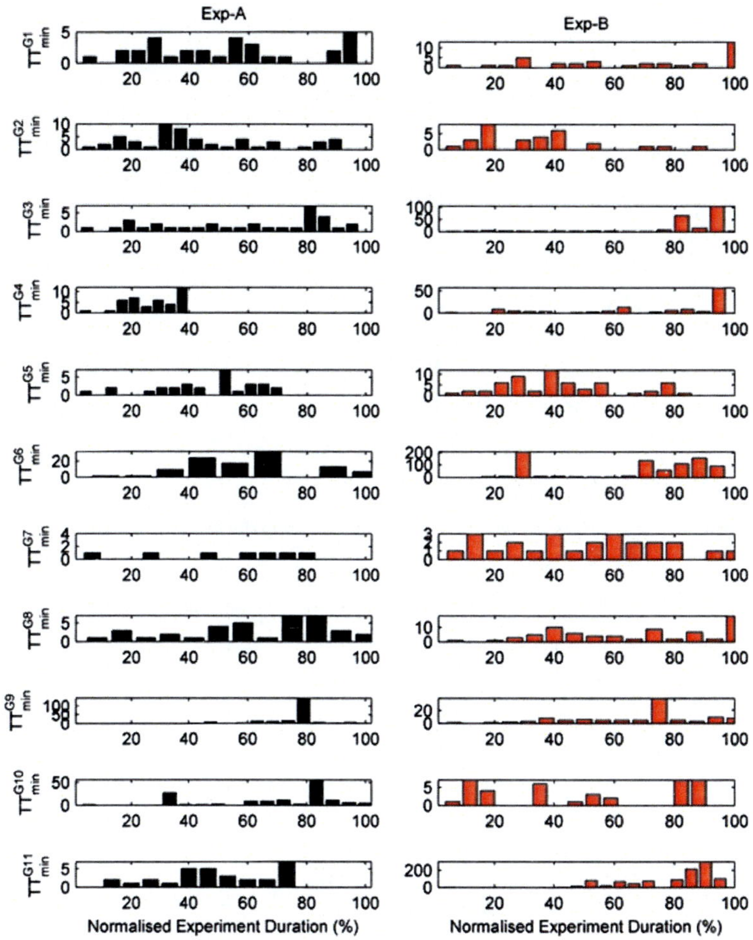

Fig. 4 Number of Turn Taking (TT) per minute of the normalized experiment duration (%), per group (G_i), and experimental condition (A, B)

Figures 5 and 6 depict the total number of actions and entities across all groups, per action and entity type, respectively, for both experimental conditions.

The reinforcement of the illusion at the middle of the normalized collaboration duration was considered as stimulation in EXP-B. However, Figs. 7 and 8 present the total number of actions and entities across all groups, per action and entity type, respectively, during the pre- and poststimulation periods for both the experiments only for comparison reasons of EXP-B to EXP-A.

The cross tabulation of the most collaboration weighting entity types ("concept", "linking phrase", and "connect") and action types ("add", "delete", and "modify text") are depicted in Fig. 9a–c, respectively.

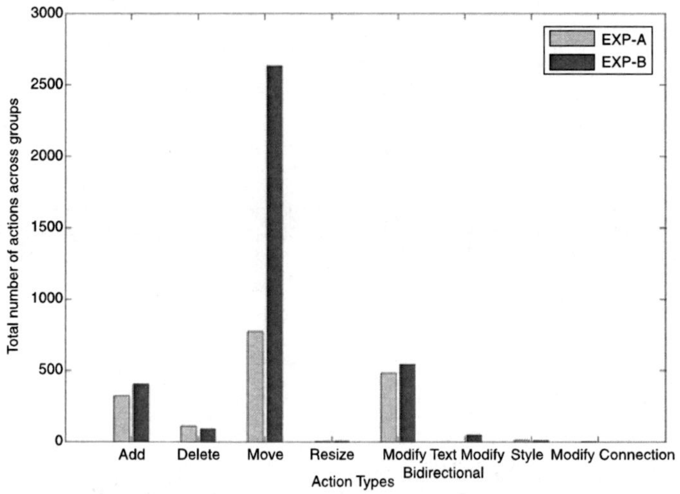

Fig. 5 Total number of actions across all groups, per action type and experiment

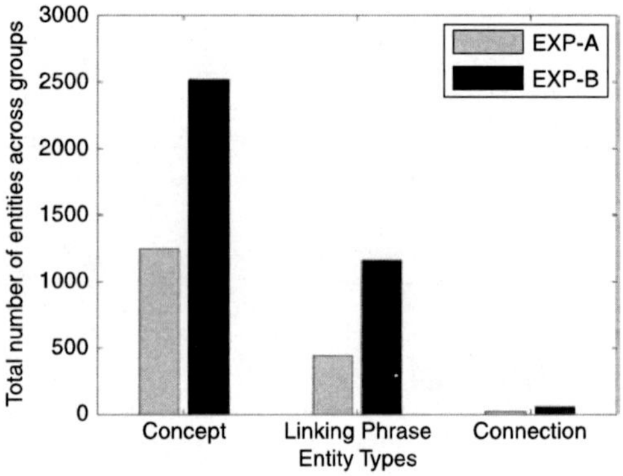

Fig. 6 Total number of entities across all groups, per entity type and experiment

Discussion

The presented results support the acceptance of H, i.e., that the provided illusionary adaptive support could impact on the QoC. More specifically, from Fig. 3 it can be noticed that the TT curve (transition of interactions between the two peers) of EXP-B overpasses the corresponding TT curve of EXP-A, showing in 8 out of the 11 groups, i.e., G1, G3, G4, G5, G6, G7, G8, G11, a clear increase, with the higher differences located at G6 and G11. This finding indicates that the total effort, in terms of the number of the TT of the interactions performed at the experimental condition, was higher than that in the control one ($p<0.05$), thus the collaborative

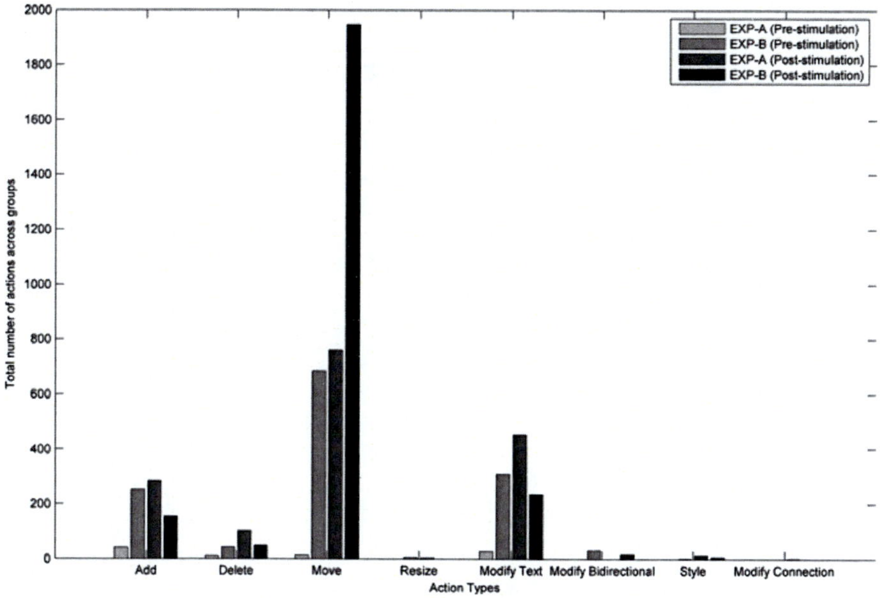

Fig. 7 Total number of actions across all groups, per action type, during the pre- and poststimulation periods per experiment

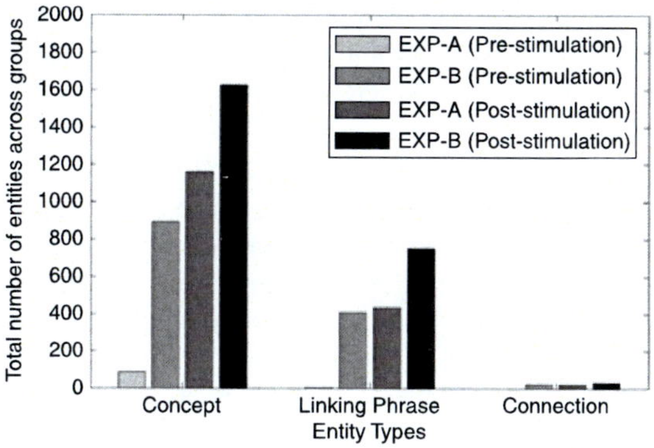

Fig. 8 Total number of entities across all groups, per entity type, during the pre- and poststimulation periods per experiment

performance was better balanced within these groups. From a more detailed examination of the characteristics of the collaboration concerning the TT per minute of the normalized experiment duration (Fig. 4), it can be noticed that the distribution of the TT in EXP-B is more uniform along the normalized time, for almost all groups. Moreover, considering the intervention at the middle of the time duration, it can be noticed that the reinforcement of the illusion in EXP-B contributed to the

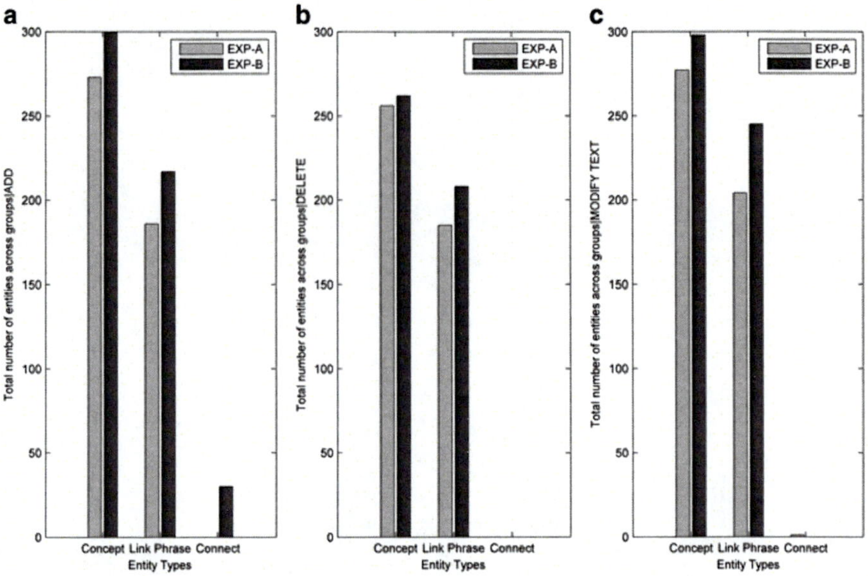

Fig. 9 Cross tabulation of the entity types and action types (**a**) "add", (**b**) "delete", and (**c**) "modify text", across groups per experiment

control of the QoC in the poststimulation duration, by increasing the value of TT per minute (e.g., in EXP-B, G4, G11). Overall, the TT indicator, as it was calculated both for the experimental duration as a whole (Fig. 3) and as a rate per minute across the normalized experimental duration (Fig. 4), provides evidence of the influence of the illusionary adaptive support to the collaborative performance of the students. Two other indicators that contributed to the acceptance of the H were the total number of actions and entities, across all groups per action, entity types and experimental condition, as it is presented in Figs. 5 and 6, respectively. From both these figures, it can be noticed that in EXP-B the total number of interactions increases, indicating a positive effect of the illusion. Moreover, it can be noticed that the most contributing action types, i.e., "add" and "modify text", and entity types, i.e., "concept" and "linking phrase", are clearly increased in EXP-B. A more in depth investigation of the number of the above interactions could be drawn from Figs. 7 and 8, for the action and entity types, respectively, where the pre- and poststimulation periods were established for both the EXP-A (only for comparison reasons) and EXP-B (as experimentally performed). From Fig. 7, it can be noticed that at the prestimulation period, the total number of actions is higher in EXP-B than in EXP-A. However, at the poststimulation duration, it is realized that the "move" action type dominated, whereas the "add", "delete", and "modify text" were sustained at high values, yet lower than the prestimulation phase. This finding is indicative of the "mean strategy" of collaboration that was performed along the groups, i.e., domination of the insertion of the information within the workspace at the beginning of the collaboration, for structuring the concept map (almost prestimulation period), and then improvement of the spatial organization of the structure of the map, on the basis of the necessary movements (poststimulation period). This gradually "maturing" collaboration is also verified from the findings in Fig. 8, where the most weighting entity types "concept" and "linking phrase", present an increase in EXP-B as compared to EXP-A, in both pre- and poststimulation periods. Moreover, the illusion of control increased their values during the poststimulation period of the EXP-B. From the results presented in Fig. 9a–c, it is clear that the total number of entities is higher for all cross tabulation combinations of action and entity types in the EXP-B as compared to the EXP-A.

The above empirical results allow the acceptance of the H within the proposed ID and extend the findings of Vandewaetere et al. (2009), about the enhancement of the learning outcome through the perceived illusion of control, from individual to collaborative settings. This effort was grounded on the conceptual framework of the Boulding's typology and contributed to its further elaboration in the area of CSCL. This framework reveals dualities within the complex social system of the collaborating dyad, i.e., designable-undesignable inputs, stable-adjustable levels, and external input-internal attractors. These clarifications highly contributed to the proposed ID, by allowing the realization of the form of the illusion (information), the timing of its provision (diminishing the assistance dilemma), the understanding of its perception mechanisms, and the expected impact at the social plane. This approach allowed handling of the intangible notion of illusion, at no cost and computational effort, within a CSCL setting that did not afford any adaptive character; thus, it moved the issue of adaptation of the support provided to the collaborators from "hard" system modeling designs to more "soft" ones, revealing possibilities of further elaborations of the boundaries and contents of the aforementioned levels.

Concluding Remarks

In this work, an instructional design (ID) was proposed that elaborates the Boulding's typology in the area of CSCL. Within the hierarchy of this typology, the focus was put at the higher levels, where the perception of adaptivity in the form of control can be illusionary triggered, in order to increase the possibilities to sustain the even higher level of social collaborative work. Through an experimental study, this research verified that the illusion of the adaptivity in the form of input provided at the lower levels of this typology may enhance the collaborative performance. These empirical results need to be justified through large-scale experiments and, perhaps, through comparison with truly adaptive settings. Efforts toward such direction are on the way, embedded within a broader perspective of lowering the ratio between investment and result in CSCL through a minimal ID.

References

Berger, J., & Schnerring, D. (1982). The effects of desire for control and extrinsic rewards on the illusion of control and gambling. *Motivation & Emotion*, 6(4), 329–335.

Boulding, K. E. (1956). General Systems Theory- The skeleton of science. *Management Science*, 11(3), 197–208.

Cañas, A. J., Hill, G., Carff, R., Suri, N., Lott, J., & Eskridge, T. (2004). CmapTools: A knowledge modeling and sharing environment. In A. J. Cañas, J. D. Novak & F. M. González (eds.), *Proceedings of the first international conference on concept mapping 'Concept maps: Theory, methodology, technology'* (pp. 125–133). Pamplona, Spain: Universidad Pública de Navarra.

Checkland, P. B. (1981). *Systems Thinking, Systems Practice*. New York: John Wiley & Sons.

Corbalan, G., Kester, L., & Merriënboer, J. (2009). Combining shared control with variability over surface features: Effects on transfer test performance and task involvement. *Computers in Human Behavior*, 25, 290–298.

Cordova, D. I., & Lepper, M. R. (1996). Intrinsic motivation and the process of learning: Beneficial effects of contextualization, personalization, and choice. *Journal of Educational Psychology*, 88, 715–730.

Dror, I. E. (2008). Technology enhanced learning: The good, the bad, and the ugly. *Pragmatics & Cognition*, 16, 215–223.

Gabriele, S. (1997). Boulding's typology elaborated: A framework for understanding school and classroom systems. *Systems Practice*, 10(3), 271–303.

Gabriele, S. (2010). The hard facts of soft social systems: Towards a theoretical and practical model for schools and other organizations. Retrieved 17 March 2011 from http://journals.isss.org/index.php/proceedings54th/search/authors?searchInitial=G.

Hadjileontiadou, S., Nikolaidou, G., & Hadjileontiadis, L. (2010). Illusionary adaptive support as a means for intrinsic motivation in CSCL settings: A case in concept mapping. In A. Jimoyiannis (ed.), *Proceedings of the 7th Panhellenic Conference with International Participation 'Information and Communication Technologies in Education'* (pp. 163–170). Korinthos, Greece: University of Peloponnese.

Kapur, M., & Rummel, N. (2009). The assistance dilemma in CSCL. In A. Dimitrakopoulou, C. O' Maley, D. Suthers, & R. Reimann (eds.), *Proceedings of the CSCL2009-symposia* (pp.37–39). NJ: International Society of the Learning Sciences.

Kinzie, M. B. (1990). Requirements and benefits of effective interactive instruction: Learner control, self regulation, and continuing motivation. *Educational Technology, Research and Development*, 38, 5–21.

Mathworks (2009). *Matlab R2009b Signal Processing Toolbox*. http://www.mathworks.com.

Novak, J. D., & Gowin, D. B. (1984). *Learning How to Learn.* New York: Cambridge University Press.

Paas, F., Tuovinen, J. E., Merrilnboer, J. J. G., & Darabi, A. (2005). A motivational perspective on the relation between mental effort and performance: Optimizing learner involvement in instruction. *Educational Technology Research and Development*, 53, 5–34.

Reeve, J., Nix, G., & Hamm, D. (2003). Testing models of the experience of self determination in intrinsic motivation and the conundrum of choice. *Journal of Educational Psychology*, 95(2), 375–392.

Reigeluth, C. (1997). Instructional theory, practitioner needs, and new directions: Some reflections. *Educational Technology*, 37(1), 42–47.

Ryan, R. M., & Deci, E. L. (2004). Autonomy is no illusion: Self-determination theory and the empirical study of authenticity, awareness and will. In J. Greenberg, S. L. Koole, & T. Pyszczynski (eds.), *Handbook of Experimental Existential Psychology* (pp. 449–479). New York: Guilford Press.

Salomon, G., & Globerson, T. (1989). When teams do not function the way they ought to. *International Journal of Educational Research*, 13, 89–100.

Schnackenberg, H. L., & Sullivan, H. J. (2000). Learner control over full and lean computer-based instruction under differing ability levels. *Educational Technology, Research and Development*, 48(2), 19–35.

Shroff, R., & Vogel, D. (2009). Assessing the factors deemed to support individual student intrinsic motivation in technology supported online and face-to-face discussions. *Journal of Information Technology Education*, 8, 59–85.

Stahl, G. (2007). Scripting group cognition. In F. Fischer, I. Kollar, H. Mandl, & J. M. Haake (eds.), *Scripting computer-supported collaborative learning* (pp. 327–336). New York, NY: Springer.

Vandewaetere, M. (2009). *The benefits and drawbacks of learner control as a means for creating adaptive learning environments*. Retrieved 8 April 2011 from http://umap09.fbk.eu/sites/umap09.fbk.eu/files/paper_164.pdf.

Vandewaetere, M., Clarebout, G., & Desmet, P. (2009). The illusion of adaptivity as instructional method in electronic learning environments. In V. Dimitrova, R. Mizoguchi, B. Boulay, & A. Graesser (eds.), *Proceedings of the 14th International Conference on Artificial Intelligence in Education: Building Learning Systems that Care: From Knowledge Representation to Affective Modelling* (pp. 769–771). The Netherlands: IOS Press.

The Design and Development of a Wiki Task in Undergraduate Education: Retrospects and Prospects

Ilias Karasavvidis and Sevasti Theodosiou

Introduction

The last decade was characterized by the gradual transition from first to the second generation of the Web. According to O'Reilly (2005), Web 2.0 can be defined in a number of ways. From a technical point of view, the affordances that second generation Web tools offer are greater when compared to the first generation ones. For example, blogs and wikis have more affordances than content management systems and threaded discussions respectively (Kim 2008; West and West 2009). Despite major technical differences, the substantial differentiation between Web 1.0 and Web 2.0 generations lies in the role users play (O'Reilly 2005). More specifically, while in the first generation of the Web users could simply read (i.e., "consume") website content, in Web 2.0 users can also contribute to its creation. This possibility turns users from information consumers into participants and "co-producers." Consequently, today the Web is best conceptualized as a platform service that relies on the architecture of participation and the wisdom of crowds (Surowiecki 2004; Tapscott and Williams 2006; Mason and Rennie 2008). Based on this fact, two are the key principles underlying Web 2.0: (a) users "add value" to technology and (b) users play an important role in content creation. For example, sites such as Wikipedia and YouTube would be inconceivable without the input of thousands of Internet users in terms of text and video respectively.

The impact of Web 2.0 on education has been substantial. This is clearly reflected in newly coined terms such as Learning 2.0, School 2.0, Classroom 2.0, and Education 2.0. The idea behind this terminology shift is that Web 2.0 technologies can contribute more to learning in comparison to the corresponding Web 1.0 technologies. As opposed to the first generation of web tools which replicated online traditional, delivery-based modes of teaching, the second generation of Web tools presupposes the

I. Karasavvidis (✉) • S. Theodosiou
Department of Preschool Education, University of Thessaly, Volos, Greece
e-mail: ikaras@uth.gr

A. Jimoyiannis (ed.), *Research on e-Learning and ICT in Education*,
DOI 10.1007/978-1-4614-1083-6_12,

active participation of students/users. This makes Web 2.0 technologies particularly appealing because they are perfectly compatible with constructivist conceptions of learning according to which students actively participate in the learning process. Moreover, the focus on communication and collaboration which many Web 2.0 tools afford makes them even more promising from a constructivist point of view. The de facto participation of students, which Web 2.0 technologies require, enables innovative constructivist practices where students do not simply consume learning materials compiled by instructors but actively contribute to the creation and processing of these materials (Palloff and Pratt 2007; Mason and Rennie 2008).

Wikis in Education

Wikis are amongst the most popular and well-known Web 2.0 tools. The most popular online encyclopedia, Wikipedia, is perhaps the prime example of wiki popularity and success. From a technical viewpoint, a wiki is a collection of interlinked Web pages the content of which can be easily modified by any user with a Web browser. Wikis are particularly interesting tools as they facilitate the collaborative creation of hypertext without the need of any previous knowledge of Hypertext Markup Language (HTML) or specific Web browser or operating system software.

However, wikis' genuine potential regarding education does not lie in their technical features but in their ability to support new collaboration and communication practices. In an attempt to conceptualize how wikis could be used in education, many different approaches have been proposed. Fore example, Guzdial et al. (2001) outlined three major wiki uses in education: (a) distributing information, (b) collaborative artifact creation, and (c) discussion and review activities. More recently, West and West (2009), following Bloom's taxonomy, proposed that wikis could be used for (a) knowledge construction, (b) critical thinking, and (c) contextual application. Generally speaking, wikis may facilitate learning, collaboration, communication, interaction, sharing, meaning-making, and reflection (see e.g., Guzdial et al. 2001; Bruns and Humphreys 2005; Lund and Smördal 2006; Nicol et al. 2005; Ras et al. 2007). Overall, a wiki may involve individual work (e.g., the creation of a webpage), collaboration (e.g., the collective creation of a text), communication (e.g., a discussion anchored on a specific webpage topic), and evaluation (e.g., a peer-review of the input made by all the members of a group).

The aforementioned pro-wiki arguments suggest that wikis have great potential. The problem is that there is a serious gap in the literature regarding how to realize their potential for educational purposes. For instance, while the model by West and West (2009) is very appealing, there is a lack of rigorous empirical evidence validating it. More specifically, the available research evidence is limited and suggests that the effective incorporation of wikis in the learning process requires radical course redesign (Rick and Guzdial 2006; Raman et al. 2005), scaffolding (Guzdial et al. 2001; Cole 2008), and high levels of course integration (Choy and Ng 2007; Wheeler et al. 2008; Cole 2008). This information might be useful as a set of general guidelines but is insufficient for using wikis in education and especially in undergraduate settings. This is further complicated by other literature findings. More specifically, research shows that students either make minimal use of course wikis or refuse to use them altogether (Rick and Guzdial 2006; Carr et al. 2007; Choy and Ng 2007; Cole 2008). Moreover, student online interaction is limited as students tend to (a) read their own contributions thereby ignoring the writings of others (Wheeler et al. 2008; Ma and Yuen 2008) and (b) make a few edits to the wiki pages (Ma and Yuen 2007; Ravid et al. 2008). Revisions are not appreciated (Wheeler et al. 2008; Vratulis and Dobson 2008) and criticism is not always well-taken by fellow students (Minocha and Thomas 2007). Finally, students' perceptions of the educational value of wikis are not always positive. In most cases students prefer to work individually, rather than collaborate on-line with fellow students (Carr et al. 2007; Ma and Yuen 2008; Ravid et al. 2008; Elgort et al. 2008). All in all, the literature suggests that regardless of the potential of wikis to contribute to student learning in higher education, their integration in courses is neither a simple nor an easy task.

Background of the Study

This work is based on data from a larger research project that explores the effective incorporation of wikis in undergraduate education settings. The program focuses on the design, development, implementation, and evaluation of wiki tasks in undergraduate courses. Drawing on the design-experiment method (Barab and Squire 2004; Collins et al. 2004; Design-Based Research Collective 2003; Cobb et al. 2003; Hoadley 2004), it aims at the design of a task that will address some of the aforementioned issues regarding wiki uses in education.

The general context of the research program is provided by an undergraduate course on learning with Information and Communication Technologies (ICT) in which the wiki was introduced. The course is compulsory for fifth semester Preschool Education students and constitutes an introduction to the use of ICT to support learning. More specifically, the course has two main objectives: (a) introduce students to the different educational software categories and the underlying learning theories and (b) render students capable of designing, teaching, and evaluating an instructional unit through educational software. In this context, the wiki is typically one of the two main compulsory course assignments.

The first design cycle took place in the 2007 winter semester and involved 38 undergraduate students. This first version of the wiki task included two main components: (a) glossary and (b) frequently asked questions (FAQs). These two components were expected to facilitate students' encounter with the wiki and provide specific and concrete routes for participation. More specifically, the writing of a glossary and FAQs was expected to facilitate the pooling of all relevant information the students as a group could access. In the process of writing concept definitions and answers, the students could use the communication functions of the wiki to discuss issues and synthesize their interpretations of the concepts and how they could be applied. To address the problem of limited student participation reported by previous studies, a minimum number for contributions per student was enforced. More specifically, each student was required to create and maintain five pages related to course concepts and make contributions to five pages created by other students. Data analysis indicated that this requirement effectively resolved the problem of limited participation as the students conformed to the minimal participation requirements set. Even though student participation had significantly increased, online interaction was still minimal (Karasavvidis 2010a, 2011).

Based on the results of the first design cycle, the task was redesigned in order to address the main limitations which had emerged. Other components were also introduced to provide more routes for participation. In addition to glossary and FAQs, the revised version of the task also comprised the following components: (a) historical information, (b) applications and examples, (c) interpretations and meaning-making, (d) lesson plans, and (e) software presentations. The rationale for the selection of these new components was that they would foster student participation and create more possibilities for online interactions. This time neither a minimal participation number was set for student contributions nor was the extent of participation dictated. The second implementation took place in the 2008 winter semester and involved 50 students. The results indicated important improvements regarding students' participation rates and the extent of contributions. However, on-line interaction still remained minimal (Karasavvidis 2010a, 2011).

Focus of the Study

The findings of the former design cycle informed the further adaptation of the wiki task and its implementation in a third design cycle. The modified task included five main components: (a) glossary, (b) frequently asked questions (FAQs), (c) applications and examples, (d) discussion of videotaped lessons, and (e) lesson plans. These components provided many different routes for student participation and online interaction. More specifically, the students could write up concept definitions, compile a list of questions and answers, describe how the concepts were applied in instructional and learning contexts, discuss exemplary lessons employing educational software which had been videotaped, and design ICT-based lesson plans.

In addition to making minor improvements to the task components based on problems which had surfaced during the previous design cycles, the main difference in the third design cycle involved online interaction. More specifically, the design of the wiki task in the third design cycle was expected to improve student participation and collaboration as well as promote online interaction because two of the task components we introduced involved either explicit discussions (e.g., of videotaped lessons) or reviews and feedback (e.g., of lesson plans).

This implementation took place in the 2009 winter semester and involved 56 undergraduate female students. The participants had an average age of 20 years 2 months and came a middle socioeconomic background. The majority of students owned computers (83%) and more than half (55%) could access the internet from home. According to the pre-course survey, the students were computer-literate and, on average, used computers for more than 2 h/day. On a 5-point Likert scale, the reported familiarity with operating system, office, and internet software was very high (operating system: $M=3.89$, SD=0.91; office: $M=3.43$, SD=0.91; browser: $M=4.62$, SD=0.66; e-mail: $M=4.45$, SD=0.91).

The present paper draws on data from the third design cycle described above and aims to address the following research questions:

(a) What is the rate of student participation in the third design cycle compared to the second one?
(b) What is the rate of online collaboration in the third design cycle compared to the second one?
(c) What is the level of online interaction in the third design cycle compared to the second one?

Method

Data Collection and Analysis

Many types of quantitative and qualitative measures were used throughout the project: questionnaires, interviews, the wiki texts produced, and system log files. MediaWiki (http://www.mediawiki.org), one of the most popular wiki clones, was the server software used for the purposes of the study. It provides advanced user-access control and keeps detailed page and user logs.

Student participation rates were operationalized in terms of page views and page edits, while online collaboration was operationalized in terms of collective edits. More specifically, the main actions a student can perform in a wiki system involve (a) view existing content and (b) add new content. Student participation was evaluated using log file information about page views and edits. The volume of page views provides a first gross measure of participation as it shows how often the students accessed the wiki pages. The volume of page edits is a more detailed measure of participation as it indicates the extent of processing that each page underwent. Finally, the number of edits per student reflects student participation levels in the creation of wiki content. Student on-line collaboration was evaluated in terms of collective page edits. We take it that the large number of student edits for a given wiki page suggests greater levels of shared editing and, consequently, collaboration for the creation of the page.

On the other hand, online interaction was operationalized in terms of the discussions held per wiki page. The five most revised wiki pages were used as a representative sample considering that these were the pages which were subjected to the most extensive processing. For each of these pages we determined the number of edits as well as the number of unique editors. Moreover, we determined whether there was a discussion in the corresponding wiki section of each wiki page and, if so, the number of unique participants.

Results

The descriptive statistics for the four main variables for the second and third design cycles are presented in Tables 1 and 2 respectively.

In the second design cycle the students created 49 pages that were viewed 6,521 times, while in the third design cycle the students created 28 pages that were viewed 8,918 times. As can be seen in the tables above, the average number of page views is much higher in the third design cycle. Despite this sizable difference, the non parametric comparison of the two means using the page as the unit of analysis did not turn out to be statistically significant (Mann–Whitney $U=589$, $z=-1{,}156$, $p=0.248$). However, the striking similarities that the two design cycles share need to be stressed. More specifically, in both cycles a small number of pages were more popular than most of all the others combined. For example, in the second design cycle 13 pages (amounting to 26% of all wiki pages) accounted for about 50% of the total number of page views while in the third design cycle 4 pages (14.29% of all wiki pages) received more than 50% of all page views. This appears to be a recurrent pattern which is interesting and requires further research.

The comparison of page edits between the two design cycles using the page as a unit of analysis indicated that the volume of edits was significantly higher in the third design cycle (Mann–Whitney $U=307$, $z=-2.47$, $p=0.013$). This means that the pages in the third design cycle were more thoroughly processed. Considering that the absolute number of page edits in the two conditions was approximately the same, this systematic difference is to be expected because the students created less wiki pages in the third cycle. On the other hand, the comparative examination of the edits per student in the two conditions using the page as the unit of analysis indicated no statistically significant differences between the two cycles (Mann–Whitney $U=1{,}314.5$, $z=-0.541$, $p=0.588$). Finally, as far as online collaboration is concerned, a non-parametric comparison indicated no statistically significant differences between the two conditions (Mann–Whitney $U=208.50$, $z=-1.89$, $p=0.059$).

The main statistics for online interaction in the second design cycle are presented in Table 3.

As can be seen in Table 3, despite the large number of edits and the many students who were involved in those edits, there were only two cases of discussions. In the first case (wiki page on Open Software) there was no actual discussion as one student posted a remark which was not further taken up by other students. In the second case (wiki page on Vygotsky) two students wrote elaborate texts which referred to the concepts featuring on the wiki page on Vygotsky. While this might technically qualify as discussion, as it was written in the discussion section of the wiki page, essentially it was not a discussion. Both student contributions involved factual information and did not address each other directly or indirectly. Given this, it is quite possible that these texts were accidentally added to the discussion section of the wiki page instead of the main one (i.e., information section). It should be noted that, for the same reason, the wiki pages on Behaviorism and Vygotsky which also included discussion sections cannot be considered as discussions.

Table 1 Wiki statistics of the second design cycle

Variable	Total	Minimum	Maximum	Mean	SD
Page views	6,521	1	388	130.42	95.29
Page edits	1,132	1	71	22.59	15.22
Edits per student	1,132	1	115	22.64	20.79
Users per page edit	–	1	44	11.4	6.43

Table 2 Wiki statistics of the third design cycle

Variable	Total	Minimum	Maximum	Mean	SD
Page views	8,918	2	2,709	318.5	523.4
Page edits	1,173	3	186	55.86	55.9
Edits per student	1,356	3	98	24.21	20.37
Users per page edit	–	1	37	15.05	11.9

Table 3 On-line interaction in the second design cycle

Page title	Number of edits	Number of unique editors	Discussion page	Number of unique discussants
Cross Disciplinary Curriculum	71	19	No	0
Behaviorism	57	24	No	0
Open Software	49	21	Yes	1
Educational Software	48	22	No	0
Vygotsky	45	17	Yes	1

Table 4 On-line interaction in the third design cycle

Page title	Number of edits	Number of unique editors	Discussion page	Number of unique discussants
Piagetian Theory	186	37	Yes	8
Information and Communication Technologies (ICT) and Education	184	29	Yes	8
Behaviorism	159	38	Yes	10
Vygotskian Theory	84	28	Yes	6
Educational Software based on Piagetian Theory: lesson plans	69	22	Yes	7

Overall, the second design cycle did not involve any discussions (Karasavvidis 2011). The main statistics regarding online interactions in the third design cycle are presented in Table 4.

In stark contrast to the second design cycle, all wiki pages involved discussions. Not only were discussions held for all the pages examined, but also the number of student participants was promising.

A qualitative examination of the discussion sections of the wiki pages indicated that the students who participated reflected on the topics and engaged in thoughtful conversations. The following excerpt from the discussion section of the page on Piagetian theory, the most thoroughly edited wiki page, is an illustration of this.

Student 1: Based on what was discussed in class, I have a question. Piaget's theory has been harshly criticized [outlines major points of criticism]...Are the experts contradicting themselves when they promote constructivism while at the same time emphasize Piaget's ideas? Or maybe Piagetian theory is not directly applied to humans but lays the foundation for new and more developed theories? Can anyone please respond to my question because sometimes theory and practice are completely unrelated (28/11/2009, 21:22).

Student 2: Regarding your question, I find Piaget's work to be very important, regardless of the criticisms it has received. As educators, isn't it our responsibility to study the theory and use it for its strengths – if any? Or compare it with other theories in order to understand why it is being disputed? ...Today researchers believe that children are more [cognitively] capable than what Piaget thought they were. This means that according to the stages [of cognitive development], learning follows the stages without taking into account the [more] advanced [cognitive] skills that children might have (3/12/2009, 11:08).

Student 3: Piaget's theory has had a huge impact not only on the theory of instruction but also on all the disciplines which study human development and more particularly cognitive development. Therefore, I think that educators should definitely study his theory (3/12/2009, 16:58).

Student 1: It would be very naive of me to believe that Piagetian theory is useless. My concern is that if university teaching only involves teacher-centered instruction, if the system uses grades as awards and punishes failures, if the exams are based on old theories, is it not natural that we might do the same in our teaching?...Shouldn't our own experiences as learners [at the University] involve more contemporary theories of learning so that we are more likely to use such theories when we enter the profession? (08/12/2009, 11:59).

Student 4: I don't think that children in the past were less [cognitively] able...it's just that nowadays there are more stimuli and children end up having more experiences. Even if you completely disagree with his theories, Piaget's work is very important... (16/12/2009, 09:52).

As can be seen in the excerpt, student 1 posed a genuine and intriguing question to which the other three students responded. The resulting discussion is authentic and provides a measure of students' understanding of Piagetian theory. This excerpt is typical of most discussions which were held in the third design cycle. The students posted remarks and questions about concepts or topics which they either found hard to understand or felt that were worth commenting and further elaborating. It is particularly promising that some of the discussions indicate explicit meaning-making attempts. Overall, both the frequency and the nature of discussions held on every wiki page represent a substantial improvement over the second design cycle and attest to the effectiveness of the task.

Discussion

Web 2.0 tools are the latest technology wave to hit education. Many authors have noted the potential of Web 2.0 tools such as wikis to promote active student learning in higher education (Guzdial et al. 2001; Cole 2008; Wheeler et al. 2008; West and

West 2009; Wheeler 2009). Given the informal nature of most such tools, the task for educators is to discover how to harness the power of Web 2.0 tools within the formalized structures of education (Wheeler and Wheeler 2009; Dohn 2009). In this sense, Laurillard (2009) argued that traditional teaching and learning approaches need to be explored in new technological contexts. Despite the many calls for exploring the potential of Web 2.0 tools for education, there is a knowledge gap regarding their effective integration in undergraduate education. Especially when it comes to wiki uses in education, the literature has revealed a number of important problems such as low student participation (Rick and Guzdial 2006; Carr et al. 2007; Choy and Ng 2007; Cole 2008) and limited online interaction (Wheeler et al. 2008; Ma and Yuen 2007, 2008; Ravid et al. 2008). It is clear that unless educators figure out how to address such issues, the contribution of wikis to learning will not match expectations. The present paper focused on the integration of a wiki in an undergraduate course and explored how to resolve the problems of student participation, collaboration and online interaction. The wiki task used was the outcome of a 3 year progressive refinement following a design experiment method.

Regarding the first research question, data analysis indicated that despite the task modifications made in the third design cycle, the anticipated improvements were not achieved. More specifically, two out of the three measures compared between the second and the third design cycles, namely page views and edits per student were not statistically significant. Regardless of systematic differences, the fact that student participation was very high without setting minimal contribution levels is particularly promising because former studies have consistently reported that participation is one of the major problems regarding wiki integration in higher education contexts (Rick and Guzdial 2006; Carr et al. 2007; Choy and Ng 2007; Cole 2008). Thus, it appears that the issue of student participation levels can be overcome to a considerable extent by adapting the nature of the wiki task. On the other hand, previous studies had indicated that students do not edit wiki pages and even when they do they tend to make a few edits (Wheeler et al. 2008; Ma and Yuen 2007, 2008; Ravid et al. 2008). The results from this study indicated that the number of page edits was significantly larger in the third design cycle. Therefore, it can be concluded that the third design cycle was successful as far as student participation is concerned and the modified wiki version led to increased student participation levels particularly in terms of editing.

Regarding the second research question, data analysis did not indicate any statistically significant differences between the two design cycles. Taking into consideration the small number of pages involved, we would have expected higher collaboration rates. In this respect, the modified wiki task was not as successful as expected when it came to on-line collaboration. This outcome replicates the findings of previous studies which report that on-line collaboration can be very difficult to achieve in a wiki context (Cole 2008; Elgort et al. 2008; Ma and Yuen 2008; Dohn 2009). Nevertheless, the average number of students involved per page edit increased in the third design cycle. This is an important improvement as it suggests that, using shared edits as a criterion, online collaboration was positively affected by modifying the wiki task.

Finally, regarding the third research question, the findings indicated that online interaction increased in the third design cycle. As opposed to the second design cycle, all the wiki pages examined involved discussions in the corresponding page sections. Some of these discussions were quite authentic and addressed issues which the students found important. Overall, the revised version of the wiki task turned out to be very successful in promoting online interactions. While the first two design cycles in the current research project have essentially replicated previous research as far as online interactions were concerned (Karasavvidis 2010a, b, 2011), the findings from the third design cycle indicate that the modified task led to increased levels of online interaction using student discussions as a criterion measure. This finding is very important because the literature suggests that students neither favor nor engage in wiki-based online interactions (Carr et al. 2007; Ma and Yuen 2008; Ravid et al. 2008; Elgort et al. 2008; Wheeler et al. 2008). What remains problematic, however, is the small number of students who participated in those discussions. Despite the considerable progress made in terms of online interactions in the third design cycle, their scale was fairly limited due to the small number of participating students. It is quite possible that all the other students who did not actively contribute also benefited from reading these discussions. Ideally, however, we would expect most – if not all – students to be actively involved in online discussions and this was not the pattern observed in the third design cycle.

To conclude, new tools create new opportunities for learning as well as new forms of learning. However, this potential for learning can not be realized in void: new tasks, activities, and practices are required to promote these new learning forms. Wikis afford new types of learning practices but there is a knowledge gap regarding such practices. The present paper attempted to fill this niche by exploring how a wiki task can be designed to promote student participation, collaboration and online interaction. The progressive refinement of the wiki task led to considerable improvements in terms of student participation and online interaction. However, it was less effective in terms of promoting online collaboration. While this is undoubtedly a small step forward, it falls short of realizing wikis' learning potential. Participation might be easier to address compared to online collaboration and interaction. Consequently, it appears that integrating wikis in education is more challenging than it was initially anticipated (Dohn 2009; Karasavvidis 2010b). Thus, more systematic research is required to determine how to achieve higher levels of online collaboration and interaction. Based on the success of discussions in the third design cycle, adapting the wiki task in a more discursive direction is a promising starting point.

References

Barab, S., & Squire, K. (2004). Design-based research: Putting a stake in the ground. *The Journal of the Learning Sciences*, 13(1), 1–14.

Bruns, A., & Humphreys, S. (2005). Wikis in teaching and assessment: The M/Cyclopedia project. *Proceedings of the ACM WikiSym 05: International Symposium on Wikis* (pp. 25–32). San Diego, CA.

Carr, T., Morrison, A., Cox, G., & Deacon, A. (2007). Weathering wikis: Net-based learning meets political science in a South African university. *Computers and Composition*, 24(3), 266–284.

Choy, S.O., & Ng, K.C. (2007). Implementing wiki software for supplementing on-line learning. *Australasian Journal of Educational Technology*, 23(2), 209–226.

Cobb, P., Confrey, J., diSessa, A., Lehrer, R., & Schauble, L. (2003). Design experiments in educational research. *Educational Researcher*, 32(1), 9–13.

Cole, M. (2008). Using wiki technology to support student engagement: Lessons from the trenches. *Computers & Education*, 52(1), 141–146.

Collins, A., Joseph, D., & Bielaczyc, K. (2004). Design Research: Theoretical and Methodological Issues. *The Journal of the Learning Sciences*, 13(1), 15–42.

Dohn, B. N. (2009). Web 2.0: Inherent tensions and evident challenges for education. *Computer Supported Collaborative Learning*, 4, 343–363.

Elgort, I., Smith, A.G., & Toland, J. (2008). Is wiki an effective platform for group course work? *Australasian Journal of Educational Technology*, 24(2), 195–210.

Guzdial, M., Rick, J., & Kehoe, C. (2001). Beyond adoption to invention: Teacher-created collaborative activities in higher education. *The Journal of the Learning Sciences*, 10(3), 265–279.

Hoadley, C.M. (2004). Methodological alignment in design-based research. *Educational Psychologist*, 39(4), 203–212.

Karasavvidis, I. (2010a). Wiki uses in higher education: exploring barriers to successful implementation. *Interactive Learning Environments*, 18(3), 219–231.

Karasavvidis, I. (2010b). Understanding wikibook-based tensions in higher education: an activity theory approach. *E-Learning and Digital Media*, 7(4), 386–394.

Karasavvidis, I. (2011). *The development and refinement of a wiki task: a design study*. Manuscript submitted for publication.

Kim, H.N. (2008). The phenomenon of blogs and theoretical model of blog use in educational contexts. *Computers & Education*, 51, 1342–1352.

Laurillard, D. (2009). The pedagogical challenges to collaborative technologies. *Computer Supported Collaborative Learning*, 4, 5–20.

Lund, A., & Smördal, O. (2006). Is there a space for the teacher in a wiki?. In D. Riehle & J. Noble (eds.), *Proceedings of the 2006 International Symposium on Wikis -WikiSym '06* (pp. 37–46). New York: ACM Press.

Ma, W.W-K., & Yuen, A.H-K. (2007). Learning news writing using emergent collaborative writing technology wiki. In J. Fong, F. L. Wang (eds), *Blended Learning. Workshop on Blended Learning* (pp. 303–314), Edinburgh, United Kingdom: Pearson.

Ma, W.W-K., & Yuen, A.H.K. (2008). A qualitative analysis on collaborative learning experience of student journalists using wiki. In J. Fong, Reggie, K. Wang, Fu Lee, W.F. (eds.), *Hybrid Learning and Education. Proceedings of the first International Conference on Hybrid Learning* (pp. 103–114), *Lecture Notes in Computer Science 5169*. Berlin: Springer-Verlag.

Mason. R., & Rennie, F. (2008). *E-learning and social networking handbook: resources for higher education*. London: Routledge.

Minocha, S., & Thomas, P. G. (2007). Collaborative learning in a wiki environment: Experiences from a software engineering course. *New Review of Hypermedia and Multimedia*, 13(2), 187–209.

Nicol, D., Littlejohn, A., & Grierson, H. (2005). The importance of structuring information and resources within shared workspaces during collaborative design learning. *Open Learning*, 20(1), 31–49.

O'Reilly, T. (2005). *What Is Web 2.0 Design Patterns and Business Models for the Next Generation of Software*. Retrieved 20 March 2009 from http://www.oreillynet.com/pub/a/oreilly/tim/news/2005/09/30/what-is-web-20.html.

Palloff, R.M., & Pratt, K. (2007). *Building on-line learning communities: effective strategies for the virtual classroom*. San Francisco: John Wiley & sons.

Raman, M., Ryan, T., & Olfman, L. (2005). Designing knowledge management systems for performance and satisfaction within a wiki environment. *Journal of Information Systems Education*, 16(3), 311–320.

Ras, E. Carbon, R. Decker, B., & Rech, J. (2007). Experience management wikis for reflective practice in software capstone projects. *IEEE Transactions on Education*, 50(4), 312–320.

Ravid, G., Kalman, Y.M., & Rafaeli, S. (2008). Wikibooks in higher education: Empowerment through on-line distributed collaboration. *Computers in Human Behavior*, 24(5), 1913–1928.

Rick, J., & Guzdial, M. (2006). Situating CoWeb: a scholarship of application. *Computer Supported Collaborative Learning*, 1(1), 89–115.

Surowiecki, J. (2004). *The wisdom of crowds: Why the many are smarter than the few and how collective wisdom shapes business, economies, societies and nations*. Anchor.

Tapscott, D., & Williams, A.D. (2006). *Wikinomics: how mass collaboration changes everything*. NY: Penguin.

The Design-Based Research Collective (2003). Design-based research: An emerging paradigm for educational inquiry. *Educational Researcher*, 32(1), 5–8.

Vratulis, V., & Dobson, T.M. (2008). Social negotiations in a wiki environment: a case study with pre-service teachers. *Educational Media International*, 45(4), 285–294.

West, J.A., & West, M.L. (2009). *Using wikis for on-line collaboration: the power of the read-write web*. San Francisco: Jossey-Bass.

Wheeler, S. (2009). Learning space mashups: Combining Web 2.0 tools to create collaborative and reflective learning spaces. *Future Internet*, 1, 3–13.

Wheeler, S., & Wheeler, D. (2009). Using wikis to promote quality learning in teacher training. *Learning, Media and Technology*, 34(1), 1–10.

Wheeler, S., Yeomans, P., & Wheeler, D. (2008). The good, the bad and the wiki: Evaluating student-generated content for collaborative learning. *British Journal of Educational Technology*, 39(6), 987–995.

Educational Blogging: Developing and Investigating a Students' Community of Inquiry

Sophia Angelaina and Athanassios Jimoyiannis

Introduction

During the last decade, Web 2.0 applications, including blogs, wikis, social networking, social bookmarking, media sharing, podcasting, etc., have received intense and growing educational and research interest (Clark et al. 2009; Ravenscroft 2009; Schroeder et al. 2010). It is widely considered that Web 2.0 applications, while not designed specifically for educational purposes, have a number of affordances that provide multiple opportunities for shared content and resources, self-directed learning, collaborative learning, ubiquitous and lifelong learning. The emerged socially based technologies of the Web 2.0 have the potential to offer enhanced learning opportunities and support students' participation in effective task-oriented personal learning spaces independent of physical, geographic, and institutional boundaries (Hall 2009; McLoughlin and Lee 2010).

Among Web 2.0 tools, blogs constitute a new content sharing and development environment supporting students' engagement, communication, interaction, collaboration, and collective intelligence. During the last years, educational blogs have captured the interest and the imagination of both educators and researchers including diverse learning groups, ranging from primary (Davis 2006; Tse et al. 2010) and secondary education (Angelaina and Jimoyiannis 2009) to higher education (Lin and Yuan 2006; Deng and Yuen 2010; Tan et al. 2010; Xie et al. 2008) and teachers' professional development as well (Loving et al. 2007; Makri and Kynigos 2007).

Literature review on educational blogging revealed a lack of a complete and consistent framework for studying and assessing students' engagement and the impact of blogging on students' learning. Farmer (2004) and Cameron and Anderson (2006) have proposed the application of the Community of Inquiry (CoI) model (Garrison et al. 2000, 2001) to blogging activities by comparing blogs' features with

S. Angelaina • A. Jimoyiannis (✉)
Department of Social and Educational Policy, University of Peloponnese, Korinthos, Greece
e-mail: ajimoyia@uop.gr

A. Jimoyiannis (ed.), *Research on e-Learning and ICT in Education*,
DOI 10.1007/978-1-4614-1083-6_13,

those of threaded discussions. However, there is not sufficient research evidence on the efficacy and the applicability of the CoI model in educational blogs. This study aims to contribute to the literature regarding the qualitative analysis of students' processes that take place in educational blogging and the evaluation of their learning experience using the framework of CoI. Twenty-one students (15 years old), coming from two K-9 classes in Greece, were involved in an educational blog which served as a project-based learning environment. The results showed that the students in the sample were made to participate actively by creating a blog CoI and learning.

Educational Blogging

The common use of blogs is for personal online journals. However, it is their open and user friendly format, and the many features incorporated such as post and commentaries organization, taglines, permanent links, etc., which have largely dominated the discussion about the educational blogs and their potential for teaching and learning. Educational blogs are currently gaining in popularity in schools and higher education institutions and they are widely promoted as collaborative tools supporting students' active learning.

It is widely considered that through well-designed educational blogs, both tutors and learners are becoming empowered, motivated, more reflective, and interactive practitioners in new learning environments. The emerging educational applications of blogs are based on their characteristics, as they are *open*, *interactive,* and *easy to create and use environments* which

- Incorporate *content posts* (often involving text, pictures, graphics, and hyperlinks) with *commentaries* to these posts, usually presented in reverse chronological order; thus a blog can work both as a personal and a group publishing area, in which every participant can exchange and share ideas, insights, comments, and recommendations with fellows.
- Provide *organized links* to recommendations of favorite or suggested websites, blogs, content resources, and events; in other words, a blog can act as a powerful personal learning portal.
- Have strong archival features; posts are automatically archived and the content is easily searchable and retrievable. Moreover, posts are syndicated using a variety of XML based standards (RSS or Atom feeds); readers interested can subscribe and be alerted to new content or discussions that have been added to the blog.

The characteristics above determine the pedagogical affordances of blogs, since they could

- Support enhanced participation and communication opportunities, promoting individual as well as group reflection on learning experiences
- Offer up-to-date information regarding changes in collaborative spaces and extend learning beyond the classroom
- Offer enhanced opportunities for collaborative content creation and, consequently, for collaborative knowledge construction

- Support authentic learning tasks through peer assessment and formative evaluation of student work
- Support blended learning activities by effectively changing the boundaries between school and formal learning; nonformal and informal learning

Since blogging enables users to exchange ideas and to share experiences and content, blogs can be an ideal environment for social constructivist learning. As a result of these communicative and collaborative attributes, blogs have been used in educational settings in many different ways, aiming at various educational objectives. Literature review suggested a growing interest in educational blogs use within the context of open learning environments. Blogs can serve in multiple ways, as an online course management tool, a discussion forum, an e-portfolio, a group blogging space, and a project-based learning environment. However, most applications of blogs in educational practice make worthy more than one of the aspects above.

Blog as Online Course Management Tool

This type of blog aims to support class work in both formal and non formal ways. The instructor posts assignments, announcements, information, and summaries of lessons. For instance, students share their learning experiences and express their thoughts to the instructor and peers through course blogs. Alternatively, a weekly topic is posted and each student posts her/his thoughts on the topic, as an assignment by the instructor. Students post examples and exercises related to course assignments as well as discuss reflections on course materials. In addition, blogs of this format could facilitate extended discussions beyond the classroom sessions. In their study Lin and Yuan (2006) followed a similar approach, where a blog was used as a reflective learning platform by engineering students.

Blog as Discussion Forum

The blog acts as a forum where students discuss and exchange information related to the course's subject, lectures, announces, and readings as well (Makri and Kynigos 2007). In addition, they can share and exchange information, thoughts and ideas on what they are learning. Yang (2009) reports on the use of a blog, created by two instructors, as a discussion forum in Taiwan. English student teachers made use of the blog as a platform to discuss about teaching theories and to critically reflect on their learning processes. In the context of teacher education, Deng and Yuen (2010) have proposed an empirically grounded framework for educational blogging that highlights four areas: self-expression, self-reflection, social interaction, and reflective dialogue. Ebner et al. (2010) investigated the use of microblogs (blogs via web interfaces and mobile devices, which are restricted to posts having up to 140 characters) and concluded that microblogging should be seen as a completely new form of communication that can support informal learning beyond classrooms.

Blog as E-Portfolio

The idea is that students set up their own blog according to the teacher assignments and guidelines; every student posts to the blog his classroom and/or homework writing assignments, tasks, and exercises. The teacher monitors students' progress and development, supports them to overcome cognitive difficulties and problems encountered, and, finally, assess the student submissions into the blog. In addition, students can share their blogs with peers in their class and receive commentaries through the comments section of their blog. Carroll et al. (2006) have developed and used an e-learning system that couples a blog with an e-portfolio component. The evaluation results showed that the integrated blogging application allowed students to assemble, reflect, and publish content for their course tasks and supported reflective learning. Blogs were effectively used in a second year university class of German language to support students' reflection on topical issues and peer-feedback on writing (Dippold 2009). Students needed to complete on their blogs a series of written tasks set by the tutor while some components were commented on by their peers and the tutor. In a case study, Farmer et al. (2008) used a trial blogging as a formative assessment exercise integrated into a first year university subject about cultural studies. The students were asked to maintain a blog throughout the 12 weeks of the semester, to reflect upon and discuss course content and/or issues that arose out of their learning experiences.

Group Blogging

Group blogging is a relatively new form of learning activity where the blog acts more as a collective or collaborative space than as an individual one. In a group blogging activity class students are divided into groups. All students in each group are expected to contribute consistently to their own group blog. The various blogs are connected and students could also post their comments to the other blogs. A case study on higher education students indicated that the incorporation of group blogging and social networking technologies within a well structured, but flexible learning environment, supports group work and creative learning processes (Philip and Nicholls 2009). Another study on group blogging, used a communities of practice philosophy to support peer assisted learning (Ladyshewsky and Gardner 2008).

Blog as a Project-Based Learning Environment

Blogs can be used as collaborative content sharing spaces to support project-based learning activities. Poling (2005) engaged elementary students from different classes in a cooperative project about natural environment. Through the blog, the students shared their reflections, completed a writing project, read, and commented on other students' posts. In a similar study, secondary education students from two different classes collaborated through a blog to implement a long-term project about the issues of doping and using drugs by athletes to improve their performance in sports (Angelaina and Jimoyiannis 2009). The analysis of students' cognitive presence, ideas sharing and debating showed that educational blogs could be effective tools to support collaborative construction of knowledge.

Blog as a Research Tool

Properly designed blogs can be used as a powerful tool supporting academic research. Blogs can constitute a platform for ongoing literature review for academic purposes (Mejias 2006). Recently, in the context of a large undergraduate lecture course in nutrition, Paulus and Spence (2010) used blogging groups to promote student learning and conceptual change through reflection and interaction in blog conversations. They found that the blog conversations were very useful to the instructors as a source of data on students' understandings and misconceptions of course topics. These misconceptions could then be addressed with further instruction.

Community of Inquiry in Educational Blogs

CoI was initially developed as a conceptual framework to guide the research and practice of collaborative learning in online environments, at first asynchronous discussion forums (Garrison et al. 2000, 2001; Garrison and Anderson 2003). The origin of CoI model was grounded in Vygotsky's theory of social construction of knowledge (1978) and the practical inquiry and critical thinking model of Dewey. The notion was also built on the important work of Henri (1992) who turned attention in online learning research to the cognitive dimension. Combining both the empirical data regarding process evaluation and learning design in online learning environments, the CoI framework could be used to define, identify and measure three constitutional elements (components) in an e-learning experience, namely the *social presence*, *teaching presence,* and *cognitive presence*. In addition, CoI model determines categories and indicators to define, identify and measure each presence in an educational blog community. Figure 1 represents the basic components and the consequent CoI indicators describing the interrelations between social, teaching, and cognitive presence, when educational blogs are used as collaborative learning environments.

The CoI analysis framework of the blogging activities includes

- Three indicators of social presence in educational blogs, e.g., *open communication*, *emotional expression*, and *group cohesion*

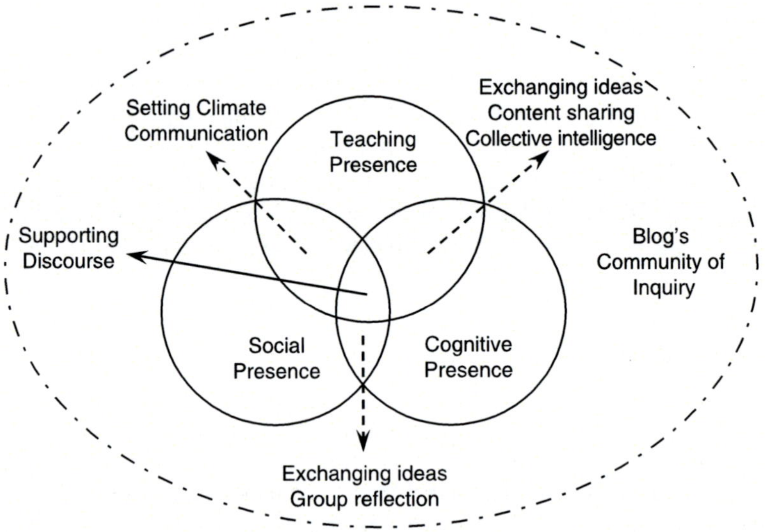

Fig. 1 Community of Inquiry (CoI) in educational blogs (adapted from Garrison et al. 2000)

- Four indicators essential to describe cognitive presence, e.g., *triggering*, *exploration*, *integration* and *resolution*
- Three indicators describing teaching presence, e.g., activities related to *instructional design and organization*, *facilitating discourse* and *direct instruction*

Cameron and Anderson (2006) first suggested the application CoI model to the design of educational blogging activities. Their main idea was to compare the features of blogs with those of threaded discussions. This study reports on the application CoI model as an analysis framework of students' engagement and presence in an educational blog-based project. Our work expands the initial CoI analysis and focuses specifically on comparing the educational affordances of blogs with those of asynchronous discussions, within which the CoI model was developed. The key idea is that an educational blog integrates a *content space* and a *discussion space*, both developed in a collaborative manner. In this paper we build on our earlier work and analysis on the use of blogs as tools to create a CoI (Angelaina and Jimoyiannis 2009).

Methodology

Design of the Educational Blog

The educational blog was designed by the authors and implemented at the first Gymnasium (lower secondary school) of Argos, Greece, in the context of the ICT subject during the year 2009–2010. Using a project-based learning approach, the blog was designed and evolved for a period of 10 weeks, as an obligatory project according to the K-9 computer science (informatics) curriculum. The main objectives were

- To engage students (15 years old) in a cross-thematic large-scale learning activity
- To integrate content knowledge from different subject areas, e.g., chemistry, biology, environmental and social sciences
- To support collaborative work and reflection between students
- To develop ICT literacy skills, namely information access, managing, integration, evaluation and, communication skills

This blog-based learning activity followed a blended learning philosophy by including classroom sessions and face-to-face discussions between the teacher and the students, individual and collaborative online work in the computer lab, and online homework (information seeking through suggested resources from the Internet, peer communication, exchanging ideas, and content information etc.). The students were independently directed to a theme coming from science education, considering it close to their interests. After debating and exchanging ideas in the classroom, with the guidance of their ICT and chemistry teachers, the students agreed and decided to investigate the "Acid Rain" problem through their class blog.

The students in the sample, though familiar with using computers and the Web, had no previous experience with educational blogs and blogging, in general. The first author was the class instructor, and the discussion facilitator in both cases (classroom and blog). Initially, he presented various types of blogs to help students understand what a blog is, how one can use it and participate in, what are the differences between posts and commentaries etc. The students were asked to reflect upon and discuss about content and/or other themes that would arise into the class blog. They were free to use the blog in any way they wish but they needed to post regularly (at least once a week on average) and to interact with other students' posts through their comments and content posts. They were informed that their active participation in the blog would be graded for the ICT course.

The Procedure

The sample included 21 students (9 boys and 12 girls) of K-9 grade from two different classes participating into the blog. The students were informed of the guidelines and details of the study in the first class meeting. They were also informed that their posts would be transcribed, that individual student identities would not be used in the analysis, that the results of the analysis available would contain no student identification, and that the analysis would have no impact on their grades.

The students were engaged into the blog not only during the ICT sessions, from the computer lab area, but also in time and place outside school, as observed from the posts details (date and time). Complete texts of posts were extracted from the blog. The data under analysis concern a time period of 9 weeks, from February to April 2010. The transcripts were analyzed using the coding scheme described in the next section.

Table 1 Blog's community of inquiry

Elements	Number of publications	Indicators		Number of publications
Social presence	22	Open communication		15
		Emotional expression		3
		Group cohesion		4
Cognitive presence	95	Triggering		14
		Exploration	Personal view	2
			Explanation	36
			Scientific knowledge	18
		Integration	Synthesis	15
			Conclusion	10
Teaching presence	14	Design and organization		1
		Facilitating discourse		7
		Direct instruction		6

Content Analysis

Content analysis was based on existing procedures used in analyzing asynchronous discussions (Gunawardena et al. 1997). Every publication on the blog is considered as the unit of analysis. Students' contributions to the blog were divided into:

(a) *Content posts*, which included content information (e.g., text, photo, visual, audio, video)
(b) *Commentaries*, which typically were publications in text format concerning questions, replies, new ideas, or comments to previous content posts

Presentation of Results

A total of 131 publications were uploaded on the blog during the investigation period; 39 content posts and 92 commentaries. The content posts uploaded were divided as following: 10 in photo format, 16 in text format, 5 in both photo and text format, and 8 in video (most of them were links to YouTube). Every publication was classified in elements and categories according to the CoI model, as shown in Table 1.

The CoI analysis showed that students, in general, were successfully engaged into the blog contributing with content posts and commentaries to their peer posts. There were differences in the number of posts and commentaries each student uploaded and the consequent learning profile into the blog. Table 2 shows the number of posts and commentaries for each member (students and teacher) in the community of blog.

Table 2 Posts and comments for each member in the community of blog

CoI member[a]	S1	S2	S3	S4	S5	S6	S7	S8	S9	S10	S11
Posts	12	1	2	1	1	3	2	2	4	–	–
Comments	2	13	3	6	12	1	6	5	6	3	4

CoI member	S12	S13	S14	S15	S16	S17	S18	S19	S20	S21	T
Posts	–	1	1	2	–	1	1	1	1	–	3
Comments	2	5	1	6	2	1	8	–	–	–	6

[a]S = Student; T = teacher

Social Presence

Social presence in online learning has been described as the ability of learners to express themselves socially and emotionally (Arbaugh 2007). There were 22 publications attributed in this category. These posts include no content information and were classified in the following categories (indicators): *emotional expression*, *open communication,* and *group cohesion*. The students used expressions similar to that in face-to-face discussions improving group cohesion, and suggested ideas supporting and enhancing dialogue. In Table 3 characteristic transcript examples of students' posts are presented. The collaborative aspects of blogging activities are expected to offer opportunities to the learners for enhanced social presence and sense of online community, which also tends to enhance their satisfaction and improve the socio-emotional climate.

Cognitive Presence

Cognitive presence includes 95 publications in total, describing the extent to which learners are able to construct and confirm meaning through sustained reflection and discourse (Garrison et al. 2001). The CoI model defines four phases essential to describe and understand cognitive presence in an educational blog.

The starting-developmental phase of the blog reflects the initiation of critical inquiry and is considered as the triggering event. In *triggering category* were classified 14 publications, which pose either a question or start a dialogue between the students. An issue, question, or problem that emerges from instruction, experience or school life is identified and recognized. In conventional educational contexts, the initial generation of topics is usually directed by the teacher who assigns or communicates learning challenges and tasks. However, most triggering events were purposively or indirectly added from the students to support discourse acting as members of the blog community.

Table 3 Coding scheme for blog's CoI

Elements	Indicators	Transcript examples
Social presence	Open communication	"My friend, it would be better if you had posted a video in Greek, not in German…"
	Emotional expression	"Very nice video. One can easily understand the problem… Congratulations!"
	Group cohesion	"S1 can you explain what is this picture about?"
Cognitive presence	Triggering	"… Why are nitrogen and sulphur oxides responsible for the acid rain since they do not contain hydrogen?"
		"… Since we have analyzed the problem of acid rain it would be better to discuss about solutions. What every one can do about this problem…"
	Exploration	
	Personal view	"…This photo shows that the major factor producing this problem is the gases coming from the industries…"
	Explanation	"Acid rain has negative consequences not only to monuments but to the environment we live as well… In this picture we can see what happens in the river when acid rain falls. It is dying because nitrogen oxide is increased and no plants, animals or fishes can live…"
	Scientific knowledge	"Acid rain is the result of the reaction of sulphur dioxide (SO_2) and nitrogen oxide with carbon hydrogen in the clouds. This reaction creates sulphur and nitrogen acid. Sulphur dioxide comes from metal industries, electric production industries and diesel cars. Nitrogen oxides are produced from the same industries and benzene cars"
	Integration	
	Synthesis	"Some other consequences are: a) reduction of agricultural production, b) increase of temperature during summer (burning heat), c) problems in tourist industry etc."
	Conclusions	"We have already mentioned some solutions regarding the problem of acid rain but I want to summarize: a) placing special filters to the industries chimneys and cars, b) using air and solar energy instead carbon and petroleum"
Teaching presence	Design and organization	"Last decades the phenomenon of acid rain is a serious environmental problem and many governments, organisations and civilians try to find solutions. At first you can explain what acid rain is?"
	Facilitating discourse	"Can you explain why a river dies of the acid rain?"
	Direct instruction	"S7, the last photo you have uploaded is not the Parthenon!"

In *exploration category* 56 publications were classified. Indicative transcripts are given in Table 3. Through these posts the students expressed a personal view, based on pre-existing knowledge, exchanged ideas and information, and gave an explanation or a new approach based on the scientific knowledge they developed. At the end of this phase, students begin to be selective with regard to what is relevant to the issue. The asynchronous nature of blogs allowed students to explore a topic before responding by looking back at archived posts and reflect on posts and commentaries provided by their peers and the instructor.

In *integration category* we have classified 25 publications that represent *synthesis of ideas* or *conclusions* formulated through the dialogue (Table 3). Once students had the opportunity, in the exploratory phase, to investigate and reflect on the topic, they were able to construct meaning through a continually evolving process of reflection and interaction. Integration phase requires active teaching presence to diagnose students' misconceptions, to provide scaffolding and comments, and to effectively support students' cognitive development and critical thinking.

According to the CoI model, the ultimate phase of students' development and progression (*resolution phase*) requires clear expectations and opportunities to apply newly created knowledge (Garrison and Arbaugh 2007). Normally, the results of the resolution phase lead to further problems and new triggering events, thus causing the process to start over. This phase was not easy to be covered since this blog was not designed to cover this particular objective. Previous studies on the CoI model with regards to asynchronous online discussions, showed a relative low rate of the resolution phase and students' difficulties to move toward higher cognitive and inquiry levels, e.g., integration and resolution (Meyer 2003; Luebeck and Bice 2005; Vaughan and Garrison 2005; Garrison and Arbaugh 2007).

Teaching Presence

There were 14 publications in the blog identified as teaching presence posts. Most of them, mainly originated from the teacher, were *direct instructions* and interventions aiming to *facilitate students' discourse*. The teacher facilitation posts appeared on the blog when the students completed dialogue on a specific topic; the aim was to support students' deriving conclusions and movement to the next topic. In a couple of cases the students exhibited a kind of teaching presence by sending specific commentaries (see Table 3).

Teaching presence is not identical to teacher presence while it fundamentally differentiates formal education from online learning environments like blogs. In blogging activities, teacher presence is expected much less tangible, since focus of individual postings may diffuse beyond the topics instigated by the teacher and the challenge of effective aggregation may mean that not all students are following and reading teacher posts and comments to the posts of others (Cameron and Anderson 2006).

Conclusions

The study presented in this paper reported on the investigation of students' engagement in an educational blog established as a project-based learning environment. The findings clearly have shown that integration of ideas and construction of meaning is directly inferred from students' participation in the CoI of the blog. Despite that the students had no previous experience in using blogs; they demonstrated enhanced interest for the project and willingness to participate in the blog activities (content and resources sharing, ideas interchanging, discussion topics, etc.). Students provided one another with social and emotional support which created a CoI continuously growing and evolving through collaboration, dialogue and encouraging students' autonomy as self-directed learners.

A unique feature of blogs is that they enable both individual reflection and peer interaction. Using a blended learning philosophy to design and implement blog-based learning activities seems to be a promising choice resulting in wider use of blogs in the context of secondary and higher education as well. The present study showed evidence that project-based blogs can support online learning groups where students are able to share content and ideas, and construct knowledge within a supportive CoI. Properly designed blogs can extend students' learning space beyond the classroom boundaries to home or personal environments, and combine formal, non formal, and informal learning. It is hoped that the CoI framework of analysis will aid educators and instructional designers to determine best practices on using blogs to enhance students' engagement, communication, and learning.

The investigation presented here has the ambition to deepen existing knowledge and give promising results on the educational affordances of educational blogs. Our future research is directed to the issues of pedagogical design of educational blogs and the consequent teachers' scaffolding strategies in order to support students' engagement, presentation and interchange of ideas, collaborative and reflective thinking.

References

Angelaina, S., & Jimoyiannis, A. (2009). The educational blog as a tool for social construction of knowledge: Analysis of students' cognitive presence. In Kariotoglou P., Spyrtou A., & Zoupidis A. (Eds.), *Proceedings of the 6th Panhellenic Conference "Teaching Sciences and New Technologies in Education"* (pp. 137–145). Florina (in Greek).

Arbaugh, J. B. (2007). An empirical verification of the Community of Inquiry framework. *Journal of Asynchronous Learning Networks*, 11, 73–85.

Cameron, D., & Anderson, T. (2006). Comparing weblogs to threaded discussion tools in online educational contexts. *International Journal of Instructional Technology and Distance Learning*, Retrieved 27 October 2010 from http://www.itdl.org/Journal/Nov_06/article01.htm.

Carroll, N. L., Calvo, R. A., & Markauskaite, L. (2006). E-portfolios and blogs: Online tools for giving young engineers a voice. *Proceedings of the 7th International Conference on Information Technology Based Higher Education and Training*, Institute of Electrical and Electronics Engineers, Sydney.

Clark, W., Logan, K., Luckin, R., Mee, A., & Oliver, M. (2009). Beyond Web 2.0: mapping the technology landscapes of young learners. *Journal of Computer Assisted Learning*, 25, 56–69.

Davis, A. (2006). Thinking and writing wrinkles bloggers. *Learning Technology Newsletter*, 8(4), 9–10, IEEE Computer Society.

Deng, L., & Yuen, A. H. K. (2010). Towards a framework for educational affordances of blogs. *Computers & Education*, 56, 441–451.

Dippold, D. (2009). Peer feedback through blogs: Student and teacher perceptions in an advanced German class, *ReCALL*, 21(1), 18–36.

Ebner, M., Lienhardt, C., Rohs, M. & Meyer, I. (2010). Microblogs in Higher Education – A chance to facilitate informal and process-oriented learning?. *Computers & Education*, 55, 92–100.

Farmer, B., Yue, A., & Brooks, C. (2008). Using blogging for higher order learning in large cohort university teaching: A case study. *Australasian Journal of Educational Technology*, 24(2), 123–136.

Farmer, J. (2004). Communication dynamics: Discussion boards, weblogs and the development of communities of inquiry in online learning environments. Retrieved 27 October 2010 from http://incsub.org/blog/2004/communication-dynamics-discussion-boards-weblogs-and-the-development-of-communities-of-inquiry-in-online-learning-environments.

Garrison, D. R., & Anderson, T. (2003). *E-Learning in the 21st century: A framework for research and practice*. London: Routledge/Falmer.

Garrison, D. R., & Arbaugh, J. B. (2007). Researching the community of inquiry framework: Review, issues and future directions. *The Internet and Higher Education*, 10(2), 157–172.

Garrison, R., Anderson, T., & Archer, W. (2000). Critical thinking in a text-based environment: Computer conferencing in higher education. *The Internet and Higher Education*, 2(2-3), 87–105.

Garrison, D. R., Anderson, T., & Archer, W. (2001). Critical thinking, cognitive presence and computer conferencing in distance education. *American Journal of Distance Education*, 5(1), 7–23.

Gunawardena, C. N., Lowe, C. A., & Anderson T. A. (1997). Analysis of a global online debate and the development of an interaction analysis model for examining social construction of knowledge in computer conferencing. *Journal of Educational Computing Research*. 17(4), 397–431.

Hall, R. (2009). Towards a fusion of formal and informal learning environments: the impact of the read/write Web. *Electronic Journal of e-Learning*, 7(1), 29–40.

Henri, F. (1992). Computer conferencing and content analysis. In A. R. Kaye (ed.), *Collaborative learning through computer conferencing: The Najaden papers* (pp. 117-136). Springer-Verlag, Berlin.

Ladyshewsky, R. K., & Gardner, P. (2008). Peer assisted learning and blogging: A strategy to promote reflective practice during clinical fieldwork. *Australasian Journal of Educational Technology*, 24(3), 241–257.

Lin, H. T., & Yuan, S. M. (2006). Taking blog as a platform of learning reflective journal. *ICWL, 2006*, 38–47.

Loving, C. C., Schroeder, C., Kang, R., Shimek, C., & Herbert, B. (2007). Blogs: enhancing links in a professional learning community of science and mathematics teachers. *Contemporary Issues in Technology and Teacher Education*, 7(3), 178–198.

Luebeck, J. L. & Bice, L. R. (2005). Online discussion as a mechanism of conceptual change among mathematics and science teachers. *Journal of Distance Education,* 20(2), 21–39.

Makri, K., & Kynigos, C. (2007). The role of blogs in studying the discourse and social practices of mathematics teachers. *Educational Technology & Society*, 10(1), 73–84.

McLoughlin, C., & Lee, M. J. W. (2010). Personalised and self-regulated learning in the Web 2.0 era: International exemplars of innovative pedagogy using social software. *Australasian Journal of Educational Technology*, 26(1), 28–43.

Mejias. U. A. (2006). The Blog as dissertation literature review?, Retrieved 26 October 2010 from http://blog.ulisesmejias.com/2006/01/25/the-blog-as-dissertation-literature-review.

Meyer, K. A. (2003). Face-to-face versus threaded discussions: The role of time and higher-order thinking. *Journal of Asynchronous Learning Networks,* 7(3), 55–65.

Paulus, T., & Spence, M. (2010). Using blogs to identify, misconceptions in a large undergraduate nutrition course. *TechTrends*, 54(5), 62–68.

Philip, R., & Nicholls, J. (2009). Group blogs: Documenting collaborative drama processes. *Australasian Journal of Educational Technology,* 25(5), 683–699.

Poling, C. (2005). Blog on building communication and collaboration among staff and students. *Learning & Leading with Technology, 32(6),* 12–15.

Ravenscroft, A. (2009). Social software, Web 2.0 and learning: status and implications of an evolving paradigm. *Journal of Computer Assisted Learning*, 25, 1–5.

Schroeder, A., Minocha, S., & Schneider C. (2010). The strengths, weaknesses, opportunities and threats of using social software in higher and further education teaching and learning. *Journal of Computer Assisted Learning*, 26, 159–174.

Tan, S. M., Ladyshewsky R. K., & Gardner P. (2010). Using blogging to promote clinical reasoning and metacognition in undergraduate physiotherapy fieldwork programs. *Australasian Journal of Educational Technology*, 26(3), 355–368.

Tse, S. K., Yuen, A. H. K., Loh, E. K. Y., Lam J. W. I., & Ng R. H. W. (2010). The impact of blogging on Hong Kong primary school students' bilingual reading literacy. *Australasian Journal of Educational Technology*, 26(2), 164–179.

Vaughan, N., & Garrison, D. R. (2005). Creating cognitive presence in a blended faculty development community. *Internet and Higher Education,* 8, 1–12.

Xie, Y., Ke, F., & Sharma, P. (2008). The effect of peer feedback for blogging on college students' reflective learning processes. *Internet and Higher Education*, 11, 18–25.

Yang, S.-H. (2009). Using blogs to enhance critical reflection and Community of Practice. *Educational Technology & Society*, 12(2), 11–21.

Experiencing 3d Simulated Space Through Different Perspectives

Maria Latsi and Chronis Kynigos

Theoretical Background

The contribution of technology to the teaching and learning of geometry is perceived to be strongly linked with interactivity, multiple interlinked representations, including symbolic ones, dynamic manipulations, and dynamic visualizations (Laborde et al. 2006). However, relatively little research has been carried out on the way the above distinct characteristics of digital media can be exploited so as to engage students in meaningful 3d geometry investigations. Aiming to understand the way in which students' intuitions and ideas concerning spatial visualization and thinking (Presmeg 2006; Arcavi 2003) are challenged in 3d digital media, we developed a set of microworlds and a set of activities adopting a constructionist theoretical perspective (Kafai and Resnick 1996). A distinct feature of the microworlds was that they were "half-baked" (Kynigos 2007), i.e., incomplete or buggy digital artifacts that students had to investigate how they work and to change and fix them.

Our pedagogical aim was to engage the students in navigating a moving entity, the turtle, to construct graphical digital objects through Logo programming and the dynamic manipulation of procedure variable values in a 3d simulated space. Research seems to conclude that carefully designed Logo-based microworlds are an effective medium in offering rich mathematical experiences and encouraging the construction of meaning in 2d through the turtle metaphor (Clements and Sarama 1997; Kynigos 1992). Navigating the turtle requires the formation of essentially novel methods of spatial orientation, where the reference point is not the position of the user's body but the turtle's body, relative to which the entire system of orientation may change. In this framework, body-syntonicity is a critical concept in 2d Turtle Geometry (Papert 1980) that refers: (a) to navigating the turtle by coordinating one's body-posture,

M. Latsi (✉) • C. Kynigos
School of Philosophy, National and Kapodistrian University of Athens, Athens, Greece
e-mail: mlatsi@ppp.uoa.gr

A. Jimoyiannis (ed.), *Research on e-Learning and ICT in Education*,
DOI 10.1007/978-1-4614-1083-6_14,

physically or imaginary, with the turtle-vehicle of motion and (b) to solving geometrical problems drawing upon ones embodied motional experiences.

Concurrently, students have to reconceptualize geometrical figures in terms of specific Logo commands, according to the distinct characteristics of Turtle Geometry (Papert 1980; Abelson and DiSessa 1981). Turtle geometry is based on a different geometrical system to those usually associated with the learning of geometry and it has been characterized as differential by Papert (1980) and as intrinsic by Abelson and DiSessa (1981) (see also Kynigos 1993). It is considered as differential since a given geometrical state of the turtle is fully defined by its relation to the turtle's immediately previous state. In a similar vein, it is characterized as intrinsic in the sense that there is no need to refer to places outside the turtle's immediate vicinity when deciding on an input to a procedure to change turtle's state. Recent extensions of Turtle Geometry in 3d space do not offer just a new perspective in the teaching and learning of geometry. New issues are raised related to the way the turtle metaphor is put to use and the way deeply rooted intuitions about experiencing space and locomotion can be exploited so as to make sense of geometric notions (Kynigos and Latsi 2007).

Recently there has been clear research interest on the perceptions students have in 3d virtual environments (Hauptman 2010) and the spatial dimensions of interactions though 3d avatars (Petrackou 2010). In mathematics education, these kinds of technological advances are investigated as far as their influences on students' learning are concerned (Hollebrands et al. 2008; Jones et al. 2010). However, to the best of our knowledge, there is little research on understandings formed by students using digital media, such as MachineLab Turtleworlds (MaLT), integrating symbolic Turtle Geometry with dynamic manipulation of the user's viewpoint of the 3d simulated space and the opportunities these media offer to revitalize the teaching of 3d geometry. The aim of our research was to investigate: (a) the way the students used the software's functionalities of changing viewpoints throughout the construction processes, (b) the interplay between the turtle metaphor and space visualization through various viewpoints, and (c) the interplay between the perception of figures considered in relation to different viewpoints and in relation to their geometric properties.

The Computational Environment

MaLT is a programmable environment for the creation and exploration of interactive virtual reality simulations developed within the ReMath project (ReMath 2005). MaLT was conceived as a constructionist microworld environment within MachineLab that extends the "Turtleworlds" turtle geometry to 3d geometrical space. Thus, an extension of Logo commands in 3d space is provided including the two conventional types of turtle turns (Reggini 1985): "uppitch/downpitch n degrees" (*up/dp n*), which pitches the turtle's nose up and down, and "leftroll/rightroll n degrees" (*lr/rr n*), which moves the turtle around its trunk/vertical axis. However, the distinct feature of MaLT is that the Logo-based Turtle Geometry is integrated with the dynamic

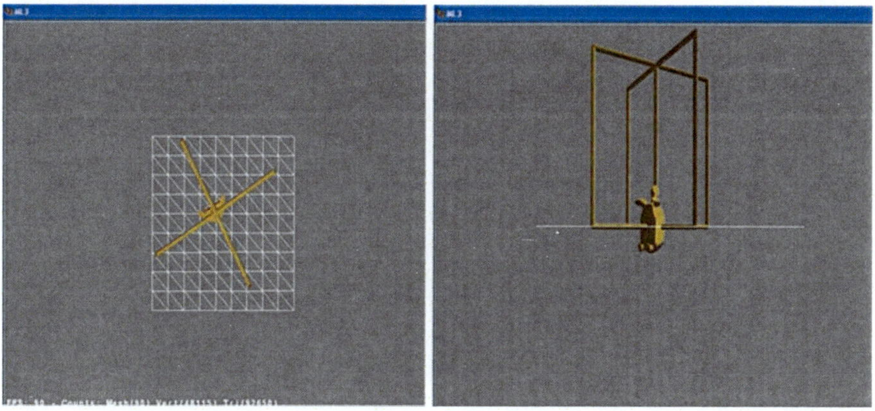

Fig. 1 The top–down and the side view of the simulated 3d space

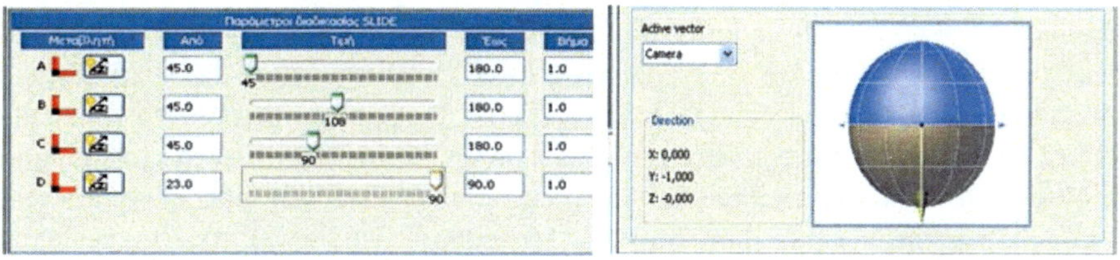

Fig. 2 The 1d variation tool on the *left* and the active vector tool on the *right*

manipulation of interactive graphical representations – a functionality characteristic of Dynamic Geometry Environments. In particular, the dynamic manipulation tools available can be divided in two categories:

- Dynamic manipulation of the viewpoint of the 3d space: (a) by using toolbar's buttons where the user can pick among three default views (front, side, top–down, as shown in Fig. 1) and (b) by manipulating through mouse a specially designed vector tool, called the active vector, where the user can define either camera's direction or camera's position (see Fig. 2).
- Dynamic manipulation of graphical figures by means of sequentially changing the variable values of the programs they create them through the use of specially designed variation tools (see Fig. 2).

Methodology

Espousing an interpretive approach in educational research (Cohen et al. 2007) in the study reported here we followed a design-based research method (Van Den Akker et al. 2006), which entailed the "engineering" of tools and task, as well as the systematic study of both the process of learning and the means of supporting it (Gravemeijer and Cobb 2006). A critical component of design-based research is that the design is conceived not just to meet local needs but to advance a theoretical agenda, to uncover, explore and confirm theoretical relationships, and to create new theoretically expressed understandings about areas for which little is known. Thus, the analysis we have carried out does not comprise any kind of quantification of qualitative data, but rather refers to a nonmathematical process of interpretation, carried out for the purpose of discovering concepts and relationships in raw data and then organizing these into a theoretical explanatory scheme.

The research took place in the sixth grade of a public primary school in Greece. The class consisted of 23 pupils, who had totally 16 45 min teaching sessions with the experimenting teacher over 2 months. The pupils worked collaboratively in mixed-gender groups of two or three in the school's computer laboratory. The tasks were designed to bring in the foreground issues concerning the mathematical nature of 3d geometrical objects through their dynamic manipulation and transformation in mathematically meaningful ways. In particular, we divided the activity sequence in two phases and we developed for each one of them a strand of two tasks. In task 1, the pupils were asked to navigate the turtle in such a way so as to simulate the take-off and the landing of an aircraft. In task 2 the pupils were asked to construct rectangles in at least two different planes of the graphical space of MaLT simulating the adjacent walls of a virtual room. In the second strand of activities, the pupils experimented with half-baked microwords. In particular, in task 3 the pupils were asked to use the 1d variation tool to control and experiment with the three variables that corresponded to different turtle turns in the half-baked microworld "Movedoor" (see Fig. 3), so as to create the simulation of a door opening and closing. The procedure was designed to have more than the variables needed. First the pupils had to decide what the role of each variable was and which values could be given to them. Then they had to build upon the half-baked microworld so as to develop a procedure that creates the simulation of a door opening and closing with the least possible variables.

In task 4, the pupils were asked to use the 1d variation tool to control the four variables corresponding to turtle turns in the "half-baked" microworld "Revolving door," so as to create the simulation of a revolving door (see Fig. 3). The procedure was designed to have more than the variables needed. First the pupils had to decide what the role of each variable was and which values could be given to them. Then, they had to build upon the half-baked microworld so as to develop a procedure that creates the simulation of a revolving door with the least possible variables. Finally, the pupils were asked to extend the procedure of the revolving door in order to create a simulation of the fan of a watermill. During the teaching sequence, the experimenting teacher intervened in the children's work by posing questions and encouraging them to clearly explain their ideas and strategies.

In order to describe the pupils' learning trajectories as they happened in real time, we adopted a participant observation methodology while the main corpus of data included video-recorded observational data, the experimenting teacher's observational notes as well as the sorting and archiving of the corpus of the pupils, work on and off computer. As far as the pupils' work on the computer is concerned we used a specially designed screen capture software – called Hypercam – which allowed us to record pupils' voices and at the same time to capture all their actions

```
to movedoor :a :b :c
uppitch(:a)
leftroll(:b)
repeat 2 [forward(7) right(:c) forward(4) right(:c)]
end
```

```
to revolving door :a :b :c :d
uppitch(:a)
leftroll(:b)
repeat 4 [repeat 2 [forward(7) right(:c) forward(4) rt(:c)] leftroll(:d)]
end
```

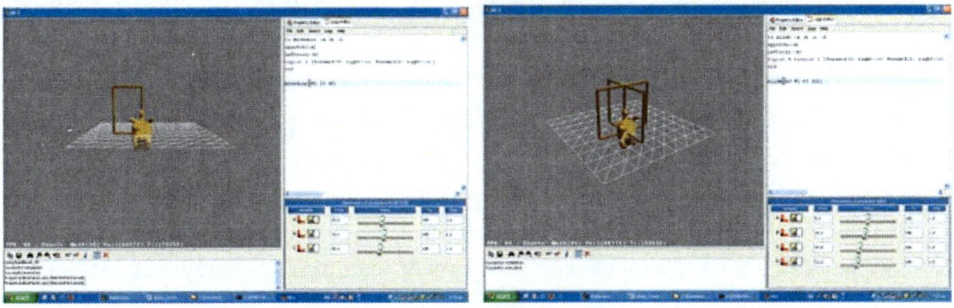

Fig. 3 The Logo code of the "Movedoor" and the "Revolving door" half-baked microworlds

on the screen. For the analysis we transcribed verbatim the audio recordings of all groups of pupils throughout the teaching sequence. Data were categorized in clusters of specific critical episodes that do not represent some quantifiable entity but are chosen to represent clearly the kind of activity that was going on in specific time in the classroom. The results presented here are based on the work of one group, consisted of one boy and one girl, and focusing on the way the viewpoint manipulation tools were used during the construction processes.

Construction Processes Through Different Perspectives

The analysis of our results has shown that the pupils' construction processes could be divided in two categories: construction processes through an intrinsic perspective and construction processes through an extrinsic perspective, depended on the point of focus and the way the simulated 3d space was experienced. This division rather reflects the two dominant perspectives people take on space (Tversky 2005); an external one when they observe space and they manipulate objects in it and an internal one when they explore an environment and when they navigate in it.

Construction Processes Through an Intrinsic Perspective

The results of the present research underline the importance of syntonizing one's body with the 3d turtle – vehicle of motion in the 3d simulated space. During the

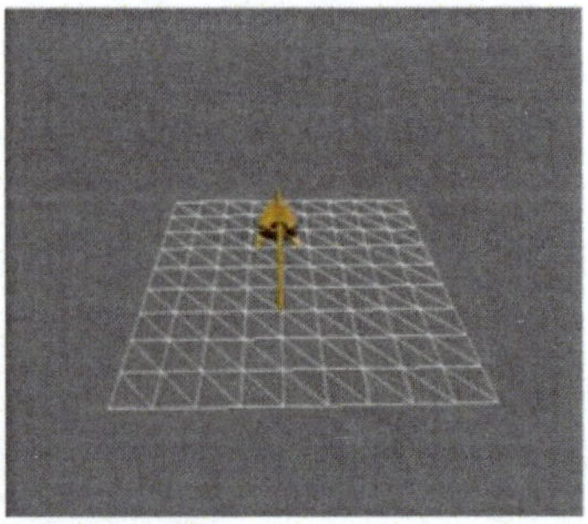

```
Uppitch(45)
Forward(2)
Downpitch(45)
Forward(2)
Downpitch(45)
Forward(2)
Uppitch(45)
```

Fig. 4 Simulating the take-off and landing of an aircraft along the *z* axis and the respective Logo code

construction processes of task 1 the pupils preferred "flying" the turtle along the *z* axis that gave the impression of depth, at a plane vertical to the display plane defined by the 2d computer screen. Moreover, they kept on working on the default front view (although slightly slanted through the use of the active vector manipulation tool) even though they did not have a clear representation of the turtle's journey (see Fig. 4).

It seems possible that the children preferred flying the turtle along the *z* axis (that gave the impression of depth) while viewing the simulated 3d space from the default front view since this way they could more easily coordinate the various frames of reference (Wickens et al. 2005) present. In order to drive the turtle in a body-syntonic way the pupils had to coordinate the following frames of reference: (a) the ego frame, defined in terms of the orientation of the trunk or location of the observer, (b) the display frame, defined in terms of the standard way of referring to things presented in the computer screen, where the right/left up/down directions are fixed, (c) the world frame, defined in terms of the fixed directions of "up" and "down," as a result of the gravitational effect, and (d) the vehicle frame of reference, defined in terms of the place and orientation of a moving entity, here the turtle.

Flying the turtle along the *z* axis, the orientation of the vehicle of motion, the turtle, coincided both with the orientation of the pupils' body in the lived-in 3d space and with the standard way of referring to the orientation of information on the computer screen as well as with the world frame of reference. The pupils' comments corroborate this result. When asked why they preferred this kind of flight they replied: "If we wanted to turn the turtle right or left, we could see from our hands. If we wanted to turn it right, let's say, we would think where our hand is and we would send it to the right."

It is interesting that the children are focusing more on body-syntonicity while not being sidetracked by the visual effects even though only an inclined line – corresponding to the "taking off" of the turtle – was clearly visible on the computer screen. This result comes in contrast to the findings of other researches in the framework of 3d computational environments that have noted pupils' preference in working in a plane parallel to the computer's screen display plane (Kynigos and Latsi 2006, 2007). Working in a plane parallel to the display plane is considered closer to pupils' experiences with 2d figures in school textbooks or with 2d Logo and would eliminate the convention used in the representation of the 3d space. However, it seems that the kind of task and the metaphor used was of critical importance: the aim was

Episode 1:

S1: Fd, more Fd, more…we should go it forward 0.5. Does it have 0.5?

S2: Wait, wait the turtle is here.

S1: Yes, but it hasn't touch the ground. Has it? Wait I have to see it. (He changes the view from side to front through the active vector tool and continues forwarding the turtle.)

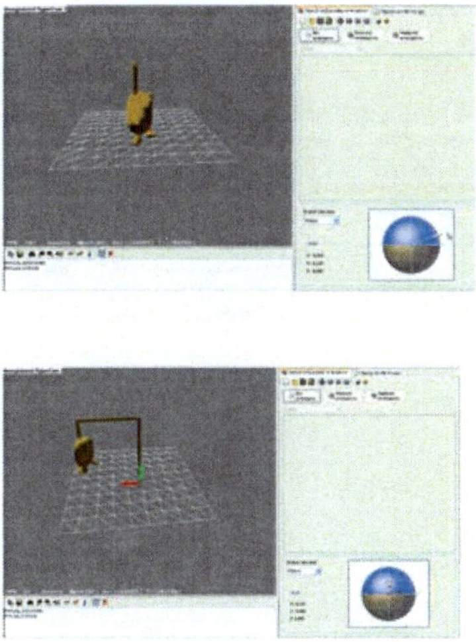

Up(180)
Dp(45)
Dp(45)
Fd(4)
Rt(90)
Rt(90)
Rt(90)
Rt(90)
Rt(90)
Fd(4)
Bk(1)
Bk(1)
Bk(1)
Fd(1)
Fd(1)
Fd(1)
Dp(45)
Rt(90)
Fd(1)
Fd(1)

Fig. 5 *First column*: Episode 1. *Second column*: Changing viewpoints. *Third column*: The respective Logo code, up to the point of the construction Episode 1 is referring to

S1: Let's see how many doors there are if the value is 720 (He plays with the 1d variation tool changing the values of the d variable). *Only one? This perspective is not convenient, I will change it* (He activates successively all the 3 default views and he opts for the top–down one).
S2 Yes, exactly like in the case of 360. It turns two rounds.

Fig. 6 Episode 2

not to construct just a slanted line or a geometrical figure but to simulate the take-off and the landing of the turtle – aircraft. In this framework, the use of the commands *uppitch/downpitch* as well as the motion of the turtle along the *z* axis, that gave the impression of depth, was rather more easily syntonized with everyday experiences and representations of flying aircrafts.

In the following tasks the pupils used extensively both the default 2d views and the active vector during their construction processes. It could be suggested that the various viewpoint manipulation tools were especially used: (a) when a bricolage construction strategy was adopted (episode 1, Fig. 5) and (b) when the pupils were experimenting with specific aspects of the half-baked microworlds (episode 2, Fig. 6). In episode 1 (see Fig. 5), the pupils are trying to construct "a wall" during task 2, giving commands to the turtle while using visual cues without having a clear strategy in mind. Their trial and error strategy is evident in the number of commands given to the turtle while they were trying to construct a parallelogram. It seems that every command is related only to the turtle's previous position and not to the whole

Fig. 7 The three default views of the revolving door half-baked microworld when the value of the *d* variable is 720

construction process and the figure's geometric properties. When it was not visually clear if they had constructed a closed figure, the pupils did not resort to the geometrical object's properties (e.g., that the opposite sides of the rectangular figure should have equal lengths) but to the viewpoint manipulation tools, so as to check if the figure was closed. Then they proceeded again forwarding the turtle little step by little step. The bricolage construction strategy followed by the pupils could not be attributed only to personal styles in programming (Turkle and Papert 1990) or to their Logo inexperience (Kafai 1995), but also to the intrinsic characteristics of Turtle Geometry. It seems that programming through the turtle metaphor promotes initially a step by step construction where emphasis is given on "guiding" the moving entity in relation to its immediately previous state rather than on the geometrical properties of the constructed objects. Following a step by step construction in 3d space, the pupils used multiple views of their construction so as to get the necessary information before giving the turtle the next command.

During task 4, the pupils initially experimented with the values of the variables of the half-baked microworld "Revolving door." They had extra difficulties in finding out the role of the: *d* variable, which determined the measure of turtle's turning and respective position in the 3d space before drawing each successive door of the revolving door model. It follows that the *d* variable determined also the position of the four rectangle doors in the 3d space as well as their position in relation to one another.

In episode 2 (Fig. 6), the pupils are conjecturing about the number of the visible rectangles (doors), if the value given to *d* is 720. However, they do not find the front default view convenient and after testing all the available default views (see Fig. 7), they choose to continue working with the top–down view active, where the number of the doors created by the turtle was more clearly visible. It should be also stressed that the preferred default view offered pupils a simplified 2d representation that possibly helped them focus on particular aspects of their construction: the turtle's rolling around its axis and the number of rectangle doors that in the top–down view were represented by line segments.

In sum, it could be argued that the pupils have initially preferred a body-syntonic way of navigating the turtle while opting for particular views that facilitated body-syntonicity, physically or imaginary. The emphasis on body-syntonicity with the turtle and generally the focus on the intrinsic characteristics of turtle geometry is rather depicted not only on the bricolage construction strategies followed but also on the preferred views that seem to have helped the pupils experience 3d space through an intrinsic perspective: get "immersed" to the 3d space through the turtle metaphor or explore it through multiple views according to challenges faced. However, as the pupils' construction strategies shifted to more analytic ones it seems that they ceased being so "immersed" in the 3d space, while starting paying more attention to the graphical results of the turtle's navigation. The multiple views that children used during their construction processes (e.g., episode 2, see Fig. 6) could not be interpreted only as a way of exploring the 3d space but also as a way of oscillating between focusing on turtle's navigation through an intrinsic perspective of the 3d space and focusing on the graphical results of its motion through an extrinsic perspective, a result that is treated in the next paragraph.

Construction Processes Through an Extrinsic Perspective

When using the turtle metaphor, pupils have to pass from the management of turtle's spatial movements to the construction of a graphic object (Fein et al. 1987), while making a distinction between the agent and the object, between the navigation of the turtle and the result of this navigation, the geometrical object. In parallel, pupils have to coordinate two different viewpoints: the viewpoint of the turtle which must be moved in an appropriate way so as to draw a figure and the viewpoint of an external observer who looks at the figural results of turtle's movement. The results of the present research suggest that as the activities unfolded, the pupils progressively adopted an extrinsic perspective of the 3d space, observing it as external viewers.

In the end of task 2 there was some free time available and the pupils spontaneously decided to try construct a closed figure building upon their experimentation during task 1. They were able to combine the flights they have previously constructed. Each take-off and landing of the turtle was used as the building block of a "peculiar" figure that came as result of four repeats of the initial turtle's journey, while turning the turtle 90° before each reexecution. It is also interesting – as it is evident in episode 3 (Fig. 8) – that the pupils adopted a more analytic programming strategy, visualizing the whole turtle's journey and explaining it to each other before entering commands to the microworld. Moreover, when they returned to the microworld they did not insert and execute the Logo commands one by one but they inserted and executed a group of Logo commands.

Another interesting point was that before starting their construction, the pupils adjusted their viewpoint through the active vector, so that there was a clear sense of perspective of the simulated 3d space (see Fig. 8). They then continued working on their construction keeping this viewpoint stable. However, this was not an occasional choice as the pupils followed the same strategy during the construction processes of the fan of the watermill during task 4: They adjusted their viewpoint so as to have again a sense of perspective (see Fig. 9) and they kept it stable throughout the whole construction process. When asked why they preferred this view, the pupils just

Episode 3:

S1: Would you like to make a design?

S2: To make a circle?

S1: To go this way and then this way and again so.

S2: Let's make a triangle. First it goes this way and then it comes back. No, I have an idea, to insert 45 so as to go this way and then again 45 so as to go this way and then again 45 (They are showing on the screen and they are using their hands so as to simulate turtle's journey).

S1: Let's make a rhombus. So not right 45 but right 90 (So far they were talking to each other and now they return to the microworld inserting the commands).

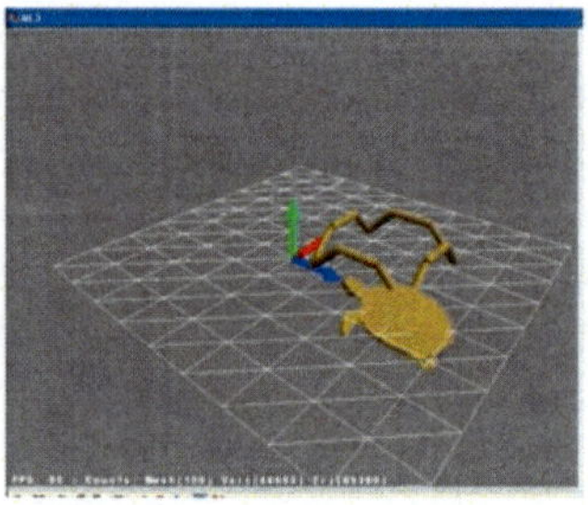

Uppitch(45)
Forward(2)
Downpitch(45)
Forward(2)
Downpitch(45)
Forward(2)
Uppitch(45)
Right(90)

Fig. 8 *First column*: Episode 3; *Second column*: The closed figure constructed by the students; *Third column*: The respective logo commands that were executed 4 times

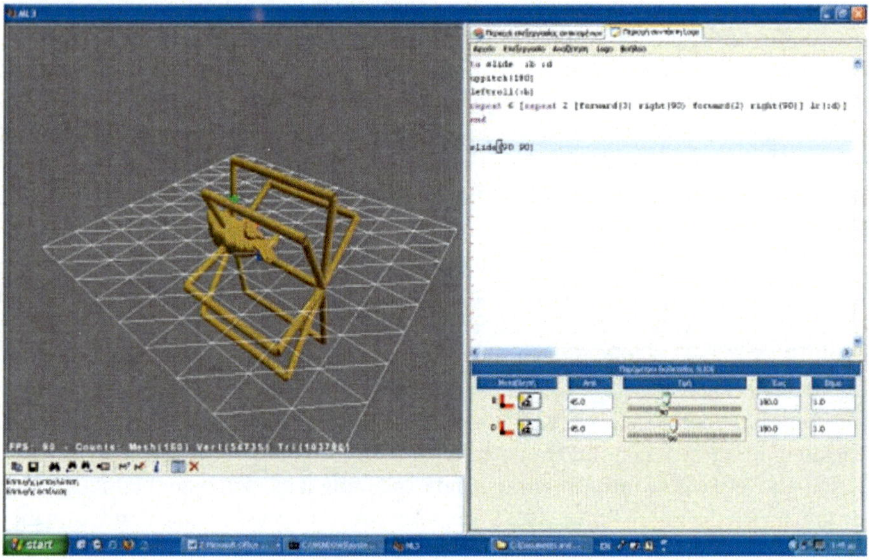

Fig. 9 The view preferred during task 4

replied: "It is more convenient because we can view the whole object." But the question that arises is: Why did the pupils keep on working with a fixed view during 3d constructions that seem to necessitate a high degree of spatial visualization and orientation? For instance would not it be easier or more body-syntonic to change viewpoints in order to decide turtle's turning before each reexecution of turtle's flight during the construction of the closed figure (episode 3, Fig. 8)? What were the reasons for this change as far as the use of the viewpoint manipulation tools is concerned as the activities unfolded? It seems that as the pupils got progressively more accustomed to the 3d turtle's motion and the software's representational infrastructure, they were not so much concerned about body-syntonicity and that it was more important for them to have a clear sense of the 3dness both of the simulated space and of the simulated objects.

Constructing the simulation of a 3d object while viewing the simulated space in perspective was probably more realistic and familiar. However, it could be also conjectured that the pupils preferred a fixed viewpoint during their constructions so as not to change position as observers and to have, thus, a stable point of reference which would probably be less cognitively demanding (Yakimanskaya 1991). A fixed 3d view rather gave the pupils a sense of space constancy, especially in cases that they adopted an analytic design strategy, as in episode 3, where they mentally visualized the whole turtle's journey before executing the relative commands so as to construct the figure. Thus, it could be argued that as the construction process became more complicated, the pupils preferred to view space from an extrinsic perspective, as external observers, focusing more on programming and geometric properties while taking into account the whole 3d space.

Conclusions

This study has tried to show that the way the available viewing angle manipulation tools were used was in a constant interplay both with the task at hand and with the construction strategies followed. When the focus was on turtle's navigation and orientation in 3d space, the body-syntonic metaphor (Papert 1980) came to the foreground while space was experienced through an intrinsic perspective (Tversky 2005): the user was immersed in space and was trying to view it from inside. In this case, the pupils used various viewpoints which helped them face specific challenges and focus on particular aspects of their construction. The intrinsic perspective and the use of multiple viewpoints seem also to be adopted in cases where a bricolage construction strategy was followed, when the pupils had not a clear idea about the actions that should be taken and when the construction was progressing command by command through trial and error. Thus, it seems that this intrinsic perspective of the simulated 3d space is rather associated – among the others – with an emphasis on the intrinsic characteristics of Turtle Geometry (Abelson and DiSessa 1981), where a given geometrical state of the turtle is fully defined by its relation only to the turtle's immediately previous state.

As the activities unfolded and as the pupils shifted focus from the management of turtle's spatial movements to the construction of a graphic object, they had started experiencing space through an extrinsic perspective, through the viewpoint of an external observer who looked at the figural results of the turtle's movement. In this case a fixed 3d view was less cognitive demanding and offered pupils both a realistic effect of familiar objects, and space and shape constancy. Moreover a holistic/external view of the 3d space was in accordance with analytic construction strategies, where the pupils were trying to visualize the turtle's journey taking into account the whole 3d space and constructed objects' geometrical properties before executing any commands on the computer. It goes without saying that there were not clear cut borders between the two perspectives and that there were a lot of instances that pupils oscillated between them according to their construction focus. This research was a tentative effort in appreciating an aspect of the large spectrum of the representational potential of a specific 3d microworld in the context of constructionist activities. Highly visual 3d Turtle Geometry microworlds, such as MaLT, seem to influence not only the kind of geometrical problems posed to students but most importantly the way students interact with the medium and the solution processes followed by them. However, a lot of further research is needed in order to investigate the way mathematical concepts can be integrated with spatial navigation and orientation in virtual environments, as well as in order to investigate the way these computational environments can be used in educational design.

References

Abelson, H., & DiSessa, A. (1981). *Turtle Geometry: The Computer as a Medium for Exploring Mathematics*. Cambridge: MIT Press.

Arcavi, A. (2003). The role of visual representations in the teaching and learning of mathematics. *Educational Studies in Mathematics*, 52(3), 215–241.

Clements, D., & Sarama, J. (1997). Children's mathematical reasoning with the turtle programming metaphor. In L. English (ed.), *Mathematical Reasoning, Analogies, Metaphors and Images* (pp. 313–338). Mahwah: Lawrence Erlbaum Publishers.

Cohen, L., Manion, L., & Morrison, K. (2007). *Research Methods in Education (6th edition)*. London: Routledge.

Fein, G., Scholnick, E., Campbell, E., Schwartz, S., & Frank, R. (1987). Computing space: A conceptual and developmental analysis of Logo. In R. E. Mayer (ed.), *Teaching and learning computer programming: Multiple research perspectives* (pp. 55–74). Hillsdale, NJ: Lawrence Erlbaum Associates.

Gravemeijer, K., & Cobb, P. (2006). Design research from the learning design perspective. In J. Van den Akker, K. Gravemeijer, S. McKenney & N. Nieveen (eds.), *Educational Design Research* (pp. 17–51). New York: Routledge.

Hauptman, H. (2010). Enhancement of spatial thinking with Virtual Spaces 1.0, *Computers & Education*, 54(1), 123–135.

Hollebrands, K., Laborde, C., & Strasser, R. (2008). Technology and the learning of geometry at the secondary level. In M. K. Heid & G. Blume (eds.), *Research on Technology in the Learning and Teaching of Mathematic, Volume 1: Research Syntheses* (pp. 155–205). Greenwich CT: Information Age.

Jones, K., Mackrell, K., & Stevenson, I. (2010). Designing digital technologies and learning activities for different geometries. In C. Hoyles & J. Lagrange (eds.), *Mathematics Education and Technology: Rethinking the Terrain, ICMI Study 17* (pp. 47–60). New York: Springer.

Kafai, Y. (1995). *Minds in play: Computer game design as a context for children's learning*. Hillsdale, NJ: Lawrence Erlbaum Associates.

Kafai, Y., & Resnick, M. (1996). *Constructionism in practice: Designing, thinking and learning in a digital world.* Mahwah: Lawrence Erlbaum Publishers.

Kynigos, C. (1992). The Turtle metaphor as a tool for children doing geometry. In C. Hoyles & R. Noss (eds.), *Learning Logo and Mathematics* (pp. 97–126). Cambridge MA: MIT press.

Kynigos, C. (1993). Childrens' inductive thinking during intrinsic and Euclidean geometrical activities in a computer programming environment. *Educational Studies in Mathematics*, 24, 177–197.

Kynigos, C. (2007). Half-baked Logo microworlds as boundary objects in integrated design. *Informatics in Education,* 6(2), 335–358.

Kynigos, C., & Latsi, M. (2006). Vectors in use in a 3d juggling game simulation. *International Journal for Technology in Mathematics Education*, 13(1), 3–10.

Kynigos, C., & Latsi, M. (2007). Turtle's navigation and manipulation of geometrical figures constructed by variable processes in 3d simulated space. *Informatics in Education,* 6(2), 359–372.

Laborde, C., Kynigos, C., Hollebrands, K., & Strasser, R. (2006). Teaching and learning geometry with technology. In A. Gutiérrez & P. Boero (eds.), *Handbook of Research on the Psychology of Mathematics Education: Past, Present and Future* (pp. 275–304). Rotterdam: Sense Publishers.

Papert, S. (1980). *MindStorms – Children, computers and powerful ideas*. London: The Harvester Press Limited.

Presmeg, N. (2006). Research on visualization in learning and teaching mathematics. In A. Gutiérrez & P. Boero (eds.), *Handbook of research on the psychology of mathematics education: Past, present and future* (pp. 205–236). Rotterdam: Sense Publishers.

Petrackou, A. (2010). Interacting through avatars: Virtual worlds as a context for online education. *Computers & Education*, 54(4), 1020–1027.

Reggini, H. C. (1985). *Ideas y formas: Explorando el espacio con Logo*. Buenos Aires: Galápago.

ReMath (2005). *Representing Mathematics with Digital Media*, European Community, 6th Framework Programme, Information Society Technologies, IST-4-26751-STP.

Turkle, S., & Papert, S. (1990). Epistemological pluralism: styles and voices within the computer culture. In I. Harel & S. Papert (eds.), *Constructionism* (pp.161–193). Norwood, NJ: Ablex Publishing Company.

Tversky, B., (2005). Functional significance of visuospatial representations. In P. Shah & A. Miyake (eds.), *The Cambridge Handbook of Visuospatial Thinking* (pp. 1–34). New York: Cambridge University Press.

Van den Akker, J., Gravemeijer, K., McKenney, S., & Nieveen, N. (2006). *Educational Design Research*. New York: Routledge.

Wickens, C., Vincow, M., & Yeh, M. (2005). Design applications of visuospatial thinking: The importance of frame of reference. In P. Shah & A. Miyake (eds.), *The Cambridge Handbook of Visuospatial Thinking* (pp. 383–425). New York: Cambridge University Press.

Yakimanskaya, I. S. (1991). The development of spatial thinking in schoolchildren. In P. S. Wilson & E. J. Davis (eds.), *Soviet Studies in Mathematics Education*, Vol. 3. Reston, Virginia: National Council of Teachers of Mathematics.

Educational Robotics and Teaching Introductory Programming Within an Interdisciplinary Framework

Anthi Karatrantou and Chris Panagiotakopoulos

Introduction

Since the late 1980s, beginning with courses and projects at MIT, robotics has been used in education in many forms, at many levels and with many purposes. Robotics, aside from being a subject in itself, has also been used as an instructional tool in a wide range of subjects, from engineering (Ringwood et al. 2005) and computer programming (Lawhead et al. 2003) to artificial intelligence (Parsons and Sklar 2004) and psychology (Miglino et al. 1999).

Within the last 20 years or so, a great many research projects have investigated the role that robotics can play at all levels of education. The literature regarding research in this area indicates that robotics is used in education with several aims, such as teaching various scientific, design-based and mathematical principles through experimentation (Rogers and Portsmore 2004), thereby developing students' ability to solve mathematical and logical problems (Lindh and Holgersson 2007), enhancing their critical thinking skills (Ricca et al. 2006), motivating them to pursue careers in science and technology and increasing their technological literacy (Ruiz-del-Solar and Avilés 2004). Robotics can also serve to engage students (Robinson 2005) and promote their skills and spirit of collaboration (Chambers et al. 2007). Moreover, robotics may be effective for at-risk or under-privileged student populations (Robinson 2005; Rogers and Portsmore 2004).

On the other hand, computational thinking is a fundamental skill for everyone, and not just for computer scientists (Wing 2006). Computer programming can be a powerful educational tool for the cultivation and development of students' cognitive skills. It is the basis for the development of a structured way of thinking and methods of dealing with problems in almost all subjects (Papert 1980). However, computer programming is a difficult process (Bravo et al. 2005); in addition to knowledge

A. Karatrantou (✉) • C. Panagiotakopoulos
Department of Primary Education, University of Patras, Patras, Greece
e-mail: a.karatrantou@eap.gr

A. Jimoyiannis (ed.), *Research on e-Learning and ICT in Education*,
DOI 10.1007/978-1-4614-1083-6_15,

of the syntax of a programming language, computer programming is a cognitive process that requires several skills (Milková and Turčáni 2006). It requires students to have the ability to construct or understand algorithms in order to solve a problem. The ability to express an algorithm for an activity is important for all subject, and even for everyday activities (Karatrantou and Panagiotakopoulos 2008). For the most part, students are confronted with difficulties when they are working with basic algorithmic structures, as well as with variables in programming (Milková and Turčáni 2006; Garner 2006). Research over the last decade has shown that Lego Mindstorms (LMs) is a powerful educational kit, suitable for teaching introductory scientific concepts, technology and programming (Niederer et al. 2003), and which allows students to work and learn within an interdisciplinary framework and to have fun at the same time, while working within a motivating environment (Garcia and Patterson-McNeill 2002).

This paper describes three pilot case studies concerning the use of LMs as an educational toolkit, with different programming software in each case. The aim of these pilot studies is to explore the extent to which the participants could manage basic programming principles, concepts and structures while working in a constructivist learning environment with LMs. Small groups of junior high school students, students in vocational secondary education and prospective primary school teachers took part in the three studies. Each group was asked to design algorithms and to create programs in order to ensure that their robotic constructions behaved in the way that was required by the worksheets that were distributed, while working within a collaborative and interdisciplinary framework.

Educational Robotics

Educational robotics promotes the construction and programming of small robots, and how they are guided using computer programs that learners have to create by themselves. Different approaches can be observed in the application of educational robotics, with the aim of developing learners' competencies such as problem-solving strategies, the formalisation of thought, socialisation and the acquisition of various concepts (Denis and Baron 1993; Alimisis 2009). Educational robotics uses computers in order to acquire, analyse, control and model various physical processes in order to make it possible for learners to acquire general skills (e.g. teamwork, critical thinking, planning and scientific observation) and scientific knowledge in such fields as experimental science and technology. Educational robotics also introduces students to advanced concepts in the fields of simulation, artificial intelligence and cognition.

In all educational robotics learning environments, students discover and use different notions which are related to scientific concepts, programming languages and technology through an interdisciplinary approach to education. The educational strategies which are developed are often linked to theories of constructivism and constructionism, and refer to active pedagogy, according to which learners build up their knowledge at their own pace (Piaget 1974; Papert 1980, 1993). In educational robotics learning environments, learners are expected to build up their knowledge and to be creative in reference to their own view of the world. They are given the opportunity to play with new ideas and technologies in a concrete way, as educational robotics provides a bridge between abstraction and reality. They can also develop problem-solving strategies and increase their level of creativity and social interaction. Moreover, in working with robotic constructions, students are offered an authentic problem-solving experience, as the procedures they are required to follow emulate those which are necessary in real-life situations (Karatrantou and Panagiotakopoulos 2008).

Several relationships between competencies and approaches in educational robotics have been outlined in the literature. One of these approaches is the programming or algorithmic approach, which concerns helping learners to develop computational thinking and the skills required for structured ways of thinking and problem solving (Denis and Baron 1993; Denis and Hubert 1999). Our work in this chapter is focussed on this approach alone.

Teaching Programming and LMs

In the early 1980s, computer programming was first recognised as an effective tool with a high cognitive value for teaching the basic concepts that can be applied to mathematics, physics and logic (Papert 1980; Howe et al. 1989) and for transferring problem-solving skills to other fields of knowledge (Ennis 1994; Pirolli and Recker 1994). However, programming requires the use of algorithms. Students' ability to construct or to understand an algorithm depends on their ability to construct a system of representation. In general, if students can express their thoughts in various systems of representation, they can make connections between concrete, intuitional and symbolic knowledge (Noss et al. 1997).

However, several studies have shown that programming is, for most students, not a very attractive activity. Students face difficulties in understanding concepts and programming structures, and only in recent years has research begun to take into account the complex factors (cognitive, educational and social) that are involved in learning when teaching programming. In the literature, problems have been reported relating to secondary school students' misunderstandings in programming, such as the implementation of the control structure for solving simple problems (Jimoyiannis 2003). Carlisle (2000) reported beginners' problems with understanding repeat structures and proposed diagrammatic representations of their understanding. High school students seem to face difficulties with the determination of conditions in control structures, as well as with their understanding of the initial values of variables. Similar types of difficulties are reported every time students use variables in their programs (Sajaniemi and Kuittinen 2005). In recent years, there has been a growing interest in designing educational activities for teaching programming based on exploratory and collaborative learning. These approaches have shifted interest from the syntactic details of a programming language to the development of problem-solving skills (analytical thinking, abstract thinking, modelling solutions) and the tools which are needed to demonstrate some of the basic concepts of programming.

Educational robotic systems meet these requirements, while also being motivating and easy to handle, making them suitable for secondary education (Wiesner and Brinda 2008).

The Lego/Logo technology appeared in the mid-1980s, as the first widely available true robotic construction kit, combining the popular Lego construction kit with the Logo programming language. In 1998, Lego released a new product called the LMs Robotic Invention System (RIS) kit, which included the Lego RCX brick with motor outputs, sensor inputs and an LCD screen. The educational version of the product, called LMs for schools, came with ROBOLAB, a graphical user-interface-based programming software. In 2006, a major upgrade was released called the LMs NXT kit. LMs NXT comes with the LEGO NXT brick, servo-motors, new sensors and the NXT-G visual programming software.

The application of every version of LMs in education is in line with the concept of constructivist learning (Piaget 1974) and the constructionist educational philosophy. Papert mentions that constructionism is built on the assumption that children perform at their best when they try to discover the specific knowledge they need for themselves. Organised or informal education can help by ensuring that the students are morally, psychologically, materially and intellectually supported in their efforts (Papert 1980, 1993). These theories state that children are much more motivated to learn when they can explore the world that surrounds them in a natural way.

Within the frame of these three pilot case studies, we will describe the ways in which Robolab and MicroWorlds EX Robotics software was used by the participants to program the RCX brick-based constructions and how NXT-G software was used to program the NXT brick-based robotic constructions.

The Case Studies

This paper describes three pilot case studies in which the LMs educational kit was used alongside different programming software in each case (MicroWorlds EX Robotics, NXT-G and Robolab). All three case studies are included in the research activities of the Computers and Educational Technology Laboratory of the Department of Primary Education at the University of Patras, Greece.

Small groups of junior high school students, students in vocational secondary education and prospective primary school teachers took part in the three pilot case studies, during which they were asked to design algorithms and create programs so that their robotic constructions would operate properly, while working in a collaborative and interdisciplinary framework. Within this framework, the students dealt with concepts relating to different scientific areas, such as light, colour, motion, circular motion etc., while trying to solve problems representing the natural complexity of the real world.

The aim of all three pilot studies was to explore the ways in which participants realise and manage basic programming principles, concepts and structures while working in a constructivist learning environment using LMs. The main focus was on the understanding and the use of control structures in programming, regardless of the programming environment used, according to modern approaches which have shifted instructors' interest from the syntactic details of a programming language to their understanding of algorithmic principals and structures and the development of problem-solving skills (Wiesner and Brinda 2008). Control structures (sequential, selection, repetition) are among the most important structures in every programming language and environment and, as mentioned above, students often face problems when handling them.

In all three case studies, a common methodology was used. The participants' work was project-based, using suitable worksheets, and consisted of two phases, the familiarisation phase and the main educational activity phase.

During the familiarisation phase, after a brief presentation of the Lego kit and the software by the teacher–researchers, a previously made robotic construction (a Lego car) was given to the students and, using the appropriate worksheets, they were asked to recognise its components (Lego pieces), to discover the role of each piece and the way it worked and to program the car in order to produce the desired simple motion and reaction.

During the main educational activity phase, the students had to work on their projects in order to ensure that their robotic construction behaved in a suitable way. While the students were working, special attention was paid to the students' efforts to complete the cycle of program development correctly (through analysis of the problem, designing algorithms, constructing the program and testing the program). Two teacher–researchers stayed with the students at all times and observed the students' brainstorms, discussions, working activities and reactions. They kept notes and intervened whenever the students needed help, mainly with scientific concepts. The role of the teacher was more like that of an experienced advisor and his or her instruction was context-driven in order to supply what was required.

Three methods were used for data collection in all of the case studies:

(a) Observation of the participants' work and notes kept by the two teacher–researchers
(b) Audio recordings of the participants' conversations while working
(c) Brief semi-constructed group interviews with the participants at the end of the activity. The focus of the interviews was on the participants' experience of using a computer, their experience of the LMs kit and the software they used, their satisfaction, the perceived usefulness of the software and the kit and their opinion of the whole procedure

First Case Study

Six students (three boys and three girls) who were attending the third grade of junior high school in Patras participated in the study. All of them had been taught the theory of basic programming and algorithm design concepts such as control structures

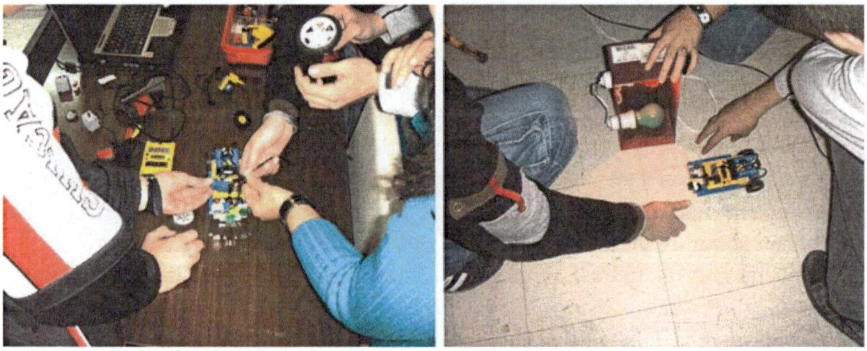

Fig. 1 Students working in groups (*left*) – The Lego car and the traffic lights (*right*)

at school. They had already been taught about sequential and selection control structures, but not about repetition control structures. They had never tried to program anything using a programming environment before. The students worked in two groups of three students each for two sessions of 2 h each, based on five worksheets (Nikolos et al. 2008).

During the first session (the familiarisation phase), the students worked on the first two worksheets in order to familiarise themselves with the Lego kit, the RCX brick and the MicroWorlds EX Robotics software. For the first worksheet, the students had to touch and recognise Lego pieces such as motors, lamps and sensors, and they experimented with controlling their functions via the programming environment. A previously constructed Lego car was given to them and the second worksheet required the students to recognise its elements and to program it to move in different directions and ways.

During the second session, the students had to work on the main educational activity. For the third worksheet, they had to add the appropriate Lego piece (sensor) to the car so that it could recognise "red" and "green" traffic lights. The traffic light construction was ready for them in order to save time. After that (in the fourth worksheet), the students had to program the stationary car in order to recognise the "red" and the "green" light and to react accordingly: to remain stationary while the red light was on, and to start moving when the green light was on. The fifth worksheet asked the students to program the car to be able to stop while moving if the red light turned on and then to start moving again when the green light turned on.

During the main educational activity, via trial and error, discussions and the exchange of ideas, the students recognised the function and the role of the light sensor as well as the physical concepts behind it with the help of the teacher–researchers. A typical example of their conversations, with agreements and disagreements, is: "We need a colour sensor"; "...but we don't have a colour sensor. We have a light sensor"; "...let's try it. Can it see the red colour of the red light?"; "....no, it doesn't see colour, it sees numbers!"; "...what are these numbers?" "... look! The number is different for the green light!"; "...oh! We have to correspond numbers to the colours" (Fig. 1).

Table 1 Students' programs in MicroWorlds EX Robotics for worksheets 4 and 5, respectively

to car	to light
waituntil [sensor1 < 450]	bon
bon	waituntil [sensor1 < 470]
End	boff
	waituntil [sensor1 < 430]
	bon
	end

The main goal of this was for the students to understand the role and the function of the repetition control structure and to use it in practice. They worked with the structure: *repeat <commands> until <condition>*. They experienced difficulties in understanding the role of the condition in the structure and how to form it in the program (Table 1).

Second Case Study

Six students (four boys and two girls) who were attending the first grade of a technical and vocational secondary education school in Patras participated in the study. None of them had been taught basic programming or algorithm design concepts at school, and they had never tried to program anything using a programming environment. Three of them had been taught about basic computer science concepts in high school. The students worked in two groups of three students each, based on appropriate worksheets for two sessions of 2 h each (Eleftherioti et al. 2010).

During the first session, the students familiarised themselves with the LMs NXT kit and the NXT-G software (familiarisation phase). A previously constructed Lego car was used. The first worksheet required the students to recognise Lego pieces such as motors, lamps and sensors on the car, and they experimented with controlling their functions via the programming environment. After that, the students had to program the Lego car to move in different directions and ways.

During the second session, the students had to work on the main educational activity. They had to add the appropriate Lego piece or pieces to the car so that the car would be able to react to a traffic light in the same way that real cars react in real life. The traffic light constructions (made of Light Emission Diodes – LEDs) were ready for them in order to save time. For the second worksheet, the students had to consecutively and constructively complete the car and program it to be able to perceive the red and the green lights and to react suitably. The car should be able to stop while moving when the red light is turned on, to remain stationary until the green light turns on and then to start moving again. The car should be able to react in the same way each time it meets a traffic light. The students found the task to be very interesting and started work on it immediately.

During each step, the students were asked to write down the algorithm (in pseudocode form) before the creation of their program. Trial and error, discussions, the

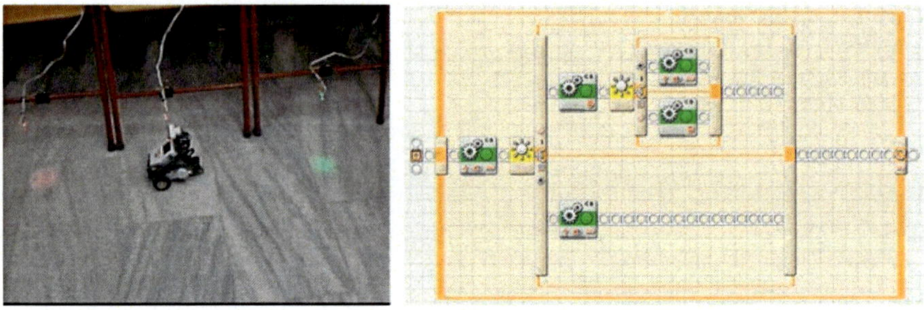

Fig. 2 One of the students' construction and one of the programs developed

exchange of ideas, arguments, agreements and disagreements took place among the students while they were working. A typical example of one of their conversations, with its agreements and disagreements, is: "We are going to use the colour sensor"; "...Where do we have to put it on the car?"; "...it can't distinguish between the red and green light... it seems to see the same light each time... what is the problem?"; "... if we use the light sensor?"; "It can measure the light intensity"; "So what...?"; "the red and the green light have different intensities..."; "Let's try it ...".

They experimented with the light and colour sensors, recognised their role and function and discussed the physics concepts that governed them with their teachers. They also experimented with the position of the sensor on the car in relation to the position of the traffic lights. They finally decided to use the light sensor, and each group placed it in a different position on the car in relation to the traffic lights. In their effort to program the car, they worked with the control structures: *repeat <commands> until <condition>* and *If <condition> then <commands>*. They also experienced difficulties in understanding the role of the condition in each control structure and how to form it in their program (Fig. 2).

Third Case Study

Nine female students who were prospective primary school teachers participated in this study. The participants worked in three groups during the eighth semester of their university course. Their average age was 22 years old. They had already completed the course requirements for their degree and were waiting to graduate from the Department of Primary Education of the University of Patras in Greece. They were able to work with a computer, using Microsoft Windows and the Microsoft Office suite of applications. They were also experienced in using computers as a teaching tool for searching for information and as a platform for educational software aimed at the primary school level. They had no prior knowledge of programming. The LMs kit with RCX brick and Robolab had been exhibited in the framework of a course entitled "Computers and Education" 1 year earlier (during the third year

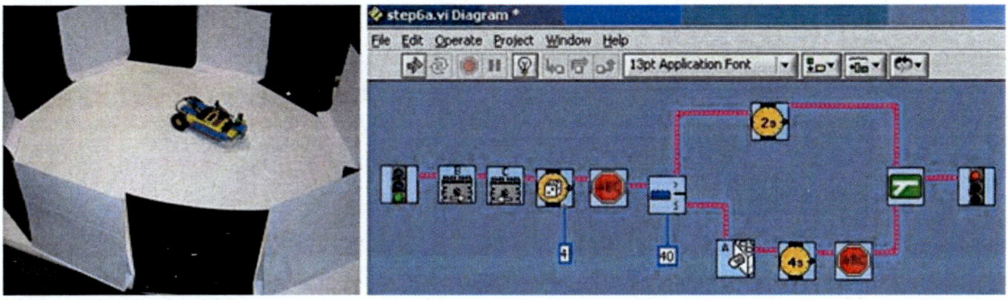

Fig. 3 The "circle" of paperboards and one of the students' programs

of their study), without the active involvement of the students. They worked for two sequential sessions of 2 h each, based on six worksheets (Karatrantou and Panagiotakopoulos 2008).

During the first session, the familiarisation phase took place with the use of a pre-constructed Lego car and the first five worksheets. After the initial process of recognising the Lego pieces on the car and experimenting with them, the students had to:

- Program the car to move forward for a specific time interval, to stop for a specific time interval, to move backwards again for a specific time interval and then to stop (first worksheet)
- Program the car to move forward for a random time interval (between 0 and x s), to stop for a specific time interval, to move backwards for a random time interval and then to stop (second worksheet)
- Program the car to turn around (in the same direction) for a specific time interval, to stop instantly, and after that to turn around again but in the opposite direction for a random time interval and then to stop (third worksheet)
- Mount a light sensor on the car. Place the car in different locations in the lab. Keep writing down the different values of the light sensor. Keep writing down the different values of the light sensor when a white or a black paperboard is been placed approximately 15–25 cm in front of the car. Write down the value of the light sensor without any paperboard in front of the car (fourth worksheet)
- Program the car to move forward when a black paperboard is placed in front of the sensor and not to respond when a white paperboard is placed in front of the sensor (fifth worksheet)

The students in each group worked in collaboration in order to accomplish their main aim during the second session (the main educational activity). The sixth worksheet presented them with the following problem: "Put the car in the middle of a circle with black and white walls – paperboards (Fig. 3). Write down the algorithm and construct the program so that the car is able to turn around for a random time interval (between 0–x seconds) and then stop, and so that if a black paperboard is placed in front of it then the green lamp will turn on. If a white paperboard is placed in front of the car, nothing should happen. This pattern should be repeated until the stop button on the RCX brick is pressed".

The students had to think of the appropriate algorithm, to think of and write down on paper the sequence of actions in their natural language (a pseudo-code) in order to describe the algorithm and to convert the pseudo-code into a program using RoboLab, in order to verify the algorithm made and to program the car.

Typical snapshots of their discussions include: "How can we make the car turn around for a certain time interval?"; "... should the wheels rotate?"; "...'Yes, of course, but how?"; "... if we make the one wheel rotate and not the other?"; "... should the car move forward at the same time?"; "...let's try to turn the car around using our hands.... Look, it turns around, and watch, the one wheel rotates forward and the other one in the opposite direction ...yes! That's it!!!" and "We say if... Is there any IF command? Can we use something for IF?"; "...How?"; "Yes, let's think of what to do with IF..."; "Well, if you (the car) see a black paperboard, move forward, if you see the white one... Do nothing?"; "How can the car see the black and white?"; "The light sensor can measure the light intensity... yes, that's it..."; "... watch in front of the black paperboard, it can measure the values lower than 45..."; "... and in front of the white paperboard higher than 45..."; "So, we found it!"

The two groups started their project immediately and, as they were working, it became obvious that their confidence was increasing and their pseudo-codes were becoming more and more accurate and more complex, involving discrete sentences. They also experimented with the light sensors and recognised their role and function. In the students' efforts to program the car, they worked with the control structures: *If <condition> then <commands>* and *repeat <commands>... times (infinite in this case)*. However, they also experienced difficulties in understanding the role of the condition in the control structure and how to form it in their program as well as with the use of the notion of a *random* value in a variable. A typical algorithm made by the students was: "The car has stopped in the middle of a paper-wall with black and white pieces of paperboard. The car starts to rotate its wheels in position B for a random time interval between 0 and 4s and then stops. If the intensity of the light is less than 40, then the green lamp should be turned on for 4s. Wait for a few seconds and then repeat the entire procedure. If the intensity of the light is higher than or equal to 40 then nothing happens – wait for a few seconds and repeat the entire procedure. The car repeats the entire procedure until we press the off button".

Qualitative Findings and Commentary

An analysis of the teachers' written notes and observations of the students' work, as well as the audio recordings, show that, in all three cases, the students' interest in the project and commitment to their work increased continually. It is important that during the project, the students tried to understand how their constructions worked and what they had to do in order to make them work properly. As they were working, it became obvious that their confidence was increasing and that their algorithms were becoming more and more accurate and complex, to the point where they involved discrete sentences. The students had the opportunity to use their experience as a guide and took advantage of their errors. The students' errors provided the teachers with the opportunity to improve the student's previous knowledge. They were provided with the necessary skills to plan a project and to carry it out to completion. At the same time, they were given a sense of community through idea sharing, and were encouraged to develop collaborative and teamwork skills. It was also observed that, from the beginning of the group work process, the males in each group showed more interest in rebuilding the car and checking whether their program worked as expected each time.

The females, on the other hand, seemed to be more inclined towards writing the pseudo-code and keeping notes. The girls also filled out their worksheets more carefully and completely, whereas the boys tended to write in short phrases or symbols (such as the program icons) instead of sentences. Other researchers have also observed similar trends in the behaviour of males and females (e.g. Fossum et al. 2001), which appear to be consistent with Papert's views about the dynamics which develop when children work with digital technology (Papert 2003), according to which girls desire all kinds of experiences while boys want to make something fast and dynamic and thus begin construction immediately.

In general, the students did not experience any major problems in recognising icons for each programming structure and command using Robolab and NXT-G. All of the groups completed their projects satisfactorily. Their solutions, as well as their entries on the worksheets, provided us with evidence that they understood the role, the function and the use of basic programming principles. At the same time, they had to combine concepts from various subject areas (such as physics and technology). This helped them to discover solutions through trial and experimentation in an interdisciplinary framework, unveiling robotics as a suitable tool with which to introduce the complexity and unpredictability of the physical world, a property which is often forgotten in the theoretical side of education.

The role of the teacher was different from normal. His/her role was more like that of an experienced advisor and his/her instruction was context-driven in order to supply what the students needed, when they needed it. The teacher had the opportunity to discern what difficulties the students experienced with concrete topics, as well as their interests and behaviours.

The interviews provided interesting answers to the questions under consideration. The students were very interested in their work with LMs and the programming environments, regardless of their previous experience and skills with computers or technology. Most of them stated that LMs helped them to understand in practice what an algorithm is and how to create a program, and that they enjoyed working and were motivated to compose an algorithm so that their construction would exhibit the desired behaviour.

In addition, the prospective teachers stated that the use of LMs can help students to think reasonably and to organise the necessary steps in order to solve a problem. It is important for children to learn to make algorithms, because algorithms are necessary in everyday life in order to solve problems in a more accurate and structured way. These participants found such activities to be interesting and useful from a pedagogical perspective, and all of them suggested that they would try to use LMs with Robolab in the future with their students.

These findings are definitely positive, but the short duration of the experiments and the limited number of the participants in each case study poses some questions: Would the students' feelings and attitudes be the same if they used LMs over a longer period of time and on a regular basis? How do we assess whether and what the students learn using robots? Would the findings be the same with a larger number of participants? These questions should be answered in further research.

Conclusions

In this paper, an effort was made to explore the extent to which participants in three different pilot case studies could manage basic programming principles, concepts and structures while working in a constructivist learning environment and in an interdisciplinary framework with LMs.

All of the participants were satisfied with their experience of the LMs environment, enjoyed their work and expressed an interest in learning and working more with it. Most of them found these educational activities to be more interesting and effective than the traditional ones. During their work and "play" with the Lego devices, as well as with lights, motors, sensors, motions and directions, they met concepts from the fields of physics, mechanics, technology and programming in practice in an interdisciplinary framework.

The results of the case studies showed that the LMs environment helped and motivated the students in all of the groups to compose the appropriate algorithms, giving them in pseudo-code in every step, and to convert them into a program.

In conclusion, the use of robots can provide a visceral, "hands-on" learning experience for students who have never programmed before and may help them to comprehend basic algorithmic principals and structures. This would serve as a bridge between our approach and a more traditional programming environment, as many research projects have shown (Fagin et al. 2001; Hirst et al. 2002). However, there is an apparent need for analysis that would provide more convincing data to support the use of robotics for educational purposes. It is very important to measure the effectiveness and perceived usefulness of these approaches in terms of learning outcomes and students' satisfaction (Malec 2001).

References

Alimisis, D. (ed.) (2009). *Teacher education in robotics – enhanced constructivist pedagogical method (TERECOP project).* Athens: ASPETE.

Bravo, C., Marcelino, M. J., Gomes, A., Esteves, M., & Mendes, A. J. (2005). Integrating educational tools for collaborative computer programming learning. *Journal of Universal Computer Science*, 11(9), 1505–1517.

Carlisle, E. G. (2000). Experiences with novices: The importance of graphical representations in supporting mental models. In A. F. Blackwell & E. Bilotta (eds.), *Proceedings of the 12th Workshop of the Psychology of Programming Interest Group* (pp. 33–44). Cozenza, Italy.

Chambers, J., Carbonaro, M., Rex, M. (2007). Scaffolding knowledge construction through robotic technology: A middle school case study. *Electronic Journal for the Integration of Technology in Education,* 6, 55–70.

Denis, B., & Hubert, S. (1999). A conceptual framework of educational robotics. In *Proceedings of the 9th International Conference on Artificial Intelligence in Education, AI-ED 99* (pp. 45–54). Le Mans: IOS Press.

Denis, B., & Baron, G. L. (1993). *Regards sur la robotique pédagogique. Actes du quatrième colloque international sur la robotique pédagogique*. Paris: INRP.

Eleftherioti, E., Karatrantou, A., & Panagiotakopoulos, C. (2010). Using Lego Mindstorms NXT for teaching computer programming in a interdisciplinary context – A pilot study. In A. Jimoyiannis (ed.), *Proceedings of 7th Panhellenic Conference with International Participation ICT in Education* (pp. 137–144). Korinthos, Greece.

Ennis, D. L. (1994). Computing, problem-solving instruction and programming instruction to increase the problem-solving ability of high school students. *Journal of Research on Computing in Education*, 26(4), 489–496.

Fagin, B., Merkle, L., & Eggers, T. (2001). Teaching computer science with robotics using Ada/ Mindstorms 2.0. *Proceedings of the 2001 Annual ACM SIGAda International Conference on Ada* (pp. 73–78). New York ACM.

Fossum, T., Haller, S., Voyles, M., & Guttschow, G. (2001). A gender-based study of elementary school children working with ROBOLAB. *Proceedings of the 2001 AAAI Spring Symposium on Robotics and Education*. Palo Alto: AAAI.

Garcia, M., & Patterson-McNeill, H. (2002). Learn how to develop software using the toy Lego Mindstorms. *Proceedings of the 7th Annual Conference on Innovation and Technology in Computer Science Education* (p. 239). New York, NY: ACM.

Garner, S. (2006). The development, use and evaluation of a program design tool in the learning and teaching of software development. *Issues in Informing Science and Information Technology*, 3, 253–260.

Hirst, J. A., Johnson, J., Petre, M., Price, A. B., & Richards, M. (2002). What is the best programming environment/language for teaching robotics using LegoMindstorms? *Artificial Life and Robotics,* 7(3), 124–131.

Howe, J.A.M., Ross, P. M., Johnson, K. R., Plane, F., & Inglis R. (1989). Teaching mathematics through programming in the classroom. In E. Soloway & J. C. Spohrer (eds.), *Studying the novice programmer* (pp. 43–55). Hillsdale, NJ: Lawrence Erlbaum.

Jimoyiannis, A. (2003). Teaching programming in senior high school: Towards a framework aiming at the development of problem solving skills. *Proceedings of 2nd Conference for ICT in Education* (pp. 706–720). Syros, Greece (in Greek).

Karatrantou, A., & Panagiotakopoulos, C. (2008). Algorithm, pseudo-code and Lego Mindstorms programming. *Proceedings of International Conference on Simulation and Programming for Autonomous Robots/Teaching with Robotics: Didactic Approaches and Experiences* (pp. 70–79). Venice, Italy.

Lawhead, P. B., Duncan, M.E., Bland, C. G., Goldweber, M., Schep, M., Barnes, D. J., & Hollingsworth, R. G. (2003). A road map for teaching introductory programming using LEGO© Mindstorms robots. *ACM SIGCSE Bulletin*, 35(2), 191–201.

Lindh, J., & Holgersson, T. (2007). Does Lego training stimulate pupils' ability to solve logical problems?. *Computers & Education*, 49(4), 1097–1111.

Malec, J. (2001). Some thoughts on robotics for education. *Proceedings of the American Association for Artificial Intelligence Symposium on Robotics and Education*. Palo Alto: Stanford University. Retrieved 5 January 2010 from http://fileadmin.cs.lth.se/cs/Personal/Jacek_Malec/psfiles/aaai01rae.pdf.

Miglino, O., Lund, H., & Cardaci, M. (1999). Robotics as an educational tool. *Journal of Interactive Learning Research*, 10(1), 25–47.

Milková, E., & Turčáni, M. (2006). Digital objects supporting development of algorithmic thinking. In A. Méndez-Vilas, A. Solano Martín, J. A. Mesa González & J. Mesa González (eds.), *Current developments in technology-assisted education* (pp. 376–380). Spain: Formatex.

Niederer, H., Sander, F., Goldberg, F., Otero, V., Jorde, D., Slotta, J., Stromme, A., Fischer, H., Lorenz, H., Tibergkien, A., & Vince, J. (2003). Research about the use of information technology in science education. In D. Psillos, P. Kariotoglou, V. Tselfes, E. Hatzikraniotis, G. Fassoulopoulos & M. Kallery (eds.), *Science Education Research in the Knowledge-based Society* (pp. 309–322). The Netherlands: Kluwer.

Nikolos, D., Karatrantou, A., & Panagiotakopoulos, C. (2008). The exploitation of MicroWorlds EX Robotics for the understanding of basic programming structures. In V. Komis (eds.), *Proceedings of 4th Panhellenic Conference in Computer Science Didactics (pp.* 221–230). Patra, Greece (in Greek).

Noss, R., Healy, L., & Hoyles, C. (1997). The construction of mathematical meanings: Connecting the visual with the symbolic. *Educational Studies in Mathematics*, 33, 203–233.

Papert, S. (1980). *Mindstorms: Children, computers, and powerful ideas*. New York: Basic Books.

Papert, S. (1993). *The children's machine*. New York: Basic Books.

Papert, S. (2003). *The children's machine: Rethinking school in the age of the computer*. New York: Basic Books.

Parsons, S., & Sklar, E. (2004). Teaching AI using LEGO Mindstorms. In L. Greenwald, Z. Dodds, A. Howard, S. Tejada & J. Weinberg (eds.), *Accessible hands-on AI and robotics education* (pp. 8–13). Technical Report SS-04-01. Menlo Park, California: American Association for Artificial Intelligence.

Piaget, J. (1974). *To Understand is to Invent*. New York: Basic Books.

Pirolli, P., & Recker, M. (1994). Learning strategies and transfer in the domain of programming. *Cognition & Instruction*, 12(3), 235–275.

Ricca, B., Lulis, E., & Bade, D. (2006). *Lego Mindstorms and the growth of critical thinking*. US: Dominican University.

Ringwood, J.V., Monaghan, K. & Maloco, J. (2005). Teaching engineering design through Lego® Mindstorms™. *European Journal of Engineering Education*, 30(1), 91–104.

Robinson, M. (2005). Robotics-driven activities: Can they improve middle school science learning?. *Bulletin of Science, Technology & Society*, 25(1), 73–84.

Rogers, C., & Portsmore, M. (2004). Bringing engineering to elementary school, *Journal of STEM Education*, 5(3/4), 17–28.

Ruiz-del-Solar, J., & Avilés, R. (2004). Robotics courses for children as a motivation tool: The Chilean experience. *IEEE Transactions on Education*, 47(4), 474–480.

Sajaniemi, J., & Kuittinen, M. (2005). An experiment on using roles of variables in teaching introductory programming. *Computer Science Education*, 15(1), 59–82.

Wiesner, B., & Brinda, T. (2008). Using robots as teaching aids in early secondary informatics education. *Proceedings of the Joint Open and Working IFIP Conference on ICT and Learning for the Net Generation*. Kuala Lumpur, Malaysia: IFIP. Retrieved 5 January 2010 from http://cs.anu.edu.au/iojs/index.php/ifip/article/viewFile/13580/506.

Wing, J. M. (2006). Computational thinking. *Communications of the ACM*, 49(3), 33–35.

Teaching Electric Circuits by Guided Inquiry in Virtual and Real Laboratory Environments

Athanasios Taramopoulos, Dimitris Psillos, and Evripides Hatzikraniotis

Introduction

For years, several researchers and teachers support that involving students in laboratory-based activities in science contributes not only to the construction of conceptual knowledge but also to the development of a scientific way of thinking. However, research studies suggest that during experimentation based on hands-on experiments, students are frequently preoccupied with handling equipment setups and taking measurements, which questions the effectiveness of laboratory based on hands-on experiments as only one of its kind environment for promoting scientific understanding (Psillos and Niedderer 2002; Niedderer et al. 2003). With the advance of ICT technology, virtual laboratories have emerged as powerful environments as well. Virtual laboratories simulate real science laboratories on a computer screen, in a visual and functional manner, by exploiting modern multimedia technology and especially user interaction, immediate and realistic variable change, and equipment handling (Kocijancic and O'Sullivan 2004). For example, using simulations to model a phenomenon or process, students can perform experiments by changing variables (e.g., resistances in a circuit) and then observe the effects of their changes (e.g., the current). In this way, students may investigate the properties of the underlying model (Ohm's law).

Recently, the increasing use of virtual laboratories in Science Education and the finding that virtual manipulatives can be as effective in teaching as real laboratory equipment (Triona and Klahr 2003; Klahr et al. 2007), has stimulated a discussion of

A. Taramopoulos (✉) • D. Psillos
Department of Elementary Education, Aristotle University of Thessaloniki, Thessaloniki, Greece
e-mail: ttar@sch.gr

E. Hatzikraniotis
Department of Physics, Aristotle University of Thessaloniki, Thessaloniki, Greece

A. Jimoyiannis (ed.), *Research on e-Learning and ICT in Education*,
DOI 10.1007/978-1-4614-1083-6_16,

redefinition of their role (Hofstein and Lunetta 2004). A large number of research studies have shown that virtual laboratories, as educational environments, are not inferior to their real counterparts (Triona and Klahr 2003; Keller et al. 2005; Klahr et al. 2007; Jaakola and Nurmi 2008) with regard to conceptual understanding as well as designing experiments. Moreover, in a number of cases results indicate that virtual laboratories may even outperform real laboratories (Zacharia and Anderson 2003; Wieman and Perkins 2005; Finkelstein et al. 2005; Zacharia 2007). On the other hand, there are also studies in which real laboratories seem superior to virtual ones (Steinberg 2003; Marshall and Young 2006). As Evagelou and Kotsis (2009) remark in their literature review, these research studies are mainly focused on University students (60%) and seldom refer to primary school pupils (20%) or high school students (20%). Furthermore, of those referring to high school students none is in the field of electric circuits, which is especially suitable for a comparison between virtual and real environments since objects with similar properties can be used in both environments.

According to the literature (Harms 2000), modern virtual laboratory environments can be categorized into five groups: Simulations, networked applet labs (Cyber Labs), Virtual Labs, Virtual Reality Labs (VR Labs), and Remote Labs. Simulations, Virtual Labs, and Virtual Reality Labs are computer applications that, mainly for speed and security reasons, are executed at the user's local computer, which restricts their use inside the school premises. Assignment of exploratory homework utilizing the virtual laboratory at home can be possible only with the use of either Remote Labs, or, more simply, Cyber Labs. However, constructing a Remote Lab (robotic lab controlled over the network), or, building a java applet requires skills which are beyond those possessed by the average teacher. Thus, during teaching, teachers may use applets available on the Internet, without being able to create their own or modify existing ones. The Open Learning and Laboratory Environment (OLLE), which is described in the next section, fills this gap by enabling the user to construct, through the virtual laboratory, an applet of his choice and use it as a Cyber Lab either locally or remotely.

In this context, the aim of the present study is to investigate whether using the affordances the modern virtual laboratories provide, embedded in a teaching-by-guided-inquiry intervention, can be successful in promoting conceptual evolution in the field of electric circuits. More specifically at first we aim to compare the improvement in conceptual understanding of junior high school students when they are involved in activities based on the VR Lab of OLLE and when they are involved in activities based on an equivalent hands-on laboratory environment, in the context of a teaching-by-guided-inquiry intervention in the field of simple electric circuits. As noted above, according to the literature, such a comparison has not been carried out for high school students. A second aim is to study the conceptual improvement observed in junior high school students in the field of electric circuits when the guided inquiry process makes use of the Cyber Labs OLLE creates. The reasons for choosing to implement OLLE and hands-on in a guided inquiry intervention is that research showed inquiry to be a powerful approach for involving students in active construction of new knowledge and enhancing students' conceptual understanding (de Jong 2006).

Description of the OLLE VR Lab and the Exported Cyber Labs

OLLE is a multifaceted virtual laboratory in the fields of Optics and Electricity developed in the Greek language (Bisdikian et al. 2006; Psillos et al. 2008). As its name suggests, it is an open virtual laboratory environment in which users construct the setup of their choice with fully and continuously functional virtual instruments.

Apart from the 3-dimensional virtual reality laboratory with navigation and rotation capabilities, zoom etc., OLLE provides its users with an additional space in the virtual lab, the model-space (Fig. 1), which depicts a 2-dimensional symbolic representation of the real laboratory setup. In the electric circuits laboratory, model-space displays in real time the schematics of the circuit constructed by the user. A detailed presentation and description of OLLE and the electric circuits laboratory has been presented previously (Psillos et al. 2008).

Another innovative aspect of OLLE is the potential to store the experimental setup in the form of a fully functional java applet. Practically, this means that from each experimental setup a new simulation can be exported, which can be executed independently of OLLE, in the form of an applet. These simulations are similar in appearance to the 2-dimensional model-space, with the addition of the freedom of handling existing in the 3-dimensional virtual lab (freedom to move an object and alter its properties). These Cyber Labs are therefore fully functional 2-dimensional symbolic multi-parametric representations of the virtual laboratory, highly consistent with the theory (Fig. 1). Moreover, the freedom of altering an object's properties is larger than it is in the virtual lab, since the virtual lab simulates the real world as closely as possible and thus obeys the real world restrictions on the range of values of the properties of the real objects.

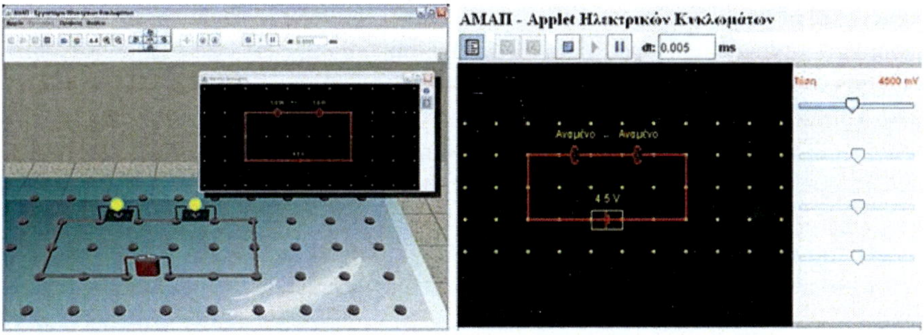

Fig. 1 The electric circuits laboratory of Open Learning and Laboratory Environment (OLLE) with the model-space (*left*) and the respective applet exported by it (*right*)

Method

The Sample

The teaching intervention took place in a junior high school of central Macedonia in Greece in the field of electric circuits during the months of January and February 2010. Teaching of physics is compulsory in junior high school, which is called Gymnasium. Thirty-two students of the third grade of Gymnasium, 15–16 years old, participated. The students were randomly assigned into two classes and had not previously attended any course relevant to electric circuits in secondary education. They had experienced some teaching and were familiarized with electric circuits in elementary school 3 years earlier.

The Teaching Intervention

It is well known that students of this age share alternative conceptions in the field of electric circuits, which are preserved despite their participation in traditional teaching approaches in Greece and elsewhere (Shipstone 1984; McDermott and Shaffer 1992; Psillos 1997; Keramidas and Psillos 2004). The aim of this intervention is to enhance students' conceptual understanding about electric circuits. Researchers have suggested that conceptual understanding may be accomplished through active construction of knowledge when students are involved in inquiry-based activities through the use of real or virtual laboratory inquiry-based experimentation (Hofstein and Lunetta 2004; Lefkos et al. 2005; Zacharia et al. 2008).

Our teaching intervention was divided into two phases. The approach in both phases of the intervention was based on guided inquiry (McDermott and Shaffer 2002; Sadeh and Zion 2009). Students were discreetly guided by the teacher and the appropriate worksheets. In the first phase, students investigated the phenomena under study by performing realistic actions either in the user-friendly virtual reality laboratory or in the real laboratory, observing immediately and repeatedly the results of their constructions. In this way a qualitative and semiquantitative model was built with which students could explain the behavior of simple electric circuits. In the second phase, students constructed virtual circuits within the networked applet labs and explored the mathematical relationships that describe the phenomena under investigation. Students worked in pairs in class, whereas they completed the worksheets individually. Homework was also carried out individually.

More specifically the first phase lasted 7 h and was performed in the school computer laboratory making use of the OLLE VR Lab (without the model-space tool) for the one class (experimental group, EG) and in the school physics laboratory for the other class (control group, CG). Both groups used the same instructional method (guided inquiry), the same instructional material and conducted the same experiments, differing only in the nature of the equipment they used (virtual vs. real).

After this phase, in order for the students to become familiar with both kinds of equipment and for us to explore any inherent differences between the two classes abilities to understand the material taught, the two classes were interchanged so that EG used real equipment and CG used virtual equipment. This additional intervention lasted 3 extra hours and dealt with the same concepts as the ones dealt with in the first phase.

The second phase was performed both at school and at home by one class (applet group, AG), exclusively utilizing the Cyber Labs OLLE exports. It lasted 5 h in class and approximately 2 h at home. Two 16-student classes participated in the first phase (groups EG and CG) and one 16-student class in the second phase (group AG). The students in the AG group at the second phase were the same as in the CG group of the first phase and thus had some experience with using both real and virtual laboratory equipment.

The content of the intervention is adapted from the school textbook of Physics, covering the larger portion of the chapter entitled "Electric Current" in the third grade of junior high school (Antoniou et al. 2008). The first phase of the intervention treated the concepts of electric circuit, electric current, intensity of electric current, electric resistance, and potential difference (voltage) in an electric circuit, under the guidance of the teacher and relevant worksheets. Teaching utilized exclusively the OLLE virtual laboratory for the EG and the real laboratory for the CG. Initially, the students constructed electric circuits with batteries and light bulbs, which were used as electric current indicators and discovered the requirements that must be met by a circuit for electric current to flow through it. Then they used ammeters to measure the intensity of the electric current and recognized that the brightness of a bulb can function as an electric current intensity indicator. Next, the students constructed circuits with bulbs connected in series and in parallel and used the ammeters to measure the intensity of the electric current at various points in the circuit and study the properties of these circuits. They found that the current flowing through a battery is not always the same but depends upon the number of bulbs and the way these are connected to it. In search for a quantity which remains constant across the battery, they used the voltmeter and were introduced to voltage. Finally, the concept of electric resistance was discussed and students connected it qualitatively to the intensity of the electric current flowing through some element when the voltage across it remains constant.

Guided inquiry activities were a crucial element in the intervention and were carried out on the basis of structured modular worksheets consisting of various steps based on a laboratory variation of the familiar Predict-Observe-Explain strategy (White and Gunstone 1992), including prediction – carrying out of the experiment – results discussion and interpretation and conclusion. In general, each worksheet referred to more than one experiment. A typical activity worksheet in this phase would contain an initial problem question to provoke a student prediction (e.g., "Do you think that the intensity of the electric current before or after a bulb is greater and why?") and then would guide the student through a sequence of steps to explore the problem (e.g., measure the intensity of the current before and after a bulb), search for the answer, and evaluate his/her prediction.

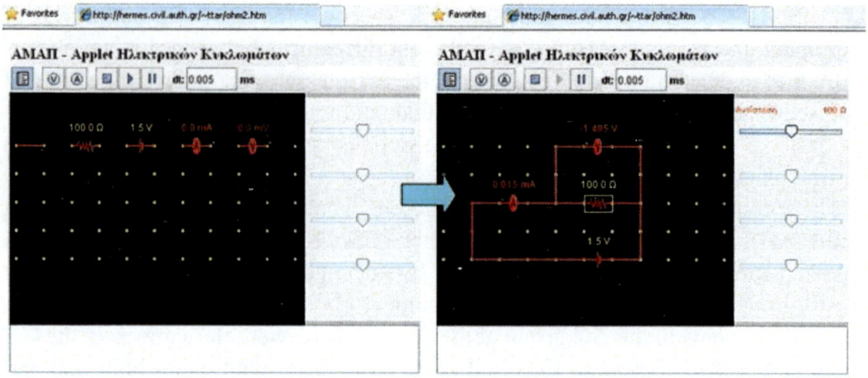

Fig. 2 An OLLE applet for exploring Ohm's law at home

In the second phase a quantitative model was suggested to students in order to explain the properties of simple electric circuits. This phase (Cyber Lab) was performed with inquiry activities at the school computer laboratory and with extensions of the theory performed by the students as extra activities at home. It dealt with Ohm's law, circuits with resistors connected in series and in parallel and Kirchhoff's two laws. In two of the activities, (connecting resistors in series and in parallel) the students were assigned extra exploratory activities at home, which were carried out using Cyber Labs via Internet. The Cyber Labs had been earlier exported by the teacher from OLLE and installed in a computer server at the Aristotle University of Thessaloniki. Students connected to this computer, either from the school computer laboratory or from home, executed the Cyber Labs within a World Wide Web browser, constructed the necessary circuits from the elements present in the Cyber Labs and examined the circuits' operation by changing various parameters, like the resistors' resistance (Fig. 2).

In this second phase, a similar pattern including guided inquiry activities was followed. A typical activity worksheet in this phase would contain an initial problem question to provoke a student prediction (e.g., "Do you think that connecting two resistors in parallel produces a larger equivalent resistance and why?") and then would guide the student through a sequence of steps in order to explore the problem (e.g., measure the intensity of the current coming into the parallel resistors circuit and the voltage at the ends of the resistors and using Ohm's law to calculate the equivalent resistor of the system), find the right answer, and evaluate his/her prediction.

Instrumentation

Students' conceptual understanding during the first phase was assessed by comparing their answers to five questions before the 7-h intervention and after it (pretest1 and posttest1). For both classes, the questions were the same in pretest1

1. **In the circuits shown below, which of the statements is correct?**

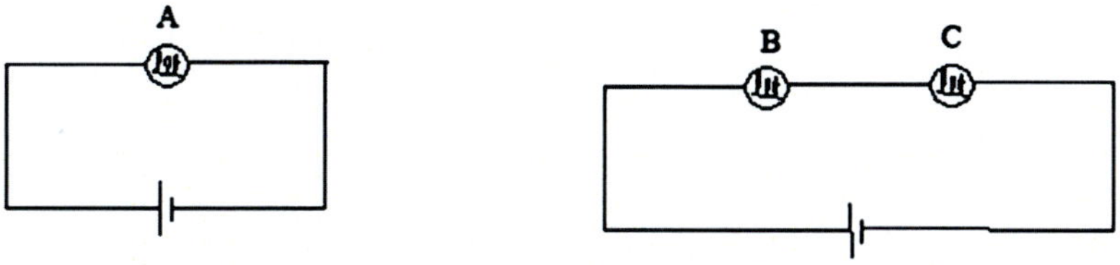

A. Bulb A brightness is greater than bulb B brightness, which is greater than bulb C brightness.
B. Bulb A brightness is less than bulb C brightness, which is less than bulb B brightness.
C. Bulb A brightness is greater than bulb B brightness, which equals to bulb C brightness.
D. Bulb A brightness is less than bulb B brightness, which equals to bulb C brightness.
E. All bulbs have the same brightness.

Fig. 3 A question of the first phase evaluation test

and posttest1 of multiple choice type, adapted from the literature (Chang et al. 1998; Keramidas and Psillos 2004) and included five possible answers to reduce random choice. The first two questions aimed at investigating the students' use of current models. The next two questions aimed at investigating the students' views for the behavior of the battery as a source in a circuit (e.g., if it gives off constant current) and the last question aimed at showing if students think that the more resistors connected in a circuit the greater its resistance is. More specifically, the first question was about the relative bulb brightness in a circuit with one bulb and a circuit with two bulbs connected in series. The second question was about relative bulb brightness in a circuit with one bulb and a circuit with two bulbs connected in parallel. The third question was about current flowing through the battery (voltage source) in circuits with one bulb, or two bulbs connected in series and in parallel. The fourth and fifth questions were about the voltage across the poles of a battery and the total resistance of bulbs in the circuits of the third question. The same posttest1 was also administered to the students after the additional 3-h intervention at the end of this phase. The translation of one question of the first phase evaluation test is shown in Fig. 3.

Similarly, in the second phase the assessment was performed by comparing the students' answers to five questions before and after the intervention (pretest2 and posttest2). Once again the questions were the same in pretest2 and posttest2, and they were multiple choice questions regarding the students' conceptual improvement. The first question aimed at investigating the use of current models, while the second one aimed at showing the students' views on the total resistance and how students relate it to the number of resistors and their connection. The last three questions aimed at finding out if students used mechanically Ohm's law and Kirchhoff's rules or have a better understanding of them. The first question was about the intensity of the current before and after it flows through two bulbs connected in series. The second question was about the change in brightness of a bulb connected in series with a second bulb, when a third bulb is added parallel to it, so that the total resistance of the circuit decreases. The third question regarded the relationship

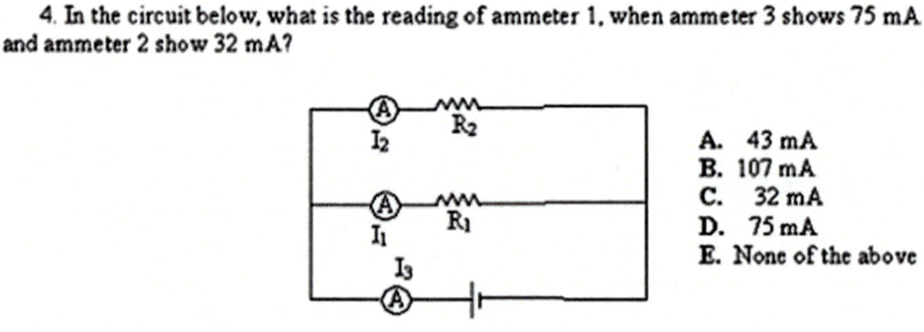

Fig. 4 A question of the second phase evaluation test

between the intensity of the current, the voltage, and the resistance of a resistor which is connected to a voltage source. The fourth and fifth questions regarded numerical applications of Kirchhoff's first and second law in a circuit with a battery and two resistors connected in parallel and, along a circuit with a battery and two resistors connected in series, respectively. The translation of one question of the second phase evaluation test is shown in Fig. 4.

Data were statistically analyzed for internal validity by calculating Cronbach α for each set. Differences in student performance between the results of pre- and posttests were examined by means of paired samples t-tests. The scores of the two classes in the first phase were compared by means of an independent samples t-test. The improvement between the pre- and posttest results was also checked by calculating the corresponding Hake gain. Hake gain is defined as the difference between the scores in pre- and posttest normalized by the maximum possible increase (Hake 1998). It is an important parameter for measuring the effectiveness of a teaching intervention since it normalizes the improvement of the student scores, thus correcting for any effects due to the students' different initial knowledge (Lenaerts et al. 2003). Recently, Hake gain has been used in small samples to monitor students' progress in experimental design skills (Lefkos et al. 2011).

Results

In the first phase for the two classes EG and CG in pretest1, Cronbach α was calculated to be 0.846 and 0.875, respectively; while in posttest1 it was calculated to be 0.802 and 0.726, respectively. In the second phase, in pretest2, Cronbach α was found equal to 0.715 and in posttest2 equal to 0.781. In all cases, the right-answer distributions were compatible with the uniform distribution according to the Kolmogorov–Smirnov test.

The average score of the experimental group (EG) in the five pretest1 questions is 0.75 right answers per student, with a standard deviation of 1.2. The average score in posttest1 is 2.7 right answers per student, with a standard deviation of 1.7.

Table 1 Results per question from the first phase

	Pretest1		Posttest1			
	Right answers		Right answers		Hake gain	
Question	EG	CG	EG	CG	EG	CG
Brightness of bulbs in series	4	5	9	11	0.42	0.55
Brightness of bulbs in parallel	3	4	10	10	0.54	0.50
Battery current intensity	1	0	7	9	0.40	0.56
Battery voltage	4	4	10	12	0.50	0.67
Total resistance	0	0	6	9	0.38	0.56
Average of right answers per question	*2.4*	*2.6*	*8.4*	*10.2*	*0.44*	*0.57*

A comparison of these scores indicates an improvement for the average student, who, from one right answer in five questions in the pretest, reached the level of about three right answers in the posttest. A statistical analysis with a paired samples *t*-test indicates that the possibility that there is no improvement can be safely ruled out since the possibility for such a scenario is 0.2% ($p=0.002<0.05$). The scores of this class per question and the corresponding Hake gains are shown in Table 1. The average number of students with a correct answer per question has increased from 2.4 (15%) to 8.4 (53%) producing a Hake gain of 0.44.

The control group (CG) in the five pretest1 questions achieved a score of 0.8 right answers per student with a standard deviation of 0.9. This is similar to the score achieved by the experimental group. The possibility that any differences between the two groups are purely statistical in nature is 87% ($p=0.87>0.05$) according to an independent samples *t*-test. The average score of the CG in posttest1 is 3.2 right answers per student with a standard deviation of 1.4. Comparison with the group's pretest scores indicates an improvement for the average student, who, as in the EG, from one right answer in five questions in the pretest1 reached the level of three right answers in the posttest1. The possibility that there is no improvement is statistically limited to 0.0% ($p=0.000<0.05$) through a paired samples *t*-test, while the Hake gain for this group is 0.57. Table 1 also shows the scores of this class per question and the Hake gains. The average number of students with a correct answer per question has increased from 2.6 (16%) to 10.2 (64%). The left graph of Fig. 5, which shows the average number of right answers per student, describes visually the student conceptual and field knowledge improvement in the first phase for both classes.

The results of Table 1 reveal that initially at each pretest question the majority of the students fail to answer correctly, whereas after the teaching intervention, about half of the students who failed to answer correctly in a pretest question changed their view to the scientifically accepted one. A closer examination of the students' views in the pre- and posttest questions reveal that the conceptions which persisted the most throughout the intervention are that two bulbs connected either in series or in parallel do not have the same brightness (the bulb being further from the battery

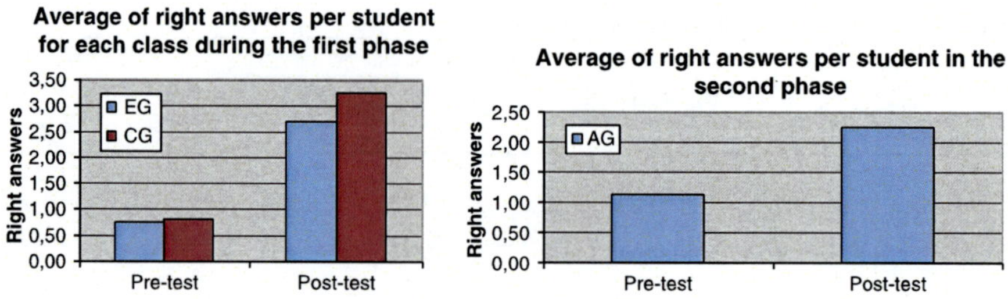

Fig. 5 The average of right answers per student for each group

Table 2 Results per question from the second phase

Question	Pretest2 Right answers	Posttest2 Right answers	Hake gain
Current continuity	6	10	0.40
Brightness of bulb in mixed connection	4	6	0.17
Ohm's law	5	8	0.27
Kirchhoff's first law	2	6	0.29
Kirchhoff's second law	1	6	0.33
Average of right answers per question	*3.6*	*7.2*	*0.29*

is believed to be dimmer), that a battery always produces electric current of the same intensity independently of the rest of the circuit connected to it and that two bulbs have always larger resistance than a single bulb regardless of the way they are connected. Although the number of students believing in these ideas decreased significantly at the end of the first phase, a number of students in both groups continued to express the same views even after constructing circuits which contradicted their initial beliefs.

During the second phase, the results for the conceptual enhancement were similar. The student scores in the five questions of pretest2 showed an average of 1.1 right answers per student with a standard deviation of 1.4. It is apparent from these scores that the knowledge the students acquired during the first phase was not adequate for them to answer the questions of this test satisfactorily. In posttest2 the results show an average of 2.3 right answers per student with a standard deviation of 1.7. A comparison of the results of the pretest2 and posttest2 again indicates an improvement in average student performance. A statistical analysis with a paired samples *t*-test shows that the case for no improvement can be discarded since the possibility for this scenario is 0.3% ($p=0.003<0.05$). Table 2 shows the right answers of the students per question and the corresponding Hake gains for the second phase. The average number of students with a correct answer per question has increased from 3.6 (23%) to 7.2 (45%) indicating a total Hake gain of 0.29. The right graph of Fig. 5 shows graphically the average number of right answers per student in the second phase.

Table 2 shows that although the average number of students answering correctly in the second phase doubled after the teaching intervention, for most questions it is less than half of the students who managed to answer correctly in posttest2. Possible reasons for this are discussed in the next section. It is noteworthy however, that there are three students (19%) sharing the conceptions described in the first phase who continue to express similar views also in the posttest of the second phase as can be inferred from their replies in the first two questions of posttest2. Furthermore, four students (25%) who answered correctly the questions in the first phase by applying the scientifically accepted ideas to simple questions, fail to apply the same ideas to answer more complex questions in pretest2 and two of them (13%) fail to do so even after the second teaching intervention in posttest2. Also, the students' alternative answers in questions 4 and 5 of posttest2 reveal a tendency of the students to prefer to add two given numbers in order to produce a result out of them than to subtract them (e.g., the majority of students tended to add currents I_2 and I_3 in order to find the current I_1 in the question of Fig. 4).

Discussion and Conclusions

The Cronbach α measurements in both phases suggest that although our research tools contained a small number of questions, they were reliable in measuring the knowledge evolution of the students. The results presented in Table 1 and Fig. 5 seem to suggest that in the first phase the control group (CG) has a greater conceptual improvement than the experimental one (EG). However, such a conclusion is not statistically valid. The small number of participating students and the relatively large standard deviations do not allow us to rule out the possibility that the difference in the scores of the two classes is purely statistical. An independent samples *t*-test between the scores of the two classes in posttest1 reveals that there is a possibility of 33% that their differences are due to statistical effects ($p=0.33>0.05$) and not due to the different nature of the laboratory environment used.

In order to further explore this phenomenon, we exchanged the classes in terms of the way teaching was performed and conducted 3 more teaching hours in which the EG used the real laboratory and the CG used the OLLE virtual laboratory. During these additional hours, students were taught again the same concepts. Afterwards, the conceptual evolution of the students was assessed with the same posttest1. It was anticipated that if the small statistically nonsignificant difference in the two classes' scores was influenced by the difference in the nature of the laboratory environment, it would decrease after the extra intervention. This however did not happen. In this test, EG scored 2.8 right answers per student with a standard deviation of 1.8, whereas the CG scored 3.3 right answers per student with a standard deviation of 1.4. The difference in the two classes' scores remained almost constant but nonsignificant despite the interchange in the teaching equipment used.

Regarding the conceptual enhancement in junior high school students in the field of electric circuits when teaching utilizes virtual equipment embedded in a guided inquiry teaching sequence, an improvement is observed both when a full

VR laboratory is used and when only the Cyber Labs exported by OLLE are used. The improvement observed in both cases shows that virtual laboratories embedded in a guided inquiry teaching sequence may contribute to the enhancement of conceptual understanding of electric circuits in junior high school students whether they are used with their realistic form or in the form of symbolic applets. A review of Tables 1 and 2 shows that the Hake gain is larger during the first phase than during the second (0.44 and 0.29, respectively). One possible explanation for this may be due to the utilization of the virtual lab in the first phase and the applets in the second. However, the smaller improvement during the second phase, which is apparent from the respective Hake gain, may be attributed to the possibly greater difficulty students may have in understanding the content of the second phase (Ohm's law and Kirchhoff's laws) and using a quantitative rather than a qualitative model for electric circuits.

Discussion among researchers is lively, and mixed results on the use and effects of virtual laboratories are reported. Some issues under study concerning their effectiveness in promoting conceptual understanding are whether virtual laboratories should be used alone and whether they are as effective as hands-on work (Finkelstein et al. 2005; Zacharia et al. 2008). Within the limitations of our small sample, the results presented here indicate that the affordances incorporated by design into modern virtual laboratories like OLLE enable them to be utilized in a teaching-by-inquiry intervention for confronting conceptual problems and enhancing content knowledge in the field of electric circuits. When compared to the real physics laboratory, the virtual laboratory produced a similar students' knowledge improvement. This answers our first research question, and suggests that knowledge improvement in the area of electrical circuits does not relate to the nature of the laboratory environment, i.e., real or virtual, used in the context of a guided inquiry approach. Such a finding for high school students is in line to findings regarding university students and supports the conclusions reached by recent studies (Jaakola and Nurmi 2008).

Besides, it is notable that significant knowledge improvement is also observed when Cyber Labs with symbolic representation of the circuit elements are exclusively used. This answers our second research question. We consider that we cannot exclude the influence of familiarization of these students with virtual manipulatives in the 3-dimensional appearance in phase one as well as that the students were actively engaged in inquiry activities during both phases. Alternatively, within the limitations of the present study, we think that such results suggest that in some fields students may successfully interact directly with virtual laboratory environments, which only provide a symbolic representation of the physical system at study. Our findings raise the question whether it is the virtual manipulatives that matter in investigative activities for promoting students' understanding of the concepts of electric circuits, and not the nature or appearance of such equipment. This opens new possibilities for incorporating virtual laboratories into science teaching and should be further researched with larger samples than in our research and in knowledge fields beyond electric circuits.

Acknowledgments The development of OLLE has been funded by the Research Academic Institution of Computer Technology (RACTI) and the Greek Ministry of Education, Lifelong Learning and Religious Affairs in the framework of the Chrysallides project.

References

Antoniou, N., Demetriadis, P., Kambouris, K., Papamihalis, K., & Papatsimpa, L. (2008). *Physics. Third grade junior high school Physics textbook.* Organization for Publishing Educational Books (OEDB), Athens (in Greek).

Bisdikian, G., Psillos, D., Hatzikraniotis, E., & Barbas, A. (2006). An Open Laboratory and Learning Environment (OLLE) in optics. In V. Dagdilelis & D. Psillos (eds.), *Proceedings of the 5th Panhellenic Conference of ICT in Education* (pp. 188-195). Thessaloniki, Greece (in Greek).

Chang, K., Liu, S., & Chen, S. (1998). A testing system for diagnosing misconceptions in DC electric circuits. *Computers & Education*, 31, 195–210.

Evagelou, F., & Kotsis, K. (2009). The qualities of researches of international literature with regard to the comparison of using virtual and real experiments in the teaching and learning of Physics. In P. Kariotoglou, A. Spirtou & A. Zoupidis (eds.), *Proceedings of the 6th Panhellenic Conference on Science Education and New Technologies in Education* (pp. 335–342) Florina, Greece (in Greek), Retrieved 15 September 2010 from http://www.uowm.gr/kodifeet/?q=el/node/89.

Finkelstein, N.D., Adams, W.K., Keller, C.J., Kohl, P.B., Perkins, K.K., Podolefsky, N.S., Reid, S., & LeMaster, R. (2005). When learning about the real world is better done virtually: A study of substituting computer simulations for laboratory equipment. *Physical Review Special Topics - Physics Education Research*, 1, 1–8.

Hake, R.R. (1998). Interactive-engagement vs. traditional methods: a six-thousand- student survey of mechanics test data for introductory physics. *American Journal of Physics,* 66(1), 64–74.

Harms, U. (2000). Virtual and remote labs in physics education. *Paper presented at the 2nd European Conference on Physics Teaching in Engineering Education (PTEE 2000)*, 14–17 June 2000, Budapest. Retrieved 25 June 2005 from http://www.bme.hu/ptee2000/papers/harms1.pdf.

Hofstein, A., & Lunetta, V. N. (2004). The laboratory in science education: foundations for the twenty-first century. *Science Education,* 88, 28–54.

Jaakola, T., & Nurmi, S. (2008). Fostering elementary school students' understanding of simple electricity by combining simulation and laboratory activities. *Journal of Computer Assisted Learning*, 24, 271–283.

de Jong, T. (2006). Computer simulations: technological advances in inquiry learning. *Science,* 312, 532–533.

Keller, C. J., Finkelstein, N. D., Perkins, K. K., & Pollock, S. J. (2005). Assessing the effectiveness of a computer simulation in conjunction with tutorials in introductory physics in undergraduate physics recitations. In P. Heron, L. McCullough & J. Marx (eds.), *Proceedings of the 2005 Physics Education Research Conference* (pp. 109–112). Melville NY: AIP Press.

Keramidas, K., & Psillos, D. (2004). Questionnaire development and students' misconceptions study in the field of electric circuits. In V. Tselfes, P. Kariotoglou & M. Patsadakis (eds.), *Proceedings of the 4th Panhellenic Conference on Science Education and New Technologies in Education* (pp. 414–421). Athens, Greece (in Greek).

Klahr, D., Triona, L.M., & Williams, C. (2007). Hands on what? the relative effectiveness of physical versus virtual materials in an engineering design project by middle school children. *Journal of Research in Science Teaching*, 44, 183–203.

Kocijancic, S., & O'Sullivan, C. (2004). Real or Virtual laboratories in science teaching. Is this actually a dilemma?. *Informatics in Education*, 3(2), 239–249.

Lefkos, I, Psillos, D., Hatzikraniotis, E., & Papadopoulos, A. (2005). A suggestion on laboratory teaching thermal radiation with the combined use of ICT. In A. Gialama, N. Jimopoulos &

A. Chloridou (eds.), *Proceedings of the 3rd Panhellenic Teachers' Conference on ICT in Education* (pp. 114–120). Siros, Greece (in Greek).

Lefkos, I., Psillos, D., & Hatzikraniotis, E. (2011). Designing experiments on thermal interactions by secondary students in a simulated laboratory environment. *Research in Science and Technological Education*, 29(2), 189–204.

Lenaerts, J., Wieme, W., & van Zele, E. (2003). Peer instruction: a case study for an introductory magnetism course. *European Journal of Physics,* 24, 7–14.

Marshall, J.A., & Young, E.S. (2006). Preservice teachers' theory development in physical and simulated environments. *Journal of Research in Science Teaching*, 43, 907–937.

McDermott, L.C., & Shaffer, P.S. (1992). Research as a guide for curriculum development: An example from introductory electricity. Part I: Investigation of student understanding. *American Journal of Physics*, 60(11), 994-1003.

McDermott, L.C., & Shaffer, P.S. (2002). *Tutorials in Introductory Physics,* Prentice Hall, New Jersey.

Niedderer H., Sander F., Goldberg F., Otero V., Jorde D., Slotta J., Stroemme A., Fisher H.E., Hucke L., Tiberghien A., & Vince J. (2003), Research about the use of information technology in Science Education. In D. Psillos, P. Kariotoglou, V. Tselfes, E. Hatzikraniotis, G. Fassoulopoulos & M. Kallery (eds.), *Science Education Research in the Knowledge Based Society* (pp. 300–312). Dordrecht Kluwer Academic Publishers.

Psillos, D. (1997). Teaching introductory electricity. *Connecting Research in Physics Education with Teacher Education,* Retrieved 22 July 2009 from http://www.physics.ohio-state.edu/~jossem/ICPE/E4.html.

Psillos, D., & Niedderer H. (2002). Issues and questions regarding the effectiveness of lab-work. In D. Psillos & H. Niedderer (Eds.), *Teaching and Learning in the Science Laboratory* (pp. 21–30). Dordrecht, NL: Kluwer.

Psillos, D., Taramopoulos, A., Hatzikraniotis, E., Barbas, A., Molohides, A., & Bisdikian, G. (2008). An Open Laboratory and Learning Environment (OLLE) in the field of electricity. In H. Aggeli & N. Valanidis (eds.), *Proceedings of the 6th Panhellenic Conference of ICT in Education* (pp. 384–391). Limasol, Cyprus (in Greek).

Sadeh, I., & Zion, M. (2009). The development of dynamic inquiry performances within an open inquiry setting: A comparison to guided inquiry setting. *Journal of Research in Science Teaching,* 46(10), 1137–1160.

Shipstone, D.M. (1984). A study of children understanding of electricity in simple DC circuits. *International Journal of Science Education,* 6(2), 185–198.

Steinberg, R. (2003). Effects of computer-based laboratory instruction on future teachers' understanding of the nature of science. *Journal of Computer in Mathematics and Science Teaching*, 22, 185–205

Triona, L.M., & Klahr, D. (2003). Point and click or grab and heft: Comparing the influence of physical and virtual instructional materials on elementary school students' ability to design experiments. *Cognition and Instruction*, 21, 149–173.

White, R., & Gunstone, R. (1992). *Probing Understanding.* The Falmer Press, London.

Wieman, C., & Perkins, K. (2005). Transforming physics education. *Physics Today*, 58, 1–36.

Zacharia, Z.C., & Anderson, O.R. (2003). The effects of an interactive computer-based simulation prior to performing a laboratory inquiry-based experiment on students' conceptual understanding of physics. *American Journal of Physics*, 71(6), 618.

Zacharia, Z.C., (2007). Comparing and combining real and virtual experimentation: an effort to enhance students' conceptual understanding of electric circuits. *Journal of Computer Assisted Learning*, 23, 120–132.

Zacharia, Z.C., Olympiou, G., & Papaevripidou, M. (2008). Effects of experimenting with physical and virtual manipulatives on students' conceptual understanding in heat and temperature. *Journal of Research in Science Teaching*, 45(9), 1021–1035.

Part IV
Learning Environments and Technologies

Games-Based Learning and Web 2.0 Technologies in Education: Motivating the "iLearner" Generation

Mark Stansfield, Thomas Connolly, Thomas Hainey, and Gavin Baxter

Introduction

Over the last decade, the area of games-based learning has evolved to provide a stimulating and engaging learning experience for younger learners who have been brought up in a technologically rich environment. Such learners can be termed digital natives (Prensky 2001) or *iLearners* who have been heavily influenced by the latest highly interactive and individual technologies such as iPods, iPhones, iPads, Wii games consoles, as well as Wi-Fi Internet access and graphic-rich multiplayer Internet gaming. In contrast, many of today's educators and teachers were largely brought up in a less technologically advanced world. Connolly et al. (2007) observed younger generation learners exhibited a cognitive preference to certain media, for example they liked portability and are more frustrated with technology that ties them to a specific location.

According to Connolly and Stansfield (2007) games-based learning can be defined as the use of a computer games-based approach to deliver, support and enhance teaching, learning, assessment and evaluation. Games-based learning has been applied to a variety of different fields such as medicine, science and mathematics, military training, language learning, computer science and business and knowledge management. Connolly et al. (2004) suggest that computer games are well suited to use within an educational environment because they build on theories of motivation, constructivism, situated learning, cognitive apprenticeship, problem-based learning and learning by doing. In addition, it can be argued that the younger generation of "iLearners" prefer video, audio and interactive media and do not read as many traditional books as previous generations, and due to shorter attention spans require learning in smaller size chunks. As result of the Internet, learners today

M. Stansfield (✉) • T. Connolly • T. Hainey • G. Baxter
School of Computing, University of the West of Scotland, Paisley, UK
e-mail: mark.stansfield@uws.ac.uk

A. Jimoyiannis (ed.), *Research on e-Learning and ICT in Education*,
DOI 10.1007/978-1-4614-1083-6_17,

learn much more collaboratively than in previous generations, thus there is an important need for educators to embrace and adopt approaches to teaching and learning that are better suited to the learning styles that the younger generation of learners now adopt and provide a more stimulating and engaging learning environment. It is as a result of this need that the next section will explore some examples of how games-based learning and interactive technologies have been used in education.

Examples of Games-Based Learning in Education

In recent years, numerous games-based learning applications have been developed for use in the classroom, in further and higher education, as well as for training. This section focuses on examples most notably within business, the classroom environment and within the context of further and higher education, highlighting how they have enhanced learning and engagement among learners.

Games-Based Learning in Business

An example of a game used for teaching business and leadership skills is SimuLearn's Virtual Leader (http://www.simulearn.net), which provides a 3D-simlation game aimed at trainers in providing accelerated learning in a wide range of business-related skills such as effective leadership, communication, team building and group dynamics, how to foster creativity, and project management. A screen shot showing some of the game's features and characters is shown in Fig. 1.

The participants in the training exercise join a group of animated artificial intelligence characters as a leader who is then provided with the task of getting the team working together in achieving a common business goal. The tasks are made more challenging as a result of the virtual team members having particular personalities, viewpoints, allies and agendas. As a result, the leader must apply certain principles relating to effective leadership in order to get the group to focus on the task in hand. Leaders are judged on how individuals in the group respond to the tasks and the actions they take. Virtual Leader has been used within the context of training with several large organisations such as Coca-Cola and Johnson & Johnson.

Games-Based Learning in Teaching Software Development Requirements Collection and Analysis

An example of a games-based learning application in this area is provided by Connolly et al. (2007) who developed a game aimed at helping further and higher

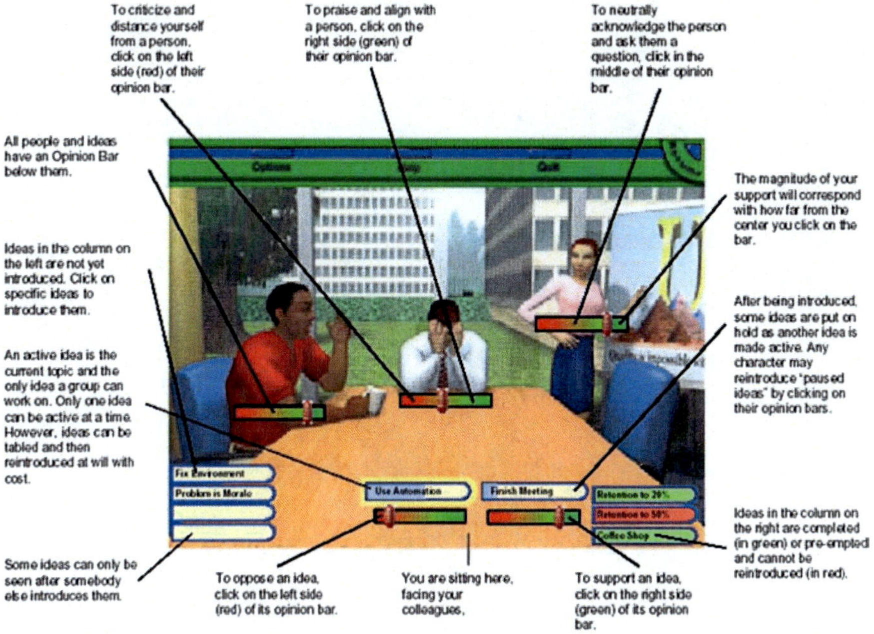

Fig. 1 Virtual Leader's interface

education students learn key skills and knowledge associated with software development requirements collection and analysis. Connolly et al. (2007) state that software development requirements collection and analysis can be considered to be a "wicked problem" as a result of what can often be viewed as incomplete, contradictory and changing requirements and solutions that are often difficult to recognise due to complex interdependencies. As a result, students often find considerable difficulty in understanding implementation-independent issues and analysing problems where there is often no single, simple or correct decision. In order to address these important issues, a simulation game "SDSim" was developed in which an example of the interface is shown on Fig. 2.

In the game, a team comprising one or more players are tasked with managing and delivering a software development project in which each player has a specific role (e.g. project manager, systems designer, team leader) and must communicate with nonplayer characters in the game to find the relevant information in order to successfully produce a high-level design that addresses the client's requirements. A detailed evaluation of further and higher education level students using the SDSim game (Hainey 2010) found that it did have a significant impact in motivating students and providing a stimulating environment within which to learn key skills and knowledge associated with software development requirements collection and analysis as compared with more traditional text book and classroom-based teaching and learning.

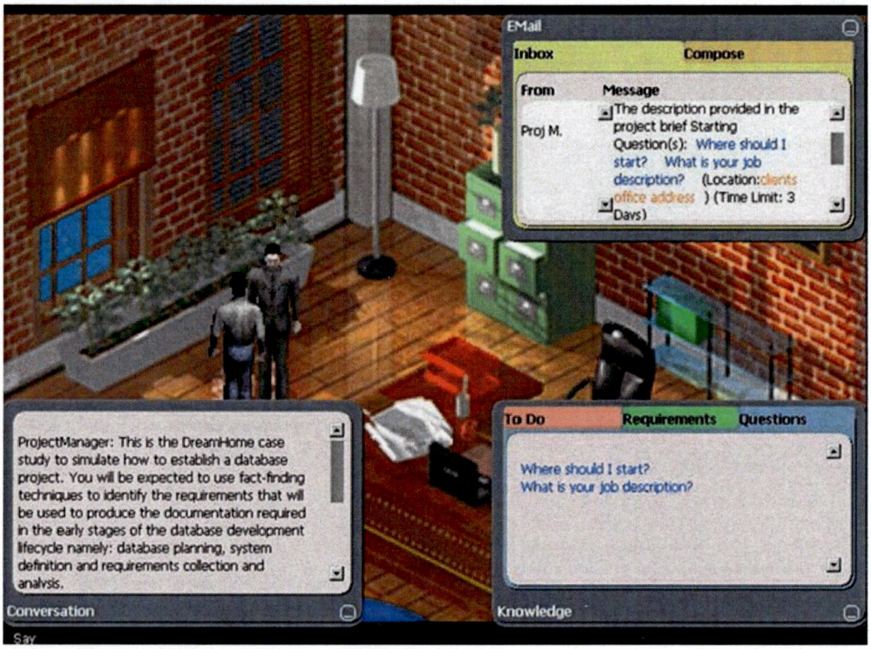

Fig. 2 SDSim game learning environment

Games-Based Learning and Interactive Technologies in Teaching Languages

In relation to using a games-based approach to teaching languages Rankin et al. (2006) in a preliminary study used EverQuest II to support the teaching of English as a second language. A screenshot from EverQuest II is shown in Fig. 3. EverQuest II is an example of a Massive Multiplayer Online Role Playing Game (MMORPG) that was found to be useful in generally reinforcing language acquisition. MMORPGs generally create a persistent universe in which hundreds of thousands of players can simultaneously interact in graphically rendered immersive worlds. By completing the quests, Rankin et al. (2006) found that the small number of players used for the purposes of their study who comprised Korean, Chinese and Castilian speakers were able to gain an appreciation for colloquial meanings, verbs and adverbs.

An example of a more detailed study into the use of games for language learning is provided by the ARGuing project (Connolly et al. 2009; Hainey et al. 2009; Tsvetkova et al. 2009). Alternate Reality Games (ARGs) are a form of interactive narrative and puzzle solving which often involve multiple media and gaming elements to tell a story that might be affected by the ideas and/or actions of the players as they take place in "real-time". The multiple media which is used to reveal the narrative to the players can involve web sites, instant messaging, text messages,

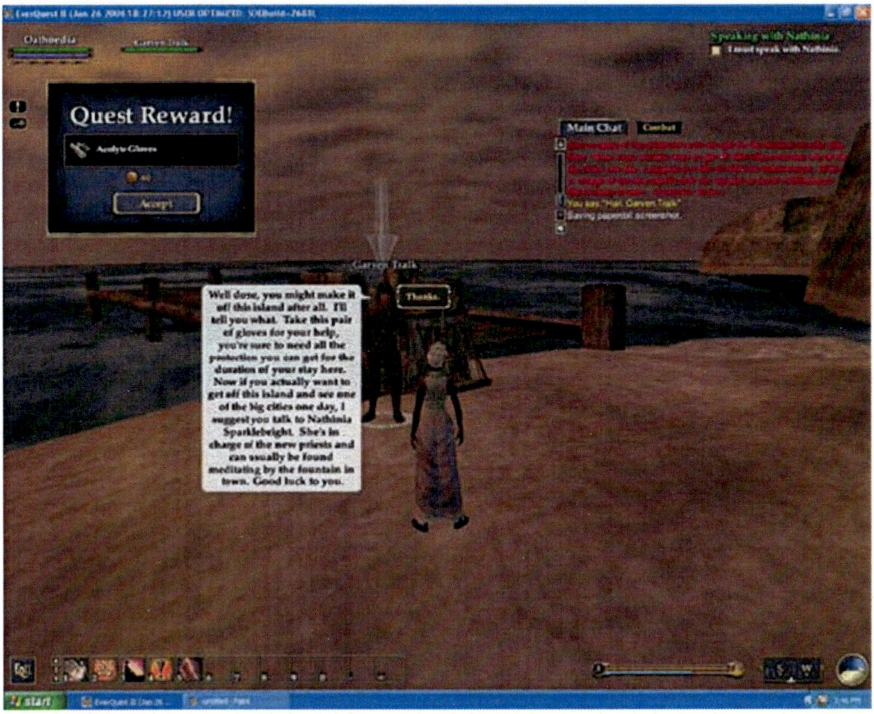

Fig. 3 Screenshot of the EverQuest II game

emails, as well as TV and newspaper adverts. As well as being a form of computer game, ARGs are heavily built around social networking in which players interact with one another and can form alliances. In the past, ARGs have been used to promote new films and TV series, as well as music CDs in which players are directed to various media in order undertake various challenges and quests in which "puppetmasters" steer players in different directions as the game's story unfolds.

The ARGuing project was part of a 2-year European Commission co-funded Comenius project entitled "ARGuing for Multilingual Motivation in Web 2.0". Web 2.0 refers to web applications that facilitate social interaction, participation, collaboration, information sharing, with tools and services including blogs, wikis, e-portfolios, video sharing, podcasting, tagging and social book marking, RSS and syndication.

The ARGuing project involved developing an ARG that was based on a set of characters who through their collective effort build a contemporary "Tower of Babel" which refers to notions and values well established in European civilisation. The ARGuing project was a cutting edge project that addressed two important needs in European education – (1) how to bridge the widening technological gap between educators and their students, (2) how to motivate students to understand the benefits of language learning at a level that impacts on their existing personal lives.

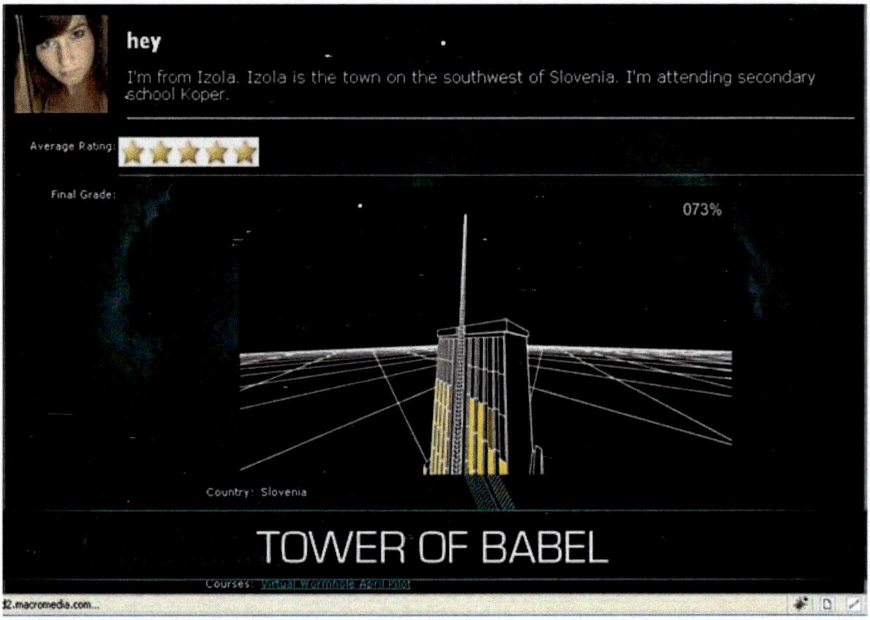

Fig. 4 Example of the "Tower of Babel" interface

The ARGuing project targeted secondary school children in which the game characters and the game participants discover how to build the foundations of the tower which are based on the principles and values of Europe – namely democracy, tolerance and respect, freedom and the rule of law and access to education. The storyline of the "Tower of Babel" is based on taking students to a future world in order to save languages that are under threat and can only be saved if students collaborate with each other and the ARG characters in bringing the different parts of Europe together and learning about each others cultures and languages.

The ARGuing project involved 328 secondary school pupils and 95 secondary school teachers from 17 European countries. Most of the quests in the ARG involved students working collaboratively with other students who were speakers of different languages in order to find information relating to a particular quest. The "building blocks" for the tower were puzzles, assignments and quests in multiple languages and in different subjects. The quests often involved a variety of tasks such as translating languages, uploading files, searching on the Internet and were delivered through forums, blogs, websites, short video clips and emails. Games were scored using two systems – building blocks awarded for the completion of a quest and an empathy score which rated players' collaboration as voted by other players. An example of the "Tower of Babel" interface is shown in Fig. 4.

In total 328 students from 28 schools across 17 European countries participated in the ARGuing project. Overall, the students' reaction to the ARG was very positive showing that the ARG was able to deliver the motivational experience expected by the students. Students believed the skills that they obtained and developed from using the ARG included problem-solving skills (48.8%), reflection skills (37.7%), analysing and classifying skills (44%), collaborative and teamwork skills (55%), leading and motivating skills (41%), critical thinking skills (32%) and creativity skills (54%). Ninety-two per cent of the students who completed the evaluation questionnaire indicated that they felt there should be more use of ICT in language learning. Of 19 language teachers who completed a post-test evaluation questionnaire 42% considered that using the ARG to be a very valuable professional experience.

Some of the issues raised by the teachers included some technical problems in using the ARG, as well as some teachers (5%) considering that it might be too difficult to monitor students' actions throughout the game. In addition, for teachers participating in the ARG, it did put immense pressure on markers to ensure that students received scores and feedback in a timely manner once they had conducted a quest so that they could continue onto the next quest. However, out of 19 teachers who completed a post ARG questionnaire:

- Seventy-nine per cent believed their students had really enjoyed the game.
- Eighty-nine per cent believed the game was appropriate for motivating their students to learn a second language.
- Eighty-nine per cent stated that they would use the game again in their language teaching.

Advantages of Games-Based Learning in Education

There are a number of advantages of using games-based learning within the context of education. Connolly and Stansfield (2007) suggest that games-based learning can provide for learners increased motivation and engagement, as well as an enhanced learning experience, improved student achievement and student retention. In addition, games-based learning can provide risk free training in a mistake friendly learning environment that allows trial and error and immediate feedback (Kriz 2003). These types of environments can be considered to invite exploration and experimentation, stimulating curiosity, discovery learning and perseverance (Connolly and Stansfield 2007).

In relation to motivation, Malone and Lepper (1987) presented a framework of intrinsic motivation in relation to computer games in that on an individual level they provide challenge (an appropriate level of difficulty and challenge, multiple goals for winning and constant feedback), fantasy (an appropriate level of immersion by assuming a particular role), curiosity (providing sensory stimulation to ensure prolonged participation), control (the ability to select choices and observe consequences of these choices). On an interpersonal level computer games can provide cooperation (assist others to achieve common goals), competition (comparing performance with that of other players), recognition (a sense of satisfaction when accomplishments are recognised). Other advantages of using games-based learning within an educational context include:

- Access to knowledge were human expertise may be scare or very expensive.
- They may encourage learners who lack interest or confidence and enhance their self-esteem (Dempsey et al. 1994).
- The versatility of using computer games was highlighted by Griffiths (2002) in which children can have access to technology that may help them overcome fears in using technology as well as assisting in the development of transferrable IT skills.
- Complex games have the potential to support cognitive processing and the development of strategic skills that can encourage greater academic performance as well as the development of social skills (Natale 2002; Connolly and Stansfield 2007).

Issues and Problems with Games-Based Learning in Education

One of the main concerns associated with the area of games-based learning that is cited is the dearth of empirical evidence supporting the validity of the approach (e.g. de Freitas 2004; Connolly et al. 2007). Games are often developed with little evaluation and concrete empirical evidence. As a result this hinders the further development and acceptance of the area of games-based learning since the area can be dismissed as lacking real evidence to substantiate claims (Hainey 2010).

Connolly and Stansfield (2007) point out that there are concerns about the negative impact on learning that games may have due to students concentrating on scoring and winning rather than the learning objectives. As well as the considerable cost that might be involved in developing games-based applications in terms of money, time and access to suitable expertise, there are also concerns that the use of some games may have a high learning curve and take significant amounts of time to work through making them unsuited to short or small-scale use within the classroom environment.

Preparing Teachers for the "iLearner" Generation

As has been shown by the examples in this chapter, games-based learning and Web 2.0 technologies can play a key role in teaching and learning across a wide range of different learner profiles from school age learners to mature learners within a training context. However, one of the key issues in attempting to engage and motivate learners is how educators can become skilled and knowledgeable in the use of such technologies within the classroom and with learners, particularly in the case of school age students who have become used to using the latest communication technologies, social networking and games-based technologies over many years. Many educators might not be as confident and knowledgeable in the use of such technologies since they were brought up in a less technologically advanced environment.

It is with these type of issues in mind that the Web 2.0 European Research Centre (Web 2.0 ERC) has been set up. The Web 2.0 ERC is a 2-year European Commission multilateral co-financed project that started in early 2010 aimed at enabling the mass of educators who find ICT confusing and frightening to have a simple and secure environment to use ICT within their class. The partners working on the project are:

- University of the West of Scotland, UK
- PROJEKTkompetenz.eu OG, Austria
- Sofia University, Bulgaria
- University of Peloponnese, Greece
- Kulturring in Berlin e.V, Germany
- Poznań University of Economics, Poland
- Çukurova University, Turkey

Many ICT tools exist and teachers do not have time nor expertise to identify the best solution for their needs. With many students using and communicating easily and openly using Web 2.0 tools (blogs, wikis, social networking, etc.), the technology gap between educators and students continues to grow despite best efforts of national and European agencies. The tools such as those described in the previous section have pedagogic value arising from sharing, communication and knowledge discovery that teachers could use to provide a more motivating, engaging, relevant and collaborative environment for students.

As a result there is a clear need for understanding how Web 2.0 tools can be used effectively within education. Thus, the objectives of the Web 2.0 ERC project are to:

- Establish a European Resource Centre for simplified and targeted Web 2.0 tools, for schools, HE and adult education.
- Provide clear examples of how to use them in class with accompanying pedagogy, guides and videos.
- Produce a customisable integrated Web 2.0 platform with single sign-on for educators to use.
- Foster and build collaborative communities to exchange best practice and for experienced Web 2.0 educators to mentor new users.

The project is aimed at significantly increasing the number of educators who can use Web 2.0 tools in a pedagogically sound way. Underpinning Web 2.0 tools and applications is an ethos of socialisation, collaboration and participation. Having a set of tools, pedagogy and guides that demonstrate how Web 2.0 can be used effectively in the classroom will provide educators and students with the means to collaborate on a European dimension and share and experience different languages and cultures.

The project is attempting to develop an innovative pedagogical framework for the use of Web 2.0 and illustrate the use of this framework with a set of pedagogical guides for the secondary, HE and adult education sectors. In addition, teacher training courses and piloting of the integrated Web 2.0 educational platform are being run during 2011 across the secondary, HE and adult education sectors. The projects include the setting up of a Community of Practice where educators from any level of education can share their experience and advice.

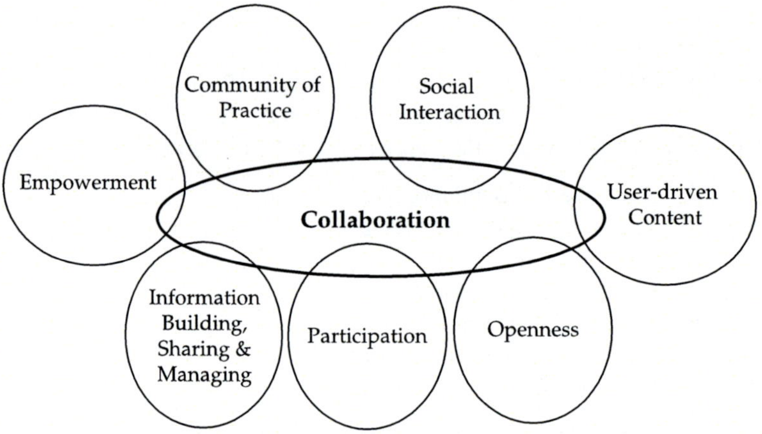

Fig. 5 Key terms commonly associated with Web 2.0

An Investigation of Empirical Evidence of the Value of Web 2.0 in Education

An extensive review of the literature was carried out at the start of the Web 2.0 ERC project into what empirical evidence exists in the academic literature in support of the education value of Web 2.0 in education. Using a set of Web 2.0 terms a number of electronic databases were searched including ACM, Science Direct, Emerald, IngentaConnect, ERIC, CINAHL Plus, EBSCO and PsychInfo and found 965 papers that matched the search terms.

A search of the academic literature published between 2004 and 2010 revealed 38 definitions of the term Web 2.0. From the various definitions of Web 2.0, several keywords feature in those papers that include – communication, sharing and collaboration. The term Web 2.0 is used to refer to a collection of tools and applications which are not focused on imparting information (or at least this is not their main or only feature) but the collaborative creation of content. Web 2.0 most often is said to include social networking platforms, wikis, blogs and tagging tools.

Examples of some of the definitions included Paroutis and Al Saleh (2009) who defined Web 2.0 as referring to "a perceived second generation of community-driven web services such as social networking sites, blogs, wikis, etc. which facilitate a more socially connected web where everyone is able to communicate, participate, collaborate and add to and edit the information space". Aharony (2009) refers to Web 2.0 as emphasising "…the value of user-generated content. It is about sharing and about communication and it opens the long tail which allows small groups of individuals to benefit from key pieces of the platform while fulfilling their own needs".

Figure 5 highlights some of the key terms and words most commonly associated with Web 2.0 that centres around the core concept of collaboration.

Common Web 2.0 tools explored in the literature included:

- Blogs (e.g. Wordpress, Twitter, Edublogs, Blogspot)
- Wikis (e.g. Wikidot, Wikispace, Wiki-site)
- Forums (e.g. phpBB, vBulletin)
- ePortfolios (e.g. Elgg, Mahara, Sakai)
- Social Networking (e.g. Facebook, Myspace, Ning)
- Social Bookmarking (e.g. Delicious, diigo, edutagger)
- Media Sharing (e.g. Flickr, Youtube, Teachertube, Podomatic)
- Document Sharing (e.g. Google docs, Zoho)

The Web 2.0 ERC project was particularly interested in empirical evidence showing the educational effectiveness of Web 2.0 tools and found only 41 papers (out of the 965) that provided some form of empirical evidence. To assess the quality of the papers, each paper was given a score along four dimensions described below. Scores of 1, 2 or 3 were used for each dimension where 3 meant high, 2 meant medium and 1 meant low on that criterion.

1. How appropriate is the research design for addressing the question, or sub-questions of this review (higher weighting for inclusion of a control group)? Papers were coded as:
    - High = 3, e.g. RCT
    - Medium = 2, e.g. Controlled study
    - Low = 1, e.g. case study, single subject-experimental design, pre-test/post-test design
2. How appropriate are the methods and analysis?
3. Generalisable to target population for this study; e.g. size and representativeness of sample: to what extent would the findings be relevant across age group, gender, ethnicity, etc?
4. To what extent can the study findings be trusted in answering the study question(s)?

The total weight of evidence for each paper was calculated by summing scores for each dimension (taking into account appropriateness of design, methods and analysis, generalisability, soundness of study methodology). Possible scores ranged from 4 to 12 where 4 is a low score and 12 a high score. A score of 7 and above was then used as a benchmark for identifying the depth and appropriateness of the underlying research within each paper that was identified. As a result of this analysis, out of the 41 papers initially identified as containing some level of empirical evidence, only eight papers scored 7 or higher.

Thus, out of an initial 965 papers that explored Web 2.0 technologies and concepts, only 0.82% of the papers actually containing any significant and detailed empirical research that was used to justify the claims being made by the authors. It was surprising that the evidence on the educational effectiveness of Web 2.0 tools is so low. Despite this apparent lack of detailed empirical evidence, the papers that did not contain empirical evidence still provided insight into some of the underlying benefits and problem areas in using Web 2.0 tools in education. The lack of empirical evidence was also found to be a factor underlying concerns expressed about much of the games-based learning literature (Connolly et al. 2007; Hainey 2010).

Conclusions

This chapter has highlighted some of the key issues that educators face if they are to continue to motivate and engage today's learners. While using games-based learning and interactive Web 2.0 technologies might pose significant hurdles for many educators from a personal, organisational and professional perspective, this chapter has provided some examples of how these technologies can be used in a positive and engaging way with a range of different learners from secondary school age through to adult learners. New projects such as the Web 2.0 European Resource Centre provide a key resource that educators from across Europe will soon be able to access and engage with other educators, learners, technologists and decision-makers in learning more about adopting such technologies and tools for their own teaching, as well as seeing examples of best practice. However, initial research has shown that there is a need for more detailed empirical research to be undertaken that can provide better evidence and insight into how games-based learning and Web 2.0 technologies actually enhance, motivate and engage learning, not just among the "iLearner Generation" but across all age groups.

Acknowledgements The ARG project reported in this chapter was supported by the EU Comenius Programme under contract 133909-2007-UK-COMENIUS-CMP. The Web 2.0 ERC project reported in this chapter was supported by the EU KA3 ICT Multilateral Projects Programme under contract 504839-LLP-1-209-1-UK-KA3-KA3MP.

References

Aharony, N. (2009). The influence of LIS students' personality characteristics on their perceptions towards Web 2.0 use. *Journal of Librarianship and Information Science*, 41, 227–242.

Connolly, T.M., Stansfield, M.H., Hainey, T., Cousins, I., Josephson, J., Rodriguez Ortiz, C., Tsvetkova, N., Stoimenova, B., & Tsvetanova, S. (2009). Arguing for multilingual motivation in Web 2.0: a games-based learning platform for language learning. In M. Pivec (ed.), *Proceedings of the 3nd European Conference on Games-based Learning (ECGBL)* (pp. 110–119). Graz, Austria.

Connolly, T. M., & Stansfield, M. H. (2007). From eLearning to games-based eLearning: Using interactive technologies in teaching an IS course. *International Journal of Information Technology Management*, 26(4), 188–208.

Connolly, T. M., Stansfield, M. H., & Hainey, T. (2007). An application of games-based learning within software engineering. *British Journal of Educational Technology*, 38(3), 416–428.

Connolly, T.M., McLellan, E., Stansfield, M. H., Ramsay, J., & Sutherland, J. (2004). Applying computer games concepts to teaching database analysis and design. In Q. Mehdi, N. Gough, D. Natkin, D. Al-Dabass (eds.), *Proceedings of the International Conference on Computer Games, AI, Design and Education* (pp. 352–359). Reading, UK.

Dempsey, J. V, Rasmussen, K., & Lucassen, B. (1994). Instructional gaming: implications for instructional technology. *Annual Meeting of the Association for Educational Communications and Technology*, 16–20 February 1994, Nashville, TN.

de Freitas, S. (2004). *Learning through Play*. Internal report. London Learning and Skills Research Centre.

Griffiths, M.D. (2002). The educational benefits of videogames. *Education and Health*. 20(3), pp. 47–51.

Hainey, T. (2010). *Using games-based learning to teach requirements collection and analysis at tertiary education level.* Unpublished PhD Thesis, University of the West of Scotland.

Hainey, T., Connolly, T., Stansfield, M., Boyle, L., Josephson, J., O'Donovan, A., Rodrigues Ortiz, C., Tsvetkova, N., Stoimenova, B., & Tsvetanova, S. (2009). Arguing for multilingual motivation in Web 2.0: an evaluation of a large-scale European pilot. In M. Pivec (ed.), *Proceedings of 3rd European Conference on Games-based Learning, ECGBL* (pp. 164–172). Graz, Austria.

Kriz, W. C. (2003). Creating effective learning environments and learning organizations through gaming simulation design. *Simulation & Gaming*, 34(4), 495–511.

Malone, T. W., & Lepper, M. R. (1987). Making learning fun: A taxonomy of intrinsic motivations for learning. In R. Snow & M. Farr (eds.), *Aptitude, learning and instruction. Volume 3: Conative and affective process analysis* (pp. 223–253). Hillsdale, NJ: Lawrence Erlbaum.

Natale, M. J. (2002). The effect of a male-oriented computer gaming culture on careers in the computer industry. *Computers and Society*, 32(2), 24–31.

Paroutis, S., & Al Saleh, A. (2009). Determinants of knowledge sharing using Web 2.0 technologies. *Journal of Knowledge Management*, 13(4), 52–63.

Prensky, M. (2001). *Digital game based learning*. McGraw-Hill.

Rankin, Y., Gold, R. & Gooch B. (2006). Playing for keeps: gaming as a language learning tool. In J. Finnegan & M. Barr (eds.), *Proceedings of the ACM SIGGRAPH Educators Program* (Article No. 44). ACM Digital Library: Association for Computing Machinery.

Tsvetkova, N., Stoimenova, B., Tsvetanova, S., Connolly, T.M., Stansfield, M.H., Hainey, T., Cousins, I., Josephson, J., Lazaro, N., Rubio, G., & Rodriguez Ortiz, C., (2009). Arguing for multilingual motivation in Web 2.0: the teacher training perspective. In M. Pivec (ed.), *Proceedings of the 3nd European Conference on Games-based Learning, ECGBL* (pp. 371–378). Graz, Austria.

Presence in a Collaborative Science Learning Activity in Second Life

Ioannis Vrellis, Nikiforos M. Papachristos, Antonis Natsis, and Tassos A. Mikropoulos

Introduction

Following Dede's description of "'Alice-in-Wonderland' multi-user virtual environments interfaces" that would "shape how people learn" (2002), nowadays, *Multi-user virtual environments* (MUVEs) are being surrounded by hype regarding their impact on and potential in education. Their support to constructivist approaches to teaching and learning seems to be of major importance for educators and researchers. MUVEs can provide rich learning experiences, enhance the sense of (social) presence of learners, and allow multifaceted interaction.

Some MUVEs have been designed specifically for educational use, like *River City*, a MUVE fostering inquiry-based learning (Ketelhut 2007), *AquaMoose3D*, a graphical MUVE for mathematics learning (Edwards et al. 2001), and *Quest Atlantis*, a 3D multi-user environment which engages children in educational tasks (Barab et al. 2005). On the other hand, general-purpose MUVEs are more widely used in many educational settings and domains of subject matter. *Second Life® (SL)* seems to be the most popular MUVE among educators. In higher education, SL has attracted a great deal of attention, with over 400 academic institutions holding a virtual presence in it (Campusin3D.com, n.d.), more and more official courses are being offered "in-world" and classes are taught in architecture, English as a second language, science, engineering, law, computer science, history, arts, etc. (Calgone and Hiles 2008). SL is a persistent (24/7) computer-generated virtual world with no pre-made content. Rather, its residents are creating the content. It is a platform with open-ended possibilities which can be utilized to develop educational virtual environments and to design learning activities.

As often happens when hype prevails, there are many issues regarding the educational affordances of MUVEs that are still under-reported such as how educators

I. Vrellis (✉) • N.M. Papachristos • A. Natsis • T. A. Mikropoulos
Department of Primary School Education, University of Ioannina, Ioannina, Greece
e-mail: ivrellis@uoi.gr

A. Jimoyiannis (ed.), *Research on e-Learning and ICT in Education*,
DOI 10.1007/978-1-4614-1083-6_18, © Springer Science+Business Media, LLC 2012

design learning activities, with specific learning goals to be conducted in MUVEs and even less data comes from empirical studies related to instructional design and pedagogy in MUVEs. A very important and unique characteristic of educational virtual environments that seems to play an important role in learning and is also not well reported is the sense of spatial and social presence (Mikropoulos 2006; Winn and Windschitl 2000; Selverian and Lombard 2010) that emerges when humans interact with and via a virtual environment.

Presence is a central conceptual phenomenon related to virtual environments, which Lombard and Ditton (1997) excellently described as "the perceptual illusion of non-mediation," the phenomenon where a person fails to perceive or acknowledge that a mediated experience is mediated. A major branch of presence conceptualization defines presence as consisting of two interrelated phenomena: spatial presence (also known as physical presence or telepresence) and social presence (Heeter 1992; Biocca 1997; Ijsselsteijn et al. 2000; Biocca and Harms 2002; Biocca et al. 2003). Spatial presence refers to the "sense of being physically located somewhere" (Ijsselsteijn et al. 2000) while social presence refers to "being with others" in a mediated environment (Heeter 1992). Many factors have been suggested as possibly affecting the sense of presence, including media form factors, content factors, and user characteristics (Ijsselsteijn et al. 2000). Presence measuring is following two major methodological strands, subjective measuring and objective-physiological measuring, but it seems that subjective post-test ratings are the most widely used methods to approach presence measuring. Among others, the following questionnaires have been developed to access presence: the Slater–Usoh–Steed (SUS) Questionnaire (Slater et al. 1994), the Presence Questionnaire (PQ) (Witmer and Singer 1998), the Igroup Presence Questionnaire (Schubert et al. 2001), and the Temple Presence Inventory (TPI) (Lombard et al. 2009).

This work is part of a research project that aims at designing learning activities in order to study learning in MUVEs in terms of learning outcomes, collaboration, and presence. In the first study of this project (Vrellis et al. 2010) an authentic, collaborative learning activity concerning light reflection was designed and developed in Second Life. First results concern educational environment design issues, collaboration, and instructional issues.

Regarding design issues, students prefer to perform the whole learning activity in the educational virtual environment. That is, they want "in-world" intuitive object manipulation, educational material, and tools that work in the environment, instead of "out of world" dialogue menus, browsers, and tools that could distract their attention from the environment and learning activity. Even though virtual environments allow object manipulation at user's will (all degrees of freedom), restricting degrees of freedom to the necessary ones, depending on the specific instructional design and educational scenario, has no negative effect on creating an engaging authentic learning task. Moreover, students prefer to perform activities in settings relevant to the specific educational scenario, even out of the conventional "classroom representation" setting.

As far as collaboration is concerned, results show that participating in collaborative learning activities conducted in MUVEs is very important for their education and they evaluated positively the presence of a tutor in the activity. They felt that they could interact with the other participants and evaluated their experience as interactive and sociable. Students prefer to collaborate through rich communication channels that do not filter out important nonverbal communication signals.

Finally, concerning instructional issues, the study reveals that pedagogical methods of constructivist approach, like scaffolding, can be implemented in SL through properly designed problem-based learning activities. This chapter presents empirical data gathered from a study regarding a problem-based physics learning activity in SL. Our aim is to gain knowledge and experience about the sense of presence (spatial and social) that emerges while students collaborate in MUVEs. This study is a step toward the investigation of the relationship between learning outcomes and presence.

Method

Virtual Environment and Learning Activity

The virtual environment was designed and developed in SL. It refers to physics learning and specifically to the reflection of light. The design of the learning activity was based on the seven principles of constructivism (Jonassen 1994):

- Provide multiple representations of reality – avoid oversimplification of instruction by representing the natural complexity of the world.
- Focus on knowledge construction not reproduction.
- Present authentic tasks.
- Provide real world, case-based learning environments.
- Foster reflective practice.
- Enable context, and content, dependent knowledge construction.
- Support collaborative construction of knowledge through social negotiation, not competition among learners for recognition.

The problem presents an authentic task in a "real" world environment. Students had to collaborate in order to shoot an apple down from a tree using a laser beam and a plane mirror (Fig. 1). They had to calculate the correct angle of the mirror in order to reflect the laser beam to the apple. Students were not allowed to use a trial and error approach. Instead, they had to use trigonometry for the calculation of the correct angle before shooting.

The following "in-world" tools were available to the students:

- Two virtual rulers for the measurement of horizontal and vertical distances.
- A poster presenting the law of reflection.
- Three posters presenting the trigonometric functions and values for sine, cosine, and tangent.
- An interactive whiteboard where students could draw sketches. The whiteboard had also a help button that presented a graphical model of the problem (Fig. 2).
- A virtual calculator.

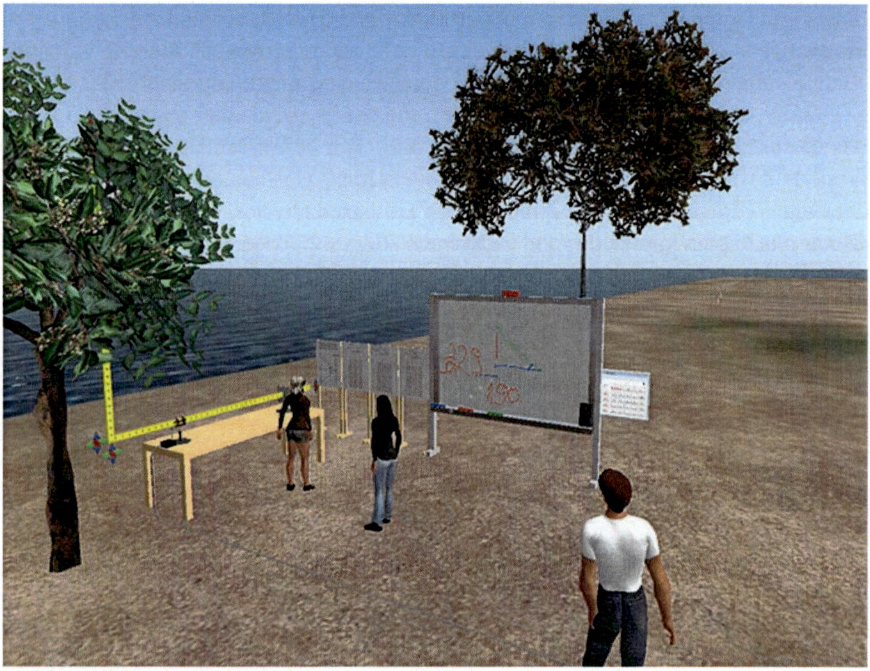

Fig. 1 The activity setting

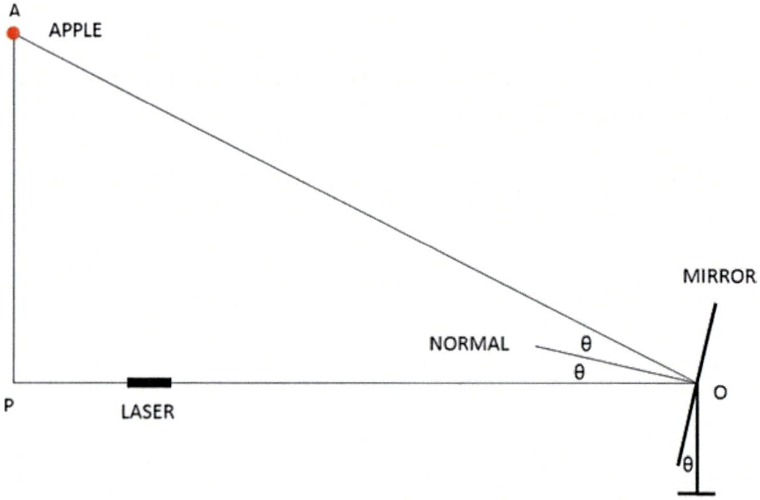

Fig. 2 A model of the problem

To solve the problem, students had to calculate the rotation angle of the mirror (θ) (Fig. 2). To do so, they had to recognize that θ=POA/2. The angle POA could be calculated through its tangent. So, first they had to measure the distances PO and PA by correctly positioning the rulers. Then, they had to divide the distances in order to find the tangent. Finally, by using the trigonometric tables, students could find the angle POA and thus θ.

Subjects

Thirty second-year, future teacher students (22 women, 8 men) of the University of Ioannina, participated in the study. Their ages were between 18 and 25 (Mean = 19.7, SD = 1.44). They all were experienced users of SL, since they had attended a class on potential educational uses of SL. Their participation was voluntary, motivated by a small bonus in their marks. The students registered in pairs for the collaborative activity.

Procedure

The empirical data was gathered from 15 sessions where a pair of students and the tutor participated. They were physically located in three different rooms and collaborated exclusively through SL. Each session lasted about 40 min. Before the experiment, the students answered a personal questionnaire on demographics, computer, and 3D-VR games experience, tendency to become involved in activities and previous knowledge related to light reflection and trigonometry.

Participants used their personal SL accounts and avatars to log in and were teleported to the Educational Approaches to Virtual Reality Technologies Lab's island in SL (Earthlab Education Island). There, they met the tutor who guided them to the activity's setting. The students and tutor communicated via the SL voice and text chat and their screens, microphones, and webcams were recorded.

The tutor made a brief introduction to the topic under study in a virtual classroom (Fig. 3). There, the students familiarized with the use of the available educational material and virtual objects and tools. After that, the participants walked outside the classroom, where the activity setting was located. The tutor posed the problem the students had to solve collaboratively and let them work, remaining nearby available to provide assistance.

After finishing the activity, the students answered a questionnaire measuring presence and took part in a debriefing interview with the tutor. The presence questionnaire used was the TPI that measures multiple dimensions of presence (Lombard et al. 2009).

Fig. 3 In the virtual classroom

Results

All pairs of students found the right solution to the problem with more or less scaffolding from the tutor. The following tables show the various dimensions of presence measured. Also some statistically significant correlations between these dimensions and the user characteristics are presented. Table 1 shows the results from the spatial presence part of the TPI questionnaire.

The overall score for spatial presence is 4.25 (SD 1.258). This value is little above the average indicating a moderate sense of spatial presence in the MUVE. This result is rather expected. SL is a desktop virtual environment that does not exploit all the available VR technologies. High scores of spatial presence are usually associated with highly immersive virtual environments.

Table 2 presents the results from the social presence – actor within medium (parasocial interaction) part of the TPI questionnaire. "In a parasocial interaction media users respond to social cues presented by persons they encounter within a medium even though it is illogical to do so" (Lombard et al. 2000).

The overall score for social presence is 5.29 (SD 0.837). The score is higher than that for spatial presence. This can be attributed to the nature of SL as a MUVE that enables social interaction and collaboration, as well as to the nature of our learning activity.

Table 1 Spatial presence

Questions	Minimum	Maximum	Mean	Standard deviation
How much did it seem as if the objects and people you saw/heard had come to the place you were?	1	7	4.37	1.771
How much did it seem as if you could reach out and touch the objects or people you saw/heard?	1	7	4.40	1.734
How often when an object seemed to be headed toward you did you want to move to get out of its way?	1	7	3.50	1.815
To what extent did you experience a sense of being there inside the environment you saw/heard?	2	7	4.77	1.591
To what extent did it seem that sounds came from specific different locations?	1	7	3.93	1.791
How often did you want to or try to touch something you saw/heard?	1	7	4.13	1.795
Did the experience seem more like looking at the events/people on a movie screen or more like looking at the events/people through a window?	1	7	4.60	1.958

Table 2 Social presence

Questions	Minimum	Maximum	Mean	Standard deviation
How often did you have the sensation that people you saw/heard could also see/hear you?	1	7	5.50	1.480
To what extent did you feel you could interact with the person or people you saw/heard?	4	7	5.63	0.928
How much did it seem as if you and the people you saw/heard both left the places where you were and went to a new place?	1	7	4.67	1.561
How much did it seem as if you and the people you saw/heard were together in the same place?	2	7	5.50	1.383
How often did it feel as if someone you saw/heard in the environment was talking directly to you?	3	7	5.70	1.291
How often did you want to or did you make eye-contact with someone you saw/heard?	1	7	4.57	1.455
Seeing and hearing a person through a medium constitutes an interaction with him or her. How much control over the interaction with the person or people you saw/heard did you feel you had?	3	7	5.47	1.279

Table 3 Social richness

Questions	Minimum	Maximum	Mean	Standard deviation
Please circle the number that best describes your evaluation of the media experience: Remote – Immediate	3	7	5.83	1.147
Please circle the number that best describes your evaluation of the media experience: Unemotional – Emotional	1	7	4.87	1.548
Please circle the number that best describes your evaluation of the media experience: Unresponsive – Responsive	4	7	6.20	0.925
Please circle the number that best describes your evaluation of the media experience: Dead – Lively	3	7	6.00	1.259
Please circle the number that best describes your evaluation of the media experience: Impersonal – Personal	1	7	5.60	1.404
Please circle the number that best describes your evaluation of the media experience: Insensitive – Sensitive	1	7	5.07	1.438
Please circle the number that best describes your evaluation of the media experience: Unsociable – Sociable	3	7	5.83	0.986

Table 4 Social realism

Questions	Minimum	Maximum	Mean	Standard deviation
The events I saw/heard would occur in the real world	3	7	5.53	1.383
The events I saw/heard could occur in the real world	1	7	5.72	1.412
The way in which the events I saw/heard occurred is a lot like the way they occur in the real world	2	7	5.20	1.400

Table 3 shows the results from the questions concerning social richness. Social richness as a dimension of presence is the extent to which users perceive the virtual environment, when it is used to interact with others, as sociable, warm, sensitive, personal, or intimate (Lombard et al. 2000).

The overall score for social richness is 5.63 (SD 0.990). The score is well above the average. Specifically, the students found their experience as highly responsive (6.20, SD 0.925) and lively (6.00, SD 1.259).

Table 4 presents the mean values for social realism. The social realism questions evaluate whether the portrayed events would or could occur in the real world.

The overall score for social richness is 5.48 (SD 1.225). This score is also high and in accordance with the previous two social dimensions of presence (social presence and social richness).

Table 5 Engagement (mental immersion)

Questions	Minimum	Maximum	Mean	Standard deviation
To what extent did you feel mentally immersed in the experience?	2	7	5.13	1.456
How involving was the experience?	3	7	5.80	1.157
How completely were your senses engaged?	2	7	5.00	1.390
To what extent did you experience a sensation of reality?	1	7	4.93	1.507
How relaxing or exciting was the experience?	1	7	5.27	1.639
How engaging was the story?	3	7	6.37	0.928

Table 6 Engagement and presence correlations

Engagement (mental immersion)		
Spatial presence	Pearson Correlation	0.587
	Sig. (2-tailed)	<0.01
Social presence	Pearson Correlation	0.643
	Sig. (2-tailed)	<0.01
Social richness	Pearson Correlation	0.739
	Sig. (2-tailed)	<0.01
Social realism	Pearson Correlation	0.487
	Sig. (2-tailed)	<0.01

Engagement with the learning activity is an important parameter that contributes to learning outcomes regardless of whether the learning environment is mediated or not.

Table 5 shows the results concerning the engagement of students in the experience. The overall score for engagement is 5.42 (SD 1.049). It is remarkable that students found the story (activity) very engaging (6.37, SD 0.928). This result indicates that the instruction design based on constructivist approaches incorporating authentic tasks engage students in the learning activity.

Below some of the statistically significant correlations found between the variables are presented.

Table 6 shows the correlations between engagement and various components of presence. It is clear that engagement and other dimensions of presence are strongly correlated. This implies that an engaging constructivist learning activity can increase the sense of presence of the learner.

Other interesting findings were the negative correlations between (subjective) computer expertise and the sense of spatial presence ($r=-0.384$, $p<0.05$) and engagement ($r=-0.437$, $p<0.05$). This would imply that the more experienced a user considers herself in computer usage, the more difficult it is for her to feel present in the MUVE. Nevertheless this finding should be regarded cautiously since no significant correlations between other subtypes of computer expertise (internet, video-games, virtual environments, SL) and presence or engagement were found.

Table 7 shows that somc variables indicating the user's tendency to become involved in activities are correlated with her sense of spatial presence.

Table 7 Tendency to become involved in activities and spatial presence

Spatial presence		
I concentrate well also on disagreeable tasks	Pearson Correlation	0.407
	Sig. (2-tailed)	<0.05
Sometimes I am so involved in a game that having the impression of being part of the game rather than moving a joystick or watching the screen	Pearson Correlation	0.440
	Sig. (2-tailed)	<0.05
I have been scared by something happening on a TV show or in a Movie	Pearson Correlation	0.522
	Sig. (2-tailed)	<0.01

Conclusions

This chapter presents empirical data about the sense of presence (spatial and social) gathered from a study regarding a collaborative problem-based physics learning activity in SL. Even though exploratory studies like this tend to generate more questions than answers, first results suggest that constructivist collaborative learning activities in a MUVE like SL have the potential to engage students. Furthermore, the social dimensions of presence scored well above average while spatial presence remained average, which is rather expected because SL is a socially oriented MUVE based on nonimmersive desktop technology. Moreover, strong positive correlations between engagement and other dimensions of presence were observed, while subjective computer expertise seemed to be negatively correlated to spatial presence and engagement, although these findings should be regarded with caution. Finally, the users' tendency to become involved in activities seems to be related to the sense of spatial presence they experience in MUVE-like environments.

The above results constitute a basis and also a motivation toward the investigation of the relationship between presence and learning outcomes from learning activities in SL.

Our next step toward this investigation includes the analysis of screen, webcam, and voice recordings in order to assess qualitative aspects of presence and collaboration.

References

Barab, S., Thomas, M., Dodge, T., Carteaux, R., & Tuzun, H. (2005). Making learning fun: Quest Atlantis, a game without guns. *Educational Technology Research and Development,* 53(1), 86–108.

Biocca, F. (1997). The Cyborg's dilemma: Progressive embodiment in virtual environments. *Journal of Computer-Mediated Communication*, 3(2), Retrieved 1 November 2010 from http://jcmc.indiana.edu/vol3/issue2/biocca2.html.

Biocca, F., & Harms, C. (2002). *Defining and measuring social presence: Contribution to the Networked Minds Theory and Measure.* In F. Gouveia & F. Biocca (eds.), Proceedings of the Fifth Annual International Workshop PRESENCE 2002 (pp. 7–36). Porto, Portugal: Universidade Fernando Pessoa.

Biocca, F., Harms, C., & Burgoon, J. K. (2003). Toward a more robust theory and measure of social presence: Review and suggested criteria. *Presence: Teleoperators and Virtual Environments,* 12(5), 456–480.

Calgone, C., & Hiles, J. (2008). *Blended Realities: A virtual tour of education in Second Life.* Retrieved 3 January 2010 from http://edumuve.com/blended/BlendedRealitiesCalongneHiles.pdf.

Campusin3D.com. (n.d.). *Second Life.* Retrieved 3 January 2010 from http://www.campusin3d.com/en/second-life.

Dede, C. (2002). Vignettes about the future of learning technologies. In D. Evans & R. Paige (eds.), *2020 visions: Transforming education and training through advanced technologies* (pp. 18–25). Washington, DC: U.S. Department of Commerce.

Edwards, E., Elliott, J., & Bruckman, A. (2001). AquaMoose 3D: Math learning in a 3D multi-user virtual world. In M. Beaudouin-Lafon & R. Jacob (eds.), *ACM CHI 2001 Conference on Human Factors in Computing Systems* (pp. 259–260). Seattle, Washington, USA.

Heeter, C. (1992). Being there: the subjective experience of presence. *Presence: Teleoperators and Virtual Environments,* 1(2), 262–271.

Ijsselsteijn, W. A., Ridder, H. d., Freeman, J., & Avons, S. E. (2000). Presence: concept, determinants, and measurement. In B. Rogowitz, T. Watson. & T. Pappas (eds.), *Proceedings of the SPIE, Human Vision and Electronic Imaging* (pp. 520–529). San Jose: SPIE.

Jonassen, D. H. (1994). Thinking technology: Toward a constructivist design model. *Educational Technology,* 34, 34–37.

Ketelhut, D. J. (2007). The impact of student self-efficacy on scientific inquiry skills: An exploratory investigation in River City, a multi-user virtual environment. *Journal of Science Education and Technology,* 16(1), 99–111.

Lombard, M., & Ditton, T. (1997). At the heart of it all: the concept of presence. *Journal of Computer-Mediated Communication,* 3(2), Retrieved 1 November 2010 from: http://www.ascusc.org/jcmc/vol3/issue2/lombard.html.

Lombard, M., Ditton, T. B., Crane, D., Davis, B., Gil-Egui, G., Horvath, K., Rossman, J., & Park, S. (2000). *Measuring presence: A literature-based approach to the development of a standardized paper-and-pencil instrument.* Paper presented at the Third International Workshop on Presence. Delft, The Netherlands.

Lombard, M., Ditton, T. B., & Weinstein, L. (2009). *Measuring presence: The Temple Presence Inventory (TPI).* Retrieved 20 November 2009 from http://astro.temple.edu/~tuc16417/papers/Lombard_et_al.pdf.

Mikropoulos, T. A. (2006). Presence: A unique characteristic in educational virtual environments. *Virtual Reality, special issue 'Using Virtual Reality in Education',* 10(3–4), 197–206.

Schubert, T., Friedmann, F., & Regenbrecht, H. (2001). The experience of presence: Factor analytic insights, *Presence: Teleoperators and Virtual Environments,* 10, 266–281.

Selverian, M. E. M., & Lombard, M. (2010). Telepresence: A 'real' component in a model to make human-computer interface factors meaningful in the virtual learning environment. *Themes in Science and Technology Education,* 2(1–2), 31–58.

Slater, M., Usoh, M., & Steed, A. (1994). Depth of presence in virtual environments. *Presence: Teleoperators and Virtual Environments,* 3, 130–144.

Vrellis, I., Papachristos, N. M., Bellou, J., Avouris, N., & Mikropoulos, T. A. (2010). Designing a collaborative learning activity in Second Life: An exploratory study in physics. In J. Mohamed, Kinshuk, D. Sampson & M. Spector (eds.), *Proceedings of the 10th IEEE International Conference on Advanced Learning Technologies* (pp. 210–214). Sousse, Tunisia: IEEE Computer Society.

Witmer, B., & Singer, M. (1998). Measuring presence in virtual environments: A presence questionnaire. *Presence,* 7(3), 225–240.

Winn, W. D., & Windschitl, M. (2000). Learning science in virtual environments: the interplay of theory and experience. *Themes in Education,* 1(4), 373–389.

Emotional Interaction in e-Learning

Konstantina Chatzara, Charalampos Karagiannidis, and Demosthenes Stamatis

Introduction and Related Work

Emotional contact is an important element in learning since it can relieve students from failure and offer them a sense of continuous support when facing negative emotions during the learning procedure. While in traditional classes educators have the ability to inspire students and create motives that can enhance the learning process, in e-learning applications the absence of face-to-face contact eliminates emotional communication. This lack of communication can act as an obstacle between the student and the learning environment. Students spend increasingly more learning time in front of their computer: for example, results from the eUSER European project reveal that 76% of adult students use the Internet in the course of organized learning activities, and that every second person taking an e-learning course reports that they would not have done it if it had not been available online (Punie et al. 2006). E-learning applications that exploit social and emotional aspects might therefore improve the quality of education for those distance learners.

In order to support the emotional process in human–computer communication, we propose the use of an agent that is represented by a graphical animated synthetic character. The agent uses expressions, gestures, and body movements to communicate with students by "talking" to them through oral and written language, expressing sympathy and comfort when they have a certain problem in the educational process.

K. Chatzara (✉) • C. Karagiannidis
Department of Special Education, University of Thessaly, Volos, Greece
e-mail: chatzara@sed.uth.gr

D. Stamatis
Department of Informatics, Alexander TEI of Thessaloniki, Thessaloniki, Greece

A. Jimoyiannis (ed.), *Research on e-Learning and ICT in Education*,
DOI 10.1007/978-1-4614-1083-6_19,

Emotional agents have been used for improving interaction in many application domains, including e-learning. Back in 1992, Bates and Elliot were the first to introduce agents with emotional behaviour (Bates et al. 1992; Elliot 1992). Three years later, Blumberg and Galyean (1995) were the first who presented emotional responses which were connected to a learning model, though this connection was not clearly defined (Beale and Creed 2009). COSMO was a research project that designed a system that could express and recognize emotions in a learning domain (Lester et al. 1999). However, the results that this could have on user's behaviour were not considered. Massaro et al. (2000) created Baldi that had emotional behaviour in the learning domain. Their research results showed that Baldi could motivate students for more learning. Maldonado et al. (2005) and Chalfoun et al. (2006) related emotional reactions to events, while Burleson (2006) introduced a learning companion in a problem-solving task application, aiming to coordinate the relationships between affect and tasks. Conati and Maclaren (2009) developed a system which accommodates the probabilistic relations between causes, effects, and emotional states of the user. Review work points out that the main question to be answered is not simply if emotional agents are more effective than agents with non-emotional behaviour, but the impact that artificial emotional intelligence has on user attitudes, perceptions, and behaviour, whether this impact is domain-related, which kind of emotional expression is appropriate and how could this be expressed (Beale and Creed 2009; Dehn and Van Mulken 2000).

In summary, research work suggests that agents may increase user's engagement in tasks and that the expressiveness of agents can create a sense of confidence between the users and the system (Lee et al. 2007). In other words: "Embodied interface agents transform the experience of interacting with a computer, making it more sociably, explicitly referencing human–human interaction. When an agent's interaction design harmonizes with its tasks and the human's needs and expectations, wonderful things can happen" (Zimmerman et al. 2005).

Emotions in Education

Our research focuses on pedagogical emotional agents and their effect on learning. Education is indeed not just the transmission of information. The human behaviour, especially its emotional part, plays a crucial role in the learning procedure (Heyward 2010). Therefore, if we are looking at designing effective learning environments, we might need to look into the emotional aspect of learning and how this is related to user's attitudes and behaviours.

Learners are affected by cognitive, social, emotional, interpersonal, and cultural factors. Emotional factors constitute a complex system that is subjective and is affected by several factors that are often interrelated. They are determined from individual's appraisal of an event and are related to individual's beliefs and attitudes of the world (Ortony et al. 1988). While operating in a learning environment, emotions are generated both from cognitive process of appraisal and from the interaction that takes place within the learning environment (learning material, other students, and educators). Student's learning performance is enhanced in environments where they can develop a positive emotional communication. It acts as a supportive base in which students can learn better (Huffman and Speer 2000).

Research has shown evidence that positive emotions improve creative problem-solving by altering the cognitive context in which cognitive activity takes place. They also affect learner's attitude, motivation, and creativity (Isen et al. 1987). Positive emotions increase satisfaction levels for the same learning material and accommodate cognitive process that leads to better learning performance and user satisfaction (Um et al. 2007).

When students are introduced to a learning task, they have beliefs and attitudes and are used to certain codes of communication that they have learnt at home and in their social background. Often students' like or dislike of a module at school is influenced from teacher's behaviour (they don't like the teacher, and they don't like the module). Negative emotions that they might have can influence their achievements at school. Even though emotions play a primary role in education (Moridis and Economides 2008), research in education is usually focused on memory, thought, reasoning, perception, and language (Oatley and Nundy 1996) and secondly in the emotional state of the learner which affects deeply the main components of learning that we addressed above (memory, thought, and so on). Effective learning systems need to accommodate the emotional factors of learning as it is reported that student's perception of their teachers' appraisals and support can play a significant role on student's academic success (Becker and Luthar 2002). Researchers show evidence that the students who develop a caring and supportive interaction with their teachers, in traditional learning, in classroom, find learning a more satisfactory experience and have a more positive attitude toward the educational processes. They are more interested in learning and have more academic achievements. Students who feel that their teachers care for them are more engaged in the learning environment (Klem and Connell 2004).

In traditional educational settings such as classrooms, the physical appearance of the educator can serve for this emotional communication between learners and educators. In e-learning environments, the absence of face-to-face communication removes the emotional element. Nowadays researchers are looking at accommodating emotions in distance learning education. Intelligent agents with emotional behaviour have been introduced in order to respond to user's behaviour and emotional state (Conati and Maclaren 2009).

Agents through their graphical representations, that are part of the application's interface, have the ability to have goals and a strategy to achieve them. This communication can be based upon appropriate rules that will allow users and agents to interact emotionally and create a sense of caring and empathy.

In our study we introduce animated lifelike agents that can facilitate interaction (in many cases, similar to face-to-face ones). We empower them with rich multimedia functions which are used for representing certain emotions. Agents can move different muscles in face and body that respond to certain expressions. The agent uses facial expressions, hand gestures, and body movements to communicate with the user. This agents' ability to combine all media in order to represent in a believable manner emotional expressions might improve the effectiveness of education (Baylor and Kim 2003; Lee et al. 2007; Chatzara et al. 2010a, b).

We are not claiming that it is possible to replace human presence with agents. The variety and complexity of emotions involved in learning and the emotional interaction that takes place between learners and educators are very complicated and it might be impossible to be represented. We are looking at incorporating some basic emotions related to learning such as encouragement and rewarding into e-learning applications and transmit them through embodied agents that possess some sort of emotional intelligence.

The Sophia Agent

Our synthetic character, Sophia, is "talking" to the user through verbal and written language and provides empathic feedback to help her recover from negative emotions as well as encourages learners to overcome academic problems (Fig. 1). The agent collects information about student's emotion and intensity of motion. The user communicates with the agent in the form of text that the user sends to the User Behaviour Manager (UBM). When designing the model we used Orthony's appraisal model of emotions (Ortony et al. 1988) that considers emotions as part of individual's behaviour which has certain characteristics (Fig. 2).

This implies that emotions are related to individual's previous experience and beliefs. Learners are not the same. They do not respond the same way to the same stimulus. Each individual might react differently to the agent's behaviour dependently of learner's profile which is updated by recording learner's behaviour when using the system. For example learners with learning difficulties (LD) might respond differently to visual cues than written instructions, at same cases, or learners with attention disorders might react differently to agent's behaviour due to their difficulty

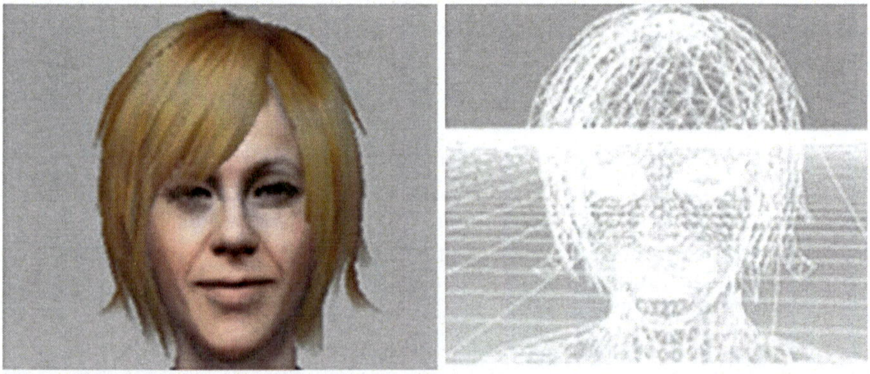

Fig. 1 Sophia, the agent

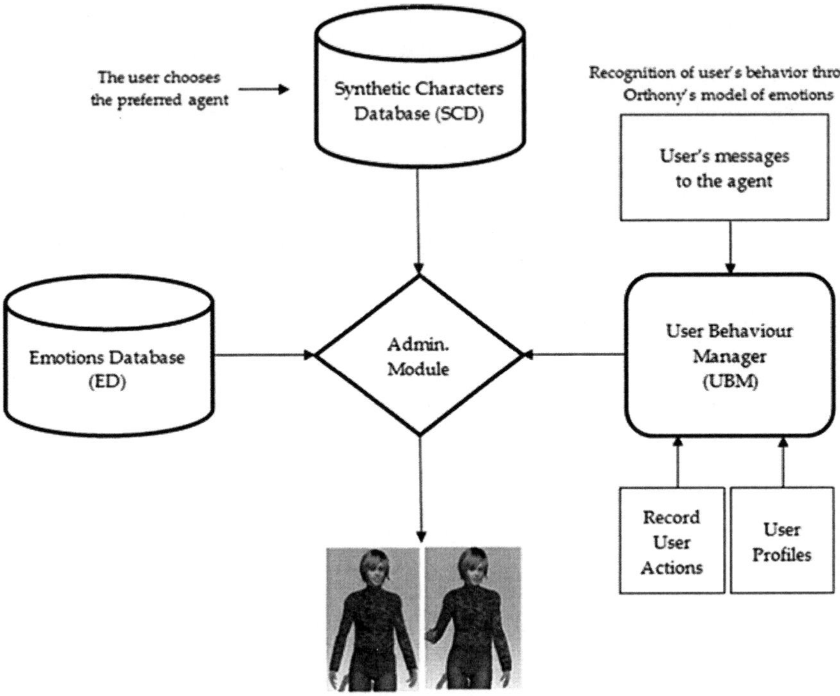

Fig. 2 Agent architecture

in keeping their attention focussed for long periods of time. Even students without LD might react differently depending on their personal learning characteristics and their personality.

UBM collects information from users' operations of the application by recording their actions and assigns an emotional state of each user following "if… then" rules. The users' performance is also taken into account, in order to make further assumptions about users' emotional state: e.g., if the user spends more time than expected in a given task, then the agent takes action and communicates with the user to indicate (in a caring way) the delay. In case the user delays the procedure due to comprehension difficulties, Sophia gives her clues for the given task and emotional support. The pedagogical agent uses an encouraging voice message that embeds emotional tones (empathic feedback) to prompt the student to express him/herself by writing messages to the agent. The user is not actually writing messages to the user but chooses from pre-given messages that correspond to user's difficulties to continue in the learning procedure. The agent chooses the appropriate behaviours from the emotion expression database, and expresses certain emotional behaviour with encouraging voice in order for the user to feel that the agent empathies with him/her. All data, recorded user's operation and direct user's input text, are collected in the UBM and categorized. In the Administrative module (AM), the appropriate emotional reactions of the agent are selected, and the appropriate emotional state of the agent is portrayed. Each student who uses the system can choose the agent they prefer to accompany them. The latest was part of the design of the application but was not incorporated when it was materialized. Users could use only one graphical representation of the agent.

The Study

Methodology and Sample

Fifty-two students took part in the evaluation of study. Their age was between 18 and 20 years old, men and women. They were students in the department of Informatics, in the Technological Institute of Thessaloniki in Greece, in the first semester of their first year of study. The sample was picked up randomly and students were asked to run the educational project and fill in questionnaires anonymously. The students were divided in two groups. One group was presented with the application with the agent and the other group with the application without the agent. There was an introduction describing the research project without giving details relating to the emotional factor that we wanted to investigate. All students were familiar with computer use as they state in the questionnaire and was expected as we are referring to first year Information Science students.

The application was covering a lesson that was part of a module that is aiming to teach communication skills to first year students. The subject matter was about Internet use as a tool of communication. We used the book metaphor and we put Sophia into an e-book which looked like a traditional study book. Users could turn pages back and forth in order to view the learning material. In the end of viewing the subject matter, students were asked to complete a multiple choice test related to the learning material presented in the application. Sophia's role was to assist users and react accordingly to their emotional state (Figs. 3 and 4).

In the end of the application, users were asked (anonymously) to complete a questionnaire that was related to user satisfaction questions.

Data Analysis

The data evoked from user's answers from the questionnaire that they were asked to fulfil in the end of the learning procedure, and from the recording of certain variables that were running during the operation of the application. Users were asked to put a five digits number in a text area in their application and they had to write the same number in the questionnaire so we could relate results. This gave us the opportunity to identify students with learning difficulties and look into this group's results separately. Through variables that were running through the operation we could collect data regarding the completion of learning tasks, the time that users needed to retry, at what points users

Fig. 3 Emotional states of Sophia

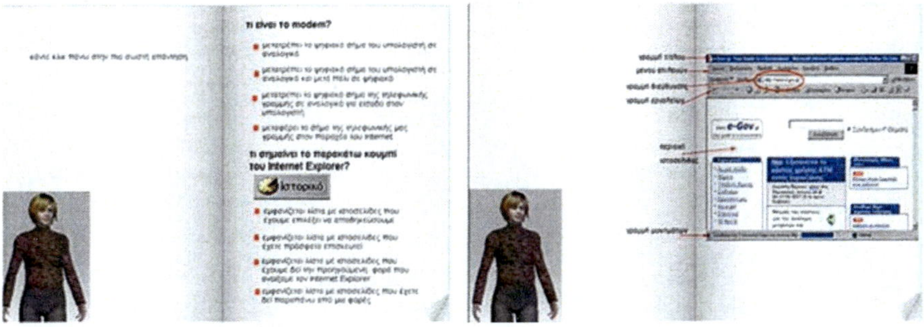

Fig. 4 Sophia in e-book

stop trying, etc. We run a quantitative analysis in the above findings and the results are presented below. For one factor, the successful completion of learning tasks, we ran a qualitative analysis. For that purpose, we used the correct and wrong answers users gave in the multiple choice test that was part of the application.

The study has shown a positive perception of Sophia. Results revealed that the caring agent may not only increase the interaction between students and the learning system, but also have positive effects on students' emotions and engage them in learning. The results of these factors have already been reported (Chatzara et al. 2010a, b), and they show that users felt that they could communicate with Sophia and that she helped them in the learning procedure (exact percentages are shown in Fig. 5a, b).

Another issue was if positive or negative emotions were revealed from this communication between the agent and users. This particular factor was included due to recent research (Fredrickson 2003) that reveals the importance of positive emotions in education. The results were analysed and show that the majority of users (61%) seem to have positive emotions toward the agent and that she helps them have positive emotions when operating the application. Exact percentages are shown in Fig. 6a. A basic problem in affective computing (Picard 2003) is that it is hard to predict user's emotional state in order for the system to react accordingly. Therefore, we asked the students to report if the system correctly identified their emotions. Results showed that 58% of students reported that Sophia identified correctly their emotions. Exact percentages are shown in Fig. 6b.

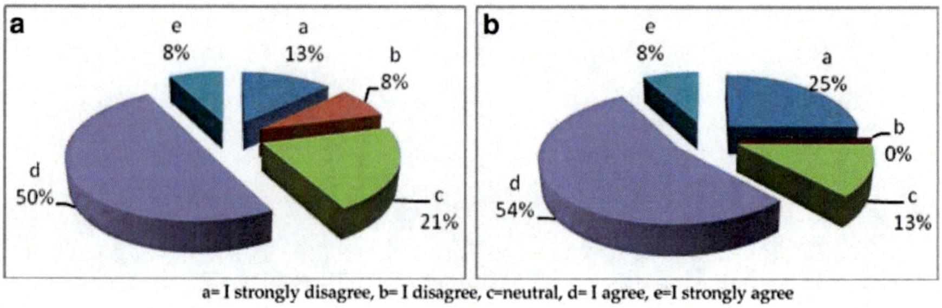

Fig. 5 Data referring to user percentages that felt that the agent (**a**) communicates with them, (**b**) helps them to complete their learning tasks (a=I strongly disagree, b=I disagree, c=neutral, d=I agree, e=I strongly agree)

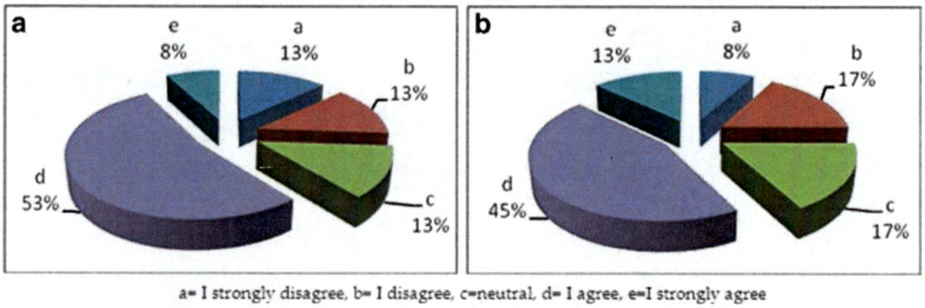

Fig. 6 Data referring to user percentages that felt that the agent (**a**) had positive emotions through their interaction with the agent, (**b**) diagnoses correctly their emotional state (a=I strongly disagree, b=I disagree, c=neutral, d=I agree, e=I strongly agree)

The notions of comfort and sympathy are often communicated in learning. Educators often comfort learners through their attitude in order to "relieve" them from negative emotions and unblock the educational procedure. We asked users if they felt that Sophia comforts them when failing at learning tasks or stay more than the expected time in the same page of the e-book. Fifty-nine percent reported that they felt that Sophia succeeded in this task (Fig. 7a). Finally, they were asked if they were satisfied overall with the operation of the learning system and the completion of learning tasks with Sophia's help. Sixty-seven percent answered positively again (Fig. 7b).

For the following qualitative results, we analysed the learning tasks that users needed to accomplish after viewing the theoretical part of the application. Since $p<0.05$ and all data >8, then the $\times 2$ criterion is fulfilled. Consequently, we assume that the success in the learning tasks is related to the agent's presence and emotional behaviour. Below there are the statistical qualitative results from which p is calculated (Table 1 and Fig. 8).

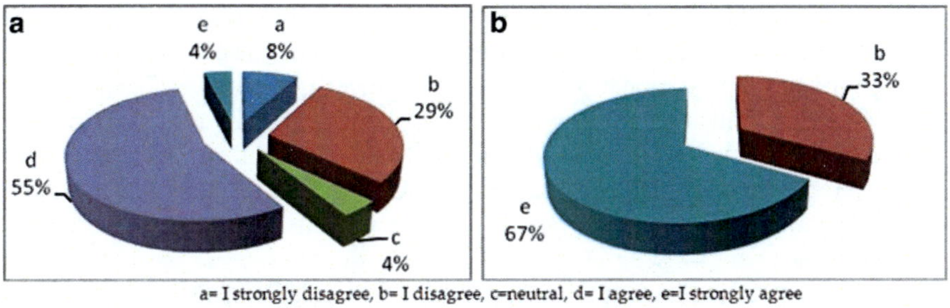

Fig. 7 Data referring to user percentages that (**a**) felt that the agent comforted them when they faced difficulties in the learning procedure, (**b**) enjoyed using the agent (a=I strongly disagree, b=I disagree, c=neutral, d=I agree, e=I strongly agree)

Table 1 Chi-square tests

	Value	df	Asymp. Sig. (2-sided)	Exact Sig. (2-sided)	Exact Sig. (1-sided)
Pearson Chi-square	12,357[a]	1	0.000		
Continuity correction[b]	11,637	1	0.001		
Likelihood ratio	12,507	1	0.000		
Fisher's exact test				0.001	0.000
Linear-by-linear association	12,336	1	0.000		
Number of valid cases	571				

[a]0 Cells (0.0%) have expected count less than 5. The minimum expected count is 57.90
[b]Computed only for a 2×2 table

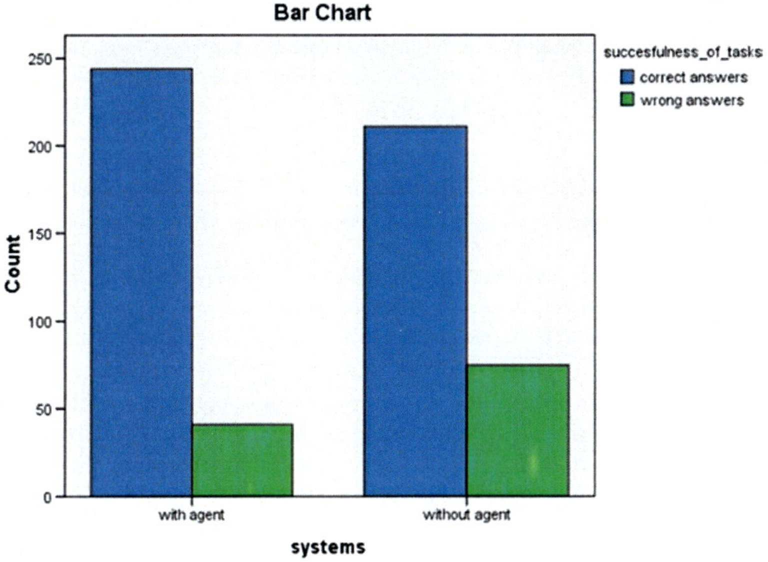

Fig. 8 Success in learning tasks

Seven out of the 52 students who took part in the study were diagnosed with learning difficulties and Attention Disorder Deficit (ADD). The questionnaires were asking for special educational needs in order to investigate whether agent's emotional behaviour will affect differently this special group and if yes in what respect. The results are supported by the statistics analysis of certain variables that were used and recorded while the user was using the applications. Results show that there is not a significant difference in results between students with ADD and students without ADD.

Based on the open type questions, a qualitative analysis of the questionnaires answered by students with ADD leads to the followings conclusions. Results have been previously reported (Chatzara et al. 2010a, b):

- The emotional agent helps them to be more concentrated in the learning tasks.
- Students had a "sense" of communicating with her.
- Three students reported that they felt they can ask Sophia's help.
- They felt that Sophia was observing them (because she was responding to their actions).
- They reported that sometimes Sophia did not have the appropriate behaviour toward them thus she did not diagnose correctly their emotional state. The same was reported by the students without ADD. Forty-two percent of users felt that sometimes Sophia could not diagnose correctly their emotional state.

The results for this special learning group indicate that emotional communication which is mediated through a visual representation of the agent, which has rich multimedia capabilities, modulates automatic attention in students with ADD and helps them to stay in the learning process.

All students who took part in the study seem to spend more time in the application with the agent than the one without Sophia. Most of them emphasize the sense of communication that they had with the agent through the visual responses that she was generating.

Conclusions

In our study, we introduced an emotional agent who is able to receive and comprehend user's emotions and respond to them by portraying emotional reactions relevant to learning. Most previous works did not investigate whether emotional reactions were perceived correctly from learners, and their direct effects on users' behaviour was less well investigated; the agent's communication skills and their effect on learner performance in the learning environment were also less examined. Our study showed that the majority of users (a) felt that the agent comforted them when they faced difficulties in the learning procedure, (b) enjoyed using the agent, (c) had positive emotions through their interaction with the agent, (d) felt that the agent diagnoses correctly their emotional state (e) had a sense of communicating with the agent, (f) felt that the agent helps them to complete the learning tasks.

Based on the results of the study, future e-learning systems can exploit the use of emotions for improving the learning process in distance education.

One of the limitations of the study is that for 42% of the users, the agent did not diagnose correctly their emotional state. Similar results were also been found by Conati and Maclaren (2009), who used educational games as a genre to identify user's emotional state (their study showed 56% accuracy in predicting user's emotions). We are currently investigating alternative ways which can increase the possibility for the agent to correctly diagnose the students' changing emotions. This is very crucial in any agent systems (and any system that supports some kind of adaptations), since otherwise the agent might respond falsely and the user could feel completely lost.

Also, we investigate how emotions can affect learning for different students through different pedagogical practices. Common pedagogical practices (such as storytelling, role playing, games, and so on) might need to be redesigned and restructured accordingly to new media formalities to incorporate user's emotional stimuli. Factors such as the context and the aesthetics of the learning environments could be employed as well. User's emotional engagement could act as cognitive support that will assist learners in understanding concepts and make the emotional element part of cognitive support (cognitive scaffolding). The social aspect of learning might be possible to increase user's attention, and offer better results in accomplishing learning tasks and a better learning experience overall.

References

Bates, J., Bryan Loyall, A., & Scott Reilly, W. (1992). *An architecture for action, emotion, and social behaviour. Technical Report CMU-CS-92-144*. Pittsburgh: School of Computer Science, Carnegie-Mellon University.

Becker, B., & Luthar, S. (2002). Social-emotional factors affecting achievement, outcomes among disadvantaged students: closing the achievement gap. *Educational Psychologist*, 37(4), 197–214.

Blumberg, B., & Galyean, T. (1995). Multi-level direction of autonomous creatures for real-time virtual environments computer graphics. In Mair S. & Cook R. (eds.), *Proceedings of the 22nd Annual Conference on Computer Graphics and Interactive Techniques* (pp. 47–54). New York, NY: ACM.

Baylor, A. L., & Kim, Y. (2003). Validating pedagogical agent roles: Expert, motivator, and mentor. In D. Lassner C. McNaught (eds.), *International Conference of EdMedia* (pp. 463–466). Chesapeake, VA: AACE.

Beale, R., & Creed, C. (2009). Affective interaction: How emotional agents affect users. *International Journal of Human-Computer Studies*, 67(9), 755–776.

Burleson, W. (2006). *Affective learning companions: strategies for empathetic agents with real-time multimodal affective sensing to foster meta-cognitive and meta-affective approaches to learning, motivation, and perseverance*. Cambridge, MA: Massachusetts Institute of Technology.

Chalfoun, P., Chaffar, S., & Frasson, C. (2006). *Predicting the emotional reaction of the learner with a machine learning techniques*. Paper presented at the Workshop on Motivational and Affective Issues at the International Conference on Intelligent Tutoring System (ITS2006), June 2006, Jhongli, Taiwan.

Chatzara, K., Karagiannidis, C., & Stamatis, D. (2010). Student's attitude and learning effectiveness of emotional agents. In M. Jemni (ed.), *Proceedings of the 10th IEEE International Conference on Advanced Learning Technologies* (pp. 558–559). Sousse, Tunisia: IEEE Publishing.

Chatzara, K., Karagiannidis, C., & Stamatis, D. (2010). An intelligent emotional agent for students with attention deficit disorder. In F. Xhafa (ed.), *Proceedings of the International Conference of Intelligent Networking and Collaborative systems* (pp. 252–258). Thessaloniki, Greece: IEEE.

Conati, C., & Maclaren, H. (2009). Empirically building and evaluating a probabilistic model of user affect. *User Modelling and User-Adapted Interaction*, 19(3), 267–303.

Dehn, D., & Van Mulken, S. (2000). The impact of animated interface agents: a review of empirical research. *International Journal of Human Computer Studies*, 52(1), 1–22.

Elliot, C. D. (1992). *The affective reasoner: a process model of emotions in a multi-agent system.* Unpublished PhD thesis. The Institute for the Learning Sciences, Northwestern University, Evanston, Illinois.

Fredrickson, B. L. (2003). The value of positive emotions. *American Scientist*, 91, 330–335.

Heyward, P. (2010). Emotional engagement through drama: Strategies to assist learning through role-play. *International Journal of Teaching and Learning in Higher Education*, 22(2), 197–203.

Huffman, L. R., & Speer, P. W. (2000). Academic performance among at-risk children: The role of developmentally appropriate practices. *Early Childhood Research Quarterly*, 15, 167–184.

Isen, A, M., Daubman, K.A., & Nowicki, G.P. (1987). Positive affect facilitates creative problem solving. *Journal of Personality and Social Psychology,* 56(6), 1122–1131.

Klem, A. M., & Connell, J. P. (2004). Relationships matter: linking teacher support to student engagement and achievement. *Journal of School Health,* 74(7), 262–73.

Lee, T. Y., Chang, C. W., & Chen, G. D. (2007). Building an interactive caring agent for students in computer-based learning environments. In M. J. Spector (ed.), *Proceedings International Conference on Advanced Learning Technologies* (pp. 300–304). Niigata, Japan.

Lester, J., Towns, S., & Fitzgerald, P. (1999). Achieving affective impact: visual emotive communication in lifelike pedagogical agents. *Artificial Intelligence in Education*, 10, 278–291.

Maldonado, H., Lee, J., Brave, S., Nass, C., Nakajima, H., Yamada, R., Iwamura, K., & Morishima, Y. (2005). We learn better together: Enhancing elearning with emotional characters. In T. Koschmann, D. Suthers, & T.W. Chan (eds.), *Computer Supportive Collaborative Learning: The Next Ten Years, Proceedings of the Sixth International Computer Supported Collaborative Learning Conference, CSCL 2005* (pp. 408–417). Mahwah, NJ: Lawrence Erlbaum Associates.

Massaro, M., Cohen, M., & Beskowm, J. (2000). Developing and evaluating conversational agents. In J. Cassell, J. Sullivan, S. Prevost & E. Churchill (eds.), *Embodied Conversational Agents* (pp. 286–318). Cambridge, MA: MIT Press.

Moridis, C., & Economides, A. A. (2008). Towards computer-aided affective learning systems: a literature review. *Journal of Educational Computing Research,* 39(4), 313–337.

Oatley, K., & Nundy, S. (1996). Rethinking the role of emotions in education. In D. Olson & N. Torrance (eds.), *Handbook of Education and Human Development: New Models of Learning, Teaching and Schooling* (pp. 257–274). Cambridge, MA: Blackwell.

Ortony, A., Clore, G. L., & Collins, A. (1988). *The Cognitive Structure of Emotions*. New York: Cambridge University Press.

Punie, Y., Zinnbauer, D., & Cabrera, M. (2006). *A review of the Impact of ICT on Learning.* Working paper prepared for DG EAC. Institute for Prospective Technological Studies (IPTS), JRC, European Commission. http://ipts.jrc.ec.europa.eu/publications/pub.cfm?id=1746.

Picard, R. W. (2003). What does it mean for a computer to 'have' emotions?. In R. Trappl, P. Petta & S. Payr (eds.), *Emotions in Humans and Artefacts* (pp. 115–148). Cambridge, MA: MIT Press.

Zimmerman, J., Ayoob, E., Forlizzi, J., & McQuaid, M. (2005). Putting a face on embodied interface agents. In S. Wensveen (ed.), *Proceedings of Designing Pleasurable Products and Interfaces* (pp. 233–248). Eindhoven, the Netherlands: Eindhoven Technical University Press.

Um, E.R., Song, H., & Plass, J. (2007). The Effect of positive emotions on multimedia learning. In C. Montgomerie & J. Seale (eds.), *Proceedings of World Conference on Educational Multimedia, Hypermedia and Telecommunications 2007* (pp. 4176–4185). Chesapeake, VA: AACE.

Virtual Models of Conic Sections

Pavel Boytchev

Introduction

People know and use conic sections for a long time. They observe these curves in many situations: the parabolic trajectory of a thrown stone, the circular waves when the stone falls in calm water, and the elliptical shadows of round objects during sunsets (see Fig. 1).

Conic sections were and still are one of the most favorite objects of mathematical study and education. Students spend hours in the classroom working with circles, ellipses, parabolas, and hyperbolas. They are presented with a concentrated view about these curves, a view that has been distilled for hundreds of years. Although mathematically correct, this view may not lead to complete rationalization, because it might be hard for students to project mathematical ideas into something more comprehensible from their everyday life.

A preliminary informal inquiry showed that it is difficult for many students to identify conic sections in a non-classroom environment. This triggered the creation of visualization tools that could introduce these curves from various perspectives. These tools are the focus of this paper.

Traditionally, conic sections are described as intersections of a plane and a cone (Downs 1993). Searching the WWW reveals that this is the predominant description of conic sections, independent on whether materials describe mathematical concepts in simple language (like Math2.org's "A conic section is the intersection of a plane and a cone") or use scientific terminology (like Wolfram MathWorld's "The conic sections are the nondegenerate curves generated by the intersections of a plane with one or two nappes of a cone").

P. Boytchev (✉)
Sofia University, Sofia, Bulgaria
e-mail: boytchev@fmi.uni-sofia.bg

A. Jimoyiannis (ed.), *Research on e-Learning and ICT in Education*,
DOI 10.1007/978-1-4614-1083-6_20,

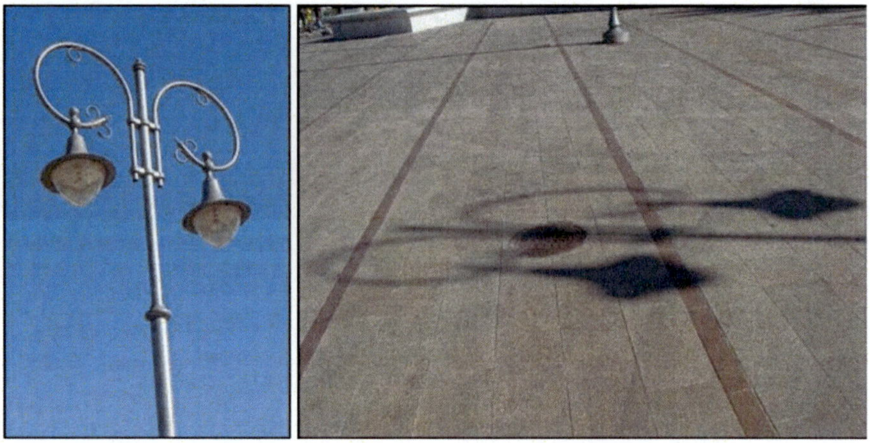

Fig. 1 Circular shapes of lamps in Korinthos, Greece, and their elliptical shadows

Unfortunately, "although intuitively and visually appealing, these definitions for the conic sections tell us little about their properties and uses" (Smith 2011). Additionally, these definitions do not always create transferable knowledge – i.e., knowledge that a person can use to bridge concepts from two distinct disciplines. There are observations that connecting is important to understand. According to Wageman (2010), "The more connections students can make the more interesting the topic becomes to them and then deeper understanding can occur."

Some educators are forced to make compromise by choosing only few aspects of the curves, those that "have important applications in the real world" (Demana et al. 2000). A few educational materials based on this traditional approach are being advertised as "the perfect set for teaching a unit on conic sections" (Nasco 2010).

The introduction of Dynamic Geometry Software (DGS) added a lot of expressiveness to the representation of conic sections and provided a playground for interesting explorations. However, DGS is still visually bound to the mathematical representation. DGS uses the conventional geometrical primitives that are not immediately relatable to concepts outside the educational environment. Even advanced DGS tools like Cabri (Schumann 2005) and the Geometer's Sketchpad (Scher 2003) represent conic sections in the traditional way. Although correct, 3D and interactive, these representations are just advanced variations of the schemes found in mathematical textbooks and in online math resources.

The author's own attempt to combine DGS with virtual reality also did not provide any significant impact. Figure 2 represents a snapshot of an interactive 3D application for experimenting with the traditional approach. It is less mathematical and more like a game, but still it is a cone intersected by a plane.

Another application of the author is a microworld developed for the *Developing Active Learning Environment for Stereometry* (DALEST) project which was co-funded by the European Union under the Socrates Program, MINERVA, 2005 Selection (Boytchev 2007). Partners in this project were several educational

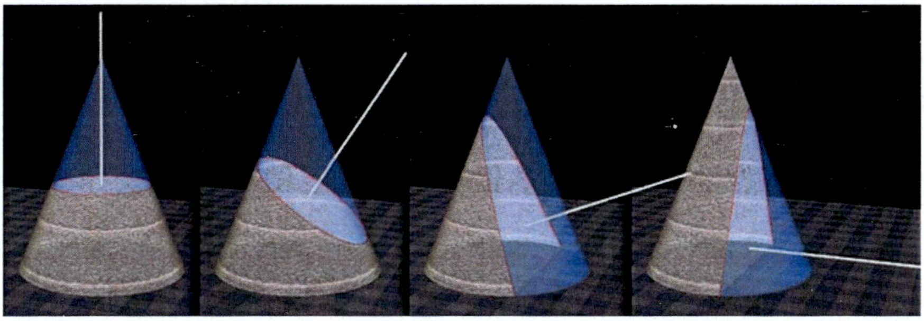

Fig. 2 Interactive 3D application for exploration of the traditional representation of conic sections

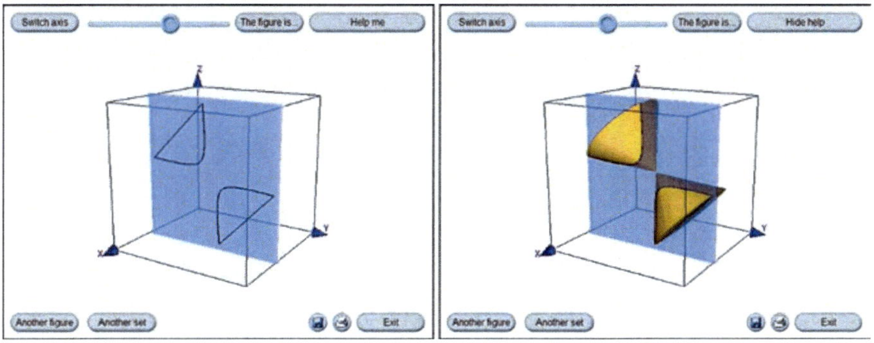

Fig. 3 Snapshots from a DALEST-Elica application for interactive exploration of the intersection of a plane and a solid

institutions across Europe. The Slider application represents the intersection of an object with a plane. By moving the plane and studying the intersection, the user has to "guess" the object. One of the subsets of activities is related to studying conic sections (Fig. 3).

Both applications (the ones shown in Figs. 2 and 3) utilized modern visualization technologies by providing the user with a game-like look-and-feel. However, like models developed by other DGS tools, the representation does not help students to resolve practical challenges like:

- Make an ellipse with a reading lamp.
- Construct a rolling mechanism that generates an ellipse.
- Draw a hyperbola using a fixed-length thread.

These applications do not provide assistance in solving the inverse problems too, like "Is this shadow a parabola or a hyperbola?" or "Where are the focal points of this ellipse?"

There are trends of bringing the reality back into Math education by constructing and using mechanical tools that relate to mathematical concepts. And interesting work is the construction of LEGO mechanisms that function as physical representation for mathematics and mathematical inquiry (Isoda et al. 2001)

The idea that initiated the work presented in this paper is to create new tools and models that describe and utilize various properties of conic sections. The main features of these tools are to present the properties of the conic sections in a way that is:

- *Unique*: The tools have to demonstrate conic sections form a perspective that is inherently unavailable in traditional hard-copy textbooks and is still difficult to implement in contemporary systems of dynamic geometry.
- *Attractive*: The tools should use virtual reality, game-like 3D models and interactive interfaces to build and then to support the student's interest in conic sections. Such attention to the visual appearance is important in order to minimize the gap between a "boring" topic in mathematics and the out-of-school entertainment.
- *Natural*: The tools should represent ideas that can be immediately related (and even applied) to real-life situations and at the same time to be still mathematically correct.

Homemade Conic Sections with Light

In 2009 the author completed an artistic project–exhibition based on computer generated images and digital photographs (Boytchev 2009). All posters feature fragments of the Mandelbrot set fractal accompanied by artistic interpretations. One of the posters depicts an area from the fractal that resembles a coordinate system with a pair of hyperbolas and their asymptotes (see Fig. 4).

The description of the poster says: *The hyperbola might have been discovered by Menaechmus, a tutor of Alexander the Great. One hundred years later Apollonius named the ellipse, parabola and hyperbola. There are many ways to construct a conic section, but the easiest one is with a table, a ball and a torch. How?* Apparently, it appears that the ball is not necessary in order to generate all types of conic sections.

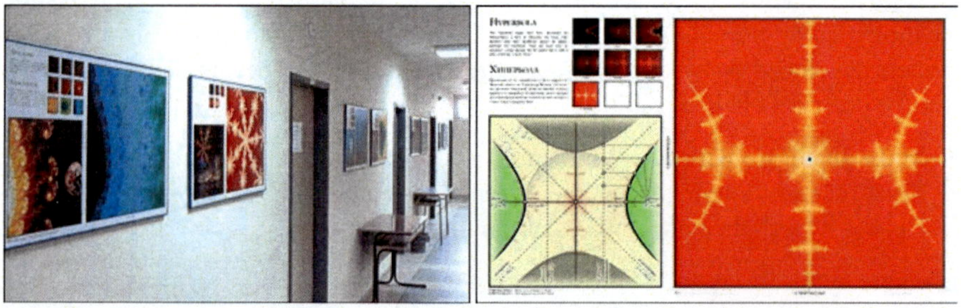

Fig. 4 The fractal exhibition and the hyperbolic shapes in the Mandelbrot set fractal

Fig. 5 All four types of conic sections generated with objects at hand

The question in the poster raises an interesting problem: Is it possible to model all conic sections at home, using only objects from our everyday life? Is it possible to classify conic sections produced in this way? To answer these questions a set of interactive 3D applications are implemented by the author. They are based on real-life "experiments" and some of them were demonstrated at the Spring Conference of the Union of Bulgarian Mathematicians in 2010. Figure 5 shows several "experiments" conducted in a hotel room using available objects and without any preliminary preparation. The "experiments" provide enough data for students to determine why the light reflection in the first photograph is a parabola, while the light in the last one makes a hyperbola.

These experiments inspired the construction of a set of interactive 3D applications. They are designed and developed within the scope of the project InnoMathEd – *Innovations in Mathematics Education on European Level* (http://www.math.uni-augsburg.de/prof/dida/innomath). Partners in this project are University of Augsburg, Bulgarian Academy of Sciences, University of South Bohemia, University of Bayreuth, Projekt Bildung Institut, German School Board Bolzano, University of Cyprus, Tyrolean Educational Service, University of Cambridge, and University of Oslo. The project addresses pupils' mathematical understanding, use of ICT and competences for lifelong learning (Bianco 2009).

The first application in the set re-explores the traditional approach that involves a cone and an intersecting plane. Snapshots of this program are shown in Fig. 2. Although the software provides an intuitive and easy-to-understand way for describing conic sections, it does not help students implement the model in real life. Instead, the model is suitable only for virtual experiments. Most of the other applications, however, are designed in a way that their ideas can be re-implemented and re-acted at home – this is crucial to our goal of having mathematical knowledge that is transferrable and applicable outside the classroom.

The next few applications in the set model just a torch and a table. The light from the torch forms a cone, while the table is an intersecting plane. The image on the table surface is the intersection of the light cone and the plane. It is straightforward to create a circle or an ellipse. However, is it also possible to generate parabolas and hyperbolas, in spite of the fact that they extend to infinity – see Fig. 6.

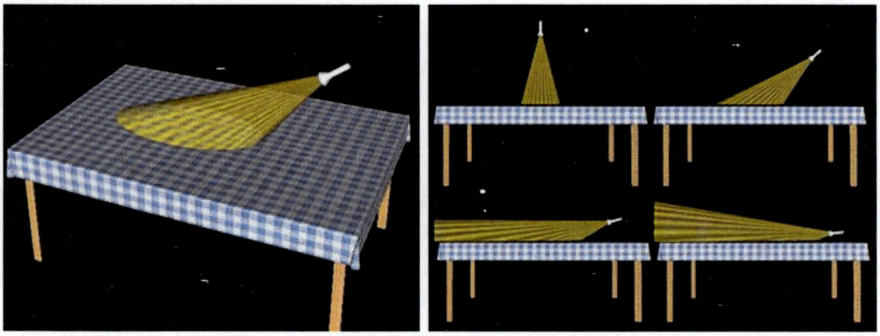

Fig. 6 Making an ellipse (*left*) and all conic sections (*right*) using a torch

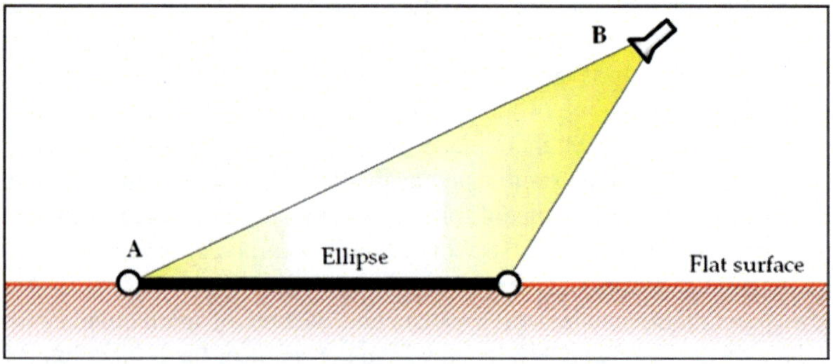

Fig. 7 Generation of an ellipse

There are simple rules that "predict" the type of the curve. These rules have a mathematical background, but they can be understood and applied by students with insufficient mathematical skills. The slope of the upper side of the light cone (segment AB in Fig. 7) determines the type of the curve. It is an ellipse (or a circle) if A is below B, a hyperbola if A is above B, and a parabola if AB is horizontal.

It is possible to rephrase the rules – if point A is below the horizon, we have an ellipse (or a circle), if A is above the horizon – hyperbola, and if it exactly at the horizon – we have generated a parabola.

The torch in the model is used to generate a light cone. If we have a traditional electrical bulb, it emits light in all directions. Yet, we are still able to generate conic sections. Figure 8 (left) shows the elliptical shadow generated by another 3D application. By moving the light, we can generate all conic sections. Again, the rules are simple. A parabola appears when the bulb is at the same level as the top of the ball, a hyperbola – when it is below it.

The position of the ball has an important mathematical meaning. The point of contact with the table is a focal point (focus) and the ball is a Dandelin sphere (Kendig 2005; Weisstein 2010). The right snapshot in Fig. 8 shows a similar application where two balls produce hyperbolic shadow and at the same time they play

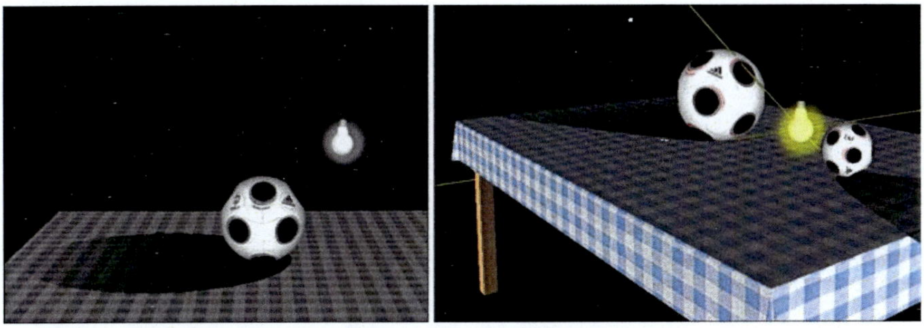

Fig. 8 Using shadows to generate an ellipse (*left*) and hyperbola (*right*)

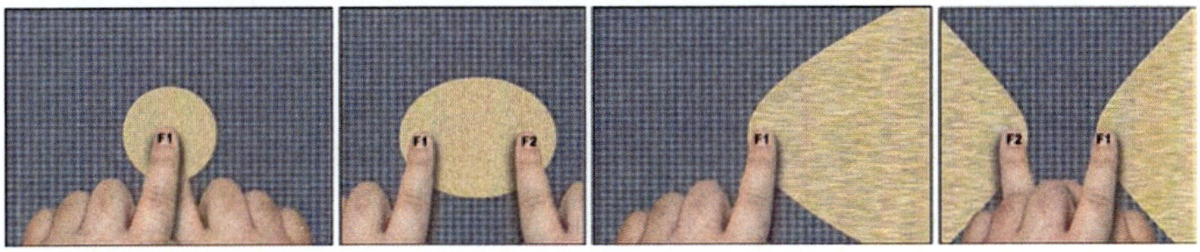

Fig. 9 The interactive pizza application

the role of two Dandelin spheres. A quick examination of the online visual resources shows that the predominant representation of Dandelin spheres is that they touch the foci of an ellipse. However, the application provides all options – students can immediately explore the Dandelin spheres of all types of conic sections.

There are a few other interactive 3D applications in the set. One of them uses just a tube. If a student looks the ground through it, the cone of sight will "cut" a conic section from the ground. The simple identification rules could be based on the horizon. If the student sees only ground – this is an ellipse. If the horizon cuts through the sight – it is a hyperbola.

The last application in the set illustrates the transition from one conic curve to another by using a virtual pizza that can be digitally deformed by pulling the focal points apart. Initially, the pizza is circular and both foci coincide – Fig. 9. If the student moves a finger to the right, the pizza becomes an ellipse. If the focus is dragged to infinity, the pizza will be a parabola. And, finally, when that hand goes beyond infinity, it "wraps" through the other side of the screen, we will produce a hyperbolic pizza.

Virtual Models of Mechanical Devices

Except for the applications using the light or the absence of light to model conic sections, the author has implemented a rich set of non-interactive 3D applications that represent models of mechanical devices drawing conic curves (Boytchev 2010a).

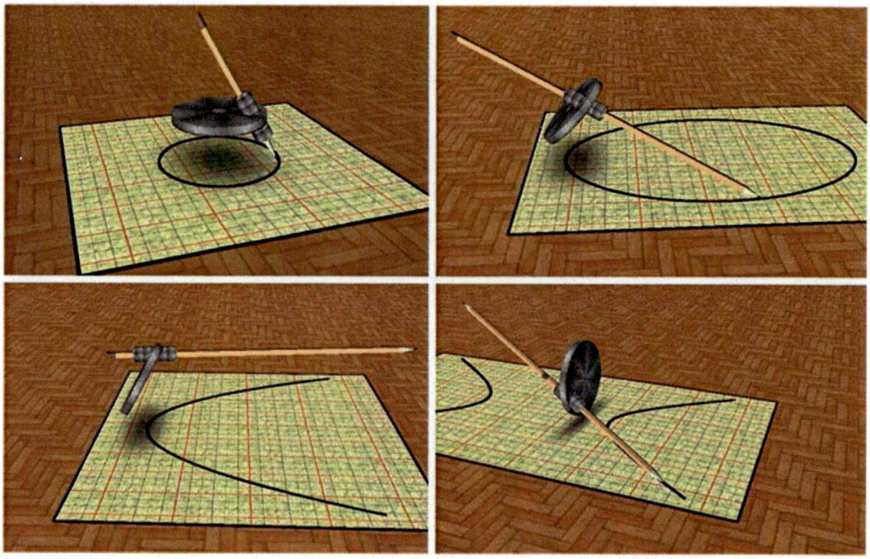

Fig. 10 Pencil attached to a disk can draw any conic section

These devices represent various methods and could foster interesting mathematical research activities for students. All devices are built by a set of primitive elements including a pencil that draws on paper.

It is easy and straightforward to model a device drawing a circle; however we should think of a more enhanced device if we need all conic sections. Figure 10 presents snapshots of such device, where the pencil can slide forward and backward controlled only by gravity.

Some of the mathematical problems occurring during the design of the animations were:

- How long should the pencil be (so that it will not slide off its holder)?
- How to model the infinities of parabolas (using finite objects)?
- How to draw both branches of hyperbolas (within a single device)?

The model in Fig. 10 recreates the conical nature of conic sections – the pencil rolls on the surface of an invisible cone (defined by the angle between the disk and the pencil) while the paper acts as an intersecting plane. The gravity forces the pencil to slide forward as much as needed to reach the paper, while the paper, itself, pushes it back.

As seen in the third snapshot, there is one specific case when the pencil becomes horizontal in its upmost position. This is the case of drawing a parabola. The tip of the pencil points to infinity (or to the horizon, if we consider the model in Figs. 6 and 7).

When the disk is vertical, there are situations when the tip of the pencil points upwards. In such cases the gravity pulls the pencil down and it touches the paper with its "back." If we use a double-sided pencil, in which both ends can draw, we

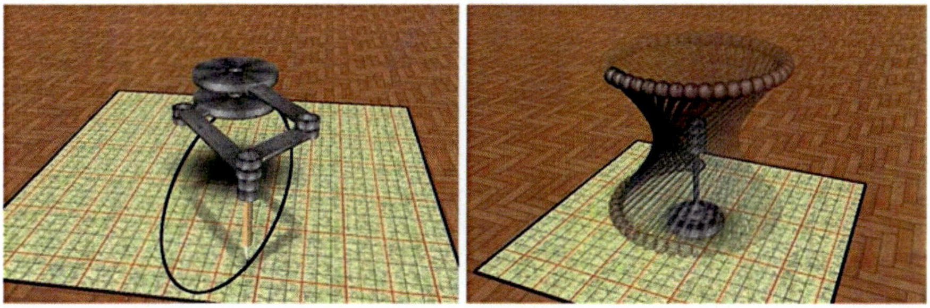

Fig. 11 Other rotational methods to generate some conic sections

will get the pencil to draw one of the hyperbola branches with one of the ends, and the other branch with the other end. This construction is shown in the last snapshot in Fig. 10. Animations of this device can be seen in YouTube playlist "Mathematical devices" (Boytchev 2010a).

The disk rotation used in the model is essential for the formation of the conic curves, but is not the only way to make them with rotation. The sum of two vectors with different lengths rotating at the same angular speed but in opposite directions is a vector that traverses an ellipse; see Fig. 11 (left). The two shorter beams represent one of the vectors; the longer ones represent the other. The construction uses a parallelogram to maintain mechanical stability and to demonstrate the commutative nature of vector addition.

The right snapshot in Fig. 11 represents a ruled surface called hyperboloid. It is created by a tilted line rotated around a vertical axis. The intersection of the hyperboloid and a horizontal plane is a circle, while the intersection with a vertical plane is a hyperbola.

Virtual Models of Existing Mechanical Devices

The models shown in Figs. 10 and 11 are not quite practical in the sense that they are suitable for generation of imaginary curves, but cannot be used for making tangible conic sections. For example, it is hard to use these devices to make elliptical windows. Carpenters have solved this problem by using a simple yet effective device called the Trammel of Archimedes (Apostol and Mnatsakanian 2009). This device can draw an ellipse with predefined major and minor axes. It also provides sufficient precision for carpentry.

Variations of the trammel are shown in Fig. 12. A fixed length segment slides along two perpendicular pairs of rails while the pencil is attached near the segment's midpoint (if the pencil is exactly in the midpoint, it will draw a circle). In reality, the devices used by carpenters are slightly different. For example, the pencil is often

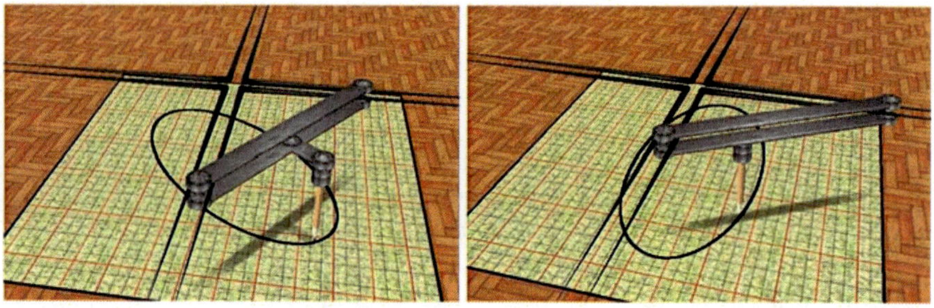

Fig. 12 Variations of the Trammel of Archimedes

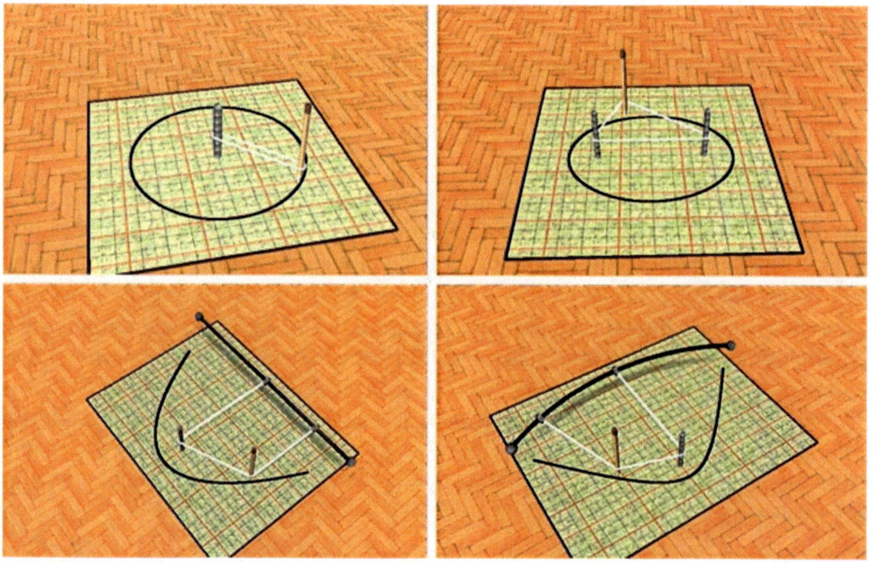

Fig. 13 A thread used to draw conic sections

attached on an extension of the sliding segment. This allows the carpenters to use much shorter rails.

The Trammel of Archimedes can draw any curve from a straight line to a circle, traversing through ellipses with various eccentricities. Unfortunately, it cannot draw a parabola or a hyperbola. Fortunately, there is another ancient method of drawing ellipses based on the property that the sum of distances from any point on the ellipse to its foci is constant. Figure 13 shows snapshots of animations visualizing all conic curves generated with a fixed-length thread. The top two cases are well known and are included just for completeness. An interesting challenge is to design a similar

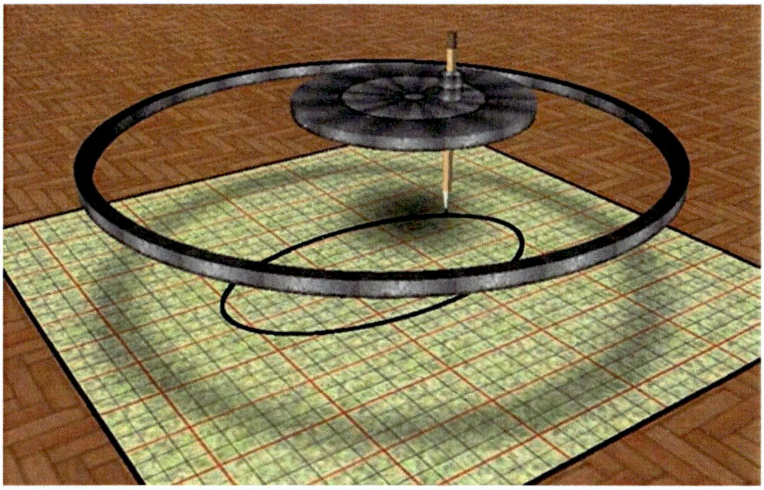

Fig. 14 A hypotrochoidal ellipse

mechanism for parabolas and hyperbolas, as long as almost all hard copy and online textbooks show only the case with an ellipse.

The lower left snapshot shows a parabola. The thread has both of its ends freely attached to a rail that is collinear to the parabola's directrix. These ends can slide along the rail keeping both sides of the thread perpendicular to the rail. The midsection of the thread embraces the pencil and the fixed focus point. A similar device is shown in the last snapshot. It has the same structure, except that the rail is a circular arc. In this case, the pencil draws a hyperbola. It is a nice mathematical exercise to prove that the curve is really a hyperbola.

The topic of modeling the construction of conic intersections is virtually unlimited. Figure 14 represents a hypotrochoidal device, where a disk rolls inside a ring. The radii of the disk and the ring are selected in such a way, that the attached pencil draws an ellipse.

Student Activities

The interactive 3D applications and the 3D animations presented in this paper are included in a set of more than 60 models of devices. Some of them draw mathematical curves, other represent mathematical transformations, construction of 3D surfaces, and even non-geometrical phenomena like normal distribution in statistics.

All these applications are rather new and they are still not used in the classroom or at home. Teaching materials are now being prepared that will utilize the full multidisciplinary power of the models. The rest of the section describes briefly some potential activities.

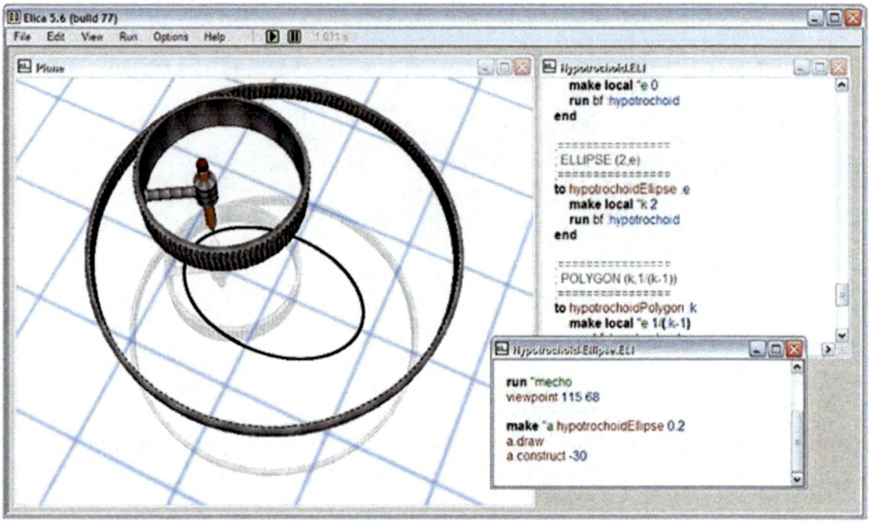

Fig. 15 A snapshot of the environment using the library for virtual mechanics

Computer Science/Computer Graphics

Each model is a program written in Elica Logo programming language. The design and the implementation of such program require skills and knowledge. Some models are very simple from programming point of view, others are quite complex. The building of precisely selected series of models can improve these skills and amass knowledge. The internal structure of models is based on concepts of the Object-oriented programming.

The power of having a complete programming control over the model allows the student to create new virtual mechanical elements. This is something which is impossible in closed software environments and in the LEGO-based models of mechanisms where the user can operate only a limited set of parts.

Physics: Mechanics

The virtual models included in the collection are not just mathematical abstractions. They comply with known physical restrictions and utilize the properties of components made of different materials. A thread can change its shape, while a solid beam cannot.

A library with virtual mechanical parts is now under development (see Fig. 15). Its purpose is simplify the construction of virtual models in non-programming contexts. The parameters of each part are customizable by the students, which only

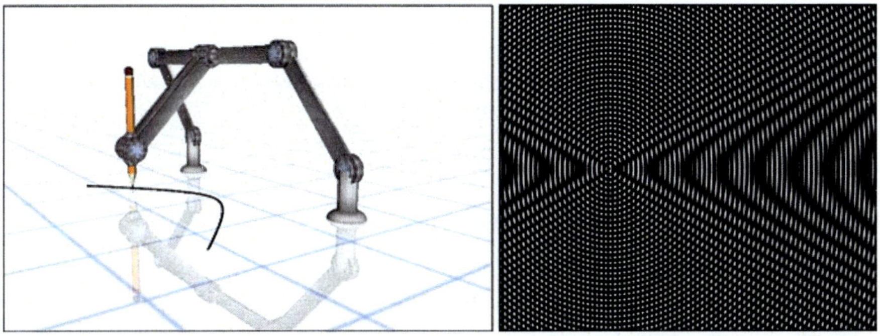

Fig. 16 Are these hyperbolas?

need to pick the desired parts and define their behavior. The first classroom application of this library is in the 2011 spring semester of the undergraduate course "Geometry of Motion" at Sofia University. Students are expected to "invent" new devices and then to implement them virtually using the library.

Mathematics: Geometry

There are many papers and web sites describing the properties of conic sections. However, the construction of virtual devices requires understanding of these properties at a higher level of abstraction. Converting a mathematical model into a mechanical one is a real mathematical and engineering challenge. Besides, mathematical challenges are hidden in the models themselves. They can be used to teach mathematical concepts and be used as an experimental playground for various tasks.

Figure 16 (left) illustrates a mathematical problem – to find whether the curve generated by the device is a hyperbola or it is just looking like a hyperbola. Also, if it draws hyperbola, could we customize the dimensions of the mechanical parts, so that it draws a degenerate hyperbola – a pair of intersecting lines? Figure 16 (right) shows a moiré pattern (Strong 1964). Is it a family of hyperbolas at various eccentricities?

Art: Animation

The collection of animations inspired the author to create a mathematical film that illustrates seven different ways of constructing ellipses (Boytchev 2010b). Although purely artistic, the making of the film was based on solving many geometrical, mechanical, and programming problems. Students may also be engaged in similar multidisciplinary activities, where, they blend scientific and artistic designs while constructing an artifact of their choice.

The InnoMathEd project provided a home for the collection and it is a nice environment to create and evaluate teaching/learning activities. The adoption of techniques from virtual reality and gaming edutainment makes the animations and the applications more appealing.

Conclusion and Future Plans

The set of virtual models and the library described in this paper are still under construction. Most likely they will never be finished as long as new models and devices are continuously being added. All models are available for free both as source codes and as 30-s clips.

The first classroom evaluation of the proposed interactive 3D models will be completed by mid-2011 within the InnoMathEd project and the results will be reported in future papers. The work described in this paper is focused solely on the design and the development of the software tools. The pedagogical aspects of their application will be researched in the next phase of the project.

The software by itself does not imply that it is effective for educational purposes, because technology in education is educationally neutral. Whether its use is effective or not in the classroom, depends on how it is used. In this respect, the presented software provides educational perspectives that are not feasible in the traditional mathematical textbooks and are not used by the modern DGS. Whether these perspectives will be utilized, is related to the actual application in the classroom.

The major expected benefits of using the presented models are: (1) to provide multiple real-life representations of conic sections; (2) to demonstrate the main properties of conics in a clear way; and (3) to build engaging and entertaining virtual environment, which utilizes the power of ICT in areas, where conventional textbooks fail.

Acknowledgments The paper is partly supported by Grant 162/2010 from Sofia University Research Fund.

References

Apostol, T., & Mnatsakanian, M. (2009). A new look at the so-called trammel of Archimedes. *American Mathematical Monthly*, 116(2), 115–133.

Bianco, T. (2009). *Needs analysis report for InnoMathEd - Innovations in Mathematics education*. Augsburg: University of Augsburg.

Boytchev, P. (2007). Enhancing spatial imagination of young students by activities in 3D ELICA applications. In P. Boyvalenkov & P. Rusev (eds.), *Proceedings of the 36th Spring Conference of the Union of Bulgarian Mathematicians* (pp. 109–119), Varna: Union of Bulgarian Mathematicians.

Boytchev, P. (2009). *Exhibition "Seduction"*. Retrieved 23 April 2011 from http://mandelbrot-set.elica.net.

Boytchev, P. (2010a). *Mathematical devices playlist at ElicaTeam's Channel*. Retrieved 23 April 2011 from http://www.youtube.com/elicateam#g/c/6534E936D46257BF.

Boytchev, P. (2010b). *Mathematical film "Ellipses…"*. Retrieved 22 April 2011 from http://www.youtube.com/watch?v=1v5Aqo6PaFw.

Demana, F., Waits, B., Foley, G., & Kennedy, D. (2000). *Precalculus: Functions and Graphs*. Chapter 8, Boston: Addison Wesley Longman.

Downs, J. (1993). *Practical Conic Sections: The Geometric Properties of Ellipses, Parabolas and Hyperbolas*. Palo Alto: Dale Seymour Publications.

Isoda, M., Suzuki, A., Ohneda, Y., Sakamoto, M., Mizutani, N., Kawasaki, N., Morozumi, T., Katajima, S., Hiroi, N., Aoyama, K., Matsuzaki, A. (2001). LEGO project – Mediational means for mathematics by mechanics. *Tsukuba Journal of Educational Study in Mathematics*, 20, 77–92.

Kendig, K. (2005). *Conics*. Cambridge: Cambridge University Press.

Wageman, J. (2010). *Conic Sections*. The North Dakota Curriculum Initiative. Retrieved 22 April 2011 from http://ndcurriculuminitiative.org/index.php/lesson_bank/lesson/conic_sections.

Nasco (2010). *Conic Sections Set~Conic Sections*. Product web page. Retrieved 29 December 2010 from http://www.enasco.com/product/TB23712T.

Scher, D. (2003). *Exploring Conic Sections with The Geometer's Sketchpad (Version 4)*. Berkeley: Key Curriculum Press

Schumann, H. (2005). Introduction to Conics with Cabri 3D. In K. Kwok (ed.), *Proceedings of 20th Mathematics Education conference* (pp. 25–38). Hong Kong: Hong Kong Institute of Mathematics Education.

Smith, B. (2011). *Conics*. Math Academy. Retrieved 22 April 2011 from http://www.mathacademy.com/pr/prime/articles/conics/index.asp.

Strong, C. (1964). Moire patterns provide both recreation and some analogues for solving problems. *Scientific American*, 211(5), 134–142.

Weisstein, E. (2010). *Dandelin Spheres*. MathWorld – A Wolfram Web Resource. Retrieved 29 December 2010 from http://mathworld.wolfram.com/DandelinSpheres.html.

Towards Community-Based Open Educational Resources: Tools for Developing and Managing IEEE LOM Application Profiles

Demetrios G. Sampson, Panagiotis Zervas, and George Chloros

Introduction

During the past years several initiatives have been developed worldwide toward the open access to Educational Resources, in the form of learning objects such as video and audio lectures (podcasts), references, workbooks and textbooks, multimedia simulations, experiments and demonstrations, as well as syllabi, curricula, courseware, and lesson plans (McGreal 2008). UNESCO (2002) has defined Open Educational Resources (OERs) as the "technology-enabled, open provision of educational resources for consultation, use and adaptation by a community of users for non-commercial purposes." The OER movement is a technology-empowered initiative that aims to create and share educational resources that are freely available online for everyone on a global level (Caswell et al. 2008). The main objective of such initiatives is to support the process of organizing, classifying, and storing digital educational resources and their associated metadata in Web-based repositories which are called Learning Object Repositories (LORs). McGreal has defined LORs as systems that "enable users to locate, evaluate and manage learning objects through the use of 'metadata', namely descriptors or tags that systematically describe many aspects of a given learning object, from its technical to its pedagogical characteristics" (McGreal 2004).

Within this context, a number of international efforts have led to the development of the IEEE Learning Objects Metadata (LOM) standard as a commonly accepted way for describing educational resources with metadata (IEEE 2002). Most of the LORs that have been developed worldwide adopt the IEEE LOM standard for describing their educational resources aiming to facilitate their

D.G. Sampson (✉) • P. Zervas
Department of Digital Systems, University of Piraeus, Piraeus, Greece

Informatics and Telematics Institute, Centre for Research and Technology Hellas, Athens, Greece
e-mail: sampson@unipi.gr

G. Chloros
Department of Digital Systems, University of Piraeus, Piraeus, Greece

A. Jimoyiannis (ed.), *Research on e-Learning and ICT in Education*,
DOI 10.1007/978-1-4614-1083-6_21,

interoperability with other LORs (McGreal 2008). However, it was recognized early enough that it is not possible for a generic standard such as IEEE LOM to fully meet specific requirements and thoroughly accommodate the particular needs of different educational communities. As a result, a common practice of generating Application Profiles (APs) of the IEEE LOM standard has emerged (Duval et al. 2002; Mason and Galatis 2007; Currier 2008; Mason and Ellis 2009). As a result, several educational communities have developed a number of APs, so as to adapt the IEEE LOM to their specific requirements and needs.

In response to this increased interest for IEEE LOM Application Profiling, a number of software tools have been developed, so as to facilitate educational communities in the process of developing and managing their own IEEE LOM APs. The aim of this book chapter is to present the practice of developing IEEE LOM APs, as well as to provide an overview of existing tools that support this process and compare them, so as to identify their strengths and weaknesses.

Application Profiles for Educational Metadata

Guidelines for Developing Application Profiles

The European Committee for Standardization (CEN/ISSS) defines an Application Profile (AP) as: "an assemblage of metadata elements selected from one or more metadata schemas and combined in a compound schema". Application profiles provide the means to express principles of modularity and extensibility. The purpose of an Application Profile is to adapt or combine existing schemas into a package that is tailored to the functional requirements of a particular application, while retaining interoperability with the original base schemas" (Smith et al. 2006).

According to IMS Global Learning Consortium, the main reasons for the development of an AP can be summarized below (IMS GLC 2005a):

- To meet technical and other requirements and preferences specific to a project, a community, a domain, and/or a region.
- To address ambiguity and generality in a specification or standard.
- To foster semantic interoperability, e.g., through the use of commonly understood vocabularies.
- To facilitate testing for conformance and successful interoperability.

However, it is important in the process of Application Profiling to support the communities, which are interesting in developing APs, with a consistent practice that will facilitate them during this process. The IMS Global Learning Consortium recognizes a number of benefits in doing this, namely (IMS GLC 2005a):

- A set of rules for constructing an AP will confine the changes that can be made, thus ensuring greater interoperability across conformant APs.

- The consistent documentation of APs will enable vendors to build products and services that reach out multiple communities with simple configuration settings for localization.
- The growing number of publicly documented APs will allow subsequent adopting communities to select and reuse elements of existing APs, rather than develop them from the scratch.
- Machine readable definitions of APs will facilitate data exchange and interoperability across different communities.

International Organizations such as IMS Global Learning Consortium and European Committee for Standardization (CEN/ISSS) have published guidelines for the development of APs with specific focus on the IEEE LOM Standard. These guidelines include the following steps (Smith et al. 2006; IMS GLC 2005b):

- *Step 1 – Selection of data elements*: During this step the data elements that the new AP will be built on are selected.
- *Step 2 – Size and smallest permitted maximum*: This step includes the definition of the size that a data element is allowed to have at a metadata instance.
- *Step 3 – Data elements from multiple namespaces*: This step aims at the definition of data elements from different namespaces, which are part of different metadata schemas.
- *Step 4 – Adding local data elements*: During this step new local data elements, which are not contained to the initial metadata schema, are added to the new AP.
- *Step 5 – Obligation of data elements*: This step aims at the definition of the mandatory data elements (i.e., the value for these data elements shall always be present), the conditional (i.e., the value for the data element shall be present only if a certain condition is satisfied), and the recommended (some APs recommend including values for specific metadata elements).
- *Step 6 – Value space*: During this step the value space of the data elements is defined. The value space defines the set of values that the data element shall derive its value from.
- *Step 7 – Relationship and dependency*: This step includes the definition of interrelationships and dependencies between data elements.
- *Step 8 – Data type profiling*: This step aims at the definition of the data types of specific metadata elements.
- *Step 9 – Application profile binding*: The final step includes the production of the AP binding, which is the conceptual data schema of the AP and should be represented in XML schema or RDF format.

Examples of Existing Application Profiles

As a result, during the past years, a number of IEEE LOM Application Profiles have been developed worldwide. Examples of well known APs are summarized below:

- *The CELEBRATE Application Profile* (Simon and Colin 2004) and its evolution, namely, the *Learning Resource Exchange (LRE) Application Profile*

Table 1 Modification types of existing IEEE LOM APs

Modification types	CELEBRATE	LRE	UK-LOM Core	JORUM	VETADATA	ANZ-LOM	DET LRM
Selection of data elements	✓	✓	✓	✓	✓	✓	✓
Size and smallest permitted maximum	✓	✓	–	✓	✓	✓	–
Data elements from multiple namespaces	–	–	–	–	–	–	–
Adding local data elements	✓	✓	–	–	–	–	–
Obligation of data elements	✓	✓	✓	✓	✓	✓	–
Value space	✓	✓	✓	✓	✓	✓	✓
Relationship and dependency	✓	✓	✓	✓	✓	✓	✓
Data type profiling	–	–	–	–	–	–	–
Application profile binding	✓	✓	–	–	✓	–	✓

(Van Assche and Massart 2007) developed by the European Schoolnet (EUN) Partnership and adopted by the LRE for Schools Repository (http://lreforschools.eun.org/).

- *The UK-LOM Core Application Profile* (UK LOM CORE 2004) and its evolution, namely, the *JORUM Application Profile* (Stevenson 2005) developed by a JISC-funded Service for Development in UK Further and Higher Education and adopted by the JORUM Web Repository (http://www.jorum.ac.uk).
- *The VET Metadata Application Profile (Vetadata)* (Australian Flexible Learning Framework 2009) developed by the Australian Flexible Learning Framework and adopted by the LORN Web Repository (http://lorn.flexiblelearning.net.au).
- *The Australia New Zealand LOM (ANZ-LOM) Application Profile* (The Le@rning Federation 2008) developed by the Le@rning Federation, a collaborative project for the development of Educational Services in Australia and New Zealand. The ANZ-LOM AP was adopted by the Le@rning Federation Web Repository (http://www.thelearningfederation.edu.au).
- *The DET Learning Resource Metadata Application Profile* (Flack 2010) developed by the Department of Education and Training of New South Wales in Australia and adopted by the Teaching and Learning exchange (TaLe) Web Repository (http://www.tale.edu.au).

Table 1 summarizes the modifications of the aforementioned APs in accordance with the steps of the guidelines described in the previous section. This can help us to extract useful conclusions about the most common types of modifications done in the developed APs.

More specifically, as we can notice from Table 1 all examined APs: (a) select a subset of data elements from the IEEE LOM Standard (step 1), (b) define the value space of the data elements (step 6), and (c) define inter-relationships and dependencies between data elements (step 7). Moreover, the majority of the examined APs: (a) define the size that a data element is allowed to have at a metadata instance (step 2), (b) define mandatory, conditional, and recommended data elements (step 5), and (c) provide the AP binding in XML Schema format (step 9). On the other hand, none of the examined APs define data elements from multiple namespaces (step 3) nor new data types for specific metadata elements (step 8). Additionally, only two of them (namely, CELEBRATE and LRE) define new local data elements which are not included at the IEEE LOM Standard.

Tools for Developing and Managing Application Profiles of the IEEE LOM Standard

Due to the increasing interest in developing community-based IEEE LOM Application Profiles, recently some tools for facilitating the development and management of IEEE LOM APs have been developed. Typically, these tools allow users to develop an IEEE LOM AP following the steps of IMS Global Learning Consortium and CEN/ISSS. In this section, a brief overview of these tools is given.

eMAP

eMAP (Chatzinotas and Sampson 2004) is an open-source standalone tool targeting non-XML experienced users. Its main functionalities include (Fig. 1):

- The creation of new IEEE LOM APs partially following the guidelines of IMS GLC and CEN/ISSS.
- Editing of IEEE LOM APs (produced by the tool) by visualizing the metadata elements in a tree structure and grouping them according to the IEEE LOM Standard categories.

IMS SchemaProf

IMS SchemaProf (IMS GLC 2007) is a standalone tool developed in the framework of the Project TELCERT (http://www.opengroup.org/telcert). It is included in a suite of tools that support the process of application profiling in learning technologies. IMS SchemaProf is targeting XML experienced users and its main functionalities include (Fig. 2):

- The creation of new IEEE LOM APs following the steps of IMS GLC and CEN/ISSS Guidelines.

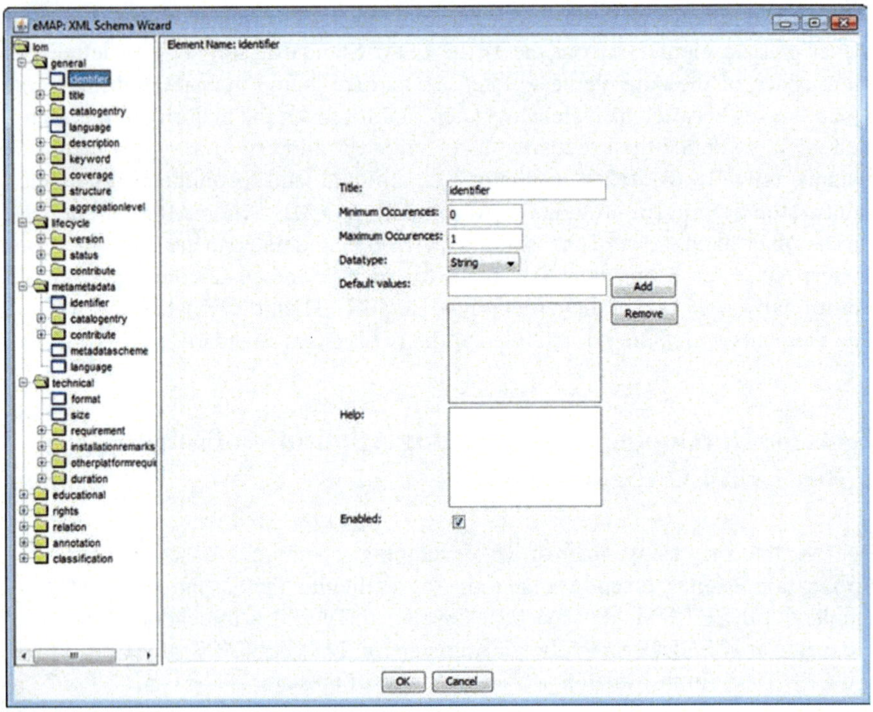

Fig. 1 Developing a new IEEE LOM AP with eMAP

- The processing and editing of existing IEEE LOM APs by visualizing all metadata elements in a tree structure and applying modifications.
- The export of an IEEE LOM AP as an XSD Schema.

ASK-LOM-AP

ASK-LOM-AP (Chloros et al. 2010) is an open-source web-based tool fully supporting the process of developing and managing IEEE LOM APs. It also incorporates the ability of educational metadata authoring based on either an existing IEEE LOM AP or a new one produced by the tool. The ASK-LOM-AP Tool is addressing non-XML experienced users, who might have limited knowledge of the IEEE LOM Standard and provide them with appropriate step-by-step wizards, which facilitate them in the process of IEEE LOM Application Profiling, as well as in the process of educational metadata authoring based on the developed APs. The main functionalities of the ASK-LOM-AP can be summarized as follows (Fig. 3):

- The creation of new IEEE LOM APs by using a step-by-step wizard conformant to the IMS GLC and CEN/ISSS Guidelines.

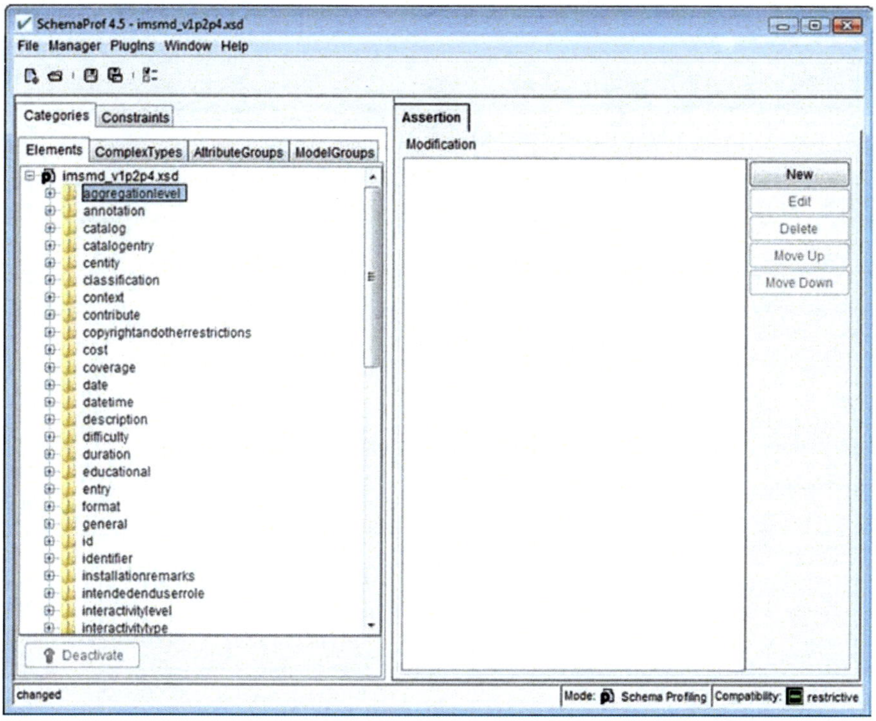

Fig. 2 Developing a new IEEE LOM AP with IMS Schema Prof

- The processing and editing of existing IEEE LOM APs by applying changes to the metadata elements and value space of the elements. Moreover the modified IEEE LOM AP can be saved to the APs Repository of the tool for future usage.
- The export of the XML Schema of a developed IEEE LOM AP with all the modifications, in accordance with the base schema of the IEEE LOM Standard, so as to be interoperable with educational metadata authoring tools.
- The authoring of educational metadata based on existing IEEE LOM APs by using a step-by-step wizard. Moreover, the educational metadata instances could be exported in XML format and imported to Learning Objects Repositories.

Comparison of Existing Tools

In order to be able to compare the existing tools for developing and managing APs, we define a comparison grid, which is based on specific requirements that such a tool should meet. The first set of requirements that an IEEE LOM Application

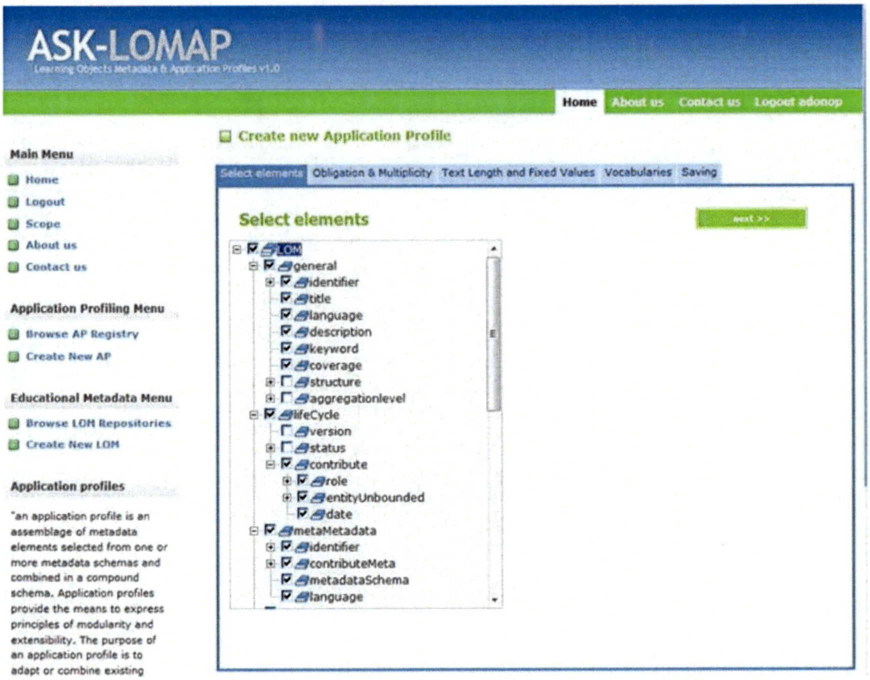

Fig. 3 Developing a new IEEE LOM AP with ASK-LOM-AP

Profiling Tool should meet is derived from the conformance of the tool with the IMS GLC and CEN/ISSS Guidelines. More specifically, these requirements can be summarized below:

- *Requirement 1*: Capability to select the IEEE LOM metadata elements which will be used for the development of a new AP.
- *Requirement 2*: Capability to define the minimum and maximum occurrence of the selected IEEE LOM metadata elements in the IEEE LOM metadata instance of the developed AP.
- *Requirement 3*: Capability to select metadata elements from other metadata schemas (not only IEEE LOM) and include them to a new AP.
- *Requirement 4*: Capability to include to a new AP, new metadata elements which are not included at the IEEE LOM metadata schema.
- *Requirement 5*: Capability to define to a new AP, the mandatory, the recommended, and the optional metadata elements.
- *Requirement 6*: Capability to define the set of values that a metadata element of a new AP shall derive its values from.
- *Requirement 7*: Capability to define relationships, as well as, dependencies between the metadata elements of a new AP.

Table 2 Requirements of IEEE LOM application profiling tools

Categories	Requirements	eMAP	IMS SchemaProf	ASK-LOM-AP
Requirements derived by IMS GLC and CEN/ ISSS Guidelines	Selection of data elements	✓	✓	✓
	Size and smallest permitted maximum	✓	✓	✓
	Data elements from multiple namespaces	–	✓	✓
	Adding local data elements	–	✓	✓
	Obligation of data elements	✓	✓	✓
	Value space	✓	✓	✓
	Relationship and dependency	–	✓	✓
	Data type profiling	–	✓	✓
	Application profile binding	–	✓	✓
Requirements derived by interoper-ability and usability issues	Interoperability of produced APs with educational metadata authoring tools	–	✓	✓
	Support authoring of educational metadata based on application profile	✓	–	✓
	Do not require XML knowledge	✓	–	✓
	It is accessible via a web-browser	–	–	✓

- *Requirement 8*: Capability to define the data types of the metadata elements of a new AP.
- *Requirement 9*: Capability to produce and export the AP binding using the XML language (in the form of an XML Schema).

The second set of requirements that an IEEE LOM Application Profiling Tool should meet is derived from interoperability and usability issues. More specifically, these requirements can be summarized below:

- *Requirement 10*: Capability to produce new APs, which can be interoperable with other tools such as educational metadata editors. This is very important because the produced APs will not be isolated from those tools.
- *Requirement 11*: Capability to author educational metadata instances based on the produced APs. This is also an important requirement because the user of the IEEE LOM Application Profiling Tool would not need to use a separate metadata editor, so as to author educational metadata instances based on the various Application Profiles developed.
- *Requirement 12*: Capability to be used by non-XML experienced users. This requirement is making the IEEE LOM Application Profiling process accessible to non-technical expert users.
- *Requirement 13*: Capability to be accessible via a web browser. This requirement maximizes the potential of sharing and reusing APs between different users and different communities of users.

Table 2 compares existing tools according to the requirements that these tools meet. The requirements are divided into two main categories, in accordance with the requirements' categories previously described.

As we can notice from Table 1, the eMAP does not meet the requirements derived by IMS GLC and CEN/ISSS Guidelines (which is reasonable since this tool was developed before these guidelines were published), whereas, both the IMS SchemaProf and the ASK-LOM-AP fully supports these Guidelines. On the other hand, the eMAP and the ASK-LOM-AP do not require from their users to be experienced in XML language, whereas, the IMS SchemaProf requires from its users adequate knowledge of XML language. Moreover, it should be noted that the eMAP and the ASK-LOM-AP provide the capability to their users to author metadata instances of a new AP, whereas, the IMS SchemaProf does not offer this capability. Finally, the eMAP and the IMS SchemaProf are standalone tools and they are not accessible online, whereas, the ASK-LOM-AP is a web-based tool fully accessible online.

Conclusions

Despite the widespread use of IEEE LOM Application Profiles by various educational communities, it appears that only limited attempts exists in the literature for the development of technological tools that support the process of IEEE LOM Application Profiling. Nevertheless, such technological efforts are much needed to make the process of developing and managing IEEE LOM APs for different educational communities more accessible to non-technical experts. In this chapter, we presented an overview of existing tools that facilitate the process of developing and managing IEEE LOM APs and we compared them based on a comparison grid that includes the key requirements which should be met by an IEEE LOM Application Profiling Tool.

The results of this comparison showed the limitations of the existing tools, namely:

- They require from their users a profound knowledge of XML structure and its syntax.
- The produced APs cannot be exported and reused by other software tools and systems.
- They do not support the process of educational metadata authoring based on the produced APs. This means that an educational community should use educational metadata authoring tools along with the produced AP, so as to author educational metadata instances based on it.
- They are not accessible online.

On the other hand, one of the examined tools, namely ASK-LOM-AP, overcomes the identified limitations and can simplify the process of developing and managing IEEE LOM APs for different educational communities.

Acknowledgments The work presented in this paper has been partly supported by the PATHWAY Project that is funded by the European Commission's Seventh Framework Programme, Supporting and coordinating actions on innovative methods in science education: teacher training on inquiry based teaching methods on a large scale in Europe (Contract No: 266624), as well as by the OpenScienceResources Project (http://www.opensciencereources.eu) that is funded by European Commission's eContentPlus Programme (Contract No: ECP- 2008 - EDU- 428045).

References

Australian Flexible Learning Framework (2009). *VET Metadata Application Profile (Vetadata)*. Retrieved 1 December 2010 from http://e-standards.flexiblelearning.net.au/vetadata/docs/vetadata-spec-v1-final2009.pdf.

Caswell, T., Henson, S., Jensen, M., & Wiley, D. (2008). Open educational resources: Enabling universal education. *The International Review of Research in Open and Distance Learning*, 9(1). Retrieved 1 December 2010 from http://www.irrodl.org/index.php/irrodl/article/view/469/1009.

Chatzinotas, S., & Sampson, D. (2004). eMAP: Design and implementation of educational metadata application profiles. In C.K. Looi, E. Sutinen, D. Sampson, I. Aedo, L. Uden & E. Kähkönen (eds.), *Proceedings of the 4th IEEE International Conference on Advanced Learning Technologies (ICALT 04)* (pp. 876–877). Los Alamitos: IEEE Computer Society.

Chloros, G., Zervas, P., & Sampson, D. (2010). ASK-LOM-AP: A Web-based tool for development and management of IEEE LOM application profiles. In M. Jemni, Kinshuk, D. Sampson, & J.M. Spector (eds.), *Proceedings of the 10th IEEE International Conference on Advanced Learning Technologies (ICALT 2010)* (pp. 138–142). Los Alamitos: IEEE Computer Society.

Currier, S. (2008). Metadata for learning resources: An update on standards activity for 2008, *ARIADNE*, 55. Retrieved 1 December 2010 from http://www.ariadne.ac.uk/issue55/currier.

Duval, E., Hodgins, W., Sutton, S., & Weibel, S.L. (2002). Metadata principles and practicalities. *D-Lib Magazine*, 8(4). Retrieved 1 December 2010 from http://www.dlib.org/dlib/april02/weibel/04weibel.html.

Flack, I. (2010). T*he Department of Education and Training Learning Resource Metadata (DETLRM) Application Profile v2.0*. Retrieved 1 December 2010 from http://www.cli.nsw.edu.au/services/standards/documents/detlrm.pdf.

IEEE Learning Technology Standards Committee (LTSC) (2002). *Draft Standard for Learning Object Metadata*. Retrieved 1 December 2010 from http://ltsc.ieee.org/wg12/files/LOM_1484_12_1_v1_Final_Draft.pdf.

IMS Global Learning Consortium (GLC) (2005a). *IMS Application ProfileGuidelines Overview*. Retrieved 1 December 2010 from http://www.imsglobal.org/ap/apv1p0/imsap_oviewv1p0.html.

IMS Global Learning Consortium (GLC) (2005b). *IMS Application Profile Guidelines Technical Manual*. Retrieved 1 December 2010 from http://www.imsglobal.org/ap/apv1p0/imsap_techv1p0.html.

IMS Global Learning Consortium (GLC) (2007). IMS Schema Profiling Tool User Manual. Retrieved 1 December 2010 from http://www.imsglobal.org/profile/IMS-SchemaProf-2p0-UserManual.pdf.

Mason, R.T., & Ellis, T.J. (2009). Extending SCORM LOM. *Issues in Informing Science and Information Technology*, 6, 864–875.

Mason, J., & Galatis, H. (2007). Theory and practice of application profile development in Australian education and training. In S. A. Sutton, A. S. Chaudhry & C. Koo (eds.), *Proceedings of the 2007 International Conference on Dublin Core and Metadata Applications: application profiles: theory and practice (DCMI '07)* (pp. 43–52). Singapore: Dublin Core Metadata Initiative and National Library Board.

McGreal, R. (2004). *Online Education Using Learning Objects*. Washington, D.C.: Falmer Press

McGreal, R. (2008). A typology of learning object repositories. In H.H. Adelsberger, Kinshuk, J. M. Pawlovski & D. Sampson (eds.), *International Handbook on Information Technologies for Education and Training* (pp. 5–28). Heidelberg: Springer.

Simon, J., & Colin, J. N. (2004). A digital licensing model for the exchange of learning objects in a federated environment. In B. Benatallah, C. Godart & S.M. Chien (eds.), *Proceedings of the IEEE Workshop on Electronic Commerce* (pp. 46–53). San Diego: IEEE Computer Society.

Smith, N., Van Coillie, M., & Duval, E. (2006). Guidelines and support for building Application profiles in e-learning. In N. Smith, M. Van Coillie, & E. Duval (eds.), *CEN/ISSS WS/LT Learning Technologies Workshop CWA* (pp. 1–26). Brussels: CEN Workshop Agreements.

Stevenson, A. (2005). *The JORUM Application Profile Version 1.0.* Retrieved 1 December 2010 from http://www.jorum.ac.uk/docs/pdf/japv1p0.pdf

The Le@rning Federation (2008). *Australia New Zealand LOM (ANZ-LOM) Metadata Application Profile.* Retrieved 1 December 2010 from http://www.thelearningfederation.edu.au/verve/_resources/ANZ-LOM.pdf.

UK Learning Object Metadata (LOM) Core (2004). Retrieved 1 December 2010 from http://metadata.cetis.ac.uk/profiles/uklomcore/uklomcore_v0p2_may04.doc.

UNESCO (2002). *Forum on the Impact of Open Courseware for Higher Education in Developing Countries-Final Report.* Retrieved 1 December 2010 from http://unesdoc.unesco.org/images/0012/001285/128515e.pdf.

Van Assche, F., & Massart, D. (2007). *The EUN Learning Resource Exchange Metadata Application Profile Version 3.0.* Retrieved 1 December 2010 from http://lre.eun.org/sites/default/files/docs/LREMAPv4p5p1.pdf.

Restrictions and Abilities of SCORM: A Path to Adaptive Course Development

Ioannis Kazanidis and Maya Satratzemi

Introduction

The growth of the Internet and with it e-learning, has led to the appearance of Learning Management Systems (LMSs), which provide a variety of features and operations including the development, management, distribution, diffusion, and presentation of educational material, as well as tools for both user and course management. However, many researchers (Conlan et al. 2002; Bouras et al. 2003; Jui-Lin Lu and Chen 2006) have raised questions in regards to the accessibility and reusability of the educational material, the interoperability between different systems and their durability over time. As a solution to the aforementioned problems, research proposes the use of technological standards for the creation of educational material (Bouras et al. 2003; Brusilovsky 2004; Jui-Lin Lu and Chen 2006; Casella et al. 2007). Some of the most well-known standards for the creation of educational material are: SCORM (Sharable Content Object Reference Model) (ADL 2009), LOM, IMS, AICC, etc. The most widespread standard, in the last years, has been SCORM which is based on SCOs (Sharable Content Objects). The exploitation of this technology not only allows the use of educational material in multiple LMSs but also facilitates the discovery and reusability of such material (Duval 2001; Krull et al. 2006).

Due to the nature of the Internet, some problems do however, arise. The courses distributed by LMSs, are available to a wide number of users, with different characteristics, cultures, learning needs and previous knowledge of the domain. Therefore, a course that is appropriate for one particular learner may not be suitable for the needs of other learners. What is more, learners have the ability to navigate freely within a

I. Kazanidis (✉)
Department of Accountancy, Kavala Institute of Technology, Kavala, Greece
e-mail: kazanidis@teikav.edu.gr

M. Satratzemi
Department of Applied Informatics, University of Macedonia, Thessaloniki, Greece

A. Jimoyiannis (ed.), *Research on e-Learning and ICT in Education*,
DOI 10.1007/978-1-4614-1083-6_22, © Springer Science+Business Media, LLC 2012

course or even visit web pages not immediately connected with the course. These characteristics have led to some major problems summarized in Murray et al. (2000), such as disorientation, cognitive overload, discontinuous flow, content readiness, and user distraction (Foss 1989). A solution proposed by a large number of researchers (Brusilovsky 1996; Pilar da Silva et al. 1998) is the incorporation of interactivity and adaptivity in online learning environments. The outcome of these research efforts was the appearance of Adaptive Educational Hypermedia Systems (AEHSs). The main objective of AEHSs is to individualize the features and operations that they provide so as to increase their functionality (Brusilovsky 1996). Their personalization is usually applied via the adaptive navigation and presentation of the educational content (Brusilovsky 2001).

From the above, it becomes clear that AEHSs mainly attempt, via adaptation, to improve the educational process and its outcome, while the standardization that many LMSs follow aims to help course developers to access and reuse educational material easily, as well as provide interoperability between different systems and platforms. As a consequence, many researchers (Specht et al. 2002; Conlan et al. 2002; Modritscher et al. 2006), turned their attention to systems, which are based on these two axes. According to Brusilovsky (2004) these systems may eventually even replace traditional LMSs.

The present work attempts to contribute to this research area. It focuses on the restrictions that are related to the production of educational content due to SCORM specifications and investigates ways in the development of dynamic and adaptive educational material which will conform to SCORM and its specifications. For further course adaptation, an adaptive LMS named ProPer is presented; while for automatic course authoring, the use of ProPer SAT (SCORM Authoring Tool) is proposed.

Technology Background

Adaptive Educational Hypermedia Systems

The main characteristic of AEHSs is the individualization of the educational process according to learner needs. The student oriented instruction allows students to follow an optimal learning path adapted to their individual characteristics, utilizing their strengths and at the same time helping them achieve a better learning outcome.

Personalized instruction through an AEHS, however, requires accurate design of both the AEHS and its courses. The problem which arises is that there is no common development framework for such systems, and therefore, a lot of time must be spent in developing them. Besides this, the development of suitably formed educational content is, most times, also required. As a consequence, precious time is spent on the development of educational material, which means that nowhere near enough attention is paid to the application of suitable educational strategies.

Learning Management Systems

LMSs and their courses are one of the most popular ways of knowledge distribution via the Internet. Yet, there is only one form of teaching for all types of learners, without meeting the individual's potential needs. The use of previously presented AEHS technologies deals with these kinds of problems. However, developers of such courses are confronted with a variety of problems: (1) lack of a predefined development standard of LMSs and its corresponding educational material, a consequence of which is that it is difficult to develop and apply educational material designed for use by one platform to another; (2) many times the upgrading of LMS in a new version requires changes in the structure of educational material; and (3) both re-use and recall of educational material require additional work from the course designers. Due to the abovementioned problems, as happens with AEHSs, many resources are expended on the programming implementation of the courses rather than on content quality and educational strategies.

The solution to these problems comes from the adoption of certain international standards and specifications in combination with the use of learning objects (LOs) of the educational material. This tendency is also confirmed from their use by the most well-known LMSs. In order for the use of LOs from different systems and courses to be successful, appropriate standards have to be adopted.

SCORM Specifications and Restrictions

Standards and specifications were developed in order to facilitate the description, packaging, sequencing, and distribution of educational content, learning activities and learner information (Campbell 2002). The description and development of suitably structured educational material comes mainly via the metadata. These standards and specifications provide reusability, accessibility, interoperability, and durability to potential software updates.

The most popular technical standard at the moment is SCORM. SCORM is a set of specifications for the development, organization, and distribution of educational content. Its goals are to enable compliant systems to import, share, reuse, and export electronic educational material. SCORM prescribes the entire development process of the educational material, from unit segregation to the definition of which metadata is essential or optional for each LO. SCORM is comprised of three main parts: the Content Aggregation Model (CAM), the SCORM Run Time Environment (RTE), and Sequencing and Navigation (SN).

SCORM, in accordance with other standards, places concrete specifications and restrictions both on the educational content and on the compatible LMSs. SCORM compliant educational content is structured from independent LOs. Each LO is composed of either assets or SCOs (Sharable Content Objects). Assets may be elementary units of knowledge, like text, sounds, images, etc. and there is no conformity rule to the standard. However, assets cannot communicate with the system and therefore, such type of content is static.

In contrast, SCOs have the ability to communicate with the system. Each SCO is composed of various assets and additionally, it includes an essential JavaScript code for communication with the system. Substantially, an SCO may be composed of one or more HTML web pages, while it follows concrete rules so as to be compatible with all the SCORM compliant LMSs. The JavaScript code, which is included in the SCOs, is in accordance with the SCORM Application Program Interface (API) and Data Model. This code has to execute concrete actions. In particular, it has to (1) locate the provided API of the LMS, (2) initialize and terminate every communication session with the LMS, (3) record and store concrete information about the learners, and (4) provide error management. The storage of information in the system's database takes place through the SCORM API. Consequently, information is dispatched for storage with the use of specific commands in concrete form.

SCORM API provides, among others, the following functions for SCO and system intercommunication (ADL 2009):

- *Initialize()*: Initializes the communication session between the SCO and the system.
- *Terminate()*: Terminates the communication session between the SCO and the system.
- *GetValue()*: Gets appropriate data from the system.
- *SetValue()*: Sends data to the system.
- *Commit()*: Promotes the permanent storage of data that has been submitted after the last call of Initialize() or Commit() functions.

The abovementioned requirements, substantially prohibit the course author from developing electronic courses in dynamic programming languages, such as, PHP, ASP, JSP, etc. using his/her own communication and adaptation techniques, as happens in most of the AEHSs. In contrast, a SCO must locate the API instance and initiate a communication session with it. Every dynamic or static presentation of the content needs to be based on the communication between the SCO and the RTE database. This communication comes with the JavaScript code, which exploits the SCORM API. In addition a SCO may not attempt to change the appearance or close the window of the RTE (Ostyn 2010).

Since each SCO must be autonomous and ready for use in any other compatible course, the use of hyperlinks to other SCOs in the package is not permitted. This restriction does not allow a connection of concrete words from the educational content to exterior content or even to a system index; practices that are applied by some AEHSs.

There are also some restrictions at the course construction level. Each course should be packaged according to the specifications of the SCORM. Apart from educational material, these specifications require the existence of a metadata XML file with the name imsmanifest.xml, which includes concrete information about the course itself and its SCOs. All the essential information about the course, such as, the place and use of educational material, course structure, SCO weight, minimal learner's progress in order for a SCO to be considered as known, possible adaptive navigation etc. should be stored in this file, according to the SCORM CAM rules. In contrast, SCORM does allow the production of personalized courses via adaptive navigation and adaptive content presentation of the educational content by the course author.

Efficient SCORM Courseware Development

This section aims to guide authors in creating a SCORM compliant course that effectively exploits SCORM API abilities. The resultant framework is tailored to the efficient construction of basic SCORM courses. For the development of a simple SCORM course, we propose a process consisting of five stages, as follows:

Resource development and collection: Initially, the author has to find or create the necessary educational material for the course. In addition, the author must download the appropriate xsd xml extension files from the (ADL 2009) website. Moreover, s/he needs to download or develop an API wrapper JavaScript that implements the SCORM API. Some of the most well-known API wrapper JavaScripts may be found in either of the following sites (Ostyn 2010; ADL 2009).

Course construction design: At this stage the instructor designs the course structure. The course is separated into concepts as well as the course map, and the relations between each concept, are defined.

Implementation of course file structure: Every course consists of folders and files. An efficient course structure organization will help the author to categorize the course educational material and subsequently to easily maintain, update, or extend it in the future. A proposed strategy that allows easy packaging of the course is to create a parent folder that includes all the course files, as well as subfolders for JavaScript files, images, CSS files and folders which includes all the necessary HTML files of every SCO of the course.

SCO development: The educational content needs to be reformed in an appropriate format in order for it to be separated into SCOs. Usually an asset, like text, image, flash, etc. may be transformed into an SCO by adding to it an HTML wrapper which contains the necessary JavaScript code.

Course manifest development: Course construction is completed by the development of the manifest file. This file includes the essential information about the course structure and sequence according to CAM. Instructors can either write the appropriate XML code in a text editor or use special graphical tools, such as Reload Editor (Reload 2010). At this stage the author needs to set all the SCO parameters and relate the SCOs with their resources. All the course files have to be referred in the manifest resources section and vice versa. In addition, even if it is not mandatory, we propose the use of metadata to describe the course content. The existence of metadata will enable the easy discovery as well as reuse of the content from other systems and users. Since most times certain learning objects, like tests, count more in user assessment, we propose the definition of a specific weight for every SCO to its parent score and thereupon to the final course score, using the sequencing rollup rules. Finally, in order to allow SCOs determine completion as well as their successful study, authors can set the minProgressMeasure and minNormalizedMeasure attributes correspondingly.

Adaptive SCORM Course Development

Using the above techniques, authors may create effective SCORM compliant courses. However, these courses are still static and do not personalize a user's study to his/her personal needs and progress. This section, therefore, focuses on the exploitation of SCORM API so as to overcome its initial restrictions and achieve the construction of adaptive courses. Since every SCO should be autonomous and suitable for use by all SCORM compliant courses and systems, the import of an extra code that would collaborate with the system so as to adapt the content, is not allowed. In order to overcome this restriction, we propose the exploitation of SCORM functionality and more specifically: (1) the use of SCORM Objectives of a course for user modeling, (2) the adaptation of educational content through JavaScript code, which will initially read the user model and later provide appropriate adaptation, and (3) the exploitation of SCORM sequencing rules in order to adapt user navigation.

SCORM CAM enables the statement of a concrete Objective, in every course, through an XML code of the course's manifest file. Later, depending on the user's actions in the course, an SCO may asses user progress on each Objective via the JavaScript code and more specifically, by using the method SetValue() of the SCORM API. Therefore, by recording the user score in particular Objectives, a user model is created which will allow the adaptation of educational content according to the data stored in the course Objectives.

Content adaptation is applied through the JavaScript code using the function GetValue() of the SCORM API. Initially, user score on the appropriate Objective will be acquired via the GetValue() function, and afterwards the JavaScript code will modulate the presentation of the educational material accordingly.

The SCORM sequencing rules make the adaptation of user navigation in a course possible. Sequence rules may determine the SCOs that the user is allowed to study, as well as their presentation sequence. These rules are formulated following the syntax: if < condition > then < action >.

In the case that the condition is true, then the appropriate action is executed. Conditions usually check user progress in a course activity. For example, if a learner does not achieve the objectives that are related to the current activity, then the system proposes the study of additional course activities (Bouras et al. 2003). The action parameter in each sequence rule defines the action that the system has to apply, if the condition is true. Sequence rules are divided according to time, into three different steps: (1) pre-condition, which is applied when the user visits a course activity, (2) post-condition, which is applied when a course activity is terminated, and (3) exit action, which is applied after exiting an activity. As a consequence, specific course activities may or may not be available to the user for study, according to the extent of course Objective coverage, in order to improve the user learning path.

ProPer

In order to achieve a more integrated adaptation of SCORM compliant courses and to study the feasibility of the development of a system that will completely adopt the SCORM standard while simultaneously providing adaptive courses, we developed an AEHS, which we named ProPer (from the initial letters of the Greek words Adaptive Environment). ProPer (Kazanidis and Satratzemi 2009a), which is available at http://proper.uom.gr, combines characteristics from both AEHSs and LMSs and provides adaptive navigation, as well as adaptive presentation of the educational content by exploiting SCORM API, which it completely adopts.

ProPer supports three types of users: students, authors, and administrators. Students are allowed to register and study courses, keep notes for every course, manually define their user model including their educational goals and preknowledge of the domain, and send feedback to the authors. Authors adopt the students' rights and additionally, may import new SCORM compliant courses. The mechanism to import a course is derived from the SCORM RTE 1.3.3 on which ProPer implementation is based. In addition, course and user models of SCORM RTE were further extended and new modules were added. Following, authors may define the course model (set course description, passwords, dates of availability, and define in which SCOs the system will display knowledge buttons that allow students to manually define whether or not they have learned each SCO educational content), keep backups, and restore their courses. Authors may also view statistics about course status as well as the actions of students in their courses (Kazanidis and Satratzemi 2010). Lastly, besides having the same rights as authors for all courses in ProPer, administrators may also administrate both users and courses.

ProPer provides adaptive technologies both for user navigation and for the presentation of the content. These technologies can be separated into two main categories: those provided by the system and those provided by the appropriate design of the educational material.

Adaptive link annotation and direct guidance of the learner are the technologies of the first category. In addition, ProPer allows the learner to declare his/her previous knowledge as well as his/her learning goals, afterwards adapting user navigation accordingly.

The technologies that belong to the second category are link hiding and the adaptive presentation of educational content according to particular user characteristics, such as learning style, knowledge in pre-required concepts, technological infrastructure, etc.

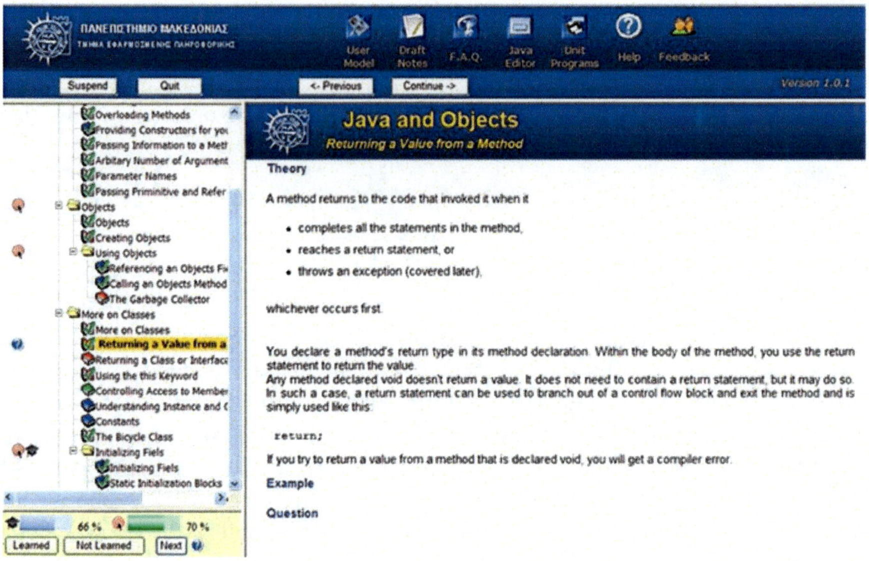

Fig. 1 ProPer interface for a Theorist user

In order to provide adaptive navigation, ProPer constructs a model for the learner based on his/her actions, and estimates learner knowledge of the domain. We propose a mechanism of user progress evaluation, according to the learner's goals and grades in each course unit. We therefore, propose: (1) the exploitation of information that can be collected via the SCORM API, like the user score in every course unit, as well as the weight of each SCO in the score of the whole course; and (2) the use of appropriate rules for the exploitation of this information, which will lead both to the adaptation of the course table of contents, as well as to the localization of the most appropriate unit for study. ProPer annotates the table of contents links according to user progress and goals, and suggests the most appropriate course unit for study by annotating the appropriate link with a green book (Fig. 1).

In order to achieve wider adaptation, we also studied the development of appropriate educational content which is adapted according to user needs. Therefore, we created adaptive courses, following the abovementioned proposed stages, that provide adaptive presentation of their content according to user characteristics, and at the same time, we propose a framework for the development of SCORM compliant courses that can be adapted to user learning style (Kazanidis and Satratzemi 2009b). More specifically, the Honey and Mumford model (1992) has been adopted, and in accordance with it users are categorized as being Activists, Reflectors, Theorists, or Pragmatists, each with its own specific learning preferences.

Adaptive courses consist of various knowledge modules on one page (Theory, Example, Question, Activity, etc.). The first SCO of these courses acquires the user learning style in accordance with the Honey and Mumford model through a questionnaire, and stores it in a SCORM objective named lstyle. All the later SCOs of the particular course read this objective value and adapt their content presentation according to the specific user learning style; e.g., if the user has been categorized as a Theorist, then the presentation of the educational material could start with the presentation of the Theory module, which is followed by an Example and a Question hint. Obviously, the sequence of these modules will be different for different learning styles. Figure 1 shows ProPer's interface and how the content of an adaptive course is presented to a user categorized as a Theorist.

In order to provide adaptive navigation and adaptive presentation, ProPer creates a user model comprising three main categories of data: (1) user knowledge of the domain, (2) user actions and goals (time spent studying a concept, number of visits, goals), and (3) independent domain data (such as: user name, password, mail, language, and privileges). User's personal data is retrieved through user registration and is static. For user knowledge representation, like the majority of AEHS, we use a multilayered overlay model which consequently, follows the domain structure. The first layer stores navigation history, i.e., data that shows whether the learner has studied a particular concept and if s/he has actually visited the corresponding web page. The second layer contains the learner's estimated knowledge on a particular concept, which is derived from a concept having been studied based on the learner's interaction with the system, and is represented as a percentage score. The third layer describes the learner's previous knowledge of the domain and can be declared in an appropriate form, either initially or during the course. Consequently, by this data being stored at different layers, it enables an independent update to take place. Thus, user knowledge data from one layer does not overwrite identical data from another.

The third category of data stores the time a learner spends on a specific concept, the number of times that s/he has visited the web page, and whether or not a concept is considered one of his/her goals. The user goal model is a combination of the overlay and stereotype models, since the user either at the start or during the actual study, can manually define his/her goals (overlay model) or select a group of goals that has been created by the tutor, which has been based on a particular category, in the range, e.g., novice – expert (stereotype model). Lastly, the learner's draft notes, feedback for tutors, and the Java Programs are stored for every course unit.

A formative evaluation of ProPer (Kazanidis and Satratzemi 2009a) was carried out in order to discover system weaknesses and check for possible improvements. After the necessary amendments, a summative evaluation followed so as to find out system usefulness and effectiveness in an online asynchronous educational process. Formative evaluation results demonstrated that with ProPer students can navigate through a course in a more goal-oriented manner enabling one to avoid unnecessary concepts, which results in faster course completion. Furthermore, summative evaluation results verified that in comparison to a simple hypermedia system, ProPer improves the learning outcome. In addition, users stated that they like studying with ProPer as they find it both simple and useful. Writers also found ProPer very easy and useful for their course delivery, since it allows them to design personalized instruction. At the same time, existent educational material can be easily retrieved, accessed, and reused taking advantage of SCORM functionality.

ProPer SAT (SCORM Authoring Tool)

As mentioned above, SCORM compliant courses were implemented for a better educational outcome. However, the development of such courses requires that the author(s) have programming knowledge. For this reason, we went one step further and developed an authoring tool, named ProPer SAT (Kazanidis and Satratzemi 2009c) which allows for the creation of SCORM compliant adaptive courses, without requiring that the author(s) have any prior programming knowledge.

ProPer SAT exploits SCORM API and utilizes the techniques presented in this paper. More specifically, it prompts the author to fill in certain predefined HTML forms, according to the type of course that s/he wants to develop (Fig. 2). In this way, the author needs only to choose the educational strategy of the course and to upload the educational content. There is, thus, no need for the author to have prior programming knowledge. In addition, ProPer SAT uses the abovementioned SCORM abilities correctly, since the SCOs that have been developed are enhanced by appropriate metadata, have a specific weight to their parents' score, grade student efforts, and can implement the presented framework for adaptive content presentation.

ProPer SAT interface is comprised of four main frames (Fig. 2). At the top of the page the toolbar functions are related to the whole course. On the left-hand side, the author may reconstruct, via a tree view table of contents, the course structure. The screen's main frame contains all the appropriate properties of course item or organization. In the case where the current selection is an item (SCO), WYSIWYG editors appear that enable the author to easily compose the educational content.

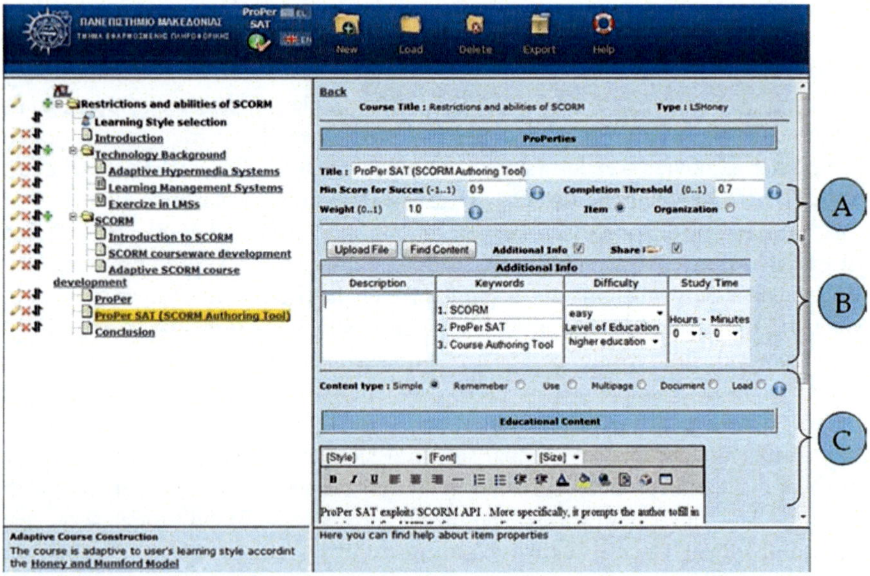

Fig. 2 ProPer SAT SCO construction interface

Section A obtains the appropriate data for user progress assessment; section B enables the easy discovery and reuse of the SCO; while section C lets the author create SCOs with adaptive content presentation according to the Honey and Mumford Model. Finally, the bottom of the screen contains information on the course type and help about available options.

ProPer SAT may create, store, and export all necessary course files in a zip file according to the third and fourth edition of SCORM 2004 standard. Therefore, this file may be imported in both ProPer and all the SCORM compliant LMSs. ProPer SAT is free for use by anyone, so long as they register in the system, which is available at http://propersat.uom.gr.

The evaluation of ProPer SAT was based on the Technology Acceptance Model (TAM), which assesses the anticipated acceptance of a particular technological system by individual users. The evaluation procedure comprised the development of SCORM compliant courses, both simple and adaptive, by authors with and without programming knowledge. This was then followed by structured interviews based on a predefined assessment questionnaire, in order to record the authors' opinion of the system. The results showed that authors found the system to be both easy and useful, stating that they intend to use it in future.

Discussion and Conclusions

This work can help authors override SCORM restrictions and create adaptive SCORM compliant courses that will provide students with personalized learning instruction. In addition, in order to achieve a better learning outcome for students, as well as fast course development for authors, future adaptive learning systems will be able to adopt the applied model presented in this work, which consists of a simple SAT and an adaptive SCORM compliant LMS. This claim has been confirmed by the evaluation results.

ProPer's main advantage is that it incorporates both adaptive technologies and LMS features, while it complies with the SCORM standard and its specifications, in contrast to most of the AEHSs which either are not completely compliant with SCORM and its specifications or incorporate limited adaptive capabilities.

In contrast to ProPer, the requirements previously presented, have not allowed most of the AEHSs to conform to SCORM specifications. Although some systems, such as OPAL (Conlan et al. 2002), and VIBORA (Morales 2003) do try to combine SCORM with adaptation, there are limitations. For instance, OPAL only uses SCORM 1.2 metadata partially and does not allow the import of SCORM courses in the way ProPer does, while adaptivity in VIBORA is limited to the dynamic sequencing of learning objects. Another system is AdeLE (Modritscher et al. 2006) which is an eye-tracking adaptive system. AdeLE supports the import of SCORM courses. However, the adaptation in AdeLE presupposes the existence of special equipment in order to record the user's eye movements. In contrast to ProPer, it cannot provide adaptation according to user learning goals and it does not support feedback during the educational process, concerning user progress. In comparison to the abovementioned systems, ProPer succeeds in combining adaptation with SCORM standard in a more efficient manner.

Other systems, similar to ProPer SAT, offer authoring tools for adaptive SCORM compliant courses in order to help authors in the course creation process. WINDS (Specht et al. 2002) creates and delivers courses based on SCORM objects but it does not support native SCORM compliant courses. It provides adaptive link annotation and adaptive presentation of educational content according to user learning style, and it incorporates an authoring tool, which helps the teacher to create adaptive courses that are based on SCOs. Another system which supports the import of SCORM courses and allows teachers to write courses which are adaptive to user learning style is AHA! (Stash 2007) in its third version. The imported courses, however, do not include all the features that AHA! offers and additional work, as well as modifications are required. In addition, it is still not possible to export its courses in a SCORM compatible form. As a consequence AHA! courses cannot be reused by other SCORM compliant systems. MOT (Power et al. 2005) is an online environment for the authoring of adaptive educational hypermedia. In MOT the author can either select an adaptive strategy that corresponds to an instructional strategy created by a different author and apply it to an arbitrary concept map or lesson map or define his/her own instructional strategy. MOT can export only courses with specific structure to pre-adapted SCORM courses in order to be used by SCORM compliant LMSs. However, these courses are only the result of a specific presentation of an adaptive course, they are not adaptive on their own.

Most of the aforementioned systems either do not completely adopt the SCORM standard and its specifications, or provide limited adaptive functionalities. ProPer SAT in contrast to the above systems, allows authors to create both static and adaptive SCORM compliant courses following simple steps. The case that it supports predefined strategies, increases system simplicity, while its conformity to SCORM enables developed courses to be delivered by any SCORM compliant LMS. In addition, ProPer SAT's internal mechanisms for sharing, discovery, and reuse of educational content, make its courses and their SCOs reusable by other course authors.

Summing up, this work presents a path for the creation of adaptive SCORM courseware. Authors may initially exploit SCORM API in order to develop either static or adaptive SCORM compliant courses. In addition, they can use ProPer for further adaptation of these courses in order to achieve a better learning outcome. This has been confirmed by ProPer's evaluation results (Kazanidis and Satratzemi 2009a), which show that students achieved a better learning outcome in less study time. Furthermore, the authoring process has been simplified with the use of ProPer SAT, where evaluation results have shown that authors found it easy and useful, while they also stated that they would use it in the future.

Although this work has attempted to exploit SCORM specifications and override the initial restrictions, more research has to be carried out in the area of applied adaptivity in SCORM. Furthermore, the possibility of SCORM API extension needs to be studied, in order to support the development of native adaptive courses, as well as to enable SCORM courses to support an appropriate user model. We, thus, intend to implement further research on various extended SCORM APIs in order to study how these extensions may facilitate personalized learning instruction for students. Finally, with the aim of enabling authors to share and reuse other authors' quality educational content more easily, friendly content sharing tools need to be implemented. For this reason, we intend to design and implement a new version of ProPer SAT that will adopt Web 2.0 abilities, and which will allow the system's users to easily share, rate, and comment on every unit of the educational content.

Acknowledgments This work was funded by the Research Committee of the University of Macedonia as part of the Basic Research Project.

References

ADL (2009). *SCORM 2004.* Advanced Distributed Learning (4th Edition).

Bouras, C., Nani, M., & Tsiatsos, T. (2003). A SCORM conformant LMS. In D. Lassner & C. McNaught (eds.), Proceedings of *Ed-Media 2003* (pp. 10–13). Honolulu, USA.

Brusilovsky, P. (1996). Methods and techniques of adaptive hypermedia. *User Modeling and User Adapted Interaction*, 6(2–3), 87–129.

Brusilovsky, P. (2001). Adaptive hypermedia. *User Modeling and User Adapted Interaction*, 11(1/2), 87–110.

Brusilovsky, P. (2004). Adaptive educational hypermedia: From generation to generation. In M. Grigoriadou, A. Raptis, S. Vosniadou, C. Kinigos (eds.), *Proceedings of the Fourth Panhellenic Conference "Information and Communication Technologies in Education"* (pp. 19–33). Athens, Greece.

Campbell, L. (2002). *Introduction to Learning Technology Interoperability Standards and CETIS.* Centre for Educational Technology Interoperability Standards, SURF Education Days, November 2002, The Hague.

Casella, G., Costagliola, G., Ferrucci, F., Polese, G., & Scanniello, G. (2007). A SCORM thin client architecture for e-learning systems based on web services. *International Journal of Distance Education Technologies,* 5(1), 13–30.

Conlan, O., Dagger, D., & Wade, V. (2002). Towards a standards-based approach to e-Learning personalization using reusable learning objects. In M. Driscoll & T. Reeves (eds.), *Proceedings of ELearn 2002, 7th World Conference on E-Learning in Corporate, Government, Healthcare & Higher Education* (pp. 210–217). Montreal, Quebec, Canada.

Duval, E. (2001). Standardized metadata for education: a status report. In C. Montgomerie & V. Karmo (eds.), *Proceedings of Ed-Media 2001* (pp. 458–463). Norfolk, VA: AACE.

Foss, C. L. (1989). *Detecting lost users: Empirical Studies on browsing hypertext.* Technical Report 972, INRIA, France.

Honey, P., & Mumford, A. (1992). *The manual of Learning Styles.* Peter Honey, Maidenhead.

Jui-Lin Lu, A., & Chen, Y. (2006). Design of a delegable SCORM conformant learning management system. *Journal of Computer Assisted Learning*, 22(6), 423–436.

Kazanidis, I., & Satratzemi, M. (2009a). Adaptivity in Pro Per: an adaptive SCORM compliant LMS. *Journal of Distance Education Technologies*, 7(2), 44–62.

Kazanidis, I., & Satratzemi, M. (2009b). Applying learning styles to SCORM compliant courses. In I. Aedo, N. Chen, Kinshuk, D. Sampson & L. Zaitseva (eds.), *Proceedings of the 9th IEEE International Conference on Advanced Learning Technologies* (pp. 147–151). Riga, Latvia: IEEE.

Kazanidis, I., & Satratzemi, M. (2009c). Efficient authoring of SCORM courseware adapted to user learning style: the case of ProPer SAT. In M. Spaniol, Q. Li, R. Klamma & R. Lau (eds.), *LNCS, 5686*, 196–205.

Kazanidis, I., & Satratzemi, M. (2010). Modeling user progress and visualizing feedback: the case of ProPer. In A. M. Cordeiro, B. Shishkov, A. Verbraeck & M. Herfert (eds.), *Proceedings of CSEDU 2010* (pp. 46–53). Valencia, Spain: INSTICC Press.

Krull, G. E., Mallinson, B. J., & Sewry, D. A. (2006). Describing online learning content to facilitate resource discovery and sharing: The development of the RU LOM Core. *Journal of Computer Assisted Learning*, 22(3), 172–181.

Modritscher, F., Garcia-Barrios, V.M., Gütl, C., & Helic, D. (2006). The first AdeLE prototype at a glance. In E. Pearson & P. Bohman (eds.), *Proceedings of Ed-Media 2006* (pp. 791–798). Orlando, Florida: AACE.

Morales, R. (2003). The VIBORA project. In A. Rossett (ed.), *Proceedings of the World Conference E-Learning in Corporate, Government, Healthcare and Higher Education* (pp. 2341–2344). Phoenix, Arizona: AACE.

Murray, T., Shen, T., Piemonte, J., Condit, C., & Tibedau, J. (2000). Adaptivity for conceptual and narrative flow in hyperbooks: The Metalink system. *Adaptive Hypermedia and Adaptive Web-based system. LNCS, 1892*, 155–166.

Ostyn (2010). *In the Eye of the SCORM*. Retrieved 10 December 2010 from http://www.ostyn.com.

Power, G., Davis, H. C., Cristea, A. I., Stewart, C., & Ashman, H. (2005). Goal oriented personalisation with SCORM. In P. Goodyear et al. (eds.), *Proceedings of the 5th IEEE International Conference on Advanced Learning Technologies* (pp. 467–471). Kaohsiung, Taiwan: IEEE.

Pilar da Silva, D., Durm, R. V., Duval, E., & Olivie, H. (1998). Concepts and documents for adaptive educational hypermedia: a model and a prototype. In P. Brusilovsky & P. De Bra (eds.), *Proceedings of Second Adaptive Hypertext and Hypermedia Workshop at the Ninth ACM International Hypertext Conference* (pp. 35–43). Pittsburgh, PA, USA.

Reload Project (2010). *Reload Editor*. Retrieved 15 December 2010 from: http://www.reload.ac.uk.

Specht, M., Kravcik, M., Klemke, R., & Pesin, L. (2002). Adaptive learning environment for teaching and learning in WINDS. In P. De Bra, P. Brusilovsky & R. Conejo (eds.), *LNCS*, 2347 pp. 572–575.

Stash, N. (2007). *Incorporating Cognitive/Learning Styles in a General-Purpose Adaptive Hypermedia System.* PhD Thesis, Eindhoven University of Technology, Netherlands.

Index

A. Jimoyiannis (ed.), *Research on e-Learning and ICT in Education*,
DOI 10.1007/978-1-4614-1083-6, © Springer Science+Business Media, LLC 2012

D

E